de Gruyter Studies in Organization 60
Human Resource Management on the Pacific Rim

de Gruyter Studies in Organization

International Management, Organization and Policy Analysis

An international and interdisciplinary book series from de Gruyter presenting comprehensive research on aspects of international management, organization studies and comparative public policy.
It will cover cross-cultural and cross-national studies of topics such as:
— management; organizations; public policy, and/or their inter-relation
— industry and regulatory policies
— business-government relations
— international organizations
— comparative institutional frameworks.

While each book in the series ideally has a comparative empirical focus, specific national studies of a general theoretical, substantive or regional interest which relate to the development of cross-cultural and comparative theory will also be encouraged.
The series is designed to stimulate and encourage the exchange of ideas across linguistic, national and cultural traditions of analysis, between academic researchers, practitioners and policy makers, and between disciplinary specialisms.
The volume will present theoretical work, empirical studies, translations and 'state-of-the art' surveys. The *international* aspects of the series will be uppermost: there will be a strong commitment to work which crosses and opens boundaries.

Editor:

Prof. Stewart R. Clegg, Faculty of Business and Technology, University of Western Sydney, Macarthur, Campbelltown, Australia

Advisory Board:

Prof. Nancy J. Adler, McGill University, Dept. of Management, Montreal, Quebec, Canada
Prof. Richard Hall, State University of New York at Albany, Dept. of Sociology, Albany, New York, USA
Prof. Gary Hamilton, University of Washington, Seattle, Washington, USA
Prof. Geert Hofstede, University of Limburg, Maastricht, The Netherlands
Prof. Pradip N. Khandwalla, Indian Institute of Management, Vastrapur, Ahmedabad, India
Prof. Surenda Munshi, Sociology Group, Indian Institute of Management, Calcutta, India
Prof. Gordon Redding, University of Hong Kong, Dept. of Management Studies, Hong Kong

Human Resource Management on the Pacific Rim

Institutions, Practices, and Attitudes

Edited by Larry F. Moore
and P. Devereaux Jennings

Walter de Gruyter · Berlin · New York 1995

Larry F. Moore, Associate Professor
Faculty of Commerce and Business Administration,
University of British Columbia,
Vancouver, B.C., Canada

P. Devereaux Jennings, Associate Professor
Faculty of Commerce and Business Administration,
University of British Columbia,
Vancouver, B.C., Canada

With 57 tables and 9 figures

∞ Printed on acid-free paper which falls within the guidelines
of the ANSI to ensure permanence and durability.

Library of Congress Cataloging-in-Publication Data

Human resource management on the Pacific Rim : institutions, practi-
ces, and attitudes / edited by Larry F. Moore and P. Devereaux
Jennings.
  (De Gruyter studies in organization ; 60)
  Includes bibliographical references.
  ISBN 3-11-014053-5 (acid-free paper)
  ISBN 3-11-014747-5 (pbk.)
  1. Personnel management — Pacific Area.   I. Moore, Larry F.
II. Jennings, P. Devereaux, 1957—   .   III. Series.
HF5549.2.P16H85   1995
658.3′0099 — dc20   94-36058
                                                          CIP

Die Deutsche Bibliothek — Cataloging-in-Publication Data

Human resource management on the Pacific Rim : institutions, practi-
ces, and attitudes / ed. by Larry F. Moore and P. Devereaux
Jennings. — Berlin ; New York : de Gruyter, 1995
  (De Gruyter studies in organization ; 60)
  ISBN 3-11-014053-5 (geb.)
  ISBN 3-11-014747-5 (brosch.)
NE: Moore, Larry F. [Hrsg.]; GT

Typesetting: converted by Knipp Satz und Bild digital, Dortmund — Printing: Gerike
GmbH, Berlin. — Binding: D. Mikolai, Berlin. — Cover Design: Johannes Rother,
Berlin. — Printed in Germany.

Table of Contents

Introduction to Human Resource Systems

Foreword

This is a very timely book! Over the past decade, a great deal of attention has been paid in the popular and business presses to "globalization", to "international management" and, most recently, to the explosion of economic growth in Asian countries. Apart from some texts on managing in international settings and a few careful empirical investigations of this topic, very little has been said about the Human Resource systems and practices in firms in different countries. Not much comparative work has been reported and there is little or nothing available that provides the researcher or the practitioner with an integrating frame or set of frames through which he or she might begin to understand, in a cross-cultural or cross-national way, how Human Resource Management systems operate. This book, *Human Resource Management on the Pacific Rim: Institutions, Practices and Attitudes*, begins to redress these omissions in the literature.

Editors Larry Moore and Dev Jennings are joined by other competent international researchers in the study of HRM systems and practices in the Pacific Rim countries of Australia, Canada, Hong Kong, Japan, New Zealand, the People's Republic of China, Singapore, South Korea, Taiwan, Thailand and the United States. Each chapter on a country includes a report of historical antecedents of current HRM practices, a presentation of data about current practices and a discussion of possible future developments in HRM in that country. Jennings and Moore provide an orienting chapter that includes a theoretical framework for understanding Human Resource Management. With Diane Cyr, they conclude the book with a comparison of findings and opinions reported by the researchers who carried out their in-country investigations.

Each chapter provides much valuable information to the researcher and to the professional HR practitioner about the nature of HRM in a particular country. What lifts the contribution of the book to another plane are the opening and closing chapters. Jennings and Moore use Neoinstitutional Theory as a major frame for understanding the nature of Human Resource Management. Neoinstitutional Theory focuses attention on the ways in which behaviors, technology and structure in organizations come into being, become accepted and are then widely used in different organizational and national settings. It is a useful perspective to help to identify the development of HRM in organizations and in nations and to compare, contrast and integrate the patterns of HRM practice across them. The theory is applied with skill and clarity and the resulting integration is very instructive.

Professors Moore and Jennings have successfully tackled a daunting task with energy and imagination. They and their co-researchers are to be admired and appreciated for providing us with this important volume on international Human Resource Management. It is a strong intellectual and practical contribution to the field. It should stimulate others to become involved in this important and exciting area of study. It comes none too soon, as we begin to recognize, in the Pacific Rim and elsewhere, that unless we become more able to understand and to manage the human dimension of our national and international enterprises, we will fall far short of the hopes and expectations of many for universal productive and prosperous employment.

Peter J. Frost

Professor and Associate Dean
Faculty of Commerce and Business Administration
University of British Columbia

Preface

Few would deny that the beginning of the 1990s has witnessed an amazing set of political and economic developments involving countries in the Pacific Region. Countries in the Pacific Region which, not long ago, were considered minor players on the economic scene have emerged as strong contenders. Others, which have been viewed as isolated and closed, have become more open and outward in focus. Some are subject to political instability and change, while others are stable and perhaps stagnating. Some represent huge markets, yet others are quite small. Expansion characterizes some, but others are slow-growing or declining economically. Some have strong, well-defined cultures, and others are marked by cultural diversity and change. Thus, it is natural to expect that human resource management systems in the Pacific Region will differ in many ways.

This book is designed to fill a strong need to provide an in-depth exploration of human resource management as practiced in major Pacific Rim countries – Australia, China, Canada, Hong Kong, Japan, Korea, New Zealand, Singapore, Taiwan, Thailand, and the United States. The central theme of the work is that managers in an increasingly global marketplace must possess specific knowledge of human resource issues and management practices within various countries, and of HR patterns and themes which characterize all countries or subsets of countries in the Pacific Region. The book is designed especially for human resource managers and other managers in organizations which are engaging or preparing to engage in business activity in the Pacific Region, and for students of international comparative human resource management.

In the late 1980s, each of the book's editors was involved in an empirical study of HR practices in his own country (Moore in Canada and Jennings in the U.S.), yet they shared a deepening interest in what was happening to HRM globally. The collapse of communism in the Soviet Union, the introduction of market socialism in the People's Republic of China, the increased incidence of the multicultural corporation, improved communication linkages, and other "global" phenomena suggested intriguing questions about how the management of human resources would be affected. Conferences in Europe and in the Far East brought together researchers and practitioners to raise and discuss emerging questions: How are human resources managed in individual countries? How are HR practices similar or different across countries? To what extent do HR practices become diffused when corporations operate in host countries? How strong is the influence of national culture, politics and economic posture in framing HR practices?

Examination of the proceedings of most of these conferences revealed a critical lack of empirically based knowledge. This seemed particularly true for the Pacific Region. The editors began to contact their combined network of researchers active in selected Pacific Region countries in order to form a team. Each chapter author or set of authors has a strong reputation and "track record" in conducting research on aspects of human resource management in their country of focus. The country authors were invited to craft their chapters so as to provide readers with a background overview of the country including some demographics, an economic profile, labor market characteristics, and a cultural perspective. Then the authors were urged to develop an empirically based discussion of human resource management; particularly focusing on characteristics of HR managers, the role of the typical HR department, and the extent of professionalism in the field. Finally, the future of HRM in each country was to be explored. The authors used their own data and drew on other research available to them. Although we encouraged authors to follow a similar format, their chapters vary somewhat in structure, displaying their unique interpretation of the state of the country's HR function. An integrative chapter extracts patterns and highlights emerging themes running through the book.

This project would not have been possible without the excellent creative contributions of the authors of the country chapters. We owe them all a tremendous debe of gratitude. We wish to thank Margaret Moore for proofreading various drafts of chapters and for many helpful comments. We also thank Irene Khoo for typing portions of the manuscript. Funding support was provided by the Centre for International Business Studies, Faculty of Commerce and Business Administration, University of British Columbia. Dr. Bianka Ralle, Managing Editor, Walter de Gruyter Publishing Company, provided competent and professional guidance throughout the book's preparation.

Vancouver, Canada
Larry F. Moore
P. Devereaux Jennings

Introduction and Theoretical Rationale

P. Devereaux Jennings and Larry F. Moore

Renewed Integration on the Pacific Rim

The Pacific Rim surrounds the Pacific Basin, an area containing the world's largest ocean – an ocean over 8,000 miles across – dotted with thousands of islands (Figure 1). The Rim is formed by a looping chain of twenty-six major countries, anchored by Tasmania at one end and Chile at the other. These countries contain over three billion people, with nearly 400 million living within a few hundred miles of the ocean. They speak at least eight different major languages and several dozen dialects, and believe in widely different religions and philosophies, ranging from Buddhism and Hinduism to Islam and Christianity (Harris and Moran, 1991; Noland, 1992; *The Great World Atlas*, 1983; Hoffman, 1992).

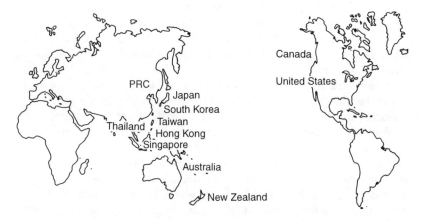

Figure 1

The sheer size and the distances involved have made consistent contact among the disparate places and peoples on the Rim difficult. Contact has been created over the centuries by different sets of integrating efforts. As early as 200 B.C., Southern Chinese traders sailed the shores of Malaysia, Burma and India, as the Han Empire began to extend its boundaries outward. Under the T'ang Dynasty (618-906) the influence of China in Asia deepened, creating lasting cultural and religious ties between China and the rest of Southeast Asia. Between 1200 and 1500 A.D. Muslim traders and proselytizers frequented cities from the coast of Thailand to the tip of Borneo; and starting in the mid-1600s, Western colonial powers began to build their long sets of economic and military chains, tying mainland ports and Pacific islands with Europe. More recently, the Second World War influenced the establishment of a new arrangement on the Rim. Formerly, "allied nations" and their supporters set up the machinery for "free market exchange" among individual, independent nation-states. In the post-war epoch, economic production and trade have become the basis for integration (Palmer and Colton, 1971; Strayer, Gatzke, and Harbison, 1974; Hoffman, 1993).

Today the countries on the Pacific Rim are responsible for over one third of the world's economic gross product (Noland, 1992). The Rim contains the world's first- and second-ranked economies – the U.S. and Japan – as well as most of the world's fastest growing economic areas. In the People's Republic of China, recent GDP growth rates have been over 10%, with parts of southern China having experienced rates of over 20% for each of the last two years (PECC, 1994:1). Korea, Taiwan, Hong Kong and Singapore have all expanded their trade base and become serious competitors in product markets like steel, electronics, clothing, and paper goods. Thailand and Indonesia have become new markets for investment, and as we compile this volume, Vietnam is beginning to open up.

Much of the economic production and exchange within these countries is directed towards other Pacific Rim counterparts. According to the OCED and World Bank, 50% of the materials for export from South Korea, Taiwan, Hong Kong, Indonesia, Thailand and Malaysia are sent to just two other Pacific Rim countries – Japan and the United States – and an additional 30% to other local Asian nations, with only 20% going outside the Pacific Rim region. The United States and Japan still export only 5-10% of their goods to other smaller economies on the Rim, but that amount has increased dramatically in the case of the U.S. (International Monetary Fund or IMF, 1992; Department of Commerce, 1992; Economic and Social Commission of Asia and the Pacific, 1992; Department of International Economic and Social Affairs, 1987).

Overlaid upon this web of market exchanges and well-developed trade link-ages are corporate ties among units of multinational companies. The largest companies of Japan and the United States are primarily multinational, with most having investments on the Pacific Rim (Gerlach, 1992; Scott, 1986; Tung, 1989). Conversely, over 30% of the major companies with investments in Canada, Hong Kong, Taiwan, Singapore, Indonesia and Thailand are foreign multinationals from other countries on the Pacific Rim (Tung, 1989).

International trade associations have been created to reinforce these economic ties. Among them, in order of increasing representativeness, are the Associa-tion of South East Asian Nations (ASEAN), the East Asian Economic Caucus (EAEC), the Asia Pacific Economic Cooperation (APEC), and the Pacific Eco-nomic Cooperation Council (PECC) (PECC, 1994:3). Whereas ASEAN only includes Brunei, Indonesia, Malaysia, the Philippines, Singapore and Thailand; PECC includes Australia, Canada, New Zealand, the United States, China, Hong

Kong, Japan, Korea, Taiwan, and the other ASEAN members. The mission of these associations ranges from aiding economic exchange to increasing political and cultural understanding. These associations also vary from tightly knit economic cooperatives to loose networks of regional subgroups. For instance, APEC has become a highly formal arrangement, particularly in the last round of talks in December, 1993; PECC is a nongovernmental organization that provides "a forum for the consideration of Pacific economic issues in an informal collaborative framework", which often is in the form of subgroup meetings on topic areas like human resources development (APEC, 1993: 1).

Together with market ties among trading partners, corporate ties among subunits and governmentally sanctioned exchange, these associations have helped create an increasingly dense spatial network linking areas of the Pacific Rim. Today the picture of the Pacific Rim is one of a vast region, undergoing a major period of integration under the impetus of economic development; and the increasing contact among the countries and cities is only accelerating the rate of change.

Inimitable Competitive Advantage of Different HRM Systems

International exchange on the Pacific Rim requires basic market machinery to be used by each exchanging partner. According to economists, once partners have adopted a market approach and implemented methods to ensure contract formation and delivery of goods, they are free to generate value using whatever competitive advantage they can find, whether it is based on natural resources or a program of development (Porter, 1990; Smith, 1776).

There has been a diffusion among Pacific Rim countries of elements essential to economic contracting, such as the use of international price information, accounting principles, insurance, and methods of risk and asset assessment (Harris and Moran, 1991; Young, 1992). But even with all the diffusion of common market elements, the economic growth and development on the Rim is quite uneven. There are "developed" industrial economies, such as those found in Australia, Canada, Hong Kong, Japan, Singapore, Taiwan, South Korea and the United States. And there are developing industrial economies, such as those found in China, Indonesia, Thailand and Vietnam. Furthermore, the "New Tigers" are growing at a much faster rate than the rest of the Rim – or the world.

A primary source of competitive advantage on the Pacific Rim seems to be how countries and the businesses in them use their human resources (Schuler, Dowling, and De Cieri, 1993). Even though there has been a substitute of capital for labor over this century, cheap unskilled labor still provides a competitive advantage in many industries. Capital intensive industries have placed an even greater premium on the availability of cheap, high-skill labor as a means of competing in rapidly changing industries. In fact, economic gurus and institutes have declared that in order to be successful in the 1990s, lower performing economies must regain control over labor, reduce costs, and re-skill their workforces (Porter, 1990; Reich, 1983). Some countries, such as Japan and Hong Kong, have succeeded in using both cheap, unskilled labor and highly skilled workers in more effective ways than their competitors. But as they expand into many different parts of the world they are facing the problem of relying on multicultural workforces to retain their advantage. Such differences in human resource use are likely to remain a central factor for competitive advantage well into the next century. In their best-selling book, *Managing Workforce 2000* (1992), Jemison and O'Mara maintain that: "Workforce 2000 could easily be renamed Workforce 1990…diversity is already an organizational fact of life."

But how "imitable" are the HR systems of more successful countries and businesses? Over the last ten years, this question has been asked by many strategists. On the one hand, industrial production and economic exchange require the acceptance of some basic HR practices and systems that seem to accompany market systems (Schuler, Dowling, and De Cieri, 1993). There is evidence that selection, in-house training, and promotion practices exist in all Pacific Rim countries, probably as a means of reaping the benefits of a firm's investment in labor (Frost and Cyr, 1990; Tung, 1990). On the other hand, by the late 1980s researchers recognized that each country faces a unique set of circumstances surrounding its workforce; and therefore it must develop practices that are in keeping with that country's traditions. Japanese quality circles were adopted extensively in the U.S. during the 1980s, but were difficult to implement and ultimately dropped by many firms. Today, strategists have gone so far as to argue that it is better to base one's competitive advantage on the unique elements of a country and its key industries. In this way one creates "inimitable", long-range advantage (Barney, 1991; 1992; Schuler, Dowling, and De Cieri, 1993).

We believe that some important imitable and inimitable elements of HR systems in different Pacific Rim countries can be identified using a Neoinstitutional Approach to the employment relationship (also see Gerlach, 1992; Pfeffer, 1994).[1] Neoinstitutional Theory focuses upon the way in which innovations in behavior, technology and structure become accepted and widely used; that is, upon the "institutionalization process" through which innovations become recognized, formalized and then legitimized in society. Once new behaviors, methods, or forms have gone through the institutionalization process in a society, they are more easily transmitted to other groups. The mechanism for their diffusion may be mimicry, pressure from one's peers and contemporaries, or direct coercion – often from the central government. For example, researchers have documented the spread of charters of human rights across the majority of nations through the creation and ratification of new constitutions or bills. This diffusion has been encouraged by the pressure on the adopting country to appear "modern and developed" to other nations and by the pressure applied by the central governments in these countries on the internal legal community to develop such principles (Meyer and Scott, 1983).

Nevertheless, neoinstitutionalists recognize that even diffused, institutionalized elements were originally embedded in the set of meanings created by the employment relationship in which they developed. The complete meaning or "signification" of the form may not be easily transmitted. Conversely, when a form is transmitted, a new context and meaning must be given to it if it is to have any significance. For example, while many constitutions discuss democratic rule, the interpretation of democratic rule varies considerably across nations (Meyer and Scott, 1983). By focusing on context and deeper interpretation, Neoinstitutional Theory underscores the role of local culture and historical condition as a source of inimitable advantage.

To understand the employment relationships on the Pacific Rim from a neoinstitutional perspective, specialists on HRM in 11 different Rim countries were asked to write a chapter in which they would discuss the historical context for similar features of the employment relationship: the external labor market, the internal labor market of the firm, and the HR manager's role. The study of similar features gives us a basis for assessing and comparing what seem to be very different work environments on the Pacific Rim. In particular, we can compare systems based on their variation in the degree of bureaucratization of these human resource elements. The specialists were also asked to address the question of meaning: "How do HRM functionaries and workers *interpret* these HR policies and practices?" "Are there critical, underlying work attitudes and values on which the HRM system depends?"

Because many of the contributors to this book are not neoinstitutionalists per se and because each chapter focuses on only one country or city, we have added a final chapter to attempt to interpret some of our findings. In particular, we compare and contrast the different features of the HRM systems around the Pacific Rim, and examine the possible sources of the similarities and differences. For example, systems vary in how much they depend on the external labor market versus internal labor markets to manage the employment relationship. Moreover, firms with internal labor markets vary in the degrees of formality and complexity in their HR function. The sources of such variation depend, in part, on how reliant a country has traditionally been on external hiring; in part, on how important it is in the nation's culture for employers and employees to create their own labor contracts; and, in part, on the ability of HR functionaries to adopt features of advanced HR systems in order to meet a firm's needs.

Knowing about these sources of variation can help both a researcher who wants to understand a country's HRM practices and a practitioner who wants to use these practices to help his or her company. Many researchers in the field of strategic HRM are trying to understand the fit between HR systems and local environments. Recent work has emphasized the need for details of local culture and history in order to help match HR systems to local environments (Adler, 1991). Similarly, practitioners are often faced with the problem of blending HR practices used in subunits of multinational corporations or joint-ventures with local traditions governing the employment relationship (Cyr, forthcoming). To provide researchers and practitioners with an interpretive lens or "frame" (Deal and Bolman, 1992) using a Neoinstitutional Approach, we discuss key elements of the HRM systems and how they apply to selected Pacific Rim countries.

Assessing Human Resource Management Systems

The Employment Relationship

Current theory in macro HRM maintains that all human resource activities take place within the context of the employment relationship. The employment relationship refers to the "set of all relations and supporting institutions between employees and employers" (Flanagan et al., 1989). In other words, HRM involves not only the classical market factors associated with work, but the structures (firms, industries, nations) in which markets operate and evolve (Kalleberg and Berg, 1987).

The operation of the employment relationship within these structures gives rise to certain enduring HRM features for study by theorists. These features vary with the different levels of analysis in which the employment relationship operates – from the external labor market system in a country, to the internal labor market in the firm, down to the specific job held by an individual (see Figure 2). In other words, the employment relationship between any specific laborer and his/her firm depends on the supply and demand of labor in the external market; the internal labor market in the firm (FILM) in which the job is embedded; all the flows attaching jobs from the internal labor markets to the external one; the specific sets of rules or practices for administering these jobs; and the individuals within them (Althauser, 1989; Baron and Bielby, 1980; Kalleberg and Berg, 1987; Pinfield and Bernier, 1994).

While a thorough description of an employment relationship requires some consideration of each of these features at the different levels of analysis, the most essential feature to consider in comparative approaches to human resource management is the firm's internal labor market – the FILM. The FILM contains all job ladders in the firm, their ports of entry, the practices for administering these ladders, and the individuals within them (Althauser, 1989; Pinfield, 1994). For instance, in large, complex firms, the FILM is equivalent to the formal and informal HR systems that exist among the firm's jobs and its longer-term employees (Pfeffer and Cohen, 1984). The features of the FILM are fewer and better understood than the employment relationship as a whole, meaning that focusing on the FILM makes it easier to assess and compare HRM systems across firms and places (Devanna, Fombrun, and Tichy, 1984; Schuler, 1987). For example, past researchers have found that the greater the complexity, the bureaucratization and the control by human resource specialists over a FILM, the less the flexibil-

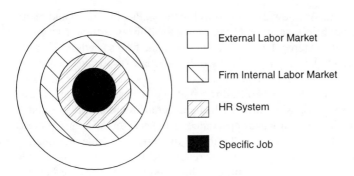

External Labor Market

Firm Internal Labor Market

HR System

Specific Job

Figure 2

ity and dynamism of the HRM system as a whole, since more elaborate, formal HRM systems have more structural or systemic inertia (Baron and Bielby, 1980; 1986; Pfeffer and Cohen, 1984). Yet, paradoxically, bureaucratized FILMs tend to encourage the development of human resource planning in the firm, making innovation in particular practices more likely (Kalleberg and Berg, 1987; Lincoln and Kalleberg, 1985).

The Neoinstitutional Approach to FILMs

The characteristics of the FILM that are most important for understanding how the FILM helps the firm fit its environments depends on one's theoretical perspective or frame. For neoinstitutionalists the most important aspect about the FILM is its degree of bureaucratization. Bureaucratization of an internal labor market is characterized by: (1) the longer term existence of an HR department; (2) the use of formalized, standardized procedures and due process to handle human resources, which include selection, retention, promotion and firing procedures; job classification, analysis and evaluation; compensation and benefits systems; safety; HR research and advancement of human rights policies (such as EEO or Affirmative Action practices); and (3) the existence of and involvement of HR managers in these distinct sets of HR practices (Baron, Dobbin, and Jennings, 1986; Baron, Jennings, and Dobbin, 1988; Edwards, 1979; Jacoby, 1985). Not surprisingly, researchers have used the number of personnel practices to measure the *degree of elaboration or complexity* of a firm's FILM (Pfeffer and Cohen, 1984; Lincoln and Kalleberg, 1985; Pinfield, 1994); they have used clusters of highly formalized practices (e.g., hiring, firing, and promotion) to measure the *degree of formalization* (Baron, Dobbin, and Jennings, 1986; Baron, Jennings, and Dobbin, 1988); and control over these practices by HR specialists to indicate the *degree of centralization* (Moore and Jennings, 1993; Saha, 1989; Thompson, 1991). Together, complexity, formalization and centralization lead to bureaucratization.

Bureaucratized FILMs allow a firm to develop the skills of workers and retain their services through internal promotion, rather than hiring different levels of skilled workers on the external labor market to match the firm's needs and hoping that the skills developed by those workers will be adequate (Doeringer and Piore, 1971). In other words, bureaucratization is a form of control over the exigencies imposed by skilled labor that relies on indirect methods such as rules, due process, and specialization of work. Nevertheless, the bureaucratic regime works to a large degree because of its rational-legal appearance. The need for rules and process to appear "fair" and "legitimate" and "rational" to both the outside and internal public is critical for the survival of the bureaucratic FILM. The bureaucratic FILM, then, has multiple sets of meanings sedimented within it, from efficiency and control to rational-legal acceptability (Baron, Jennings, and Dobbin, 1988).[2]

Sources of the bureaucratized FILM. The development of highly bureaucratic methods of labor control in North America and Britain grew out of a lengthy and only partially understood chain of events, but at least depended on: (1) the treatment of labor as a "resource", just like any other resource or commodity in the firm (Edwards, 1979; Gordon, Edwards, and Reich, 1982); (2) the allocation of labor by trained managers, who were also responsible for controlling labor's reaction (Jacoby, 1985); (3) the training of laborers in firm-specific skills to allow for a more efficient, long-term production of value-added goods (Doeringer and Piore, 1971); and (4) the acceptance by labor of the conditions of hiring, firing and promotion as being "fair" – governed by rules that appeared to follow due process and external legalities (Baron, Dobbins, and Jennings, 1986; Baron, Jennings, and Dobbin, 1988; Edwards, 1979; Jacoby, 1985).

Over time new behaviors, rules or forms were created as alternatives to the existing way of doing things as a means of making sense out of a confusing reality and to overcome pressing problems of the day (see Figure 3). Neoinstitutionalists argue that such innovations often begin at a pre-conscious level; that is, their use may not even be directly recognized by the actors. The innovations are part of "sense-making" – an epistemological quest to establish what we can take as "fact" in everyday life (Berger and Luckmann, 1967, p. 15; Powell and DiMaggio, 1991). For instance, one of the original personnel departments (at National Cash Register in the 1890s) was used to handle a large volume of applicants who could not be sorted rationally and allocated to different parts of a rapidly growing company. The waves of immigration during the late 1800s made it even more difficult to find information on applicants, necessitating some standardized interviewing and skills testing for basic jobs. The personnel department was an experimental arrangement to deal with this uncertainty generated by the quantity and quality of workers in the external labor market (Jacoby, 1983; 1985; Springer and Spring, 1991).

After the creation of these new behaviors, rules or forms, the essential moment in institutionalization process is the "legitimation" of that action. Legitimation refers to implicit or explicit acceptance of some set of behaviors, rules or forms

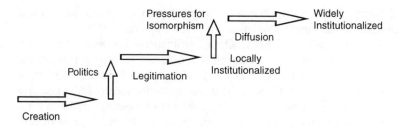

Figure 3

by a recognized authority in society. Typically, this authority has been the central government or "State". During World War I and World War II in North America, Britain, and Australia, firms involved in wartime industries were encouraged by the federal governments in these countries to use centralized hiring, training and promotion methods to allocate labor efficiently. This facilitated the acceptance of personnel departments within firms as legitimate subunits (Jacoby, 1983; 1985; Nkomo, 1980).

Political strategies usually play a key role in legitimation. The bureaucratization of the FILM has been aided by the professionalization of HRM. During this century HRM practitioners have claimed unique expertise in HR matters. HRM associations have lobbied the federal and local governments in the U.S. and in other countries (e.g., Canada and Hong Kong) to recognize the need for well-trained HR managers. Once the premise of specialized training has been accepted by the government, HR specialists have been able to set up certification programs to control entry into the occupation and to further specialize HRM training (Saffarti-Larson, 1977; Starr, 1982). This step towards professionalization further reinforces the need for firms to use certified practitioners to deal with labor problems, such as employee counselling in EAPs. The reliance on trained officials is a central part of bureaucratization (Moore and Jennings, 1993; Weber, 1924).

Once legitimated, these behaviors, rules or forms are well on the way to becoming "institutionalized". The most advanced and recognizable point of the institutionalization process is the creation of a new, physical institution in society, such as the central bank or the United Nations. In the case of HRM, the creation of the elaborate HR departments with professional staff members to administer bureaucratic practices is one of the most salient features of the institutionalization of bureaucratic control.[3] Nevertheless, many institutions are not manifested physically, but simply as well-understood notions – such as the notion of "the employee a citizen of the corporation". "Citizenship" or "full-time membership" implies certain obligations and rights. In the past, these obligations included high commitment to the firm and a right to lifetime employment as a reward. The characteristics of corporate citizenship are currently being redefined around the world to no longer include a long-term horizon. In fact, it is even unclear that the HR department will have a role in the interpretation and protection of these employee rights in the future (Dobbin et al., 1993; Edelman, 1992).

Diffusion of the bureaucratic FILM. Once legitimated or institutionalized, new behaviors, rules and forms may be diffused to different sectors or parts of the world that are without them. According to DiMaggio and Powell (1983), there are three sets of processes that lead to diffusion: mimetic, normative, or coercive isomorphism – where "isomorphism" simply refers to becoming similar in form or appearance to something else. An institution or institutionalized form may simply be mimicked because it is perceived as a possible way to proceed in the new environment. An institution may also be adopted because normative pressure is put on others to convince them that these new behaviors, rules or forms are proper. Finally, an institution may be adopted because of direct force or coercion. Sometimes more than one pressure is at work. In the case of the bureaucratic FILM, the central governments in Australia, Canada, New Zealand and the U.S. appear to have encouraged the adoption of bureaucratic policies, thereby creating highly visible models for other organizations to try to copy (Baron, Dobbin, and Jennings, 1986; Edelman, 1992). The central government of the U.S. has also "asked" more local governments, who are part of the same "government sector", to follow the federal example; and the central government has threatened to use force, such as withdrawal of local funding, if local governments do not comply (Dobbin et al., 1993; Edelman, 1992). The spread of the bureaucratic FILM within some of the countries in our study, then, has occurred through all three isomorphic processes.

As the new behavior, rule or form diffuses, it is overlaid on older methods. The bureaucratic method of control does not directly replace the earlier methods of handling labor in the employment relationship, but it is sedimented on top of them (Baron, Dobbin, and Jennings, 1986; Clegg, 1981; Edwards, 1979). These earlier methods are sometimes employed in part within the new methods. For instance, job classification and job evaluation are used by HRM practitioners in bureaucratized personnel departments, even though these practices were developed to allocate and evaluate labor efficiently within a mass production system guided by a technical method of labor control. Furthermore, vestiges of these older regimes of control may be recognized, even after their function is no longer evident. Welfare practices developed in the 1920s, such as employee holidays, employee information booklets, and employee recognition programs, were still to be found in firms in the 1940s, long after a home-grown, welfare approach had been supplanted by the more legalistic one associated with bureaucratization.

As firms in North America downsize and strip their personnel departments of funding and staff, many bureaucratic practices are still in place, such as the use of job classification and job evaluation procedures. What is unclear at this point is what new methods are replacing the older ones at the core of the employment relationship. One question that we encouraged our contributors to consider is "what is beyond the bureaucratic regime?". In particular, are we developing a decentralized yet professionally controlled method of handling the employment relationship?

The Neoinstitutional Approach and Strategic HRM

The Neoinstitutional Approach is in keeping with some of the central ideas of the strategic human resources management (SHRM) approach, which currently dominates macro human resources management theory (Jennings, 1994). SHRM theorists maintain that the primary function of the HR unit in a firm is to cope with the external labor market that the firm faces and to handle internal coordination and control problems associated with the firm's human resources (Hickson et al., 1971; Hinings et al., 1974; Schuler, 1987; Schuler, Dowling, and De Cieri, 1993). Like neoinstitutionalists, SHRM theorists have used a systems- and levels-type framework for describing the external environment. Beer et al. (1984), Boxall (1992), Schuler (1987) and others have included social and political factors that affect the firm and its HR units. While some of this inclusion of social and political dimensions is merely an attempt to make the dimensions of SHRM more relevant (e.g., see Lengnick-Hall and Lengnick-Hall, 1988 for a review), reconceptualizing the firm's role in the general environment has given a new level of prominence to the environment and a more synthetic picture of the relationship of the firm to it. For instance, Beer et al.'s formulation (1984) notes that the industry of the firm and particularly the labor market(s) on which the firm draws are tightly interwoven with the HR unit. The consequence is that staffing models must incorporate external personnel flows if they are to be of use (also see Stewman, 1986; Pinfield, 1994).

To cope with these external and internal problems, SHRM theorists argue that the HR manager must be proactive; s/he must invent new HR practices and take part in business planning and implementation. "If the [HR department] has no process by which it engages in strategic planning at the corporate or business level, it will not be possible for the human resource function to develop a strategic thrust since the human resource strategy flows from the corporate or business strategy" (Devanna, Fombrun, and Tichy, 1984:50). To a neoinstitutionalist, this is equivalent to saying that HR managers must use political strategies to push innovations in HRM, if they want such innovations to become accepted (legitimated) within the firm. In fact, neoinstitutionalists and SHRM theorists both focus on coherent sets of personnel practices as manifestations of innovative HR systems. Devanna, Fombrun, and Tichy (1984) describe five essential clusters of HR strategic activities within firms that must be matched with strategic needs: compensation, staffing, performance appraisal, training, and planning. These clusters are the same ones involved in bureaucratic control (Baron, Dobbin, and Jennings, 1986; Moore and Jennings, 1993).

However, neoinstitutionalists make fewer assumptions than SHRM theorists about the conditions prior to and proceeding institutionalization. They do not assume that there are necessarily HR managers in a firm or an HR unit in order for the employment relationship to be managed strategically. Nor do neoinstitutionalists assume that strategically designed systems are even the goal of HRM; instead, there may be no particular goal in advance, just the evolution of new systems out of an intricate process of creation, politicization, legitimation, and final institutionalization. In fact, to be successful in a firm SHRM requires the institutionalization of some key elements of human resource management in the firm, such as the acceptance of HRM as an important method to help the firm fit its environment or the active participation of HR managers in the development of corporate strategy. In this sense, strategic human resources management entails some elements of the Neoinstitutional Approach. The advantage of using the latter approach for examining the Pacific Rim is that neoinstitutionalists are actually able to examine the assumptions made by SHRM theorists about the environment and the existence of HR managers. For instance, some countries such as the People's Republic of China do not even have companies that use a recognizeable, formal HR system or designate any one person as an HR manager.

At least one major difference of opinion exists between the SHRM and the Neoinstitutional Approach: They disagree about the role of usefulness or "rationality" versus simple acceptance or "legitimacy" as the basis for adopting new HR practices. Neoinstitutionalists argue that such adoption may not be performance-oriented and that internal politicking is usually around only one central question – whether it is acceptable or legitimate for HRM to participate in strategy formulation. Thus, adoption may be based on mimicry, normative pressure or coercion – none of which may be an attempt to improve the performance of the firm or be "rational". The efforts of HR managers and HR units must be to maintain their acceptance by the rest of the firm as a legitimate function with unique insight into employment-relationship problems.

A direct implication of this view is that neoinstitutionalists see HR managers as proactive, but in a retrenched direction – as defenders of the HR faith in re-structuring firms. They would argue that much of what is espoused as "SHRM" is actually more ideology than theory or practice. HR specialists are just using SHRM as a knowledge base for legitimating their profession.[4] Like other professional knowledge, SHRM requires some knowledge of abstract theory (e.g., I/O psychology), the ability to diagnose situations, and the prescription of treatments through a process of inference (Abbott, 1988:35-58). There are also specific technologies involved with administering a complete SHRM program, including the use of psychometrics for employee evaluation and cost/benefit analysis of the HR unit's contribution to the bottom line (Dyer and Holder, 1988; Nininger, 1982; Tsui, 1987). If an HR department has adopted several SHRM practices and reports heavy involvement in them, it will have taken a big step towards legitimation and, indeed, professionalization of its HR staff.[5]

The Neoinstitutional and Cultural Approaches to HRM

The Neoinstitutional Approach is also in keeping with much of the Cultural Approach to macro HRM (Adler, 1991; Frost, 1989; Frost and Egri, 1989; Steers et al., 1990). The Cultural Approach maintains that HRM must be understood within the specific cultural setting in which HRM is being practiced (Frost and Cyr, 1990; Steers et al., 1990), and that HRM must incorporate the concept of culture into HR theory if successful implementation of HR in different countries is possible (Adler, 1991; Frost, 1989). Like the Neoinstitutional Approach, it stresses the need to examine social rules in the context of the cultural environment, and it places weight on the subjective nature of rule construction and application. Furthermore, both approaches single out the importance of the normative system within an organization – the underlying values embedded in norms and rules – as critical for the behavior that we see in everyday life.

However, neoinstitutionalists disagree with culture theorists about the source of rules and how important sense-making really is. Frost and Egri (1989) emphasize the role of "deeper politics" in the creation of the "surface politics", which beget innovations such as the use of bureaucratic HR practices; whereas, Baron, Jennings, and Dobbin (1988) and Tolbert and Zucker (1983) note that politics may create some initial innovations in an organizational field, but other firms will adopt highly innovative practices for non-political reasons – because of an almost irrational copying urge. Steers et al. highlight the role of the specific socio-cultural history of Korea in the development of its industries' HR practices; but Hamilton and Biggart (1988) stress the willingness of Korean industry to adopt foreign employment practices as it develops along a path similar to industry in these other nations. If firms are so willing to just mimic behavior or copy rules and structures because of some perceived rationale that these elements will benefit the firm, then the actual meaning underlying these behaviors is likely to be secondary, since meaning is developed over time through use and is tied to specific contexts.

Therefore, while the Cultural Approach is useful for description – especially for elaborating the meaning of practices and the context for their interpretation – it is not as good for systematically assessing the wide variety of sources of these practices and their differences.

Studying the Pacific Rim

The interpretive frame provided by the Neoinstitutional Approach appears more useful than the SHRM or Cultural Approach for studying the commonalities and differences in HR systems around the Pacific Rim. It helps identify essential elements of the employment relationship; it focuses on the historical processes underlying the evolution of HR systems; it emphasizes the importance of sense-making and legitimacy in sectors such as HRM where the technique or methods are hard to standardize and objectively measure; and it looks to the process of diffusion as a source of new systems in different countries.

Assessing Each Country's HRM System

In keeping with the Neoinstitutional Approach, our contributors examine the following sets of elements in each country:

- the country context, from the societal level down to the level of the HR manager;
- the state's role in the employment relationship;
- the array of practices found in any particular firm's internal labor market (FILM);
- the role of HR managers and HR knowledge in administration of the firm's internal labor market;
- the interpretation of HR practices and policies by managers and workers;
- the creation of new employment practices deep in the work place or adoption of new practices from other countries.

The context of the HRM system includes background history of the country – with an eye towards economic development – and the supply and demand of labor in the external market. The role of the State is considered in terms of its overall intervention into the economy, along with its effect on the legal framework underpinning the HRM system. The array of practices refers not simply to practices under the control of HR functionaries, but to all employment practices – from hiring policies to long-term HR planning. Similarly, the administration of HRM activities involves the interpretation and application of these practices not just by HR managers, but by other managers and workers in the firm. The process of interpreting and applying these practices often leads to the development of new practices or the adoption of practices currently used elsewhere. The conclusion of each chapter considers the meaningfulness of current practices and the future development of HRM in that country.

Comparing HRM Systems across Countries

The final chapter of the book compares and contrasts the HRM systems found in different countries and examines some of the underlying sources of similarities and differences. Among all the elements examined in the Neoinstitutional Approach, we have argued that the firm's internal labor market (FILM) is most directly related to the type of HR system used by an organization. Therefore, one of the first points for comparing HR systems will be in terms of the FILM's characteristics – its degree of complexity, formalization, centralization, and, ultimately, bureaucratization.

In addition, each chapter will examine the role of the HR manager in the administration of the HRM system and the degree of professionalization of HRM in each country. One might suspect that the degree of involvement of the HR manager and professionalization covary with bureaucratization, but that remains to be seen on careful examination of each case. Even if these factors do covary, the actual use and meaning of the practices within an HR system may diverge in two highly bureaucratic regimes. For example, in Western Canada the meaning of affirmative action legislation in an HR department is typically quite different than in departments in the Pacific Northwest of the U.S., even though firms in both regions tend to be involved with such practices. Affirmative action takes a back seat to employee rights described under the Charter of Rights in British Columbia and in Alberta, as well as to labor codes in both provinces, partly because these other rights are so newly defined. In contrast, in the U.S. affirmative action is a much newer, additional guarantee beyond the Bill of Rights, and has been the focus of more legal battles. The degree of embeddedness – the importance of context in other words – for the meaning of different practices will also be considered.

Finally, the last chapter will take a second look at some sources of the differences in HR systems. These sources include the supply and demand for labor in the external labor market, the degree of State intervention, and the role historically played by HRM in the country – in other words, the socio-historical context around the FILMs in each country. For instance, two reasons for the importance of affirmative action in large U.S. firms is the history of civil rights litigation in that country and the current demographic composition of the U.S. working population (Edelman, 1992; Sutton et al., 1993). The institutional framework established by the federal and local governments and the continuing pressures of racial unrest act as environmental stimuli for the elaboration of more HR policies. In Canada, there has traditionally been a split jurisdiction between federal and provincial levels on human rights issues, such as those surrounding affirmative action. This has slowed the development of an institutional framework and enforcement of equal rights laws. Furthermore, the social unrest in Canada has been more focused on the differences between the Francophone and Anglophone populations than on differences between races.

The authors will conclude with a discussion of how similarities and differences in HR systems might relate to long-range, strategic competitiveness of organizations within the economies of different Pacific Rim countries. By studying eleven of the most important Pacific Rim countries, we hope to provide at least some well-documented observations about HR systems in different countries and to highlight some possible avenues for more sweeping analyses of more specific questions in future research. Our framework for these observations should also be useful both for researchers hoping to learn more about specific questions and for practitioners who wish to organize their thinking about comparative differences.

Endnotes

1. Pieper (1991) mentions a similar approach to understanding HR systems – one based on Habmeras and Heidegger, which requires an understanding of the signification of each practice in a given context. The Neoinstitutional School in sociology (Meyer and Scott, 1983; Powell and DiMaggio, 1991) has some of its roots in phenomenology (Berger and Luckmann, 1967), but has also focused on more structural and organizational elements at a mid-range theory level (Blau and Scott, 1962; Selznick, 1948) than European scholars working in that tradition.
2. Neoinstitutionalists also agree with Neo-Marxists that bureaucratized FILMs represent a distinct type of control "regime" over labor in the firm (Edwards, 1979). Control in this regime over labor is based on the application of standardized, formal procedures to the hiring, development, evaluation, promotion and firing of labor. These procedures are implemented by professional HR staffs, and adjudicated not only by management but also by the different levels of government in society.
3. Of course, at the margin the institutionalized power of HR professionals is limited and always in flux.
4. A knowledge base is the foundation of the occupation and convinces society that this particular occupation alone can fill the professional niche among other professions (Abbott, 1988; Cullen, 1985).
5. There are other knowledge bases or "ideologies" for professional development and management of the employment relationship besides "SHRM". The major alternative to SHRM is "industrial relations management" (IRM), which is based on the industrial relations model of the employment relationship developed in the early post-World War II era (see Dunlop, 1950; Kochan and Cappelli, 1984). In the IRM model, HR specialists are primarily concerned with mediating the relationship between management and labor in order to keep the industrial system in balance. The most important HR activities are not strategic manpower planning or HR research, but contract negotiation and grievance administration. If an HR department is heavily involved in these IRM practices and, as in the above case, it is also able to take part in strategic business planning, we believe IRM will have become a legitimated approach in the firm and benefits will accrue to members of the occupation. We will see this split between SHRM and IRM approaches to human resources most predominately in Australia, New Zealand, and Canada.

References

Abbott, A. (1988). *The System of Professions: An Essay on the Division of Expert Labor*. Chicago, IL: University of Chicago Press.
Adler, N. (1991). *International Dimensions of Organizational Behavior*. (2nd ed.) Boston, MA: PWS-Kent.
Althauser, R. (1989). "Internal Labor Markets." *Annual Review of Sociology*, 15, 143-161.
APEC (1993). "APEC Ministerial Meeting, Seattle." *APEC-HRD-NEDM Newsletter*, 1(2), 1-12.
APRRC (1992). "ASEAN Celebrates 25 Years." *APRRC Newsletter*, 2(3), 1-12.

Baron, J.N. and W.T. Bielby (1980). "Bringing the Firm Back in: Stratification, Segmentation and the Organization of Work." *American Sociological Review*, 45, 737-765.

Baron, J.N. and W.T. Bielby (1983). "Organizations, Technology, and Worker Attachment to the Firm." *Research in Social Stratification and Mobility*, 2, 77-113.

Baron, J.N. and W.T. Bielby (1986). "The Proliferation of Job Titles in Organizations." *Administrative Science Quarterly*, 7, 561-586.

Baron, J.N., F. Dobbin and P.D. Jennings (1986). "War and Peace: The Evolution of Modern Personnel Administration in U.S. Industry." *American Journal of Sociology*, 92 (2), 350-383.

Baron, J.N., P.D. Jennings and F. Dobbin (1988). "Mission Control? The Development of Personnel Systems in U.S. Industry." *American Sociological Review*, 53, 497-514.

Barney, J. (1991). "Firm Resources and Sustained Competitive Advantage." *Journal of Management*, 17 (10), 99-120.

Barney, J. (1992). "Integrating Organizational Behavior and Strategy Formulation Research: A Resource Based Analysis." In P. Shrivastava, A. Huff and J. Dutton (eds.), *Advances in Strategic Management: A Research Annual, Vol. 8.* Greenwich, CT: JAI Press.

Beer, M., B. Spector, P.R. Lawrence, D. Quinn Mills & R.E. Walton (1984). *Managing Human Assets.* New York: Free Press.

Berger, P.L. and T. Luckmann (1967). *The Social Construction of Reality.* New York: Doubleday.

Bernstein, I. (1960). *The Lean Years: A History of American Workers, 1920-1933.* Boston: Houghton-Mifflin.

Bernstein, I. (1970). *The Turbulent Years.* Boston: Houghton-Mifflin.

Blau, P.M. and W.R. Scott (1962). *Formal Organizations.* San Francisco: Chandler Press.

Boxall, P. (1992). "Public Policy and Human Resource Management: Developments in the New Zealand Case." *Asia Pacific Journal of Human Resources*, 30 (2), 2-9.

Carlson, D. (1945). "Annual Report of the President." *Personnel Administration*, 7 (10), 18-19.

Clegg, S. (1981). "Organization and Control." *Administrative Science Quarterly*, 26, 545-262.

Creighton, A. (1990). "Some Aspects of the Emergence of Formal Organizations." Talk presented at the University of British Columbia, Fall.

Cullen, J.B. (1985). "Professional Differentiation and Occupational Earnings." *Work and Occupations*, 12 (3), 351-372.

Cyr, D. (Forthcoming). *International Joint Ventures: The Strategic Human Resource Management Challenge.* New York: Quorum Books.

Deal, T. and L. Bolman (1992). *Reframing Organization Theory.* San Francisco: Jossey-Bass.

Deal, T. and A. Kennedy (1982). *Corporate Cultures.* Reading, MA: Addison-Wesley.

Dept. of Commerce, U.S. Govt. (1993). *Statistical Abstract of the United States, 1993.* Washington, DC: U.S. Govt. Printing Office.

Dept. of International Economic and Social Affairs, United Nations. (1987). *Yearbook of International Trade Statistics.* New York: United Nations Publishing.

Devanna, M.A., C. Fombrun and N. Tichy (1984). "Human Resources Management: A Strategic Perspective." *Organizational Dynamics*, Winter, 51-67.

DiMaggio, P. (1985). "Interest and Agency in Institutional Theory." Paper presented at UCLA/NSF Conference on Institutional Theory.

DiMaggio, P. and W.W. Powell (1983). "The Iron Cage Revisited: Institutional Isomorphism and Collective Rationality in Organizational Fields." *American Sociological Review*, 48, 147-160.

Dobbin, F.R. (1992). "The Origins of Private Insurance, 1920-1950." *American Journal of Sociology*, 97 (5), 1416-1450.

Dobbin, F.R. and T. Boychuk (1993). "Job Autonomy and National Context: Evidence from Nine Nations." Paper presented at the American Sociological Annual Meeting, 1991.

Dobbin, F.R., L. Edelman, J.W. Meyer, W.R. Scott and A. Swidler (1988). "The Expansion of Due Process in Organizations." In L. Zucker (ed.), *Institutional Patterns and Organizations*, Cambridge, MA: Ballinger, 70-98.

Dobbin, F.R., J.R. Sutton, J.W. Meyer and W.R. Scott (1994). "Equal Opportunity Law and the Construction of Internal Labor Markets." *American Journal of Sociology*, 99 (4), 396-427.

Dobbin, F.R., W.R. Sutton, J.W. Meyer and W.R. Scott (1991). "The Renaissance of Internal Labor Markets: The Effects of Affirmative Action." Paper presented at SCOR Conference, Asilomar, CA.

Doeringer, P.B. and M.J. Piore (1971). *Internal Labor Markets and Manpower Analysis*. Lexington, MA: Lexington Books.

Dunlop, J.T. (1950). *Wage Determination Under Trade Unions*. New York: August M. Kelley.

Dyer, L. and G.W. Holder (1988). "A Strategic Perspective of Human Resources Management." In L. Dyer and J. Tolman (eds.), *HRM: Evolving Roles and Responsibilites*. Washington, DC: Bureau of National Affairs, 1/1-1/45.

Economic and Social Commission of Asia and the Pacific, United Nations (1993). *Statistical Yearbook of Asia and the Pacific, 1992*. New York: United Nations Statistics Division.

Edelman, L.B. (1992). "Legal Ambiguity and Symbolic Structures: Organizational Mediation of Civil Rights Laws." *American Journal of Sociology*, 97 (6), 1531-1576.

Edwards, R. (1979). *Contested Terrain: The Transformation of the Workplace in the Twentieth Century*. New York: Basic Books.

Flanagan, R.J., L.M. Kahn, R.S. Smith and R.G. Ehrenberg (1989). *Economics of the Employment Relationship*. Glenview, IL: Scott, Foresman and Company.

Fombrun, C., N. Tichy and M.A. Devanna (1984). *Strategic Human Resources Management*. New York: John Wiley and Sons.

Frost, P.J. (1989). "The Role of Organizational Power and Politics in Human Resource Management." *Research in Personnel and Human Resources Management*, Supplement 1. Greenwich, CT: JAI Press.

Frost, P.J. and D. Cyr (1990). "Selective Frames, Findings, and Futures: A Review of the Second Conference on International Personnel and Human Resources Management." *Research in Personnel in Human Resources Management*, Supplement 2. Greenwich, CT: JAI Press.

Frost, P.J. and C.T. Egri (1989). "The Political Process of Innovation." In L.L. Cummings and B.M. Staw (eds.), *Research in Organizational Behavior*, Vol. 13. Greenwich, CT: JAI Press.

Gerlach, M. (1992). *Alliance Capitalism: The Social Organization of Japanese Business*. Berkeley, CA: University of California Press.

Gibb, H. (1993). "Spanning the Pacific for Growth: APEC's 15 Economies Strengthen Their Links". *Briefing of North-South Institute*, 1993-B35.

Gordon, D.M., R. Edwards and M. Reich (1982). *Segmented Work, Divided Workers*. London: Cambridge University Press.

Hamilton, G. and N. Woolsey Biggart (1988). "Market, Culture, and Authority: A Comparative Analysis of Management and Organization in Far East Asia." *American Journal of Sociology*, 94 Supplement, pp. 52-94.

Harris, P.R. and R.T. Moran (1991). *Managing Cultural Differences*. London: Gulf Publishing Co.

Harrison, J. (1994). *Manage the People Issues, the Dollars Will Flow.* Vancouver: KPGM Management Consulting.

Hickson, D.J., C.R. Hinings, C.A. Lee, R.E. Schneck and J.M. Pennings (1971). "A Strategic Contingencies Theory of Intraorganizational Power." *Administrative Science Quarterly*, 14 (3), 378-397.

Hinings, C.R., D.J. Hickson, J.M. Pennings and R.E. Schneck (1974). "Structural Conditions of Intraorganizational Power." *Administrative Science Quarterly*, 19 (1), 22-44.

Hoffman, M.S. (1992). *The World Almanac and Book of Facts*. New York: Pharos Book.

Hofstede, G. (1980). *Culture's Consequences: International Differences in Work-related Values*. Beverly Hill: Sage Publications.

International Monetary Fund (1992). *The Direction of Trade Statistics*. Washington, D.C.: Statistics Division of the IMF.

Jacoby, S.M. (1983). "The Early Years of Personnel Management in the United States: 1900-1930: The Rise and Fall of Professionalism." Unpublished manuscript.

Jacoby, S.M. (1985). *Employing Bureaucracy: Managers, Unions, and the Transformation of Work in American Industry, 1900-1945*. New York: Columbia University Press.

Jemison, D. and P. O'Mara (1992). *Managing Workforce 2000: Gaining the Diversity Edge.* San Francisco: Jossey-Bass Publishing.

Jennings, P.D. (1994). "Viewing Macro HRM from Without." *Research in Personnel and Human Resources Management*. Vol. 12. Greenwich, CT: JAI Press, pp. 1-40.

Kalleberg, A.L. and I. Berg (1987). *Work and Industry: Structure, Market and Processes.* New York: Plenum Press.

Kochan, T.A. and P. Cappelli (1984). "The Transformation of The Industrial Relations and Personnel Function." In P. Osterman (ed.), *Internal Labor Markets*. Cambridge, MA: MIT Press..

Leonard, J.S. (1984). "The Impact of Affirmative Action on Employment." *Journal of Labor Economics*, 2 (4), 439-463.

Lengnick-Hall, C. and M.L. Lengnick-Hall (1988). "Strategic Human Resources Management: A Review of the Literature and a Proposed Typology." *Academy of Management Review*, 13 (3), 454-470.

Lincoln, J.R. and A.L. Kalleberg (1985). "Work Organization and Workforce Commitment: A Study of Plants and Employees in the U.S. and Japan." *American Sociological Review*, 50, 738-760.

McPhillips, D. (1990). "Pay Equity and Employment Equity." IRM Division Seminar Series, University of British Columbia, Vancouver.

Meyer, J.W. and B. Rowan (1977). "Institutionalized Organizations: Formal Structure as Myth and Ceremony." *American Journal of Sociology*, 83 (Sept.), 340-363.

Meyer, J.W. and W.R. Scott (1983). *Organizational Environments: Ritual and Rationality.* Beverly Hills: Sage.

Moore, L.F. and P.D. Jennings (1993). "Canadian Human Resources Management at the Crossroads." *Asia Pacific Journal of Human Resources*, 31 (2), 12-25.

Nininger, J.R. (1982). *Managing Human Resources: A Strategic Perspective.* Ottawa: The Conference Board.

Nkomo, S.M. (1980). "Stage Three in Personnel Administration: Strategic Human Resources Management." *Personnel*, 57, 69-77.

Noland, M. (1992). *Pacific Basin Developing Countries: Prospects for the Future.* Washington, DC: Institute for International Economics.

Palmer, R.R. and J. Colton (1971). *A History of the Modern World.* New York, NY: Knopf Press.

PECC (1994). "Pacific Economic Cooperation Council." CANCPEC Secretariat: Jan., 1-3.

Pfeffer, J. (1992). *Managing with Power.* Cambridge, MA: Harvard Business School Press.

Pfeffer, J. (1994). *Competitive Advantage Through People.* Boston: Harvard Business School Press.

Pfeffer, J. and Y. Cohen (1984). "Determinants of Internal Labor Markets in Organizations." *Adminstrative Science Quarterly*, 29, 550-73.

Pfeffer, J. and G.R. Salancik (1978). *The External Control of Organizations: A Resource Dependence Perspective.* New York: Harper and Row.

Pieper, R. (1991). *Human Resource Management: An International Comparison.* Berlin: Walter de Gruyter.

Pinfield, L.T. (1994). *The Operation of Internal Labor Markets: Staffing Practices and Vacancy Chains.* San Francisco, CA: Jossey-Bass.

Pinfield, L.T. and M.F. Bernier (1994). "Internal Labor Markets: Towards a Coherent Conceptualization." *Research in Personnel and Human Resources Management*, Vol. 12. Greenwich, CT: JAI Press.

Porter, M. (1990). *Competitive Strategy: Techniques for Analyzing Industries and Competitors.* New York: Free Press.

Powell, W.W. and P.J. DiMaggio (1991). *The New Institutionalism in Organizational Analysis.* Chicago: University of Chicago Press.

Reader's Digest (1983). *The Great World Atlas.* New York: Reader's Digest Magazine.

Reich, R. (1983). *The Next American Frontier.* New York: Penguin Books.

Saffarti-Larson, M.S. (1977). *The Rise of Professionalism: A Sociological Analysis.* Berkeley: University of California Press.

Saha, S.K. (1989). "Variations in the Practice of Human Resource Management: A Review." *Canadian Journal of Admistrative Sciences*, 34, 37-45.

Schuler, R.S. (1987). *Personnel and Human Resource Management.* (3rd ed.) St. Paul, MN: West Publishing.

Schuler, R.S., P.J. Dowling and H. De Cieri (1993). "An Integrative Framework of Strategic International Human Resources Management." *Journal of Management*, 19 (2), 419-459.

Scott, J. (1986). *Capitalist Property and Financial Power.* Brighton: Wheatsheaf Books.

Scott, W.R. (1987). "The Adolescence of Institutional Theory." *Administrative Science Quarterly*, 32, 493-511.

Selznick, P. (1948). "Foundations of the Theory of Organization." *American Sociological Review*, 13, 23-35.

Smith, Adam (1776). *An Enquiry into the Nature and Causes of the Wealth of Nations*. Chicago: University of Chicago Press.

Springer B. and S. Springer (1991). "Human Resources Management in the U.S. – Celebration of its Centenary." In R. Pieper (ed.), *Human Resource Management: An International Comparison*. Berlin: Walter de Gruyter.

Starr, P. (1982). *The Social Transformation of American Medicine*. New York: Basic Books.

Strayer, J.R., H.W. Gatzke and E.H. Harbison (1974). *The Mainstream of Civilization: To 1715*. New York, NY: Harcourt, Brace Jovanovich.

Steers, R.M., Y.K. Shin, G.R. Ungson and S. Nam (1990). "Korean Corporate Culture: A Comparative Analysis." *Research in Personnel and Human Resources Management*. Supplement 2, 247-262.

Stewman, S. (1986). "Demographic Models of Internal Labor Markets." *Administrative Science Quarterly*, 31, 212-247.

Sutton, J.R., F. Dobbin, J.W. Meyer and W.R. Scott (1993). "The Legalization of the Workplace." *American Journal of Sociology*, 100, 944-971.

Tichy, N., C.J. Fombrun and M.A. Devanna (1982). "Strategic Human Resource Management." *Sloan Management Review*, 24, 47-60.

Thompson, M. (1991). "Canadian Industrial Relations." In G.J. Bamber and R.D. Lansbury (eds.) *Comparative Industrial Relations*. (2nd ed.) George Allen and Unwin.

Tolbert, P.S. and L.G. Zucker (1983). "Institutional Sources of Change in the Formal Structure of Organizations: The Diffusion of Civil Service Reforms, 1980-1935." *Administrative Science Quarterly*, 23, 22-39.

Tsui, A. (1987). "Defining the Activities and Effectiveness of the Human Resource Department: A Multiple Constituency Approach." *Human Resources Management*, 26 (1), 35-69.

Tung, R. (1989). "Strategic Management of Resources in the Multinational Enterprise." *Human Resources Management*, 23 (2), 129-144.

Tung, R. (1990). "International Human Resource Management Policies and Practices: A Comparative Analysis." *Research in Personnel and Human Resources Management*. Supplement 2. Greenwich, CT: JAI Press.

Weber, M. (1924). *The Theory of Social and Economic Organization*. Glencoe, IL: The Free Press.

Young, S. (1992). "Globalism and Regionalism: Complements or Competitors?" Paper presented at PAFTAD's Conference on the Pacific Dynamism and the International Economic System. Washington, DC: Institute for International Economics.

Zucker, L.G. (1987). "Institutional Theories of Organizations." *Annual Review of Sociology*, 13, 671-670.

HRM in Selected Pacific Rim Countries

Human Resource Management in Australia

Diane Shelton

Introduction

Human resource management (HRM) in Australia is in a very critical phase of development. Recent changes in the international economic standing of Australia have created an "economic crisis" mentality that is having a lasting impact on business and politics in this country. These changes are perhaps best typified by the then Treasurer Paul Keating's famous "banana republic" statement:

We must let Australians know truthfully, honestly, just what sort of an international hole Australia is in. The price of our commodities is as bad in real terms as during the Depression. That is a fact of Australian life now...

If this Government can't get the adjustment, get manufacturing going again, and keep moderate wage outcomes and a sensible economic policy, then Australia is basically done for. We will end up being a third-rate economy.

If Australia is so undisciplined, so disinterested in its salvation, that the government must slow the economy down to zero growth [to control imports], then you know you are a banana republic (*Age*, May 15, 1986).

Keating's comment reflected the reality that Australia is no longer the "Lucky Country" enjoying a very comfortable standard of living from the consistent proceeds of the export of primary products. Changes in international trade, particularly the formation of the EC and the growth of trade blocs, and increasing protection in agricultural industry in the EC and the USA, together with increasing competition in the commodities market from new players like Argentina and South America have meant that Australia's certain income is diminishing; and little effort had been made to supplement it through alternative exports. The prolonged period of relative prosperity has enabled the development of a highly regulated and highly protected economy in Australia. The Australian workforce – employees and managers alike – have not been used to the idea of needing to be internationally competitive (Stace, 1987).

The reality of the recession, the historically and unacceptably high levels of unemployment (around 10.5% in 1992), international credit downgrading by Moodys and the increase in the current account deficit (for the calendar year 1991 a deficit of 3.5% of GDP, the third highest among OECD countries), have all combined over the last five years to focus Australian business, government, academia and the population on the need to work more productively and more effectively.

The implications for HRM in Australia are far reaching. The need to restructure the economy has meant that the key economic systems are under very close scrutiny. The industrial relations system, the regulation of the labour market and the structure and management of work practices at the workplace level are all being revised. The trend is to move away from our highly regulated, centralised system to a more flexible, decentralised system and to develop a more highly trained, better managed and flexible workforce. HRM has been identified as an important strategic tool in changing the Australian workplace culture from one of complacency to one of competitiveness (Dunphy, 1987; Stace, 1987; Collins, 1987). The question of whether or not HRM is the panacea for which the Australian economy has been looking is a significant one. It is unlikely that a single approach is going to be able to deliver all the outcomes required. However, I believe that through more sophisticated and culturally sensitive HRM management, the Australian workforce can be markedly improved into the next century.

The current situation reflects the early stages of this series of changes in work-place management. As will be seen from the various empirical studies cited in this chapter, Australian managers have become much more aware of the centrality of human resources in the business enterprise. However, there is still a lack of commitment to fully integrating human resource strategies with overall business strategies. There is still too much rhetoric about the importance of people and not enough change in management practices. In many cases this is not simply a result of a lack of true commitment but more a lack of understanding of just how to implement the changes in ways that are integrated with the overall business pro-cesses. Human resource professionals have a central role to play in educating and developing management understanding of how to reorganise and reconceptualise management. In order to trace some of these changes in workplace practice and policies in Australia and the development of the awareness of the need for change, this chapter will provide a brief geo-political overview of Australia, a review of the development of industrial relations in Australia and a picture of the current position of HRM in Australian organisations.

Australia – A Brief Geo-political Overview

Australia is a large island continent (7.5 million square kilometres) situated in the Asia Pacific region but possessing a strong Western cultural and political tradition. The nation's cultural inheritance and its geographical positioning is an accident of history and one that is only now, in the 1990s, beginning to be fully appreciated by most Australians.

Australia was "discovered" by a British naval captain, James Cook, in 1770 (there is evidence of earlier exploration of the "Great South Land" by the Dutch, the Spanish and the French) and was formally annexed by the British Crown in 1788 at the time of the First Settlement at Sydney Cove. The country was, of course, already inhabited by aborigines who migrated from South-East Asia at least 40,000 years ago. Estimates of the aboriginal population of Australia at the time of European settlement vary considerably from 300,000 to 750,000 (ABS, 1992a). What is not disputed, however, is that an aboriginal way of life was well established. At the time of settlement the British Crown ignored the legal right of the aborigines and proclaimed the land *Terra Nullis* signifying that the land was uninhabited; thus, at one stroke dispossessing the aboriginal population. *Terra Nullis* has only just been adjudged a "legal fiction" in the landmark Mabo decision handed down by the Supreme Court of Australia in 1993 opening the way for land right claims by contemporary aborigines. For most of the past two hundred years, however, the history of Australia has been one of British settlement and development.[1]

Australia's regional position, in South-East Asia, has played very little part in the development of its economic, social and political practices during its relatively short history. Founded initially as a British penal colony – transportation of convicts to New South Wales was not abolished until 1850 and the practice continued in Tasmania until 1853 (ABS, 1992a) – the country derived many of its practices and traditions directly from Britain. Most new settlers in the nineteenth century came from Britain and the substantial Chinese migration that accompanied the 1850s gold rush was officially regulated in 1861 and restricted in Queensland in 1878 (ABS, 1992a). Although, non-British European immigration increased substantially after the Second World War and South-East Asian immigration increased significantly after the Vietnam War, the first 150 years of modern Australian settlement was shaped by British assumptions, norms and values. As a significant member of the British Commonwealth, Australia has continually strengthened these ties. So Australia has been in the somewhat anomalous situation of being culturally British (at least for the first 150 years) and geographically Asian.

Indeed, the Australian nation is not only a member of the British Common-wealth of Nations but the titular head of Australia is still the Queen of England, represented in Australia by the Governor General in Canberra and in the various states by state governors. The question of national identity has been raised re-cently in the debate over whether or not Australia should become a republic with a President as head of state rather than the Queen of England as the titular head of state. The pro-republicans, lead by the current Prime Minister Paul Keating, suggest that it is time for Australia to cut the last largely ceremonial ties with Britain and establish a more distinctly Australian identity in keeping with the increasingly multicultural nation that we have become. The monarchists naturally argue for continuity with the past and for the stability and security of a system that has been shown to work.

The significance of this current debate is that it reflects the underlying uncertainty on the part of many Australians about just how to define themselves as a nation and about how they would like to see themselves develop into the next century. Australians have only really started to look to the implications of their regional position as part of Asia during the last two decades. This shift in focus from Europe and the USA to Asia has been prompted by economic necessity. The formation of the EEC led to a decrease in trade with Britain and the developing economies in Asia offer a large potential market. Australia's largest trading partners as of 1993 are Japan, mainland China, Hong Kong and the USA (ABS, 1993). There has also been considerable increase in non-European immigration over the last twenty years (ABS, 1992a) which has also prompted more interest in the cultures and history of Asia. In the 1990s Australia may be seen as a country which still has very strong affiliations with Western countries but also as one with an emerging Asia-Pacific identity (refer to media coverage of Prime Minister Keating's September, 1992 trip to Japan, especially *The Age* and *The Australian*; Korporaal, 1992; Grattan, 1992).

This awareness of the importance and significance of Asia for Australia is reflected in the wide-ranging relationships that Australia has now developed with its ASEAN neighbours (Indonesia, Malaysia, the Philippines, Thailand, Singapore and Brunei). The issue of trade is an important one with the Asia Pacific region currently accounting for 71% of merchandise exports and 66% of merchandise imports (ABS, 1991).

The most important development in this area was the Australian initiative to establish APEC (the Asia Pacific Economic Council) in Seoul in January, 1989. APEC comprises the six ASEAN nations – Indonesia, Malaysia, the Philippines, Thailand, Singapore and Brunei – and Australia, Japan, the Republic of Korea, New Zealand, Canada, the USA, China, Taiwan and Hong Kong. The main aims of APEC are to provide a forum for open discussion of international trade and development, to lobby for multilateral trade liberalisation in GATT negotiations and to identify specific areas for further cooperation. APEC has now passed its formative stages and is acknowledged as the pre-eminent forum for economic cooperation in the region. The success of the most recent APEC conference in Seattle in 1993 was a strong indicator of the strength of this forum.

However, cultural relations are also seen as important and a programme of cultural activities is now administered by the Department of Foreign Affairs and Trade. The major emphasis for the programme is on South-East Asia, the South Pacific, North and East Asia, South Asia and Indian Ocean countries (ABS, 1991). The programme includes overseas tours of all types of performing and visual arts, promotion of Australian literature and literary studies, promotion of general Australian studies, cultural assistance, visitor exchange, book gifts and sporting gifts and exchanges.

Politics

Politically, the Australian system is heavily indebted to the British system. As a British colony until 1900, Australian laws were British laws except where altered by the colonial legislatures. Many principles of British law still dominate the Australian legal system. In 1900 the Australian Constitution was enacted and a federal system of government instituted. Under this system, power is shared by the central federal government and the six states and two territories, which are New South Wales, Victoria, Queensland, Tasmania, South Australia, Western Australia, The Northern Territory and The Australian Capital Territory.

The federal government can only make statute laws on the subjects listed in the Constitution, mainly in Section 51. These include: defence, foreign affairs, and customs and excise. The States retain the right to legislate on most other matters such as education, industrial health and safety, and local government. The majority of law-making powers are "concurrent powers" shared by state and federal governments.

Federal power in Australia is currently held by the Labour Party while power in five of the six states is held by the Liberal Party. The Labour Party in Australia has held federal power since 1983 after a long period of almost continuous Liberal Party rule (the exception here was the Whitlam Labour government from 1972-75). The Labour Party of the 1990s can be broadly categorised as a social democratic party with a belief in the importance of social service safety networks at the same time as acknowledging the need to stimulate a strong free market economy. The Liberal Party has traditionally been the more conservative party, advocating the importance of individual development, a strong business sector and small government. Numerous complications arise in coordinating the varying philosophical assumptions across state and federal governments, and these problems are clearly seen in the area of industrial relations. An example of how the problems are played out is given below in the section on industrial relations.

The power that is crucial to human resource management is the industrial relations power. Under Sec. 51 (xxxv) of the federal Constitution, the federal government can legislate for the settlement of interstate industrial disputes. If a conflict arises between a valid federal industrial law and a valid state law, the Constitution, in Section 109, provides that the federal law shall prevail (Robbins et al, 1986). This sharing of power has understandably led to some friction and long-standing tension between the states and the federal government. A description of the current balance of industrial power in Australia forms an important backdrop to an understanding of the development and practice of human resource management in Australia. This issue will be covered in the next section on industrial relations.

Australian Industrial Relations

Industrial relations has developed a very high profile in Australia in the 1990s. With combined effects of recession, increasing international competition, de-creasing stability in financial markets, decreasing stability in commodity markets and a worsening balance of trade, the question of how to transform the lagging Australian economy is central to any political discussion. Politicians, economists, businessmen and trade unionists are increasingly arguing about the role and in-fluence of the current centralised and highly regulated industrial relations system on workplace productivity and initiative. Indeed, a system which has been sub-stantially in place since 1904, albeit with many marginal changes, is now being seriously challenged from a number of directions. There is general agreement among all parties that some change is required. The most contentious issue is how much and how radical a change is necessary? How far down the path to unregu-lated enterprise-based bargaining does the country need to go and how far is the country likely to want to go? The implications for human resource management in this debate are far reaching.

The industrial relations system in Australia is characterised by a highly regu-lated system of awards and a compulsory conciliation and arbitration policy. The main parties in Australian industrial relations are governments, state and federal; tribunals, state and federal; employers and employees. Whilst the governments have been involved in framing and enforcing statutory workplace rules – examples here would include the various state legislations concerning EEO (equal employ-ment opportunity) and OSHWA (occupational safety, health and welfare) – they have generally left the regulation of workplace conflict and disagreement to the in-dependent tribunals. The tribunals, in particular the Australian Industrial Relations Commission (AIRC), are central to the compulsory arbitration and conciliation system that lies at the heart of industrial relations in Australia.

The other major players comprise the peak employee body, the Australian Council of Trade Unions (ACTU) and the peak employer bodies, the Business Council of Australia (BCA) and the Australian Chamber of Commerce and Indus-try (ACCI). It would be fair to observe that the ACTU has been more successful in developing a strong and united voice in industrial relations policy debates in the country than have either of the employer bodies. The BCA is beginning to emerge as a stronger and more united advocate of employers in the last five years, and the recent round of mergers which has resulted in the formation in 1992 of the ACCI should result in a much stronger and more integrated voice for employers than previously has been the case.

An impressive system of state and federal machinery has been generated to administer and regulate industrial relations from a relatively centralised position (see Figure 1 for an indication of how the federal system works). State tribunals are free to legislate on a wide variety of industrial relations issues and have been responsible for the development of a number of important employment

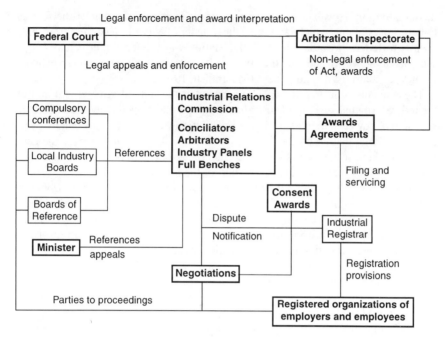

Figure 1:   The Federal System

conditions like workers' compensation, long-service leave, safety legislation and anti-discrimination legislation. The state systems are varied in their structures and procedures and this reflects the political and philosophical differences of the individual state governments.

This difference is no more evident than in the state of Victoria since the election to power of the Liberal Party under the leadership of J.G. Kennett in late 1992. Kennett's government immediately passed legislation to radically transform the existing centralised system and facilitate a more voluntarist and decentralized system. The legislation abolished all state awards, established the requirement for all employers and employees to enter collective or individual agreements, made unionism voluntary, excluded unions from the enterprise agreement process, banned all industrial action in specified essential services industries and made voting compulsory for all industrial action, which in any case could not exceed five days.

This legislation was perceived by those on the right as in the vanguard of the new model competitive Australian workplace, and the impact of the legislation was very closely monitored by other state Liberal governments and by the federal Liberal opposition. The impact was marked. The Victorian legislature pushed through the changes in a tough and uncompromising way that created a strong and polarized reaction. There were popular mass demonstrations and much adverse media attention. However, the most significant response was that of the federal Labour government, which facilitated the transfer of Victorian workers from state awards to federal awards where the legislation was rendered ineffectual. Large sections of the workforce took the opportunity to make this change and so to avoid the new decentralised state system (MacIntosh, 1993).

These events reinforce the role and power of the federal government and of the federal tribunal system in Australia. Although the states do have considerable substantive power in the field of industrial relations; ultimately, they can by over-ruled to a large degree by the federal jurisdiction. This is increasingly the case in an era where so much business is carried on across state boundaries, and thus more employees legitimately become part of the federal system.

Federal tribunals are also dominant in the area of wages, where nearly 40% of the workforce comes under federal tribunal jurisdiction (Deery and Plowman, 1991, p. 123). Whilst the Industrial Relations Act (1988) still provides for compul-sory arbitration of industrial disputes, the commission has flexibility in resolving disputes through conciliation, and legalistic bureaucracy is minimized. However, the undoubtedly centralised nature of the system has had a strong influence on the prevalent attitudes of both managers and employees.

The genesis of the current state of affairs in industrial relations in this country is related to a long standing political and social history. Workplaces have been the "takers" rather than the "makers" of industrial relations policy. The origins of the system lie in the labour unrest of the 1890s which resulted in strikes and lockouts that threatened the social stability of the young colony. After foundation in 1900, legislators attempted to frame an Act that would enshrine some principles that would ensure industrial harmony and economic stability (Deery and Plowman, 1991). The decision to adopt compulsory arbitration was in part influenced by the experiences of the states of New South Wales and South Australia which had legislated for voluntary arbitration in the 1890s, but to no real effect. A further factor contributing to the acceptance of the Act was the passing of the *Excise Tariff Act* in 1906. This Act provided for trade protection through tariffs and also imposed an excise on employers who did not pay fair and reasonable wages. So, in essence, it provided trade protection for manufacturers in return for the payment of fair and reasonable wages. Thus, the interests of both employers and employees were linked through the legislative machinery. This structural linking of industry protection and government intervention in the setting of the "basic wage" has had the effect of undermining a sense of economic reality among both employers and employees. Australia's economy was strong enough to sustain this degree of protection for most of this century. However, this is no longer the case. Australia's GDP has fallen to the bottom third of the OECD rankings after having been near the top until the 1960s (OECD Survey, 1991/1992). Need for change is clearly indicated.

Although the Act has been one of the most frequently amended Common-wealth Acts, sustaining more than 70 amendments from 1904 to 1988 (Deery and

Plowman, 1991), it has nevertheless retained its essential characteristics over a period of more than 80 years and provided a significant and stable set of guiding principles for industrial relations in Australia. It was repealed and replaced by the *Industrial Relations Act 1988*, which has a more contemporary emphasis on the promotion of consensus and collaboration in the workplace and less emphasis on the machinery of industrial regulation. However, the centralised nature of the system remains, as does the place of compulsory conciliation and arbitration.

There are three major concepts implicit in the Australian industrial relations system: the concept of the basic wage, the concept of comparative wage justice, and the concept of the capacity to pay (Hill, 1987). These three concepts encapsulate some of the values and norms central to the Australian ethos. The basic or "living" wage concept was introduced in the 1907 Harvester Award and reflected a view that all workers were entitled to a minimum level of remuneration to provide for "the normal *needs* of the average employee regarded as a human being in a civilised society" (Higgins, 1968, p. 3). It was further emphasised that this "needs" component of the wage should be seen as an irreducible minimum: "unless society is to be perpetually in industrial unrest, it is necessary to keep this living wage as a thing sacrosanct beyond the reach of bargaining" (Higgins, 1968, p. 53).

Fair play and egalitarianism are reflected in the concept of comparative wage justice, where the setting of wage relativities provides for some equalization of wages and working conditions across industries. Thus "employees doing the same work for different employers or in different industries should by and large receive the same amount of pay..." (Engineering Oil Industry Case 1970, 134 CAR, p. 165, cited in Deery and Plowman, 1991, p. 340-341). This principle has become an important mechanism for transmitting wage gains from one award to another – the "flow-on effect" – and has resulted in the development of significant central wage cases which in effect have set the standards for numerous related awards.

The third concept, that of "capacity to pay", refers to the capacity of the industry to pay. That is, wage bargaining is predicated on the capacity of the industry as a whole to pay and is not related to the current level of profits of individual firms. From the outset the Industrial Court took the view that its obligation was to award a fair wage and not to be influenced by the level of firm profit. "The Act is not an Act for profit sharing, but for securing peace in industries..." (Seaman's Case 1911, 5 CAR 164, cited in Deery and Plowman, 1991, p. 338).

All of these principles – the basic wage, comparative wage justice and capacity to pay – have the effect of shifting industrial bargaining away from the enterprise, away from the primary participants in the workplace and away from the economic realities of the market place. They demonstrate a greater preoccupation with social principles than with economic realities (Hill, 1987). There are many who would argue that as Australia has moved into the increasingly competitive global market place of the late twentieth century, it is no longer possible to ignore the realities

of the market and that Australia as a nation has to work to reconstruct industry
and the industrial relations system.

The calls for change come quite unanimously from all quarters. The most contentious issue is how much and how radical a change is necessary. The politically
conservative Liberal Party (currently in federal opposition, 1994) has proposed
a radical restructuring of the industrial relations system which will, over time,
disband the current centralized system in favour of enterprise-based bargaining
(Liberal coalition, 1991 and Liberal coalition, 1992). The main employer groups,
the Business Council of Australia (BCA) and the Australian Chamber of Commerce and Industry (ACCI), support and actively lobby for this position. The
BCA commissioned and published a report into Australian industry in 1989 and
subsequently published its study, *Enterprise Based Bargaining Units: A Better
Way of Working* (BCA, 1989). This BCA report argues for reform of the current
industrial relations system with a move to what it calls employee relations (BCA,
1989, p. 5). The authors of the report, Hilmer et al, claim that employee relations
would signal a shift to greater emphasis on the enterprise as the site of workplace
bargaining, greater responsiveness on the part of Australian firms to the demands
of the market place, increased concern for the development of a common purpose at work between management and employees and the production of a more
competitive and productive culture in the workplace (BCA, 1989, p. 8).

The two other major players in the Australian industrial system – the unions and
the federal government (currently the Labour Party, 1993) – have expressed similar
desires to see some of the more restrictive machinery of the system modified
and reconfigured to facilitate greater productivity and growth in the economy.
The Australian Council of Trade Unions (ACTU), Australia's major trade union
group at the national level and a dominant force in industrial relations, produced
a report in 1987, *Australia Reconstructed*, which stressed the need for greater
flexibility in the system to allow for enterprise-based agreements, the reduction of
the number of unions, a move to industry-or enterprise-based unions away from
craft or occupational unions and a greater degree of consensus and collaboration
in the workplace. This stance has been consistently supported and elaborated by
the Labour government's initiatives in award restructuring and the development
of industry policy. All groups have a common desire to move towards a more
flexible and responsive system.

The difference then lies in the role of the centralised system (Palmer, 1988;
Marginson, 1991; Frenkel and Peetz, 1990). The opponents of the current system
argue that its cumbersome machinery and centralised nature are profoundly at
odds with any proposal to decentralise and "free-up" the system; further, that
it is the very nature of the current system that works against productivity and
initiative in the Australian economy (Drago et al, 1992; BCA, 1989; Niland,
1990). Supporters of the current system argue that since 1983, a very large number
of enterprise-based agreements have been negotiated and registered with the
Industrial Relations Commission (Callus et al, 1991; Jorgensen, 1991; Groves,

1990) and that this demonstrates the inherent flexibility of the system. They also suggest that the existence of the system provides a "safety net" for those employees who may be unable to negotiate directly and equally with management (Shaw, 1990).

While the debate is ongoing and far from resolved, there have in fact been many changes to the industrial relations system during the 1980s. This series of reforms to industrial relations began with the election of the Hawke Labour government in 1983 and the historic Accord summit, which was held soon after the election. The Accord was a bipartite agreement between the Australian Labour Party (ALP) and the ACTU. Its key concept was that the path to economic recovery should be one of consensus and collaboration. The initial summit meeting to launch the Accord in April of 1983 included representatives of government, unions and business. The Accord communique stressed the shift to corporatist, consensual negotiations on industry, prices and incomes policies (Dabscheck, 1989). Over the 1980s the Accord has been renegotiated several times with reference to wage indexation, industry restructuring and micro-economic reform relating to training. As an income policy it has been a clear success – the Accord has brought about significant falls in real wages and the longest period of industrial peace in more than twenty years (Lewis and Spiers, 1990).

More importantly, the Accord has provided a mechanism for generating change from within the current industrial relations system (National Wage Case Decision, October 1991).[2] It has facilitated cooperation and negotiation between the government, the unions and some of the key players in business, and has been a significant factor in enabling the government to make quite radical changes to industry through targeted deregulation (Jamieson and Westcott, 1992). At the same time, it has resisted the pressure to move too quickly to a completely open market system. As such, it protects the core values of egalitarianism and fair play that were built into the original *Conciliation and Arbitration Act*.

The Labour Force and Industrial Relations Practices

Australia has a population of 17 million people (1991) with 71% of them living in the state or territory capitals (OECD, 1991/1992). So the population density of 2.2 people to the square kilometre masks the real pattern of distribution. Australia is a very urbanized society and there is an increasing trend of rural to urban migration. Further, the major population regions in the south-east and south-west of the country rarely extend more than 200 or 300 kilometres inland.

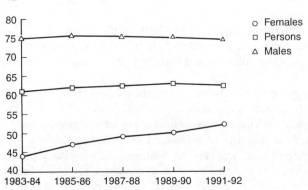

Figure 2: Participation Rates, Annual Average
Source: ABS (1992b)

Employment Rates over Time

The size and composition of the labour force in Australia varies over time to reflect changing social and economic realities. As can be seen in Figure 2, the annual average participation rate for males declined from 75.6% in 1986-87 to 74.5% in 1991-92. At the same time the annual average participation rate for women has risen from 48.7% in 1986-87 to 52.2% in 1990-91. The increasing number of women in the workforce has resulted in a number of significant changes in both the industrial relations arena and in human resource management. This will be discussed in more detail below. The fall in male participation rates reflects the recession and the rise in unemployment rates to an historic high of 10.8% in 1992 (ABS, 1992a).

Migration has always been an important component in the growth of population in Australia. In the period 1971-1989 migration is estimated to have contributed 40% of total population growth (ABS, 1991). Indeed, recent growth in the population is due more to migration than to natural increase (1988 and 1989). However, the composition of the migrant intake has been changing over the last two decades. Although British migrants remain the most numerous settlers, they have declined in absolute numbers and as a proportion of the whole. There has been an increase in the number of arrivals from Asian countries, particularly from Vietnam, the Philippines, Malaysia and Hong Kong, who account for 20.4% of arrivals from 1986 to 1989 (ABS, 1991). The Australian government's policy of multiculturalism has encouraged the development of cultural diversity in the country. This has led to an increasing emphasis on plurality and difference. The very homogeneous Anglicised Australian ethos of the 1950s has been replaced by a much more heterogenous multicultural society.

The participation rate of different migrant groups is outlined in Table 1. From this it can be seen that migrants from non-English speaking countries are relatively disadvantaged in obtaining jobs. In particular, the Lebanese and those from

Table 1:   Labour Force by Birthplace

	Labour Force ('000)	Participation Rate (%)	Unemployment Rate (%)
Born in Australia	6410.3	65.2	10
Born outside Australia	2197.6	60.9	12.8
English Speaking Countries	945.1	65.1	10.2
Other countries	1252.5	58.1	14.7
New Zealand	184.1	77.2	12.6
Germany	67.7	60.8	12.1
Greece	77.7	55.4	9.6
Italy	135.6	48.6	11.7
Netherlands	62.4	59.1	4.2
UK and Ireland	682.5	61.6	9.9
Yugoslavia	113.6	65	14.8
Lebanon	33.7	50.1	37.3
Malaysia	44.2	62.9	13.9
Philippines	42.4	67.3	17.7
Vietnam	65.7	58.5	30.2
China	60.7	63.6	14
The Americas	78.7	71.3	13.9
India	38	65.8	11.5
Other	133.1	69.7	9.1

Source: *The Labour Force, Australia*: ABS (1992b)

the Middle East and North Africa, and the Vietnamese have very high rates of unemployment. This has meant that the federal government has needed to in-stitute a variety of programmes to stimulate job opportunities for these groups. The large number of migrants in the work force has also presented challenges for management in dealing with diversity, and a number of large organisations have put in place special training for both employees at the management level and on the shop floor to facilitate management of a multicultural workforce.

Although the recession is having an impact on special HR programmes within organisations, the number of women now participating in the Australian workforce (42% of total workforce, Callus et al, 1990) means that organisations cannot ignore their special needs. Table 2 indicates the rate of female participation in the labour force in 1990. This table shows the large number of women who are employed part-time in the labour force. This pattern of employment is a result of a number of socioeconomic factors, but one result is that relatively few women enjoy the same conditions of employment as full-time male employees. Part-time employees in

Table 2:   Employment in Australia, January 1990 (by gender)

	Number employed	Percentage of total	Employed full-time (%)	Employed part-time (%)
Women	3126,500	40.5	31.6	83.7
Men	4586,100	59	68.4	22.9

Source: ABS (1992b)

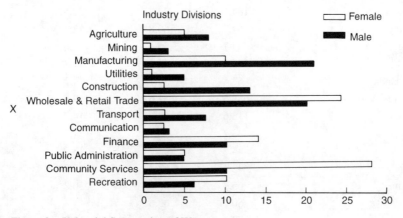

Figure 3:   Industrial Segregation of Women
Source: Department of Employment, Education and Training (1990)

general tend to be less likely to have superannuation entitlements, job tenure, training and development, leave entitlements and so on.

Distribution of women in the workforce tells a more disturbing story about the status of women at work in the Australian labour force. Figures 3 and 4 show the segregation of women by industry and occupation in Australia in 1990. As can be seen, women are over represented in community services, retail trade, recreation industries, clerical positions and sales positions. Table 3 indicates the state of pay equity across occupations. These figures demonstrate the failure of the Australian government and of Australian business to redress the imbalance in remuneration for men and women.

The current distribution of women in the workforce indicates that there are still serious structural problems limiting the most effective utilisation of their skills. Whilst the female participation rate is now almost equal to that of men in the workforce, they are employed in a narrow band of industries and disproportionately employed in part-time positions at the lower levels of the organisation. Quince and Lansbury report that only 13% of women in Australian organisations are at the managerial level, even in industries where there is a high level of female participation (Quince and Lansbury, 1988). Women in management tend to be

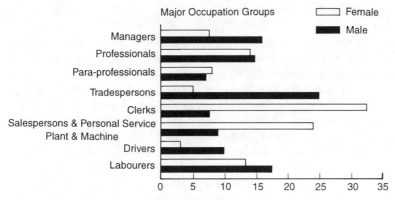

Figure 4:   Occupational Segregation of Women
Source: Department of Employment, Education and Training (1990)

Table 3:   Average Weekly Total Earnings for Adult Male and Female: Full-time Non-managerial Employees by Major Occupational Groups, Australia, May 1988

	Male	Female	Ratio
Professionals	595	527	.88
Para-professionals	535	498	.93
Trade persons	423	336	.79
Clerks	444	381	.86
Sales/personal service	442	366	.83
Machine operators	421	306	.73
Labourers	374	324	.86
All occupations	449	401	.89

Source: ABS (1992c)

clustered in the 'caring' occupations in the organisation – quite often the human resource or personnel area.

The Australian governments, both federal and state, have enacted equal employment opportunity legislation and this has been in place since the early 1980s (Kramer, 1991). However, the more subtle forms of systemic discrimination require organisation-based HR policies that are directed at redressing the inequities in the system. The challenge here for HRM is to identify ways of organising work that facilitates the best use of all employees. Some specific issues include the avoidance of sexual segregation of the workforce, the career implications of part-time work and "gaps" in career paths and the lack of child-care facilities (Carmody, 1991). These areas need attention not only in terms of equity but also because it is now recognised that the wastage of capability, expertise and effectiveness in not promoting women workers is costing Australia dearly.

Industrial Relations Practices

The study of industrial relations in Australia has tended to concentrate on analysis at the state and federal level rather than at the workplace or enterprise level. This has been a natural outcome of such a centralised system. However, greater attention is now being paid to the actual structure and workplace practices in Australian industry and a much clearer picture is emerging of how work is structured and managed within and across industries (Deery and Gahan, 1991). A very important and significant piece of work in this area is the recently published *Industrial Relations at Work: The Australian Workplace Industrial Relations Survey* (Callus et al, 1991, hereafter referred to as AWIRS). AWIRS consisted of two surveys: first, a survey of 2,004 workplaces with a minimum of 20 employees covering all states and territories and all industries except agriculture and defence; and secondly, a telephone survey of managers at 349 workplaces with between 5 and 19 employees. This survey provides a wealth of information about Australians at work and is well worth close analysis.

AWIRS confirms that Australia has a very uneven distribution of employment. The sample representing 68% of all Australian wage and salary earners demonstrates that while workplaces with 500 or more employees only constituted 1% of total workplaces, they employed a disproportionate 24% of the workforce. At the other end of the scale, workplaces employing 50 employees or less made up 87% of the total of workplaces but employed only 34% of the workforce. So while it is true that there are many small businesses in Australia, a disproportionate number of employees work in a very small number of organisations. Thus, what happens in a small number of large workplaces is likely to have a very significant impact on all employees. The question of organisational status revealed that half of all workplaces with more than 5 employees were part of a larger organisation. Indeed, in large workplaces of more than 200 employees 96% were part of a larger organisation. This finding has implications for workplace autonomy and regulation.

Trade unions are a prominent fact of Australian organisational life. There are currently approximately 299 unions operating in Australia (Callus et al, 1991) despite the ACTU's efforts to reduce the number to a more manageable 20 (ACTU, 1987). However, AWIRS reveals some interesting data about the distribution of unionism across workplaces and industries. From the survey it was estimated that 43% of Australian workplaces were unionised and that union membership stood at about 54% of total employees. Seventy percent of the union-free workplaces had 19 or fewer employees while only 4% of large workplaces of 500 or more employees were union-free. Union density varied with sector, with much higher densities in the public sector (74%), and industry: mining (88%), electricity, gas and water (83%), transport and storage (81%), wholesale and retail trade (30%), finance and business services (36%), and recreation and personal services (45%). Twenty-two percent of unionised workplaces had some form of management-union agreement to ensure 100% union membership of non-managerial employees; that is, a "closed-shop" provision. The closed shop was more likely to be the case in mining and communication.

Some of the more significant facts to emerge from AWIRS are the patterns of distribution of employees across workplaces, the increasing participation rate of women, the increasing incidence of part-time work and the patterns of unionism. For the current debate on the role and impact of the industrial relations system, these data tend to suggest that the necessary flexibility required to restructure Australian industry is available from within the system. The study draws attention to the centralisation of management decision-making that is a corollary of the high proportion of workplaces that are part of larger enterprises. This study also suggests that Australia has a tendency to centralisation in both management and labour processes.

The Rise of HRM in Australia

Nomenclature, as much as anything else, has signalled a significant shift in the role and status of human resource management in Australia in the last decade. Many organisations have changed the name of their personnel departments to HRM departments or employee relations departments (AWIRS, 1992), and now advertise for positions in HRM rather than in personnel. The peak professional body representing human resource management practitioners changed its name from the *Institute of Personnel Management Australia* to *Australian Human Resources Institute* as recently as March 1992. There has also been a considerable shift in the status assigned to managers in HRM, a trend reflected in their positions on senior management boards and committees, their reporting relationships within the organisations and in their levels of remuneration. What was once seen as an organisational "dead-end", primarily the province of female employees, is now enjoying enhanced prestige as an important component of organisation-wide strategy (Lansbury and Quince, 1988; BCA, 1990; NBEET, 1990; Schuler, 1988). The questions of how and why the change came about, the extent of any real substantive difference between Personnel and Human Resource Management, and the sustainability of the change are all the subjects of much academic and practitioner debate in Australia in the 1990s (Wright, 1993). In order to gain some insight into this contemporary debate, an overview of HR management in Australia is necessary.

HRM in Australia – The Background

Professional personnel management in Australia can be traced back to the period of the Second World War when manpower shortages and the demands of the war effort required the smooth assimilation of a large number of women into the workforce, many in very non-traditional roles (Cochrane, 1985).[3] The Australian government sponsored a series of courses in industrial welfare and personnel services at the universities of Sydney and Melbourne in 1941 (Gardner and Palmer, 1992). The graduates of these courses then went on to form the first association of personnel managers in Australia in 1943. A national association, the Institute of Personnel Management Australia (IPMA), was formed in 1951 and fully ratified with a constitution in December 1952. Forty-nine years later the name has just been changed to Australian Human Resources Institute – a reflection of the broader capacity and scope of the institute. AHRI sees itself as playing a role in leading HR strategic thinking and direction. AHRI currently has a membership of over 9,000.

Dexter Dunphy (1989) traces the development of the personnel function in Australia from the 1960s to the 1980s. He argues that "personnel" was basically a "housekeeping" operational level function in the 1960s and 1970s. The picture he draws of Australian organisations in the 1960s and 1970s is one of little management sophistication with a fundamental conception of employees as costs to be minimised rather than as assets to be managed. The personnel departments in organisations at that time were largely low-level departments concerned with hiring, remuneration, entitlements and retirement. There was enormous emphasis on record-keeping and on operationalising rather than on developing personnel policies. Heads of personnel departments were quite likely to have had little or no specific training or education in management and had often drifted into the job. Dunphy points to the prevalence of functionally structured organisations in Australia at the time and suggests that the general stability and predictability of organisational reality did not prompt any real proactivity on the part of managers. He suggests that it was the development of the more complex divisionalised form of organisation and the growing volatility of the general business environment of the late 1970s and 1980s that prompted the shift to more sophisticated management in general; and in particular, to more emphasis on strategy in management, and to the development of a more integrated and strategic human resource management approach.

In the late 1980s the Australian government recognised the importance of HRM in its efforts to restructure industry and promote a more productive business environment. The Accord, as renegotiated in March 1987, August 1988 and May 1989, specifically acknowledged the necessity of micro-economic reform. Such reforms related to issues central to HRM like multi-skilling, broad banding, changes to work patterns, and shifts in workplace authority and responsibility. Central to all of this is, of course, training. The government's priority on training is clearly signalled in the 1990 Training Guarantee Act. This Act stipulates that all organisations with payrolls of more than $A200,000 must spend a minimum of 1% (rising to 1.5% in 1991) of that payroll on training.

Government legislation for training highlights both the emphasis the government places on training as a way to develop an informed, flexible workforce, and the perception that Australian organisations have long undervalued the development of their people. Understandably, such a level of government intervention provoked debate on the issue. However, the overall investment of Australian organisations in their staff was far below comparable OECD countries (OECD, 1991/1992) – in 1990 Australian firms were spending on average 2.2% of turnover on training while German and Japanese firms were spending approximately 5% of turnover on training (Smith, 1993) – and this lack of investment was seen as one of the prime reasons for the poor performance of the Australian economy. The implications for HRM are clear: training has now become mandatory in sizeable Australian companies, with the result that there is an unprecedented need for detailed and professional training programmes.

HRM may actually provide a framework for analysis and theorising about workplace practices that has not been possible from within the study of industrial relations in Australia (Boxall and Dowling, 1990). Because of the centralised and institutionalised nature of industrial relations in Australia, most of the analysis and theorising has been focussed at the macro level. HRM allows a shift to the study of workplaces that re-examines the role of management, that provides frameworks for understanding enterprise level relations and for understanding indirect and informal management-employee relations (Boxall and Dowling, 1990, p. 209).

HRM in Organisations

While politicians, economists, academics and business strategists all agree that HRM is now a very important part of the overall economic effort, it is less clear that this message has been heeded by the average Australian manager. It is pertinent then to look at how many of the more proactive, strategic elements of HRM have been picked up by Australian organisations.

Human Resource Management Practices

A study of management development by the National Board of Employment, Education and Training (NBEET, 1990) found that there was a discernible trend towards well-developed human resource policies in large Australian organisations. Job analysis and performance appraisal appear to be central to Australian HR practices, primarily because they are seen to be directly related to identification of performance gaps and training needs. However, the study also showed that size was an important variable related to the incidence of formal HR programmes (NBEET, 1990). Smaller business units "are subject to the constraints of scale of operation" (NBEET, 1990, p. 27). As there are a large number of small workplaces (87% of all workplaces employ less than 50 employees) in Australia employing approximately 34% of the workforce (Callus et al, 1991), this would argue for the involvement of government in providing industry-related training and development programmes.

The NBEET survey found that on average Australian managers spent 3.9 days a year on training programmes, with 34% spending no time at all. The areas of greatest managerial deficiency were identified as "entrepreneurship, developing subordinates, bias to action [and] creativity and vision" (NBEET, 1990, p. 13); however, these areas received the smallest time budget – 10% of time allocated – while functional expertise, which had been identified as an area of strength, was allocated 40% of time budget (NBEET, 1990, p. 15). This suggests some lingering doubts about the efficacy of the "softer" areas of management training. Comparisons between the NBEET survey and the Ralph Report on management development (1981) show an increase in training effort of about 5% per annum. The increase in time budget from 1,700 days to 2,500 days appears mainly to be due to increased participation – the proportion of managers attending programmes increased from 60% to 75%. Also, the proportion of senior managers holding postgraduate qualifications has increased from 14% to 31% while the proportion holding no formal qualification has fallen from 28% to 13%.

Another survey of HR policies of 27 leading Australian organisations by the BCA revealed a very strong awareness of the importance of human resource management as a strategic tool. HR was seen as crucial to competitive edge (BCA, 1990). The expenditure of budget on training varied from 2.5%-10% of total payroll; far in excess of the government's mandatory 1%. However, it was recognised that training was not a panacea; that it needed to be clearly directed to areas of deficiency within the organisation and that a total integrated HR approach was necessary. It was also suggested that naive management failed to identify areas of need and tended to use training in an undirected and unsophisticated way (BCA, 1990). These companies all used specialist HRM managers and consciously tied HRM into overall strategic planning.

As mentioned above, training has been identified as a crucial component of an economic recovery and the Training Guarantee Scheme (TGS) was implemented in 1990 in an attempt to encourage greater investment in training and hence in the development of a more flexible and educated workforce. Early assessments of the TGS have been mixed with reports of widespread dissatisfaction on the part of employers who see the scheme as yet another impost on doing business (Smith, 1993). However, the findings of the now annual Training Expenditure Survey conducted by the Australian Bureau of Statistics indicate that the overall expenditure on training has indeed increased (Smith, 1993). There is some doubt about just how the money is being spent with some evidence that more training is being provided at the managerial level than at the shopfloor level (Waters-Marsh and Thompson, 1993) and that the range in investment in training is thus narrowing. At this early stage, it has been noted that the TGS has not been an unqualified success. Rather, it does seem to have increased employer awareness of the necessity of training and investment in human resource, but it has not been able to influence the range of training offered. There is a very important role here for the human resource professional. It is vital that training in firms be more clearly related to the overall firm business strategy and that all training efforts be assessed and evaluated in light of these strategies. If an increased investment in training is to be maintained, it needs to be seen to be effective in delivering improvements in business performance at the level of the firm as well as at the level of the national economy.

Performance appraisal is the most universally practised human resource management programme in Australian organisations. A 1990 review of performance appraisal and management practice in Australia indicated that 83% of organisations surveyed had a performance appraisal system (Collins and Wood, 1990, p. 443). Traditionally, managerial level employees are more likely to have PA systems while performance management for blue-collar workers is more likely to involve monitoring by bundy clocks and direct supervision (Callus et al, 1991). This lack of overall programmes, and the lack of sophistication in the programmes being used for blue-collar workers, seems at odds with the emphasis being placed on productivity by both government and business leaders alike.

PA is being used for multiple purposes in Australian organisations. Identification of training needs (83%) and employee counselling (80%) are the two most common reasons given for usage with allocation of performance-based rewards (64%) the next most commonly cited reason. The ranking of these reasons reflects the current focus on training. With the freeing up of the labour market under new enterprise-based bargaining systems it can be assumed that the allocation of performance-based rewards will increase in importance. The problems associated with the dual function of PA systems – the need to both develop and evaluate staff – will be exacerbated by this trend.

The AWIRS study (mentioned above) surveyed companies on changes in management practices in the five years prior to the survey. Tables 4 and 5 show the extent of the changes designed to improve efficiency and communication that were implemented during that period. It can be seen from the figures that more companies were interested in changes that they felt would deliver efficiency improvements and that staff appraisal and training were the most commonly cited changes here.

Table 6 shows the findings of a survey conducted by the National Institute of Labour Studies at Flinders University that was designed to record the number of workplace changes attributable to award restructuring in the mid-1980s. As can be seen from the findings, the most common changes were reduction in job classifications, establishment of skills-based career paths, multi-skilling and reduction of demarcation lines. All of these changes could be seen as indicators of a move towards a more deregulated and flexible workplace. The perceived significance of the changes shows that it is the more qualitative changes towards commitment to continuous improvement and changed workplace culture that are the ones that

Table 4:   Efficiency Changes in Workplace Management

Innovation	% of Workplaces
Staff Appraisal	56
Job Redesign	38
Formal Training	48
Incentive Schemes	27
Quality Circles	26
Total Quality	26
Computer Integration	19
Semi-autonomous Groups	16
Skills Audit	16
J-I-T system	7
None of the above	14

Source: Gardner and Palmer (1992) based on Callus et al (1991, p. 93)

Table 5:   Communication Changes in Workplace Management

Innovation	% of Workplaces
Meetings of Managers & Employees	49
Newsletter	21
MBWA	17
Social Functions	12
Suggestion Schemes	10
Working Parties	9
Formal Joint Committees	7
Employees on Board	3
None of the Above	42

Source: Gardner and Palmer (1992) based on Callus et al (1991, p. 93)

are most highly valued. This is a very interesting finding notwithstanding the fact that only a small proportion of companies reported any such changes. It indicates that managers are aware of how important morale, motivation and commitment are to productivity; and it reflects a shift in management thinking if not yet in management practices.

Australia's perceived need to move from a centralised industrial relations system to a decentralised system focused around enterprise-based employment agreements relies heavily on a massive increase in the extent and frequency of joint consultation between employers and employees at the enterprise level. The current estimates on the incidence of Joint Consultative Committees (JCCs) in Australian

Table 6:   Workplace Changes: Award Restructuring and Perceived Value

Workplace Changes	Introduced through Award Restructuring	Importance of Change (Mean Value)
Reduction in Job Classifications	53	2.55
Establishment of New Skills-related Career Paths	48	2.73
New Training Arrangements	34	3.04
Reduced Demarcation Lines	37	2.84
Multi-skilling	44	3.15
Consultative/Employee Participation	36	3.07
Flexible Working Arrangements	23	2.43
Averaging or Removal of Penalty Rates	8	2.45
Altered Terms for Part-time and Casual Employment	9	1.98
Reduction in Overstaffing	13	3.00
New Forms of Work Organisation	16	2.91
Review of Sick Leave Provisions	4	1.87
Annualised Pay	4	1.96
Greater Flexibility in the Taking of Annual Leave	4	1.72
Compensating Overtime with Time off	3	1.84
Greater Communication with Employees	10	3.34
Changed Workplace Culture	12	3.43
Commitment to Continuous Improvement	10	3.52
Performance-based Pay	5	2.72

Source: Sloan (1993) unpublished survey analysis

workplaces indicate a substantial increase over the last 5 years. By 1990, 14% of workplaces employing more than 20 staff had JCCs – in public sector workplaces this figure was 28% (Lansbury and Marchington, 1993). However, these findings also indicate how much more needs to be done to facilitate consultative management practices in a decentralised system. One of the problems is that both parties – employers and employees – need to shift from strategies of negotiation and advocacy that were successful under the centralised system to strategies of communication and consultation that are required for success under an enterprise-based system. Again, the human resource professional is best placed to advise on and to provide the training and development necessary to facilitate this shift in management thinking and practice.

Attributes of Human Resource Managers

A composite picture of the Australian "Personnel Manager" is presented by
Deery and Dowling in a survey they conducted in 1984. The sample consisted
of members of the Institute of Personnel Management Australia (IPMA) (now
the Australian Human Resources Institute). The findings strongly support a view
of HR managers becoming increasingly professionalised. Seventy-eight percent
of the respondents were tertiary trained with qualifications in Commerce (31%)
and Personnel (20%). Over 50% began their careers in personnel or industrial
relations with this figure rising to 73% for those respondents under 40 years of
age. Clearly, younger HR managers see the area as offering a professional career
path and one that requires a specific knowledge base. Women represented only
20% of the sample (though this is higher than the figure for women managers
in general, 13%) (Quince and Lansbury, 1988). However, age is again a strong
moderating variable here with 69% of the female respondents being under 40
years of age. This study also suggests that HR managers tend to be multiskilled
and to perform a range of personnel tasks. The major activities of the respondents
were recruitment and selection, dispute handling, wage and salary administration,
and training and development (Deery and Dowling, 1988, p. 21).

The AWIRS survey (Callus et al, 1991) confirms some of these findings but
also provides more information about the role of the specialist HR manager in
Australian organisations. AWIRS found that 34% of workplaces had at least
one manager who had special responsibility for the management of employees
(Callus et al, 1991, p. 84). The absence of specialist managers in the other 66% of
workplaces was due to two factors. The first was size. Size was the variable most
strongly correlated with the incidence of specialist managers. Small organisations
do not have the economies of scale to make it feasible to have a manager purely
designated for HR issues. The second factor was related to being part of a larger
organisation. For 52% of workplaces without specialist managers, there was a
specialist manager in a different part of the organisation. The implication is that
the HRM and industrial relations function were carried out at a corporate level.
Of those workplaces with specialist managers, the most commonly used title was
still "Personnel", with "Human Resources" and "Employee Relations" the next
most popular (Callus et al, 1991).

This survey found that specialist managers characteristically had an average
of 11 years experience in the field: 50% of them had relevant tertiary level
qualifications, and there was relatively high employment mobility among the
group with 77% having worked in their current position for less than 5 years.
The proportion of women specialist managers had risen from 20% to 31% – a
trend suggested in the Dowling and Deery findings. At 68% of the workplaces
the specialist manager reported directly to the most senior manager. Personnel
type tasks – training, induction and negotiation – appeared to be the province of
both specialist and generalist managers. Seventy-eight percent of managers not

primarily concerned with the management of employees reported that they spent a good deal of time on at least some personnel tasks (Callus et al, 1991). This suggests that HRM is increasingly decentralised and clearly significant within the enterprise.

Studies by Deery and Purcell (1989) found that organisations were tending to have a board member responsible for employee relations. Overall, 46% of companies surveyed had a such a position while in companies with more than 10,000 employees the percentage rose to 61% (Deery and Purcell, 1989). This trend clearly puts human resource managers in a stronger position to influence company policy and to begin to integrate HR strategies and business strategies.

Conclusion

Human resource management professionals have become increasingly important in Australia over the last decade. The reasons for this mirror trends in other Western capitalist economies: the increasing importance of the international marketplace and the need for competitive work practices; the requirement for organisations to differentiate themselves in terms of quality of workforce; demographic changes in the characteristics of employees that require more sophisticated management; the growing sophistication of workplace technologies that require more flexible work structures; and, finally, in the late 1980s and early 1990s, the effects of the recession which impact directly on employment practices in organisations. Human resource management has been targeted as a strategic tool that can make a difference to the organisation, the industry and the nation in their competitive positioning in any market (Boxall and Dowling, 1990; BCA, 1989; Dunphy, 1987; Stace, 1987). Consequently, the HR professional of the nineties needs to be well trained, well remunerated, well positioned and proactive.

A disturbing finding which reflects the lag between theory and practice in human resource management in Australia is that only 13% of organisations reported a direct link between their performance management system and their corporate objectives, strategic and business plans, and departmental objectives. Twelve percent of organisations reported no relationship between these two areas at all (Collins and Wood, 1990). This is a disturbing finding given the emphasis that has been placed on the importance of *strategic* human resource management practices in Australia's effort to become internationally competitive. It would appear that even though a number of leading Australian organisations (BCA, 1990; Lewis et al, 1988) are adopting such a strategic approach to human resource management, there are still a great many medium- and large-sized Australian organisations who have not fully realised the importance and potential of such an approach.

Not surprisingly, downsizing has been shown to be a key feature of Australian HR practice over the last five years. An interim report from *Workforce 2000*, a study commissioned by the BCA, indicated that in 1991, 75% of respondents had reduced their workforce. Seventy-three percent forecast continuing reductions in 1992 while 62% expected the trend to continue over the next five years (Giles, 1992). However, such downsizing is accompanied by corporate and industry restructuring which has the effect of leading to employment growth in certain areas. The implications for the HR professional are increased emphasis on redundancy, and in some cases, redeployment programmes, increased need for industry and organisation specific training, manpower planning and career succession programmes, and more innovative and flexible remuneration packages for skilled employees. There appears to be a trend, albeit still quite a small one, to the use of sub-contractors and part-time workers. This implies that the workforce will become increasingly differentiated along these lines and employers will need to develop the HR expertise to manage the two diverse groups. The BCA survey found that organisations were becoming increasingly selective about the HR policies they introduced. Policies were seen to be more tailored to specific industries and organisations and that these respondents at least were attempting to use HR programmes as part of their competitive strategy (Giles, 1992, p. 9).

The wide-ranging surveys on HR practices and policies over the last five years would tend to suggest that the picture in Australia is a rather mixed one. It does seem that HRM is now perceived as a significant part of overall management practice. The status of HR managers in terms of who they report to and of the range of strategic decisions into which they have input has clearly risen quite considerably. The number of HR managers with professional qualifications is similarly encouraging. However, overall HR practice would still seem to be lagging considerably behind the rhetoric.

The demands on HRM in Australia are only going to increase in the next few years. There is a clear and inexorable move to a much more decentralised industrial relations system in this country. Both major political parties are moving in the same general direction on this issue – although the Labour Party's view would be seen as a form of regulated enterprise-based bargaining, while the Liberal Coalition would like to see a more deregulated form of enterprise-based bargaining. Either way the responsibility for negotiating individual and collective remuneration packages is going to move much closer to the individual workplace and to the HR manager in a way that is unprecedented in this country. Probably the biggest challenge facing HRM in Australia is how to incorporate the requirements of industrial relations and human resource management at the workplace in programmes that combine equitable conditions for all employees, optimal conditions for organisational level productivity, and effective economic outcomes for the nation.

Endnotes

1. This is not to underplay the role of the various migrant groups who have contributed so massively to the development of Australia as a modern nation. However, for the purposes of tracing the origins of the social, political and economic systems in Australia, it is the British heritage that has had the most influence over the first 150 years of European settlement.
2. For a detailed analysis of the move to decentralization of the wage fixation system under the Accord see Judith Sloan (1993).
3. Welfarism was a prominent part of Australian Management practice long before this period. For a fuller discussion, see P.G. Patmore (1991).

References

ABS (Australian Bureau of Statistics) (1991). *Year Book Australia 1991*. Cat. No. 1301.0 (casebound). Canberra: Commonwealth Government Printer.

ABS (1992a). *Year Book Australia 1992*. Cat. No. 1301.0 (casebound). Canberra: Commonwealth Government Printer.

ABS (1992b). *The Labour Force, Australia: Historical Summary, 1978-1989*. Cat. No. 6204.0. Canberra: Commonwealth Government Printer.

ABS (1992c). *Distribution and Composition of Employee Earnings and Hours, Australia*. Cat. No. 6306.0. Canberra: Commonwealth Government Printer.

ABS (1993). *Year Book Australia 1993*. Cat. No. 1301.0 (casebound). Canberra: Commonwealth Government Printer.

Australian Council of Trade Unions/Trade Development Council [ACTU/TDC] (1987). *Australia Reconstructed*. Canberra: Australian Government Publishing Service.

Boxall, P. and P. Dowling (1990). "Human Resource Management and the Industrial Relations Tradition." *Labour & Industry*, 3(2-3), 195-214.

BCA [Business Council of Australia, Industrial Relations Study Commission] (1989). *Enterprise-Based Bargaining Units: A Better Way of Working*. Melbourne: Business Council of Australia.

BCA [Business Council of Australia] (1990). *Training Australians: A Better Way of Working*. Melbourne: Business Council of Australia.

Callus, R., A. Morehead, M. Cully and J. Buchanan (1991). *Industrial Relations at Work: The Australian Workplace Industrial Relations Survey*. Canberra: Australian Government Publishing Service.

Carmody, H. (1991). "The Need to Focus on People Investment." *Work and People*, 14(1), 13-16.

Cochrane, P. (1985). "Company Time: Management, Ideology and the Labour Process, 1940-1960." *Labour History*, 48, 54-68.

Collins, R. (1987). "The Strategic Contributions of the Personnel Function." *Human Resource Management Australia*, 25, 3, 5-21

Collins, R and R. Wood (1990). "National Survey of Performance Appraisal and Management Practices: August 1990." *Personnel Management*. Sydney: CCH Australia.

Dabscheck, B. (1989). *Australian Industrial Relations in the 1980s*. Melbourne: Oxford University Press Australia.

Deery, S. and P. Dowling (1988). "The Australian Personnel Manager and Industrial Relations Practitioner: Responsibilities, Characteristics and Attitudes." In G. Palmer (ed.). *Australian Personnel Management: A Reader*. Melbourne: The MacMillan Company of Australia Pty.

Deery, S. and P. Gahan (1991). "The Workplace Survey and Management Structures." *The Journal of Industrial Relations*, 33, 502-518.

Deery, S. and D. Plowman (1991). *Australian Industrial Relations* (3rd. ed.). Sydney: McGraw-Hill.

Deery, S. and J. Purcell (1989). "Strategic Choices in Industrial Relations Management in Large Organisations." *Journal of Industrial Relations*, 31(4), 462-463.

Department of Employment, Education and Training (1990). *Women's Work, Women's Pay: Industrial and Occupational Segregation of Women in the Australian Workforce*. Canberra: AGPS.

Drago, R., M. Wooden and J. Sloan (1992). *Productive Relations? Australian Industrial Relations and Workplace Performance*. Sydney: Allen and Unwin.

Dunphy, D. (1990). "The Historical Development of Human Resource Management in Australia." *Human Resource Management Australia*, 25, 2, 40-47.

Federal Coalition Party (1991). *Fightback: The Liberal and National Parties' Plan to Rebuild and Reward Australia*. Canberra: Commonwealth Government Printer.

Federal Coalition Party (1992). *Jobsback: The Federal Coalition's Industrial Relations Policy*. Canberra: Commonwealth Government Printer.

Frenkel, S. and D. Peetz (1990). "Enterprise Bargaining: The BCAs Report on Industrial Relations Reform." *The Journal of Industrial Relations*, March, 69-99.

Gardner, M. and G. Palmer (1992). *Employment Relations: Industrial Relations and Human Resource Management in Australia*. Macmillan, Australia.

Giles, P. (1992). "The HR Policies You are Using in the 1990s." *HR Monthly*, September, 8-10.

Grattan, M. (1992). "PM Hoists his Trade Flag for a Changed Australia." *The Age*, September 26.

Groves, D. (1990). "Award Restructuring at the Workplace." *Work and People*, 13(3), 37-45.

Higgins, H. (1968). *A New Province for Law and Order*. London: Dawson. (Originally published in 1922.)

Hill, J. (1987). "Australian Industrial Relations and the 'National Character'." In G. Ford, J. Hearn and R. Lansbury (eds.). *Australian Labour Relations: Readings*. (4th ed.) South Melbourne: The MacMillan Company of Australia.

Jamieson, S. and M. Westcott (1992). "Review of Industrial Relations – 1991." *Asia Pacific Journal of Human Resources*, 30(2), 51-58.

Jorgensen, L. (1991). "Breaking Down the 'Them' and 'Us' Attitude at Gemco." *Work and People*, 14(1), 28-33.

Korporaal, G. (1992). "Pacesetting for an Asian Shift." *The Age*, September 25.

Kramer, R. (1991). "Australian Developments in Equal Employment Opportunity and Affirmative Action." *Equal Opportunities International*, 10(5), 5-13.

Lansbury, R. and M. Marchington (1993). "Joint Consultation and Industrial Relations: Experience from Australia and Overseas." *Asia Pacific Journal of Human Resources*, 31(3), 62-82.

Lansbury, R. and A. Quince (1988). "Management and Professional Employees in Large Scale Organisations: An Australian Study." *Employee Relations*, 10(5), 2-55.

Lewis, P. and D. Spiers (1990). "Six Years of the Accord: An Assessment." *The Journal of Industrial Relations*, March, 53-68.

Lewis, G., J. Clark and B. Moss (1988). "BHP Reorganizes for Global Competition." *Long Range Planning*, 21(3), 18-26.

MacIntosh, M. (1993). "Australian Industrial Relations in 1992: Another Turning Point?" *Asia Pacific Journal of Human Resources*, 31(3), 52-64.

Marginson, P. (1991). "Beyond Size and Sector: A View from Overseas." *The Journal of Industrial Relations*, 33(4), 586-600.

National Board of Employment, Education and Training [NBEET] (1990). *Interim Report on the Benchmark Study of Management Development in Australian Private Enterprises.* Canberra: Australian Government Publishing Service.

National Women's Consultative Council (1990). *Pay Equity for Women in Australia.* Canberra: AGPS.

Niland, J. (1990). "The Light on the Horizon: Essentials of an Enterprise Focus." In M. Easson and J. Shaw (eds.). *Transforming Industrial Relations.* New South Wales: Pluto Press.

OECD (1989/1990; 1991/1992). *OECD Economic Surveys.* Paris.

Palmer, G. (1988). "Human Resource Management and Organisational Analysis." In G. Palmer (ed.). *Australian Personnel Management: A Reader.* Melbourne: The MacMillan Company of Australia Pty.

Patmore, P.G. (1991). *Australia Labour History.* Melbourne: Longman Cheshire.

Plowman, D. (1992). "An Uneasy Conjunction: Opting Out and the Arbitration System." *The Journal of Industrial Relations*, 34(2), 284-306.

Quince, A. and D. Lansbury (1988). "Two Steps Forward But Going Nowhere? Women and Management in Australia." *Employee Relations*, 10(6), 26-31.

Robbins, S., P. Low and M. Mourell (1986). *Managing Human Resources.* Sydney: Prentice-Hall of Australia Pty.

Scherer, P. (1987). "The Nature of the Australian Industrial Relations System: A Forum of State Syndicalism?" In Ford, G.W., J. Hearn and R. Lansbury (eds.). *Australian Labour Relations: Readings.* (4th ed.) Melbourne: The MacMillan Company of Australia.

Schuler, R. (1988). "Personnel and Human Resource Management Choices and Organisational Strategy." *Human Resource Management Australia*, February, 81-100.

Shaw, J. (1990). "Are Radical Changes Needed in the New South Wales Industrial Relations System?" In M. Easson and J. Shaw (eds.). *Transforming Industrial Relations.* New South Wales: Pluto Press.

Sloan, J. (1993). "Wage Fixing Under Accord Mark VII and the Role of National Wage Principles." *Australian Bulletin of Labour*, 19(3), 218-240.

Smith, A. (1993). "Australian Training and Development in 1992." *Asia Pacific Journal of Human Resources*, 31, 2, 65-74.

Stace, D. (1987). "The Value-Added Organisation: Trends in Human Resource Management." *Human Resource Management Australia*, 25, 3, 52-62.

Waters-March, T. and B. Thompson (1993). "The Training Guarantee Scheme: A Longitudinal Study in the Australian Metals Industry." *Asia Pacific Journal of Human Resources*, 31(3), 30-43.

Wright, C. (1993). "From Personnel to Human Resource Management: A Review of Australian Employment Relations Developments During the 1970s and 1980s." *Industrial Relations Working Papers*, Working Paper No. 94, The University of New South Wales.

Wooden, M. (1993). "The Australian Labour Market – September 1993." *Australian Bulletin of Labour*, 19(3), 165-183.

Human Resource Management in Canada

Larry F. Moore and P. Devereaux Jennings

The Country and the Economy:
Historical Background and Present Configuration

In order to foster a more complete understanding of human resource management (HRM) as practiced in Canada, this chapter contains two background sections. The first section provides a brief geo-political summary and the second offers a perspective on the history and characteristics of Canadian industrial relations, the framework of labor legislation, and government support programs. Following these "stage setting" sections, the history, present state, and future prospects of HRM are explored, utilizing the results of current empirical research where available.

Canada has been depicted as a land of diversity (Anderson and Frideres, 1981; Clark, 1965; Kanungo, 1980; Malcolm, 1985; Mann, 1971). It is the largest country in the Western hemisphere and the second largest in the world, with a land mass ranging from its vast fertile prairies and farmlands, to its great expanses of mountains, rocks and lakes and its frozen tundra and snowy vistas of the Arctic north. Canada's outline is convoluted, but its greatest east-west distance is 5,500 km with an extreme north-south distance of 4,650 km, and roughly 10 million square kilometres of land mass including freshwater lakes and rivers.

There is no permanent settlement in approximately 90% of Canada. About 60% of its population lives between the U.S. border and a 1050 km east-west line from Quebec City to Sault Ste Marie, Ontario. Canada's population is increasing, although the rate of growth is slowing due to a declining birth rate. The five-year growth for the 1986-91 period was 7.9%. Over the last 25 years there has been a continued redistribution of population. The Atlantic provinces and Quebec have showed declines, Ontario and the prairie provinces have changed very little, and British Columbia on the west coast has increased somewhat. Population growth in the metropolitan areas has been well above the national average, especially in Toronto, Montreal and Vancouver composing together about one third of the country's people (Statistics Canada, 1992). Sixty-one percent of Canadians speak English as their only mother tongue while 24% speak French. Nonetheless, linguistic diversity is greater today than it was 25 years ago. The proportion of the population whose mother tongue is Asian or Middle Eastern has grown considerably, although there was little change in the number of persons whose native language was of European origin. These patterns reflect immigration trends of the past few years (Badets, 1993).

Family size has been shrinking and now (1992) the average Canadian family has 3.1 members, due mainly to lower fertility rates. There has been a marked growth in families with no children at home, but even so, 70% of Canada's families have children at home and 77% of these families are traditional husband-wife-child families. Still, the number of single-parent families has been increasing at a much faster rate than before. The majority (82%) of single-parent families are headed by women. Most of these must work or go on welfare to make ends meet (La Novara, 1993).

Politically, Canada consists of ten provinces and two territories, organized as a federal union with a strong central government. Until 1982, Canada was a dominion of Britain, with governing powers defined by the British North American Act of 1867. In essence, the BNA Act was a constitution which established for Canada a parliamentary system similar in many respects to that of the U.K. Provided for under this scheme is the Queen's representative (the Governor General), an elected House of Commons, an appointed Senate with life tenure, and a judicial system grounded in British statute and common law and usage. Formulation of public policy usually begins with individual ministers working in cooperation with civil servants. Cabinet chooses which policies it wishes to present to Parliament. All executive acts must be authorized by law and laws are enacted by Parliament. Administration of legislation is accomplished through a well-developed public service (ministries, departments, commissions, special boards, Crown corporations and other agencies).

There is a multi-party political system with no restriction on the number of parties which can advance candidates for public office. Historically, three parties have tended to dominate the federal political scene: the Progressive Conservatives (in power until October, 1993), the Liberals (constituting the official opposition) and the New Democratic Party. In October, 1993, a federal election was held, the outcome of which may greatly affect the distribution of political power in Canada. The Liberal party was returned to power winning a strong majority of parliamentary seats (177 out of 295 seats). Both the Conservative and the New Democratic Party failed to retain enough seats to maintain their designations as official parties. Two relatively new parties – Bloc Quebecois and Reform – nearly tied for second place; the BQ dominating by only two seats (54-52) to become officially designated the Opposition. At great risk of oversimplification, the Liberals seem inclined to favor limited government intervention in commerce, social reform programs, and moving toward a Canadianized democratic system deemphasizing class structure (Horowitz, 1971). The Bloc Quebecois is mainly confined to the province of Quebec and is striving for greater autonomy for Quebec or even independence from the rest of the country. The Reform Party could be characterized as right-wing, espousing the ideals of individualism, private industry, fiscal responsibility, increased recognition of provincial concerns, and limits on government spending for social and other programs. The strength of the Reform Party is mainly in western Canada. It remains to be seen whether the

Reform Party and the BQ have sufficient common interests to work in coalition on national issues.

In 1982, Canada adopted a new Constitution which establishes protection of basic rights and freedoms necessary to a democratic society and a unified country (Statistics Canada, 1988) including: freedom of conscience and religion; freedom of opinion and expression; peaceful assembly; the right to vote and seek office; mobility rights; equality rights allowing no discrimination based on race, national or ethnic origin, color, religion, sex, age, or mental or physical disability; minority education rights; language rights (equality of status for English and French in public institutions); and native people's rights.

In each of the ten provinces, there is a unicameral legislature consisting of a lieutenant-governor and a legislative assembly. Under the Constitution, several important areas of jurisdiction are left to the provinces, e.g., educational policy, natural resources, and health care. Although the federal internal revenue service (Revenue Canada) collects tax revenue, through a system of transfer payments, the federal government remits funds to the provinces to help finance these services. There is some federal/provincial coordination, but basically the provinces develop their own administrative arrangements in these areas. Not infrequently, ambiguity arises around which level of government actually has jurisdiction; thus the Canadian federation is somewhat loose and the distribution of political power between the federal and the various provincial governments is a dynamic balance. The federal/provincial balance regarding employment and labor relations will be discussed below.

The Industrial Relations Setting in Canada

History and Traditions

Industrial relations in Canada, as in other countries, have been shaped by economic, political, and social forces. Basically, industrial relations in North America is a conflict between individual and collective interests. Throughout its history, immigrants and refugees have been attracted to Canada by the promise of relatively cheap land, freedom from class restriction and regulation of occupation, and the chance to become financially independent. Unfortunately, for many new settlers, the notion of Canada as a land of easy opportunity turned out to be a myth. Without neighborly cooperation, life in early-day Canada would have been almost impossible, due to the extremes of climate and geography (Broadfoot, 1976). In the growing cities of Halifax, Toronto, and Montreal, immigrants needed the support of trades associations to find work, to help heighten self-esteem, and to provide a sense of "community" (Morton, 1989).

After 1850, as an industrial economy began to emerge in Canada and the railway canal systems increased labor mobility, craft-based unionism spread rapidly, largely from England. These craft unions were oriented towards maintaining membership qualifications and preventing mass immigration from undermining wages, although an anti-conspiracy law threatened all unions. Soon after the amalgamation of Canada's provinces and territories into a loose federation in 1867, the new nation passed the Trade Unions Act, legalizing union activity. However, strikes remained illegal and an attempt to form a Canadian Labour Union failed.

Characterized by a number of internecine struggles, Canadian trade unionism evolved and strengthened. During the next three decades, the development of industrial unions followed Canada's rise in industrialization – in mining, railways, construction, logging, and factory work. Labor-management confrontation dates to the early 1900s when Canada experienced some of its most violent and disruptive strikes. Labor shortages during World War One, combined with the development of several entirely new industries, led to further unionization and politization. After World War One, the Canadian labor movement fragmented and lost ground, and in 1926 the Privy Council decided that labor relations were in the constitutional domain of the provinces and not the federal government (Morton, 1989).

Industrial relations in Canada were strongly influenced by events in the United States in the 1930s. With the passage of the Wagner Act in 1935, U.S. employers were forced to recognize a democratically elected union. Although the great U.S. organizing drive by the Congress of Industrial Organizations (CIO) failed to thrive in Canada's auto plants in Ontario, the stage was set for CIO organizing gains in World War Two's newly emerging war industries. Wartime organizing had reduced the distinction between traditional craft and industrial union categories as both had to deal with the internal political threat of Communist influence.

The Canadian Labour Congress, the national federation of trade unions, was formed in 1956, shortly after the AFL-CIO merger in the United States. Despite the formation of the CLC, the labor movement in Canada failed to make political gains as the country returned to a conservative, anti-union posture in the face of rising competition, especially from Japan. In the 1960s, technological change posed a challenge to union membership in many instances and provincial governments were largely unsympathetic to the labor movement's demands for protection against loss of membership.

As in other industrialized, mixed capitalistic countries, an increasingly complex economic system based on regulations and protections, coupled with the bureaucratization effects of two world wars resulted in a large civil service infrastructure in Canada. In the mid-1960s, efforts to maintain budgetary control led to civil service dissatisfaction with wage and benefit packages (comparatively lower than for the private sector). In the late 1960s, the federal government enacted the Public Service Staff Relations Act, providing for compulsory arbitration and the right to strike. Provincial governments generally followed the central government's lead. The Canadian Union of Public Employees soon formed from merging public service unions to become Canada's largest union. Largely as a result of this public-sector unionization, the country experienced an upsurge of union growth generally. The strong CUPE influence within the CLC led to pressure on the U.S.-based international unions to provide more autonomy or full independence to their Canadian affiliates, and national Canadian unions came to represent the majority of Canadian workers.

By the mid-1970s, trade unionism in Canada had sustained a number of important advances. The right to organize was enhanced by a new federal labor code in 1971 (the Canada Labour Code) and by compatible legislation in the three western provinces. Issues of technological change, occupational health, and safety could now be negotiated and dealt with more easily. Public servants were at last full-fledged union members with full rights. However, these changes and concessions came at a time when Canada's economy was beginning to experience double-digit inflation, due to various factors including a decline of the U.S. dollar's value in world currency markets, a further decline of the Canadian dollar against its U.S. counterpart, dramatically increased oil prices, and the need to finance through tax increases, a growing deficit in the national balance of payments. Beginning in the 1970s and continuing into the 1980s many of Canada's older, established industries underwent drastic change and several new industries developed, particularly in the service sector.

Labor Market Characteristics:
Changing Structure of Employment Demand and Supply

Canadian human resource management is profoundly affected by the changing state of the country's labor force. Recently, a number of events have impacted the Canadian economy, including the strengthening of foreign competition, changes in population demographics, increased female participation in the work force, deregulation, negotiation of a free trade agreement with the United States, deindustrialization, and a deep recession. In turn, in complex ways not completely understood, Canada's labor force has experienced sharp changes. A number of general trends have been delineated by Stone and Meltz (1993, pp. 45-55).

1. Since the early 1970s there has been increased participation in Canada's labor force (from around 58% in 1971 to a projected 68% in 2000).
2. Female participation in the labor force has increased dramatically (from around 38% in 1971 to a projected 62% in 2000), while the rate for males has remained steady at about 76%. The participation of females has increased most in the 25-44 age group. Many in this age group are working mothers or are childless.
3. The median age of the working population is increasing. The proportion of working youths (15-24 years) will decline from around 20% in 1990 to a projected low point of 16% of the labor force by 2021 (Foot, 1982).

4. The number of part-time workers on a voluntary basis has increased at more than twice the rate of full-timers over the last decade and the practice of work-sharing has increased. Part-time workers tend to be concentrated in the trade (24% of all employees) and service (25% of all employees) industries.

5. Since 1970, the composition of immigrant groups into Canada has shifted markedly away from the traditional European and United States sources toward non-European immigration, especially from Asia, Africa, the Caribbean, and Central and South America. The majority of immigrants arrive as young adults (between the ages of 20 and 39 years) and their average dependency ratio is much lower than for native born Canadians (the proportion under age 14 and 65 or over). More immigrants (78%) live in large urban areas than do native-born Canadians (47%), and more than a third of Canadian immigrants speak a first language other than French or English. A recent Economic Council study (*New Faces in the Crowd*, 1991) concludes that economic performance of immigrants compares very favourably with similarly qualified native-born Canadians and that they adjust reasonably well to the labor market in a short time and constitute a significant component in the labor pool. Nonetheless, this changing mix has the potential for intergroup conflict and prejudice and may provide challenges for human resource managers in the future.

6. The employment pattern across Canadian industry has been and is projected to be diverging. In the goods-producing category, for the 1981-88 period, only the construction industry showed any growth in employment. There were declines in employment in manufacturing, primary (other than agriculture), and in agriculture. On the other hand, in the service-producing industries including public administration, there was significant growth except for transportation, utilities and communications, which posted a slight decline. Recent census data indicates an even steeper decline in employment in the goods-producing industries overall, but moderate increases in the service industries except for wholesale and trade. Canada's overall employment between 1988 and 1992 has declined very slightly (see Table 1).

7. A highly unionized public sector (including the federal, provincial, and municipal civil services, health care, education, and government enterprises) now employs nearly one third of Canada's workforce (Ponak and Thompson, 1989). A number of important differences impinge upon human resource management in this sector. Public sector employers are more subject to political influence but less affected by economic forces. Some public institutions can legislate. Management structures and responsibilities are more diffused. In collective bargaining, profit and loss calculations are often inappropriate; competitive and market considerations are usually not at issue; but public employers have to be very aware of public and political reactions. Furthermore, there are employee differences. White collar and professional employees are over-represented in the public sector. Bargaining units are often determined legislatively and bargaining scope is often constrained by statute. If strikes are

Table 1: Employment and Employment Growth by Industry Sector

	Employment in thousands			Percentage change	
	1981	1988	1992	1981–88	1988–92
Goods-producing industries	3,711	3,696	3,307	−0.40	−10.52
Manufacturing	2,124	2,104	1,788	−0.94	−15.02
Construction	651	726	681	11.52	−6.20
Primary (other than agriculture)	321	294	257	−8.41	−12.59
Agriculture	488	444	433	−9.02	−2.48
Service-producing industries	7,290	8,549	8,933	17.27	4.49
Finance, insurance real estate	594	728	763	22.56	4.81
Community, business, personal service	3,262	4,062	4,408	24.52	8.52
Wholesale and retail trade	1,884	2,168	2,155	15.07	−.60
Transportation, utilities, communications	911	904	922	−0.77	1.99
Public administration	767	815	834	6.26	2.33
Total all industries	11,001	12,245	12,240	11.31	−.04

Source: Statistics Canada (1993b, pp. 49–54)

permitted, the preconditions are usually more stringent than for private sector unions. Overall, unionized public employees have been less prone to strike than unionized private sector employees as senior decision-makers have experimented with alternate and innovational schemes, e.g., interest arbitration, final offer selection, the controlled strike, and "choice of procedures" (Ponak and Thompson, 1989).

Framework of Employment Legislation

In Canada, to a considerable extent, legal regulations shape human resource policies and constrain HRM practices (Sack and Lee, 1989). Less than 40% of the Canadian work force is unionized and not all aspects of the employee relationship are covered by collective agreements; hence, employment legislation is designed to provide coverage and protection for all workers (McPhillips and England, 1989). Compliance with legal requirements means maintaining specific records and creates much paperwork. Canada has a particular problem because its employment relations laws are established by thirteen separate jurisdictions made up of ten provinces, two territories, and the federal government. Firms doing business in more than one province may encounter certain difficulties and confusions because each province and territory has separate human rights and labor standards laws and procedures for interpretation and enforcement. Federal labor and employment laws cover less than 10% of the labor force; basically, those employees of interprovincial and international firms whose operations cross provincial boundaries or constitute federally linked Crown corporations.

In addition, Canada's new federal Constitution has a Charter of Rights and Freedoms which is designed to provide protection against discrimination concerning race, national or ethnic origin, color, religion, sex, age, or mental or physical disability. Because the Charter is relatively recent, some of its specific clauses are being tested in the courts and interpretations under the Charter as it applies to employee rights and standards are prone to change.

McPhillips and England (1989) have described Canada's framework of human resource legislation in four broad categories: work standards, individual contracts of employment, human rights, and occupational health and safety. Within each of these categories, specific statutes lay out the (often minimum) requirements, rights and duties. For example, most jurisdiction have legislation covering wage protection, minimum wage, hours of work and overtime, annual vacation, statutory holidays, maternity leave, and termination procedures. Employers, of course, are free to provide greater than minimum levels of specified benefits and management bargains to establish a collective agreement which specifies benefits far in excess of the statutory minima.

Human rights legislation applies to all employees, union and non-union. Both employers and unions are prohibited from discriminating against workers. In practice, an employee generally perceiving discrimination on the part of an employer will seek early redress through the formal grievance process rather than going to the human rights council in the jurisdiction. Although Canada has seen much expansion in its framework of employment legislation in recent years, McPhillips and England (1989) identify some major problem areas: employees often are unaware of their rights; employees may fear employer reprisal; understaffed agencies often do not effectively police the laws; and legal remedies are often inadequate. Thus, a major challenge facing Canadian human resource managers and their trade union counterparts will be to work toward making the legislative framework and its specific elements more operationally effective.

Government Support and Employment Programs

Since the early 1980s, Canada's labor market has been suffering from a serious imbalance made up of both structural and aggregate components (Kaliski, 1985). Structurally, there are mismatches between the levels of skills or experience possessed by individuals available for employment in certain occupations and those required for acceptable job performance. Additionally, the location of individual job seekers often lies in a part of the country where there are few vacant jobs. In

Canada, aggregate imbalance is usually cyclical, where there is an overall excess supply of or demand for labor occurring regardless of individual characteristics or occupations. Both components contribute to what has amounted to a chronically high rate of unemployment in Canada (Kumar, 1983; MacDonald Commission, 1985, Vol. 2, p. 587).

A critical concern for federal policy makers is to (1) diagnose the source of imbalance, and (2) to design and implement effective remedial programs. This concern has been the central theme of three major government task force reports released between 1981 and 1982 (Employment and Immigration Canada, 1981; Economic Council of Canada, 1982; House of Commons, 1982), Volume 2 of the Royal Commission on the Economic Union and Development Prospects for Canada (MacDonald Commission, 1985), and several other conferences and special reports (cf. Gera, 1991).

The fact that theories concerning the impact of labor market policy are unreliable for making cause-effect inferences justifies the extensive empirical research undertaken by Canadian governmental bodies to assess the relative effectiveness and efficiency of various programs. The three task forces and the other smaller studies concurred that many of the occupational training and job creation programs carried out by the Canadian Employment and Immigration Commission (CEIC) in the 1970s and 1980s tended to focus more on temporary reduction of unemployment than on long-term creation of productive employment. Job creation programs implemented during this period largely failed to develop demand which would be self-sustaining over a long duration. CEIC's placement services, counselling and consultative facilities, and the information and forecasting systems were all found to be inadequate in dealing with the exceedingly inefficient adjustment mechanism of the "natural" labor market.

The present concern with the inadequate past performance and future direction of government-sponsored programs is to a very large degree due to drastic shifts in labor supply and demand anticipated in the 1990s. Canada entered the 1990s in a major recession. There is an upward trend in the chronically high aggregate unemployment rate (approximately 11% in 1993). Long-term unemployment disparities have worsened. Moreover, the burden of unemployment has been distributed unevenly across different demographic groups. Some groups in our society incur disproportionately high levels of unemployment; e.g., older workers, those with relatively little formal education, and persons who lose their jobs involuntarily (Gera, 1991). Occupationally, groups of people with certain skills, particularly those in the higher skilled manufacturing trades and in engineering have been in short supply. Industrial and regional imbalances have been produced by unstable factors such as fluctuating prices and the timing of several megaprojects.

The Canadian Employment and Immigration Commission has been attempting to develop an up-to-date labor market intelligence system of high quality which would be linked to an integrated series of more consistent, better informed, better targeted, and better coordinated labor market policies and programs.

The Canadian Occupational Projection System (COPS) forecasts both supply and demand by regions. COPS is designed as a means of pooling knowledge from across the entire economy and integrates subjective judgement by experts in various sectors with data derived from mechanical modelling. Thus, COPS takes into consideration such factors as shifts in the skill-mix of the workforce, inter-occupational mobility, substitution in response to changes in wages or supply conditions, modifications in participation rates, or changes in price and productivity (Kaliski, 1985).

In June, 1985, Canadian Jobs Strategy (CJS) was brought into being as a major part of the CIEC's Human Resource Development Programs (several earlier, short-term programs were allowed to diminish). The CJS is intended to support training programs or strategies which have public policy objectives, which are directed at specific target groups, and which are aimed at improving long-term employment prospects for individuals (Milkovich et al., 1988). Furthermore, CJS attempts to encourage the participation of regional and local governmental and private organizations, including unions, in joint ventures and initiatives.

Canada's twelve separate provincial and territorial jurisdictions each have a range of human resource programs aimed at improving job opportunities for employees. For example, in the area of employment equity, human rights statutes and employment equity programs have widely been introduced to ensure that members of designated groups (based on gender, disability status, visible minority and aboriginal status) have the same probability of obtaining a job as do others with the same qualifications (Milkovich et al., 1988). Growing public awareness of discrimination in employment has caused some provincial governments to establish special services to assist employers in introducing and developing employment equity programs (EEPs). On the other hand, EEPs remain controversial; especially where strict quotas are set on the number of women and minorities to be hired. Nonetheless, it is very likely that increased public pressure and legislation will cause large numbers of Canadian organizations to develop EEPs. The human resource department may be expected to be centrally involved in developing and implementing these and other programs where human resource issues span provincial, community, and company interests.

Some Tensions and Crosscurrents in the IR Scene

In the early 1990s, the arena of industrial relations is filled with dynamic tension. That is, several complex underlying forces are in flux and may well be moving in countervailing directions. Figure 1 illustrates these forces and shows their major oppositional alignment. Additionally, there are crosscurrents of tension between all of these forces.

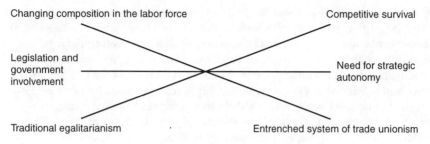

Figure 1: Countervailing Tensions in Canadian Industrial Relations

Competitive survival versus traditional egalitarianism. For many years, Canada has been characterized as a high wage-cost nation with an expensive system of social supports including universal medical service, unemployment insurance, welfare protection, and education. Economically, the country has been comparatively well placed (OECD, 1991/1992). Yet, there are serious challenges to Canada's economic position. In 1988, Canada entered into a major tariff reduction agreement with the U.S. (dubbed the Free Trade Agreement) where most industrial commodities are permitted to be transported and sold across the common border without tariffs and other trade restrictions. In 1992, Canada and the U.S. entered into negotiations with Mexico to form a North American Free Trade Agreement (NAFTA). Individual Canadian industries are likely to be affected differently, but it may be concluded that the overall effect of the FTA has been to intensify competition and to increase pressures to reduce costs generally. NAFTA will likely exacerbate these effects and may increase the number of Canadian firms which seek to establish plants in the U.S. or Mexico or leave Canada altogether. Concomitantly, because much of the output from Canada's extractive industries (e.g., forest products, mining, and fishing), its agricultural sector (e.g., grain and meat products), and its manufacturing industries (e.g., automobiles and parts) is marketed internationally, both the price and quantity of goods sold are affected negatively (Porter, 1991). Effects of the world-wide recession may be translated into increasing pressure on human resource departments to hold the line or reduce labor costs. The search for labor cost savings is becoming ever more critical as Canadian organizations attempt to survive in a global marketplace where competitors' labor costs are significantly lower (Economic Council of Canada, 1990).

Of course, labor unions and their leaders have an opposing agenda. Their goals include maintaining or increasing members' wages and benefits, obtaining job security, and improving work conditions; all of which add to labor costs. Traditionally, labor and management relations in Canada have been adversarial, despite meagre recent attempts at cooperation (Kochan, Katz, and McKersie, 1986; Thompson and Verma, 1988).

Legislation and government involvement versus a need for strategic autonomy.
Over the past quarter century, a body of law has developed which is designed to
supplement collective agreements and provide protection to all employees: work
standards, contracts of employment, fundamental human rights, and occupational
health and safety. Federal legislation applies to about 10% of the Canadian work
force and provincial laws provide reasonably similar coverage for other employees, both union and non-union. Needless to say, human resource managers must
be acutely aware of the complex and sometimes confusing network of legislation
which constrains and shapes their managerial roles.

At the same time, HR managers, because of the relentlessly increasing labor cost
component of produced goods and services throughout the Canadian economy,
are under constant pressure to seek strategic and competitive advantages for their
organizations (Porter, 1991).

*Changing composition of the labor force versus an entrenched system of trade
unionism.* For nearly two decades, Canada's employment growth has been much
more dramatic in the service-producing industries, which are more prone to employ part-time and female workers who are more likely to be unorganized or have
weaker ties to a union (Stone and Meltz, 1993). Adjustments of the Canadian
labor market due to the 1981-82 recession resulted in accelerating the elimination
of older, long-tenure workers and increasing the hiring of younger workers in
the sectors of growth (Gera, 1991). On the immigration scene, whereas Europe
used to be the main source of immigrants, newcomers to Canada are now more
likely to hail from Asia, Africa, the Caribbean, or Latin America and congregate
disproportionately in Canada's three largest cities (Economic Council of Canada,
1991a). The net effect of these shifts has been that the addition of new union
members did not keep pace with the growth in the labor force during the 1980s.
Consequently, the typical unionist is now likely to work in a government office
and belong to a Canadian union rather than an international union. About one third
are female (Ponak, Gunderson, and Anderson, 1989). Canadian unions have been
forced to respond to the changing attitudes, needs, and interests of their members.
At the same time, in some unions, the spectre of loss of membership has created
defensiveness and a hesitation to cooperate with management or government.

In an atmosphere where the public has increasingly grown impatient with the
inconvenience of strikes and slowdowns, and where tax increases and escalating
goods and service costs have often been attributed to union demands, HR managers are challenged to break the old adversarial pattern. Better ways must be
found of eliciting union cooperation in joint efforts to improve Canadian union-
management relations and labor cost effectiveness.

Brief History of the HRM Field in Canada

Interestingly, the historical evolution of the human resource management field in Canada is reflected in titles. World War One necessitated advances in selection and duty assignment procedures. Industrial firms were expended to meet the war effort. During and after the war, firms increasingly began to recognize the importance of careful treatment of employees, at least in a physical sense. Some firms began to create a "staff clerk" or "industrial welfare worker" position to keep rudimentary records on employees and employee-related activities.

The Canadian union movement in the 1920s and 1930s led employers to rely more and more on "personnel specialists" to deal more effectively with organized workers. Unionization stimulated the improvement of job descriptions, wage schemes, and several new types of benefits. The early personnel specialists were largely self-educated, although the newly formed Montreal Personnel Association in 1934, created a 10-week night course for its nine members, using materials from the Canadian National Railway, the Canadian Pacific Railway, Bell Telephone, C-I-L, Sun Life Insurance, and McGill University (Personnel Association of Toronto, 1986).

The personnel and industrial relations function gained importance during and following World War Two. Once again, industry expanded rapidly and became more sophisticated. Major advances were made in industrial psychology; particularly in selection testing and in placement and training. During the late 1940s and 1950s, Canada experienced some additions and changes in labor legislation and regulations. Clearly, administering the personnel function in an effective way meant acquiring more specialized skills. The federal government sponsored special extension courses in personnel administration at Dalhousie, Queens, the University of Manitoba, and the University of British Columbia. Nonetheless, the typical "personnel administrator" was not formally trained and acquired his position more often by expediency than by conscious career choice. In fact, many firms used the personnel administrator's position as a temporary assignment for managers being groomed for transfer or promotion to a line position in some other functional area.

The human relations movement in the late 1950s through the mid 1960s had a major impact on the personnel and industrial relation function. Because of the wide attention given to the work of behaviourial scientists such as Elton Mayo (1945), Douglas McGregor (1960), and Rensis Likert (1961), managers began seriously to focus on their organizations as social systems. Newly discovered possibilities for improving employee effectiveness included promising techniques in job design, employee participation, communication, and conflict management (to name a few). As the personnel function became much more proactive, its leader often held the more prestigious title of "personnel manager". The new personnel manager often had some university training as well, but usually not in personnel administration and industrial relations *per se*. Unfortunately, some of the new human relations ideas were prematurely or inappropriately packaged and promoted as "cure-alls" in management development programs which became faddish during this period (Campbell, 1971; Milkovich et al., 1988).

By the late 1960s, personnel management and industrial relations courses leading to a recognized specialty were offered in most universities in Canada. During the early Trudeau era (1968-79), the former National Employment Service, the Department of Labor, and the Immigration Services of the Department of Citizenship and Immigration were brought together to establish the Department of Manpower and Immigration (Canada Manpower). This new federal agency was charged with improving Canada's human capital through training, mobility facilitation, and job creation (Economic Council of Canada, 1971). A number of programs were created, furnishing opportunities for many firms to take advantage of the possibilities for training enhancement and more effective resource acquisition. Many of the programs involved joint participation with provincial governments (Milkovich et al., 1988). Canada probably was the first western industrialized country to undertake this sort of joint industry/government participation in HR development on a national scale. Personnel managers were afforded the opportunity to increase their stature in their organizations by spearheading these programs, many of which could be shown to be directly cost effective.

The struggle for professional recognition and for acceptance (clout) at the senior organizational level continued to characterize the Canadian "human resource manager" during the 1970s and 1980s. One indication of continuing acceptance of HR management in Canada is the remarkable growth in numbers of HR managers from about 4,000 in 1971 to about 25,000 in 1981. Continued growth at a slower pace is projected for the 1990s (CEIC, 1986). Canada had approximately 44,000 HR managers and an additional 44,000 HR officers in 1991.

Some scholars have argued that, particularly during the past decade, the human resource function in Canada has grown increasingly distinct from HR management in the United States (Milkovich et al., 1988). There are several reasons for this view. Politically, there has been a resurgence in national feeling, centering around the 1982 Constitution and its accompanying human rights provisions, many of which have been or are being translated directly into employment regulations. Canada has not experienced a decline in unionization like the U.S. The imperative for effective labor-management negotiations continues to be a prime concern of organizations in Canada, especially in the public service arena. Many foreign-owned firms with subsidiaries in Canada have decentralized their operations, allowing their Canadian HR managers more autonomy in strategic decision-making where peculiarly Canadian issues are concerned (Milkovich et al., 1988). Many organizations located in Canada's major metropolitan areas (Toronto, Montreal, and Vancouver) are faced with the HR opportunities and problems inherent in an increasingly multicultural work force (Economic Council of Canada, 1991a) in a country which espouses the ideology of preserving cultural diversity (a mosaic) in contrast with the U.S. ideology of cultural homogeneity (a melting pot). Prima facie evidence of a tendency toward Canadianization of the HRM profession is provided by the proliferation of Canadian HR textbooks within the last ten years (e.g., Jain, 1978; Werther et al., 1990; Stone and Meltz, 1988; Milkovich et al., 1988; Dolan and Schuler, 1987; Anderson et al., 1989). As will be discussed in more detail below, distinctive HR professional associations have developed regionally, although a national federation existed for several years prior to 1982.

Present State of Canadian Human Resource Management

The current form and scope of Canadian human resource management has been the focus of a small number of recent research efforts (Kumar, 1980; Thacker and Cattaneo, 1987; Blake, 1988; Saunders and Leck, 1989; Moore and Robinson, 1989; Murray, Whitehead, and Blake, 1990; Jennings and Moore, 1991; Jennings, 1992). A comprehensive Canada-wide study of HR managers and management remains to be undertaken. However, existing research does provide answers to several questions about Canadian human resource management as it is currently practiced. What are the characteristics of those persons who are engaged in HRM? What role do HR managers perform? How is this role impacting on the organization? Has this role changed? To what extent is HRM a profession?

HR Managers in Profile

Ninety-two percent of the Moore and Robinson (1989) sample of western Canadian HR practitioners were performing a managerial role at some level in their departments. Thus, the characteristics of this group will be used to provide a profile of the HR managerial group. Murray, Whitehead, and Blake (1990) illuminate the profile of the senior HR manager in large firms.

Overall, the respondent group was composed of 62% males and 38% females. The median age was 38 years with a range of 21 to 77. The average salary received was C$30,000 with a range of C$16,000 - C$130,000. Male practitioners' salaries were significantly higher than those for females (C$56,551 vs. C$40,369, p<.05). There was a positive relationship between managerial level and salary. Census figures for 1991 confirm these relationships and indicate that HR managers' average salary levels for male HR managers are slightly higher than for the average Canadian manager. Female HR managers, on the other hand, earned 16% more than the average for female managers generally (Statistics Canada, 1993a).

Western Canadian HR managers are quite highly educated, and many are trained specifically in the field, as shown in Table 2

Compared to a Western Canadian study of HR managers (primarily located in the province of British Columbia) conducted 20 years ago (Moore and Longbottom, 1971), a much larger proportion of present-day managers have had specific

Table 2:   Education Pattern of HR Managers

Level of Education	Percent	Field of Study	Percent
High School	9	HRM related	33
Some university	9	General management	17
College diploma	17	Arts emphasis	30
University degree	50	Science emphasis	5
Some masters work	1	Other	8
Masters degree	14		

training in the HR field (33% vs. 22% earlier) and the proportion obtaining university training in general has increased from 53% to 64%. Moreover, this comparison does not include the 17% in the present study who earned a diploma in one of the technical or community colleges not in existence until recently.

In general, the respondents in the Moore and Robinson (1989) study were experienced managers who held fairly senior positions in the organization's hierarchy. About one fourth reported directly to the president or chief executive officer (CEO), and 32% were two levels from the top. On average, these managers had been with their present organization for eight years and had spent six years in HRM with that firm. Overall, the managers had an average of 11.5 years' experience in the field (sd = 7.0). About one third of the managers held positions in government organizations and about two thirds work in organizations not engaged in primary industry. Nonetheless, in the average organization represented, 42% of the employees were union members.

Compared to the past, how do Canadian HR practitioners perceive themselves? Moore and Robinson (1989) probed the extent of agreement with several statements about HR people which were written for a Canadian study 30 years ago (Colmen, Green, and Futransky, 1959). The statements and comparative percentage agreements are presented in Table 3.

A visual examination of these comparative data provides a consistent impression that personnel or HR managers perceive themselves as more 'managerial' than in the past, but at the same time a greater percentage identifies a primary responsibility directed at employees rather than management. This seeming contradiction may reflect the current tendency for enlightened HR managers to recognize the plurality of their role. That is, HR managers can only enhance their strategic influence by establishing an effective linkage between top management and the employees, resulting in mutual understanding, cooperation, and heightened overall effectiveness. In essence, these findings seem to indicate a gradual upgrading of the field rather than a dramatic gain or breakthrough in any one area of activity. Of course, these data only reflect the way HR managers view themselves. Managers representing other functional areas may hold differing views.

Table 3:   Canadian HR Managers' Self-perceptions: Then and Now

Perception	Percent agreement	
	1959	1988
Supervisors outside the personnel office view personnel as a nuisance, not an aid	46	35
Most personnel people keep up with recent developments in their field	59	64
Personnel people have provided vigorous leadership needed to support merit principles in such actions as selection and promotion	40	58
Personnel people stick together too much – speaking their own language and remaining aloof from those outside the field	55	33
Personnel people usually know more about the operating programs they service than line officials give them credit for	74	68
Few personnel people actually practice with their own staffs what they preach to operating officials	59	43
Most personnel people are prone to hide behind rules and regulations as an excuse for a lack of positive action	47	27
Most personnel programs have the respect of employees in the organization they serve	50	50
The primary responsibility of the personnel office is to management rather than to employees	54	41

Source: Moore and Robinson (1989, p. 105)

Murray, Whitehead, and Blake (1990) report that, although 40% of the most senior HR managers have titles that do not contain the designation of Vice-President, most SHRMs do report directly to the CEO or the immediate second in command. In Canada's largest organizations, most HR functions maintain a corporate presence plus a dotted-line (advisory) relationship to subsidiary HR units which are operational staff departments serving the line managers at that level. One important indicator of any manager's potential for having real impact on organizational strategy is how that manager is perceived by his or her CEO. The way the manager is seen to behave affects the way the CEO will interact with that person and his or her department. Murray and his colleagues found that the CEOs perceived their senior HR executives more as professional specialists than organizational generalists, although they were perceived as "good" but not outstanding either as generalists or specialists.

In the Canadian organizations studied by Murray, Whitehead, and Blake (1990), corporate-level senior HR managers were very often used in a consulting (or advisory) role both on HR and on operational policy issues, with the effective decision-making authority more often in the hands of corporate-level senior line management. Once a policy decision is taken, however, the senior HR manager has much responsibility for implementation. Blake (1988) reported three factors which are important determinants of the amount of influence a senior HR executive has on corporate-level decision-making: support of the CEO, credibility, and acceptance by peers. The CEOs Blake interviewed overwhelmingly felt that their SHRE's influence had increased in the past five years; however, the CEOs believed the SHREs must develop a more holistic understanding of business, as well as a "bottom line" orientation.

In Canada, while it is not common for senior HR executives to move up to the CEO position, a good performance record and a generalist background can enable them to move higher in the organization outside the human resource function. Thus, to have real organization influence, the HR executive must strive to become both a professional HR specialist and a generalist in his or her organization's business arena.

The Human Resources Department

Moore and Robinson (1989) asked HR managers a series of questions about their departments, designed to shed some light on specific areas of strategic and tactical responsibility and involvement. How central is the HR department in various key areas and how has the role of the department changed?

First, the researchers looked at the degree of departmental involvement in decision making in 24 specific areas and how that involvement had changed over the past five years (see Table 4). In general, involvement in all areas seems to have increased. On average, for each area listed, 48-83% of the respondents felt it had increased; and in no area did more than 28% feel that it had decreased. Areas in which the HR department appeared to be more involved are employee benefits, counselling, and compensation – approximately three fourths of the sample felt that involvement had increased.

Those areas cited as having the least increase in involvement include voluntary separation, transfers, and time off work. In these areas only about half felt involvement had increased. If the overall perspective is accurate, then the level of tactical centrality in administering the HR function has increased dramatically over the past five years.

Historically, there has been much concern and scepticism about the relative lack of involvement that HR departments have had at the strategic level in organizations. In many organizations, top management regarded careful attention to human resources as a planning input as unnecessary and a waste of time. The HR

Table 4: HR Departmental Involvement in Specific Human Resource Decisions

	Percent reporting high/sole involvement	Percent increased involvement over past 5 years
Recruiting	79	70
Involuntary separation	78	77
Compensation	73	79
Human resource policy	71	73
Benefits	70	81
Grievances	67	61
Hiring	64	63
Selection	64	68
Contract negotiation	62	63
HR planning	60	76
Performance appraisal	57	77
Counselling	56	83
HR research	55	68
Training and development	53	76
Control/discipline	50	69
Voluntary separation	44	59
Organization review	43	64
Safety	42	65
Affirmative action/EEO	39	70
Promotion	36	63
Transfer	36	57
Job design	35	66
Incentive payment	34	62
Time off/on work	30	48

Source: Moore and Jennings (1993, p. 17)

department often had little influence in major decisions affecting the firm's future destiny (Wolf, 1980; Mealiea and Lee, 1980). Recent North American evidence suggests that human resource policy and planning is becoming more feasible with the evolution of sophisticated data systems, and the need to integrate HR activities with organizational strategy is now more widely recognized (Mahoney and Deckop, 1986; Anthony, Perrewe, and Kacmar, 1993).

In a series of questions, Moore and Robinson (1989) attempted to examine the extent to which Western Canadian HR departments were perceived to be involved in planning at the strategic level. Two thirds to three fourths of the respondents indicated that their departments participated to a larger or very large extent in developing HR strategies, and in initiating and implementing HR programs, but less than 45% saw their departments as having strong involvement in planning at the corporate or overall level. On the other hand, compared to the level of participation in strategic planning five years ago, the respondents perceived significantly greater (p<.05) involvement both in strategic decisions specifically focused on human resource issues and programs and in overall organization planning. The perceived extent of increased involvement at both the functional (HR) and the overall (corporate) levels of planning was about the same.

A major area of interest is how the role of the Canadian HR department has changed or grown in the last five years. Based on open-ended questions a wide variety of responses were received and categorized into general areas. Consistent with the results discussed above, only 12% of the respondents felt their departments had not grown or changed. Approximately 25% made a general statement that a new HR department had developed or that their department had grown considerably. Most respondents were quite specific in attributing their department's development to its taking on greater responsibilities and handling these in a more professional manner. HR staff members were seen as having become more professionalised in their approach and abilities. As a result, their department was now more involved in decision making and/or had a greater impact on the organization as a whole.

Respondents were asked to indicate what they believed were the internal and external factors that accounted for this change. Again, the responses were diverse but they fell into some broad areas. With regard to internal factors, 26% did not respond. Of those who did, many attributed the change to the impact of senior management. Respondents mentioned such things as the philosophy of the president, senior management's commitment, and executive succession. The second most commonly mentioned set of factors related to the HR department itself: a new and/or more professional staff, good HR management, and the quality of the department's output. Departmental downsizing or restructuring in adjusting to organizational needs was also mentioned rather often (e.g., a realization that specialized advice was necessary, or that complexities of legislation required a growth or change in the HR department). Amazingly, regarding external factors, more than 50% offered no reply. Of those factors that were mentioned, government legislation was by far the most common. Competition and financially related factors were second.

Even though the role played by the HR department in organizations was perceived by Western Canadian respondents to have grown and developed in recent years, 54% felt that the relative prestige of the department was best characterized as medium (although 32% chose "high"). Perception of departmental prestige was significantly related to level in the hierarchy. HR practitioners occupying more senior positions had a greater tendency to perceive their department as having a higher level of prestige.

About two thirds of the respondents indicated that their department had extensive contacts with HR departments in other organizations, suggesting the existence of a network linking members of this field for the purpose of sharing information on programs and so on. Many types of HR programs are shared in this way, but no clear pattern could be discerned.

Finally, respondents were asked how satisfied they were with a number of specific features of their present role of job. The highest mean levels of satisfaction on a scale of 1-5 were: sense of competence on the job (4.08), having a lot of responsibility (4.05), professional satisfaction (3.99), and fit between interests and skills on the job (3.96). Areas where there was least satisfaction were: having to do things that should not be part of my job, and (too much) time spent away from major responsibilities.

The overall pattern of responses obtained by Moore and Robinson (1989) regarding the HR department suggests that people who fill HR roles perceived the HR function as growing in importance and professional stature within the organization. The HR department was viewed as a place where there are real opportunities to exercise HR skills in areas where much responsibility is required and where competence is put to test. On the other hand, although the department appears to play a major role in setting and implementing HR policy and programs, there still is a certain lack of influence and participation in strategic business planning. Saunders and Leck's (1989) study of HR management policies in Canada's largest business organizations suggests that while HR department influence remains lower than ideal, organization size is related to the adoption of formal HR mechanisms in some areas of decision-making. In general, then, the available evidence shows the HR departments in Canadian organizations have been gaining strategic and tactical importance but that they still lack prestige and clout in many firms. Encouragingly, HR practitioners and their CEOs both expect that HR managers will become even more involved with strategic decisions in the future (Blake, 1988; Moore and Robinson, 1989; Murray, Whitehead, and Blake, 1990; Saunders and Leck, 1989).

The Murray, Whitehead, and Blake (1990) study of HR management in large Canadian organizations found that the use of outside consultants is becoming more common, especially in rapidly evolving areas such as employee benefits, training, computerized HR information systems, and government regulations and legislation affecting labor relations. Interestingly, the more highly educated the HR specialists were, the more often consultants were used (r=.32; p<.01).

According to Murray et al. (1990), measurement of the HR department's impact and effectiveness remains mainly subjective. In 45% of their sample no kind of HR evaluation was conducted. Where an evaluation occurred, it was typically a qualitative appraisal; and made against a set of strategic departmental objectives in only about half of the departments. U.S. and Canadian controlled firms operating in Canada were more likely to use quantitative forms of HR department evaluation than were European controlled firms. Firms experiencing cutbacks, as opposed

Table 5:   Professional Dimensions of HR as a Profession
           (seen as descriptive by western Canadian practitioners)

Professional Dimension	Percent indicating descriptive
A body of specialized knowledge including standardized terminology	87
Widely recognized certification based on standardized terminology	31
Code of ethics	55
Members oriented towards a service objective	85
Recognized by the general public as a profession	60
Limited access to the field, based on acquisition of standard skills/knowledge	63
A professional society or association, which, among other things, represents and gives voice to the entire field	61
Practitioners are licensed	8
Close collegiality among practitioners	73

Source: Moore and Robinson (1989, p. 101)

to growing firms, were more likely to use quantitative evaluation of their HR departments. Firms experiencing comparatively low growth were more likely to evaluate their HR activities against strategic plans. Thus, it appears that the more competitive or difficult the firm's environment, the greater the likelihood that the HR function will be rigorously evaluated.

Human Resource Management as a Profession

To provide an indication of the extent to which Western Canadian HR managers see their field as a profession, Moore and Robinson (1989) identified several dimensions which have been used to characterize professional occupations (cf. Abrahamson, 1967; Kleingartner, 1969; Ritzer and Trice, 1969). The managers were asked how well each dimension described the HRM field. The responses were dichotomized into descriptive or not descriptive categories as shown in Table 5.

Based on the pattern of responses in Table 5, the professional dimensions most descriptive of HRM include a body of specialized knowledge and a membership oriented towards a service objective. Other dimensions are less descriptive, particularly with regard to license or certification requirements. Only 60% view their field as being publically recognized as a distinct profession. At least three fourths of the respondents felt that improvement is needed on all dimensions except licensing and collegiality, and even in these two areas, over half the sample called for improvement (58% and 62% respectively). Clearly, there is much interest in becoming still more professional as a field but not necessarily in securing formal recognition through licensing or certification arrangements. In common with many other Canadian professionals such as engineers, accountants, radiologists, and nurses, the *de facto* amount of professional status is much more dependent on his or her demonstrated competence at work day after day than on paper qualifications. Nonetheless, the Human Resource Professionals Association of Ontario sponsors a professional designation program which is enshrined in legislation in the province of Ontario. Designation as a *Certified Human Resource Professional* is granted based on satisfaction of certain standards of educational background and/or experience as an HR practitioner. The province of Alberta also grants the CHRP designation, although there is no legislative status involved. Several other provinces are considering some form of professional designation as well, although a Canada-wide certification program leading to professional designation is not in place at present.

Moore and Robinson's (1989) survey contained one question regarding the steps the respondent had taken to upgrade professionally during the last two years. In general, HR practitioners in Western Canada put considerable effort into continually improving themselves. Only 3% left the item vacant and most respondents could list at least two activities. The most common activity was attendance at HR-related seminars, courses and workshops. Three fourths of the sample had been involved in such programs. More commonly mentioned courses included computer training, association-sponsored seminars, and courses offered by local colleges or universities. Another major activity for about 25% of the respondents was reading career-related literature from periodicals to recent legislative changes. As indicated earlier, most of these respondents are well trained and they clearly have a strong desire to stay current in their field. Other less frequently mentioned upgrading activities included participation in HRM associations, networking, attending conferences, and participation in certificate or diploma programs (where they exist).

Similarly, at the senior level, Murray, Whitehead, and Blake (1990) found HR managers keeping up with their field by attending conferences and reading both the professional HR literature and business periodicals, especially those regarding the environment in which their company operates. Murray and his colleagues found the 75% of the SRHMs had careers entirely in HR, but they typically had moved from one company to another, increasing their authority and responsibility with each move.

In the Canadian context, professionalization appears to be worthwhile for a career-oriented HR manager. Jennings and Moore (1991) found that increasing job complexity and education were associated with increased salary and autonomy. Increased interdepartmental contact (a more effective internal network) and increased involvement in strategic decision making lead to more salary, autonomy and satisfaction. Working in an HR department with a legitimated (formally recognized) ideology (policy orientation with integrated practices) yields more rewards than working in a department without a legitimated ideology. In Canada, organizational size is related to professionalization of the HR function. Because the body of HR knowledge is expanding and becoming more complex, there are more sophisticated tools with which to manage, hence more interest in using these effectively. There is a pervasive feeling that the real professional challenges in the next decade lie in integrating HRM theory and practices with overall organization strategies (cf. Blake, 1988; Mahoney and Deckop, 1986; Murray, Whitehead, and Blake, 1990; Anthony, Perrew, and Kacmar, 1993).

Canadian Human Resources Management: A Field in Transition

Clearly, the field of human resource management in Canada has undergone a steady stream of important changes. Moore and Robinson (1989) asked respondents to indicate what they believed to be the three most significant changes in the field in the last five years. A wide range of replies were given and some consistent patterns emerged. By far, the most significant change appears to surround the issue of government legislation. About half the respondents mentioned that government policy had either changed or increased and many mentioned such issues as pay and employment equity, labor relations law and human rights legislation. Greater acceptance of the HR field was another frequently listed change, with about one third of the respondents mentioning the higher profile, responsibility or importance of HRM in organizations. Changes created by economic conditions were also frequently mentioned; 28% of the respondents cited such factors as the downsizing of the HR department and/or the organization, and the HR department being required to become more cost conscious as a result of economic changes in the environment.

Practitioners see a similar set of environmental factors influencing HRM's development in the next five years as in the last five. More than two thirds of the Western Canadian practitioners felt that changes in government legislation will have a significant impact on the field in the near future. Almost half of the respondents felt that equity legislation would have a considerable impact, and nearly an eighth mentioned government-related issues specifically surrounding human rights and the Charter of Rights in the new Canadian Constitution. Other forces mentioned by at least one fourth of the sample included changes in work structure, including part-time work and early retirement, changes in provincial labor laws, benefits and compensation issues such as the rising cost of benefits, pension reforms and the need for flexibility, and the HR impact from technological change and computerization.

Given the similarities of these future trends to those of the past, it is likely that the responses of the HR function and HR managers will contunue to be similar to those in the past. The HR function will have an increased involvement in strategic decision-making, particularly in the area of employment equity and in developing methods to incorporate aboriginal peoples into the mainstream of the Canadian workforce. HR managers will continue to improve their training and professional standing. For instance, the Human Resource Management Associaltion (HRMA) of British Columbia is presently considering a certification procedure for its members which would involve four elements: 1) committee evaluation of current knowledge, 2) standardized course work, 3) a period of practical service, and 4) some type of formal examination (Argue, 1993). Ontario's province-wide certification system for HR practitioners involves, among other things, standardized courses offered at the college/university level.

Because of NAFTA and other global economic shifts, we believe that Canada is facing a different set of pressures today, and that these must be recognized by HR managers. The need for advanced training and for flexibility in the workforce will increase the volatility of employment and careers. International competition will exert enormous cost-cutting pressures on firms, which experience shows will be transmitted directly to the HR function. Unlike the past, the real expertise in HRM may end up residing not in large HR departments, but in small, external part-time consulting firms that specialize in training, legal issues and pay systems, and in other managers in the firm who have added HR knowledge to their repertoire of skills. This scenario suggests that the environment still appears to be dictating the form and function of HRM. In an atmosphere where the public has grown increasingly impatient with the inconvenience of strikes and slowdowns, and where tax increases and escalating goods and service costs have often been attributed to union demands, HR managers must try to break the old adversarial patterns between management and labor. Better ways must be found for eliciting cooperation in joint efforts to improve Canadian union-management relations and labor cost effectiveness. In these endeavors, HR practitioners as a group need to be less reactive and more proactive. Internationally, the Canadian HR field stands to benefit greatly from forging links (e.g., establishing communication networks, and exchanging technology and information) with its global counterparts in the Pacific Region and elsewhere.

References

Abrahamson, M. (1967). *The Professional in the Organization* Chicago: Rand McNally.
Anderson, A.B. and J.S. Frideres (1981). *Ethnicity in Canada: Theoretical Perspectives.* Toronto: Butterworths.
Anderson, J.C., M. Gunderson and A. Ponak (1989). *Union-Management Relations in Canada.* Don Mills: Addison-Wesley.
Anthony, W., P.L. Perrewe and K.M. Kacmar (1993). *Strategic Human Resource Management.* Fort Worth, TX: Dryden Press.

Argue, G. (1993). From a personal interview with the president of the British Columbia Human Resources Management Association, conducted 15 January, 1993.

Badets, J. (1993). "Canada's Immigrants: Recent Trends." *Canadian Social Trends*, Statistics Canada Cat. No. 11-008E, pp. 8-11.

Blake, R.W. (1988). "The Role of the Senior Human Resource Executive: Orientation and Influence." In T.H. Stone and A. Petit (eds.) *Proceedings of the Administrative Sciences Association of Canada*, Personnel and Human Resources Division, Saint Mary's University: Halifax, NS, pp. 62-71.

Broadfoot, B. (1976). *The Pioneer Years 1895-1914*. Toronto: Doubleday Canada.

Campbell, J.P. (1971). "Personnel Training and Development." *Annual Review of Psychology*, 22, 565-602.

CEIC (Canada Employment and Immigration Commission) (1986). *Reference Growth Scenario*. Ottawa: Supplies and Services Canada.

Clark, G. (1965). *Canada: the Uneasy Neighbor*. Toronto: McClelland and Stewart.

Colmen, J.C., D.E. Green, and D. Futransky (1959). "What Personnel Workers Think of Their Jobs and Profession." *Personnel Administration*, 23, 8-15.

Dolan, S.L. and R.S. Schuler (1987). *Personnel and Human Resource Management in Canada*. St. Paul, MN: West Publishing.

Economic Council of Canada (1971). *Eighth Annual Review*. Ottawa: Supplies and Services Canada.

Economic Council of Canada (1982). *In Short Supply: Jobs and Skills in the 1980s*. Ottawa: Supplies and Services Canada.

Economic Council of Canada (1990). *Twenty-Seventh Annual Review*. Ottawa: Supplies and Services Canada.

Economic Council of Canada (1991a). *Twenty-Eighth Annual Review*. Ottawa: Supplies and Services Canada.

Economic Council of Canada (1991b). *New Faces in Economic and Social Impacts of Immigration*. Ottawa: Supplies and Services Canada.

Foot, D.K. (1982). *Canada's Population Outlook, Demographic Futures and Economic Challenges*. Ottawa: Canadian Institute for Public Policy.

Gera, S. (1991). *Canadian Unemployment: Lessons from the 80s and Challenges for the 90s*. Ottawa: Supplies and Services Canada.

House of Commons (1982). *Work for Tomorrow: Employment Opportunities for the 80s*. Ottawa: Supplies and Services Canada.

Horowitz, G. (1971). "Conservatism, Liberalism and Socialism in Canada: An Interpretation." In W.E. Mann (ed.) *Canada: A Sociological Profile* (2nd ed.). Toronto: Copp Clark, pp. 8-23.

Jain, H.C. (1978). *Contemporary Issues in Canadian Personnel Administration*. Scarborough, ON: Prentice-Hall.

Jennings, P.D. (1992). "SHRM Makes a Difference: The Impact of SHRM on the HR Manager's Job, Training and Salary." Working Paper, Faculty of Commerce and Business Administration, University of British Columbia, Vancouver, Canada.

Jennings, P.D. and L.F. Moore (1991). "A Comparison of the Functional, Political and Institutional Perspectives on Professional Rewards: The Case of the Human Resource Specialists." Working Paper, Faculty of Commerce and Business Administration, University of British Columbia, Vancouver, Canada.

Kaliski, S.F. (1985). "Trends, Changes, and Imbalances: A Survey of the Canadian Labour Market." In *Work and Pay: The Canadian Labour Market*, vol. 17, prepared for the Royal Commission on the Economic Union and Development Prospects for Canada. Toronto: University of Toronto Press.

Kanungo, R. (1980). *Biculturalism and Management*. Toronto: Butterworths.

Kleingartner, A. (1969). "Professionalism and Engineering Unionism." *Industrial Relations*, 8, 224-235.

Kochan, T.A., H.C. Katz and R.B. McKersie (1986). *The Transformation of American Industrial Relations*. New York: Basic Books.

Kumar, P. (1980). *Professionalism in the Canadian Personnel Administration Function: Report of a Survey*. Kingston, ON: Industrial Relations Centre, Queens University.

Kumar, P. (1983). "Introduction and Summary." In *Canadian Labour Markets in the 1980s: Proceedings of a Conference held at Queens University at Kingston, Feb. 25-26, 1983*. Kingston, ON: Industrial Relations Centre, Queens University, pp. 1-6.

La Novara, P. (1993). "Changes in Family Living," *Canadian Social Trends*. Statistics Canada, Cat. No. 11-008E, pp. 12-14.

Likert, R. (1961). *New Patterns of Management*. New York: McGraw-Hill.

MacDonald Commission (1985). See Royal Commission on the Economic Union and Development Prospects for Canada.

Mahoney, T.A. and J.R. Deckop (1986). "Evolution of Concept and Practice in Personnel Administration/Human Resources Management." *Journal of Management*, 12, 223-241.

Malcom, A.H. (1985). *The Canadians*. Markham, ON: Fitzhenry and Whiteside.

Mann, W.E. (1971). *Canada: A Sociological Profile* (2nd ed.). Toronto: Copp Clark.

Mayo, E. (1945). *The Social Problems of an Industrial Civilization*. Cambridge, MA: Harvard University Press.

McGregor, D. (1960). *The Human Side of Enterprise*. New York: McGraw-Hill.

McPhillips, D. and G. England (1989). "Employment Legislation in Canada." In J.C. Anderson, M. Gunderson and A. Ponak (eds.) *Union-Management Relations in Canada* (2nd ed.). Don Mills, ON: Addison-Wesley, pp. 43-69.

Mealiea, L.W. and D. Lee (1980). "Contemporary Personnel Practices in Canadian Firms: An Empirical Evaluation." *Relations Industrielles*, 35, pp. 410-420.

Milkovich, G.T., W.F. Glueck, R.T. Barth and S.L. McShane (1988). *Canadian Personnel/Human Resource Management: A Diagnostic Approach*. Plano, TX: Business Publications.

Moore, L.F. and N. Bu (1990). "Human Resource Planning in Canada: A Perspective." *Asia Pacific HRM*, 28, pp. 5-22.

Moore, L.F. and P.D. Jennings (1993). "Canadian Human Resource Management at the Crossroads." *Asia Pacific Journal of Human Resources*, 31(2), pp. 12-25.

Moore, L.F. and R. Longbottom (1971). "B.C. Study of Personnel Managers: Preliminary Items of Interest." *Canadian Personnel and Industrial Relations Journal*, 18, pp. 45-49.

Moore, L.F. and S. Robinson (1989). "Human Resource Management Present and Future: Highlights from a Western Canadian Survey of Practitioner Perceptions." In A. Petit and A.V. Subbarau (eds.) *Proceedings of the Administrative Sciences Association of Canada*. Montreal, PQ: Personnel and Human Resources Division, McGill University, pp. 100-110.

Morton, D. (1989). "The History of the Canadian Labour Movement." In J.C. Anderson, M. Gunderson and A. Ponak (eds.) *Union-Management Relations in Canada* (2nd ed.). Don Mills, ON: Addison-Wesley, pp. 155-181.

Murray, V.V., D. Whitehead and W. Blake (1990). "Managing the HR Function: The Prentice-Hall Survey." In *Human Resources in Canada*. Toronto: Prentice-Hall, 15543-15582.

OECD (1990/1991) (1991/1992). *Economic Survey Series*. Geneva: OECD.

Personnel Association of Toronto (1986). *PAT: The First 50 Years (Building the Human Resources Function)*. Toronto: PAT.

Ponak, A., M. Gunderson and J.C. Anderson (1989). "Back to the Future." In J.C. Anderson, M. Gunderson and A. Ponak (eds.) *Union-Management Relations in Canada* (2nd ed.). Don Mills, ON: Addison-Wesley, pp. 465-485.

Ponak, A. and M. Thompson (1989). "Public Sector Collective Bargaining." In J.C. Anderson, M. Gunderson and A. Ponak (eds.) *Union-Management Relations in Canada* (2nd ed.). Don Mills, ON: Addison-Wesley, pp. 373-406.

Porter, M.E. (1991). *Canada at the Crossroads: The Reality of a New Competitive Environment*. Ottawa: Business Council on National Issues and the Government of Canada.

Ritzer, G. and H.M. Trice (1969). *An Occupation in Conflict: A Study of the Personnel Manager*. Ithaca, NY: New York State School of Industrial and Labor Relations.

Royal Commission on the Economic Union and Development Prospects for Canada (1985). *Report, Vol.2* Ottawa: Queen's Printer, p. 587.

Sack, J. and T. Lee (1989). "The Role of the State in Canadian Labour Relations." *Relations Industrielles*, 44, 195-221.

Saunders, D.M. and J.D. Leck (1989). "Human Resource Management Policies: A Descriptive Study." In A. Petit and A.V. Subbarau (eds.) *Proceedings of the Administrative Sciences Association of Canada*. Personnel and Human Resources Division, McGill University: Montreal, PQ, pp. 142-151.

Statistics Canada (1988). *Canada Yearbook*. Ottawa: Supplies and Services Canada.

Statistics Canada (1989). *Labour Force Annual Averages 1981-1988*. Ottawa: Supplies and Services, Canada.

Statistics Canada (1990). *Canadian Statistical Review*. Ottawa: Supplies and Services Canada.

Statistics Canada (1992). *Canada Yearbook*. Ottawa: Supplies and Services Canada.

Statistics Canada (1993a). *Employment Income by Occupation*. Ottawa: Industry, Science and Technology, Canada.

Statistics Canada (1993b). *Historical Labour Force Statistics 1992*. Ottawa: Supplies and Services, Canada.

Stone, T.H. and N.M. Meltz (1988). *Human Resource Management in Canada* (2nd ed.). Toronto: Holt, Rinehart and Winston.

Stone, T.H. and N.M. Meltz (1993). *Human Resource Management in Canada* (3rd ed.). Toronto: Holt, Rinehart and Winston.

Thacker, J.W. and R.J. Cattaneo (1987). "The Canadian Personnel Function: Status and Practices." In T.H. Stone and J. Le Louarn (eds.) *Proceedings of the Administrative Sciences Association of Canada*. Personnel and Human Resources Interest Group, University of Toronto: Toronto, ON, pp. 56-66.

Thompson, M. and A. Verma (1988). "Managerial Strategies in Industrial Relations in the 1980s: The Canadian Experience." Working Paper 1272, Faculty of Commerce, University of British Columbia, Vancouver.

Werther, W.B., K. Davis, H.F. Schwind, T.P. Haridas and F.C. Miner (1990). *Canadian Human Resource Management* (3rd ed.). Toronto: McGraw-Hill Ryerson.

Wolf, W.B. (1980). *Top Management of the Personnel Function: Current Issues and Practices*. Ithaca, NY: New York State School of Industrial and Labor Relations.

Human Resource Management in Hong Kong

Wai Keung Poon

This chapter provides background information about Hong Kong for those who have never been there, and acquaints readers with the state of the art in human resource management in the territory for business or educational purposes. The contents of the chapter will be presented in the following sequence: first, the historical background of Hong Kong will be discussed, followed by the development of its industrial and commercial activities. Then, against this background, the work ethic of the Hong Kong people is examined to see what role it plays in the prosperity of the territory. Hong Kong's personnel practices are analyzed in the traditional framework of the discipline, although in view of the length of the chapter, the unique characteristics of these practices are highlighted to facilitate comparison of the Hong Kong situation with that of other countries in the region.[1]

Historical Background

Hong Kong is composed of three parts: Hong Kong Island, Kowloon and the New Territories. Situated at the Pearl River estuary, Hong Kong was no more than a mountainous fishing village at the southern tip of China one hundred and fifty years ago.

Hong Kong first came on the scene of international politics as a result of the so-called Victorian Free Trade Movement, in which the spirit of adventure and missionary causes sent British people to Hong Kong and elsewhere. According to a booklet published by the Hong Kong Government (Hong Kong Government Information Services, n.d.), foreign countries were frustrated by the closed door policy of China in the nineteenth century which discouraged free trade. Foreign merchants who were lucky enough to be able to do business in the single port of Canton in south China were only allowed to stay there for half the year and required to leave in the summer.

The situation probably explained the eagerness of the British merchants to set up a trading post off the coast. Due to the weakness of the Chinese government at that time, Hong Kong Island had already been frequented by British merchants in 1841 and, as a result of the Anglo-Chinese war of 1839-42, it was officially ceded to Britain in August 1842. It appeared that Britain was not content with the small size of the island (about 75 square kilometres) and, after another war in 1858-60, forced the Chinese government to cede Kowloon and Stonecutters' Island (about 9.7 square kilometres). Last but not least, the Chinese government was pressured in 1898 to lease to Britain for ninety-nine years a much larger piece of land known as the New Territories. The move eventually brought the Colony's total land area to 1,030 square kilometres.

The development of Hong Kong was marked with turbulence. Due to its geographical location and unique political characteristics, people from mainland China came and went in times of trouble in the motherland, such as the Japanese occupation in the Second World War, the toppling of the Imperial regime, the civil war, the Cultural Revolution and so on. Such turbulence, to some extent, was reflected in the change of population in the territory. At the beginning of the century, for instance, the population was about 300,000. In the decade following the toppling of the Imperial government in China, the population swelled to 625,000. In 1941, the population reached 1,640,000, only to decrease to half a million at the end of the Second World War. From then on, it grew to break the two million mark in 1950 and was estimated to be 4,103,500 at the end of 1972 (England and Rear, 1975, p.2). In 1993, the figure stood at 5.9 million (*Asiaweek*, 1993a). The general trend has been a steep 13-degree rise since 1946 (Census and Statistics Department, Hong Kong, 1990, p.111).

The latest turbulence is the change of ownership of Hong Kong. Since the People's Republic of China (PRC) came into existence in 1949, it has repeatedly emphasized that it will not honour the treaties which gave Hong Kong away a century ago. At any rate, the lease which allowed the New Territories to come under British rule will expire on June 30, 1997. China and Britain finally decided to hold talks on the future of Hong Kong in the early 1980s.

Inevitably, the talks were punctuated with arguments and strong feelings. The foreign exchange and stock markets were extremely volatile as the middle class was thrown into disarray. The Hong Kong dollar was battered so much that the Hong Kong government had to peg the Hong Kong dollar to the US dollar in October, 1983 to restore financial stability in the territory. The official exchange rate of the Hong Kong dollar to its US counterpart has been 7.8 to 1 since that time. The emergency measure has far-reaching implications, as will be seen when the topic of inflation is discussed later.

After a series of hard negotiations and bargaining efforts, China and Britain finally came to terms with each other when they signed the Joint Declaration in December, 1984, stipulating that Hong Kong would return to Chinese rule on June 30, 1997. To help put the minds of Hong Kong people at ease, the Chinese government proposed a framework of "one-country-two-systems", meaning that while reverting to Chinese sovereignty Hong Kong would be allowed to maintain its status quo for fifty years beyond 1997 in the form of a Special Administrative Region. The term "1997" has since been the talk of the town not only in Hong Kong but also in many parts of the world. Hong Kong people travelling abroad these days are often greeted with the question, "What will you do after 1997?" as if doomsday were just around the corner. However, at home people seem less concerned now than two years ago. They generally go about their business and brush aside the 1997 issue for the time being. Two factors contribute to this mentality. The first is the continuous economic reform of China and the prosperity that goes with it. The second is the serious recession in countries such as USA, Canada, and Australia which are the favourites of the prospective emigrants (*Asiaweek*, 1993b).

Hong Kong's Changing Political and Economic System

As a British colony, the power of the Hong Kong government originally came from the Chartered Letters Patent and the Royal Instruction proclaimed by the British Crown in 1843 (Cheng, 1985, p. 6). These two documents later underwent minor revisions and are now known as the "Letters Patent" and "Royal Instructions". In essence, the Governor is appointed by the Queen. He presides over the meetings of the Executive Council which acts as the advisory body, and he consults it on all important policy matters. Until very recently, the Governor also presided over the meetings of the Legislative Council, which functions "to scrutinize government policies, to enact laws and to control public spending" (Cheng, 1985, p. 11). The day-to-day administration of the territory rests with the civil service, the size of which stood at 182,387 in 1992 (Employment and Earnings Statistics Section, Census and Statistics Department, Hong Kong, 1993, p. 14).

Both the Executive and the Legislative Councils comprise official as well as unofficial members. In the past, with the exception of the Commander of the British forces, the official members were all senior members of the local civil service. As far as the unofficial members were concerned, they were appointed by the Governor on grounds of social influence or professional expertise. Most, if not all, of them came from well-to-do families and subscribed to the middle-class values of the society.

Although the Councils were not representative in the absence of elected members, the situation might not be a simple case of commission or omission on the part of the Governor, or the British government for that matter. There were indeed arguments that the political development of the territory had long been under the scrutiny of China. To the extent that China did not want Hong Kong to admit anti-communist politicians to its legislature through election, it was more than willing to let sleeping dogs lie (Employment and Earnings Statistics Section, 1993, p. 23).

In line with the British model, the judiciary is in principle independent of the administrative arm, upholding the spirit of a separate legal system which prevails in so many developed countries. This helps to give investors the confidence to put their money in the territories. Although Article IX of the Letters Patent gives the

Crown the right to make laws for Hong Kong in matters related to peace, order and good government, the latter has actually been left alone in most cases to do its own job (Penlington, 1978, pp. 17-18). In comparison with the British system, the relationship between the executive and the judiciary is indeed much closer here (Penlington, 1978, p. 40), but certainly not at the expense of the British constitutional principles.

In the recent Joint Declaration between Britain and China, one of the promises was to let "Hong Kong people rule Hong Kong". Consequently, 18 seats from the Legislative Council were up for direct elections in September, 1991. The United Democrats ended up winning 12 of the 18 seats and enabled Hong Kong to reach, in the words of the British Foreign Secretary Mr. Douglas Hurd, "a new point in its history". The admission of the elected members to the Legislative Council has since led to drastic changes in the political scene and its impact on the human resource management practice is beginning to be felt, as shall be discussed later.

Only time will tell whether the new balance in the political system will benefit Hong Kong more than the old balance.[2] For the time being, strong arguments can be put forward to prove the efficiency and effectiveness of the old system. Indeed, in view of the past success of Hong Kong, it appears that a British legal and administrative framework and the local Chinese residents together could work wonders. To begin with, the economic philosophy of the Hong Kong government was essentially "positive non-intervention" and "intervention only as a final option", giving rise to a system in which people carried their own weight and adventurers could be handsomely rewarded. Consequently, Hong Kong has been well known for low taxation and the fact that a government budget deficit is the exception rather than the rule.

Nevertheless, the influence and degree of intervention by the government has increased over time. During the early post- World War II era, the government relied heavily on a laissez-faire policy. Hong Kong depended on the influx of refugees from places such as Shanghai, who brought with them money and expertise in the manufacturing area which, coupled with the ample supply of labor, formed a solid basis for Hong Kong's industrial expansion. One can get some idea about the pace of change from the fact that, in 1948, Hong Kong products sent abroad were worth $240,000,000 and that in 1963 the corresponding figure was $3,831,000,000 (Penlington, 1978, p. 13).

However, the prosperity of Hong Kong brought with it opportunities and problems. During the 1970s, the Hong Kong government made tremendous efforts to improve the living standard of its people. By adhering to a policy of charging high prices for land, the government generated money which was used, among other things, to provide social welfare and free education programs. The move on the education front, coupled with the fact that family planning had been widely accepted by the local people and had begun to bear fruit, drastically changed the supply of the work force. By way of illustration, the crude birth rate per 1,000 persons dropped from 28.1 in 1965 to 17.0 in 1980 and the labor force participa-

Table 1:   Labor Force Participation Rates in Hong Kong (Age group: 15–19; %)

	1971	1981
Male	50.4	41.8
Female	56.4	40.3

Source: Cheng (1985, p. 54)

tion rates of the 15-19 age group also declined significantly from 1971 to 1981 (see Table 1).

Gone were the days when low labor costs gave Hong Kong's manufacturing sector the edge over its competitors. The challenges which the industry faced then came both from within and without. The rapid increase in wages soon put Hong Kong in a much less enviable position when compared with other "little dragons" of Asia such as Taiwan and South Korea. The persistently high cost of land also made many manufacturing concerns ponder the alternative of relocating their plants in other parts of the region.

Decision-makers in the terrritory's governing body were finally convinced that cheap production costs were a thing of the past and that a different ball game would have to be played if Hong Kong were to survive. The end product of their pooled wisdom was diversification, meaning that Hong Kong should be prepared to venture out from its traditional industrial base and move into areas where competition would still be in its favor. Emphasis has since been placed on "higher productivity and diversification into more sophisticated product lines and new industries" (Hong Kong Government, 1973, p. 13).

To facilitate structural transition, the Hong Kong government set up the first polytechnic institution in 1972 to buttress local talent in jobs such as technician, designer and so on. An important factor in luring foreign investment was the availability of skilled workers and technicians. For example, Japanese industries, in the process of internationalization, first made their products in their homeland and exported them to other countries. Later, they began to manufacture their products in the importing countries. In that connection, the Japanese manufacturers establishing plants in Hong Kong wanted to be ensured that their operations would be supported by local talent being trained for such purposes (Poon, 1989).

Although the new government policy in Hong Kong was logically sound, it was not without drawbacks. For one thing, the government intervention was, at best, limited and indirect. Because of its purported "laissez faire" philosophy, the government did not want to subsidize the local industry the way some of its counterparts did in other parts of the Pacific region. A case in point was the small amount of grant money which the government allocated for research and development activities on a yearly basis. Moreover, the 1997 issue was still in the minds of many industrialists; so much so that there was obvious reluctance on their part to commit to long-term investments.

Nevertheless, Hong Kong still had important competitive advantages as an economic player. First, the success of Hong Kong had long been a result of the flexibility and adaptability of its people. Consequently, despite the periodical bumpy ride, Hong Kong still managed to flourish after the mid-seventies. Indeed, "the growth rate in terms of GDP per capita at constant value were 9.3 per cent during the four years from 1975-80" (Cheng, 1985, p. 127).

Second, and equally important, Hong Kong had become a major financial centre. Hong Kong's time zone helped it to secure an important role in the international financial market because, together with New York and London, financial transactions all over the world could take place almost round the clock. As a result, 84 of the top 100 banks had operations in the territories in 1990 (Labor Department, Hong Kong, 1991, p. 3) and the total market capitalization of the stock market increased from HK$131,640 million dollars in 1982 (The Stock Exchange of Hong Kong Ltd., 1988, p. 51) to HK$1,332,184 million in 1992 (The Stock Exchange of Hong Kong Ltd., 1992, p. 10).

Third, the opening up of China in the late 70s also boosted Hong Kong's role as a bridge between the mainland and the outside world. At a time when it appeared that Hong Kong could no longer compete on the grounds of low labor costs, the special economic zones in the southern part of China suddenly helped to extend the economic frontier. Many manufacturing concerns then rushed to move their plants there to benefit from the ample supply of cheap labor. This middle-man function was particularly evident in areas such as technology, finance and management. Such developments, coupled with the booming tourist industry, resulted in the growing importance of the tertiary sector in Hong Kong's national income.

And last but not least, the manufacturing sector itself underwent a face lifting when foreign investments came into the territory. Multinationals such as Motorola contributed to the fast growth of the electronic industry and helped to a certain extent to balance out the effect of the dwindling textile industry on local employment. The United States and Japan have been two of the most important sources of foreign capital since the 1950s. They provided, for instance, "43 and 32 per-cent respectively of the HK$702,310 million invested in the 442 factories either wholly or partly owned by overseas interests in early 1981" (Cheng, 1985, p. 64). In 1991, manufacturing establishments with fifty percent overseas interest and up account for slightly more than one percent of the total figure (Industrial Pro-duction Statistics Section, Census and Statistics Department, Hong Kong, 1991, p. 21).

The economic euphoria from these changes ran into serious challenges between the early 1980s and 1989. Dominating the scene in the early 1980s was the Sino-British negotiation on Hong Kong's future. Much has been said about this previously. What needs to be added at this point are the implications for human resources management of the Joint Declaration and the government's counter responses.

Quite a number of people started to apply for emigration when the 1997 issue had been clarified. The mentality underlying the exodus mainly fell into two categories. First, there were people who wanted to play safe. What they intended to do was to spend some time abroad, get a foreign passport and then return to Hong Kong for as long as they would like without the 1997 shadow hanging over their heads. Secondly, there were those who wanted to give their children a choice so that, when the going got tough, they would not be blamed by their children for lack of foresight. Much less mentioned was some people's concern about the deteriorating living environment of the territory.

Hong Kong's exodus was widely known as the brain drain because it typically involved middle and senior managers, professionals and so on. The confidence crisis came to its peak after the Tiananmen massacre in 1989, when China crushed the students' pro-democracy movement with military forces. In order to help Hong Kong bridge the troubled waters, a series of remedial measures were announced in the Governor's speech in October, 1989 and afterwards which included a massive airport and port development, more tertiary places for local students, and British citizenship for a selected group of people without their having to leave Hong Kong. Furthermore, in 1990 the government launched the Importation Scheme.

In numerical terms, post-secondary first year, first degree places were to increase from about 7,000 in 1990 to about 15,000 in 1995; a growth of more than 100% in five years' time (*South China Morning Post*, 1989). Under the British Nationality (Hong Kong) Act 1990, fifty thousand heads of households in the territory might be recommended by the Governor for British citizenship. The quota was to be allocated to four classes of applicants with the lion's share going to the General Occupational Class (36,200 places), to be followed by the Disciplined Services Class, the Sensitive Service Class and the Entrepreneurs Class, in that order (Hong Kong Government, 1990). Apparently, the government was determined to tackle the brain drain issue on two fronts. First, by providing British citizenship to people who formed the skeleton of the business sector and civil service without requiring them to stay in Britain, it was hoped that the smooth running of the community could be continued. Concern was particularly reflected in the number of places allocated to the Disciplined Services because, in times of turbulence, law and order appeared to be the backbone of stability. Second, from a long-term perspective, the expansion in tertiary education clearly demonstrated the government's commitment for a more stable supply of local talent.

However, the labor shortage continued as China grew and foreign emigration opportunities increased, putting enormous pressure on local employers during wage and salary reviews (Marriage, 1991). The rapid increase of wages and salaries, in turn, fuelled the inflation spiral and the vicious circle went on and on. The situation, of course, did not go unnoticed. Due to the restructuring of the economy, labor shortages in areas such as construction, hotel, retailing business and so on had long been recognized; and the port and airport development could only intensify the problems particularly in the construction industry. The General

Table 2:   Unemployment Rates in Hong Kong between 1980 and 1991

Year	Unemployment Rate (%)
1980	3.8
1981	4.0
1982	3.6
1983	4.5
1984	3.9
1985	3.2
1986	2.8
1987	1.7
1988	1.4
1989	1.1
1990	1.3
1991	1.9

Source: Nyaw (1993, p. 4)

Labor Importation Scheme was launched in 1990 to allow employers to bring in imported labor on a contractual basis. All these developments can be put in better perspective vis-à-vis the historical unemployment rates in Table 2.

The reaction to the Scheme was understandably mixed. Those who stood to benefit would certainly subscribe to it. The losers, in this case mainly workers laid off in the manufacturing sector, and their sympathizers either in the unions or the Legislative Council, were resentful. The major complaint of the unemployed was that, regardless of their past contribution to the success of Hong Kong, they were deprived of their livelihood at a time when prosperity prevailed. In an attempt to make everybody happy, the government set up a Provisional Retraining Fund Board in early 1992 to help to retrain workers who wanted to seek new opportunities in other areas of employment. Such activities will most likely remain in the limelight in the personnel field for some time to come.

At the same time, there was the massive airport and port development, which was intended to restore confidence in the future of the territory. With a price tag of HK\$127 billion, the government was sending out a message loud and clear that it had "confidence and strength to meet the challenge". As the economy of Hong Kong increasingly relied on that of China, the development probably was also aimed at boosting the economy of the territory in the face of possible austere conditions in the mainland as an aftermath of the June 4 incident. However, what the Governor probably did not anticipate was the strong opposition from the Chinese side. In essence, China was very concerned about the financial implications of the project for the post-1997 government of Hong Kong and the last thing it wanted was for the British to withdraw with glory while leaving behind a formidable debt.

A sense of distrust was clearly displayed when a top Chinese official summed up the general feelings of his colleagues by defining the proposal as one of "you throw the party and I end up paying the bill". The comment only revealed the tip of the iceberg. In the days that followed, the Hong Kong government ran into difficulties every now and then when trying to secure the approval of China in getting things off the ground. Worse still, in the course of mutual manipulation, the amount of trust decreased even further. The Hong Kong Governor desperately tried to improve the degree of trust with China but to no avail. Things did not change appreciably even after the British Prime Minister risked his reputation by being the first head of state to visit China after the June 4 incident. Despite the signing of the so-called Airport Memorandum on that occasion, there were continual disagreements on the interpretation of the relevant documents.

The Governor of Hong Kong was replaced in 1992 by the British government amid rumors that some large business firms backed by British capital were unhappy about the lack of protection given to their interests. The speech delivered by the new Governor in October, 1992, outlined his political reform proposal which, if implemented, would give Hong Kong people more democracy than was previously agreed. China was definitely not happy with the proposal and when it started to show its discontent it left no room for doubt about its bitterness. The stock market was among the first to react to the row and went on a roller coaster ride. To combat the British "offensive", China made it known that it would not hesitate to set up a "second stove" if things went from bad to worse, meaning that it would set up its own legislature to replace the one which might be formed on the blueprint of the political reform proposal.[3]

Whether people liked it or not, Hong Kong became a very political city overnight. The Governor, for instance, made use of every opportunity to publicize his reform proposal and, quite recently, agreed to be interviewed and featured on the Larry King Show in one of the most popular TV networks in the United States. China, in return, garnered the support of a group of influencial people under the title of Hong Kong Advisors and, when the Special Administrative Region Preparatory Committee was set up around July, 1993 to oversee the transition of the territory, it could only add to the impression that China was hoping for the best while preparing for the worst. When a breakthrough will arrive is anybody's guess. For the time being, it probably is safe to say that China and Britain are still miles apart on political issues.

For those who are familiar with the history and orientation of the two governments, the development has indeed been ironic. Just imagine that Communist China is linking up with the rich businessmen and influential people to wrestle with the Governor of Hong Kong who used to be the chairman of the Conservative Party of Britain and is now gaining his political support from the middle and lower classes. As far as the writer is concerned, the confrontation has its deep roots in the lack of trust between the two parties. China seems to be suspicious of the motives of Britain and afraid that the latter may seek any advantage including protecting its post-1997 interests by doing everything it can to perpetuate its influence. And, after the June 4 incident and all the frustrations arising from the airport project, Britain may be less sure whether China would actually give Hong Kong the kind of autonomy which has been promised. As long as both parties are trying their best to gain the upper hand in the political struggle, the negotiation for a settlement of the constitutional reform is anything but smooth; and the Hong Kong community is likely to become polarized.

The Development of HRM in Hong Kong

To the extent that Hong Kong has no natural resources, the success of the territory must depend heavily on its human factor. It so happens that the traditional Chinese culture has placed tremendous emphasis on values such as diligence, frugality, harmony, and education, which are all important to help the economy to get off the ground and bridge troubled waters when the going occasionally gets tough. The fact that the Chinese people are inclined to save their earnings and work hard enables them to react promptly and constructively when opportunities arise.

In the absence of any significant social welfare programs, Hong Kong people are used to carrying their own weight – so much so that motivation is seldom a problem in the work place. This was particularly true before the 1970s when the economy was not as robust and many of the new immigrants found themselves in a highly uncertain environment. Those who eventually chose to seek employment instead of starting their own business, tended to see their job as a lifelong commitment. Their relationship with their employers could become a paternalistic one if the latter rewarded their loyalty by treating them as members of the family or enterprise. The ensuing harmony could go a long way towards enhancing productivity (Waters, 1991, pp. 57-58).

Most Chinese people are still working hard today although probably for different reasons. Hong Kong has been gradually transforming itself into an affluent society and, unlike their counterparts in the past, people are less likely to work hard for the sole reason of supporting themselves or their families. In this connection, Maslow's theory of a hierarchy of needs generally applies although it can be supplemented with empirical findings in the territory.

An unpublished survey carried out by the writer for an electronics factory as part of a training project at the end of the 70s found that female workers in different age categories had different needs. Those who were between 14 and 17, for example, were more concerned about staying with their friends, so much so that they were inclined to follow suit if their friends joined another factory for monetary reasons. While those in the 18-21 age category placed more emphasis on self development, it was for those who were older and married that money really counted. The findings appeared to be in line with common sense. Given the priority of education in the value system of the community, the female

Table 3: Vacancy Rates in Hong Kong between 1985 and 1990

Year	Manufacturing Sector	Tertiary Sector
1985	2.31	1.07
1986	3.56	1.42
1987	5.8	3.44
1988	6.12	4.22
1989	5.19	3.78
1990	4.72	3.37

Source: Labor Department, Hong Kong (1991, p. 11)

workers coming from low-income families were inclined to treat their jobs in the electronics factory as a stepping stone in their pursuit of a brighter future. By the same token, given the high living standard of Hong Kong, those who were married faced genuine pressure to bring home extra money to meet the ever increasing daily expenses.

Prosperity and the free education program in Hong Kong also help to change the job market and expectations within the work force. Currently, one of the jobs which is most difficult to fill is office assistant (a euphemism for messenger). Young workers can be extremely egocentric. It is not unusual for them to work hard, save up some money, and then resign from their jobs for a tour which may last from three months to one year. People with better educational backgrounds or training are very aggressive. When they think about promotion, they have in mind a time frame of less than one year. For many white-collar jobs, long-term benefits such as pensions have very little appeal because people do not want to guess what the future will hold. After all, "one bird in the hand is better than two in the bush". To a very great extent, many local employees are spoiled because the labor shortage in the territory has given them much stronger bargaining power. The vacancy rates in Table 3 testify to this scenario.

Not surprisingly, the use of formal HR practices and the development of the discipline has been retarded by individualism and the labor shortage. Although the products of Hong Kong successfully broke into the foreign markets around the middle of the century, they were soon met with resentment and protests. In essence, Hong Kong was accused of outdoing its competitors by building its strength on exploited labor. A case in point was the hardship experienced by workers in Britain who had lost their jobs because their production cost was no match to that of Hong Kong. Consequently, they worked with the unionists to lobby the Parliament to bring pressure to bear upon Hong Kong.

To a certain extent, the accusation regarding labor exploitation was justified. Most, if not all, appointed members in the legislature were either businessmen or closely connected with the business sector. In the absence of any elected member to represent the interests of the work force, there was probably not much incentive to better the lot of workers at the expense of the capitalists. The daily life of an ordinary worker was vividly depicted in the remark: "When the worker returned home from long hours in the shop or factory he returned to noise, heat, stench, gross overcrowding and an almost total absence of privacy" (England and Rear, 1981, Plate 1).

The tables began to turn when the predicament received attention in the report after the 1967 riots and the appointment of Sir Murray Maclehose as Governor in 1971. The new Governor appeared to be sympathetic to the underdogs in the society and the subsequent government policies did reflect his attitudes. The stage was set, as it were, for some radical changes in the area of labor legislation. In the writer's view, the fact that appointed members in the legislature went along with the changes was more a political consideration than anything else. At least some of them had probably been given to understand that change was the order of the day and that the most effective way to ward off accusations from abroad was to do something.

The periods that followed saw the increase of labor ordinances by leaps and bounds. The legal implications alone were reasons enough to have a full-time professional to set one's house in order. The growth of personnel management as a profession was also buttressed by the increasingly accessible training available in the institutions of higher learning, including those abroad. As mentioned above, the Chinese people place a lot of emphasis on education. Given a chance, they would prefer to equip themselves with as much education and/or training as possible. This mentality was vital both for the prosperity of Hong Kong and the development of any given profession.

A very significant impact came from the founding of the Hong Kong Institute of Personnel Management (HKIPM). The growth of the Institute followed the pattern of most professional bodies in the United Kingdom. Indeed, the founding members themselves were members of the Institute of Personnel Management in the UK. As the development of HKIPM has marked the progress of the local personnel management profession, it is important to briefly trace its history in the past 16 years. The discussion below draws heavily on information from the various issues of its newsletter.

Current HR Practices

The term HRM implies a systems approach to handle the human resource within an organization. As such, its role is seen as shifting "from protector and screener (as in personnel management) to planner and change agent" (Dessler, 1991, p. 698). The fact that manpower planning is receiving wide attention among personnel practitioners reflects this change of focus. Human resource management topics generally include job analysis, manpower planning, recruitment and selection, training and development, salary administration, performance appraisal, industrial relations, industrial safety and perhaps others. In view of the length of the chapter, no attempt is made to cover all these in detail. On the basis of the writer's exposure to HRM systems in the Western countries, he will highlight the unique characteristics of the local system for comparison purposes.

By far, the most comprehensive and thorough study of personnel management practice in Hong Kong was done in 1989. It was a joint project among three institutions, including HKIPM. The study was based on a modified version of a study conducted in the UK in 1986 and was carried out in two separate parts. Large companies with more than 200 staff were sent questionnaires which comprised 159 questions in 26 pages. The response rate was 14%. On the other hand, 1,983 companies hiring either between 100 and 199 employees or between 20 and 99 employees were sent questionnaires consisting of 45 questions which were the condensed version of those sent to the large companies. The response rate was 11% (Kirkbride and Tang, 1989).

Despite the relatively low response rate and the possibility of "overstat(ing) the sophistication of personnel management in the territory", the study is often quoted and mentioned. For the purpose of this chapter, relevant findings from the study will be discussed under selected headings together with information from other sources.

Staffing

Kirkbride and Tang (1989) identified the three methods most preferred by large companies to forecast required staffing levels: 1) maintenance of present staffing ratios (64%), 2) projected sales/orders (60%), and 3) careful guesswork (45%). Generally speaking, personnel managers in Hong Kong were well aware of the two different sides of manpower planning. On the supply side, their reaction to the labor shortage situation in Hong Kong was helped by their ability to think beyond geographical borders. In the early 1990s, The Royal Hong Kong Jockey Club, for example, made an effort to contact its former computer staff who had emigrated to Australia and successfully arranged to tap the latter's computer expertise without having them come back to Hong Kong. Cathay Pacific Airlines, the local flag carrier, also tried to reduce its overhead cost by moving its accounting operation to southern China to benefit from the cheap labor cost there. At one time, efforts sponsored by the Hong Kong government were also made to bring back emigrants from Canada, the US, and Australia. The program, however, never got off the ground as potential candidates found the offer unattractive without substantive housing subsidies or allowances.

Recruitment and Selection

On the retention side, it was demonstrated by a personnel practitioner that putting oneself in the shoes of the staff could go a long way. The person mentioned here was a personnel manager of a financial company in the central district who, when faced with high labor turnover rate, found his solution in a pantry. It was a well-known fact that having lunch could be a big problem for people working in the central district because of the limited number of inexpensive eating places there. Those who could only afford to eat at the fast food outlets would have to spend most of their one-hour lunch time waiting in a long queue. The personnel manager then installed a small pantry in the office and equipped it with simple but useful appliances including a microwave oven. The result? A group of much happier clerical staff and a decreased turnover rate, at least up to the time when the story was told in a HKIPM gathering.

In connection with recruitment and selection, Francesco (1981) found that advertising in English newspapers was often used for managerial and professional positions, but Chinese newspapers were used in advertising for factory workers. The practice has not changed in the course of time although the term "manual jobs" instead of "factory workers" was used in a later study by Kirkbride and Tang (1989). Both studies concluded that personal referral was used by more than 70% of the respondents for recruitment of people in this category. Not mentioned was the common practice of offering a bonus to the employee who successfully helped to bring in a new recruit for a specified period of time.

Two more elements remained unchanged over time. The first was the tight labor market. The two studies cited in the previous paragraph were eight years apart. A tight labor market was cited by Francesco (1981) as a major factor which seemed to discourage the use of more sophisticated recruitment methods. In the study by Kirkbride and Tang (1989), 53% of the respondents saw the labor shortage as the hindering factor in their recruitment efforts. The second element undergoing little change was the selection process. Both studies identify the interview and the application blank as two of the most popular methods used. Both studies also reported the use of tests for the selection of clerical staff although a direct comparison between them was not possible due to differences in terminology.

As indicated earlier, the tight labor market has been a dominant factor in the personnel scene in recent years. Consequently, salary administration reflects this external constraint. Having said that, we must quickly add that performance appraisal is also a major factor used to determine salary increases. Kirkbride and Tang (1989), for example, found, for all grades of employees, that performance appraisal is used by approximately three-fourths of firms to assess past performance and by about two-thirds to help improve current performance and assign salary increases.

Performance Appraisal

In terms of appraisal methods, the results-oriented/MBO type was most commonly used for the managerial/professional staff, just as alpha-numeric rating was for the manual/technician and clerical/supervisory staff. For all three grades, the written report was the second most commonly used method (Kirkbridge and Tang, 1989, p. 35).

Despite the frequent use of interviews as part of the appraisal exercise, only 20% of the respondents in the study of Kirkbride and Tang provided their interviewers with the necessary training. The implication of this oversight was shown in an unpublished survey conducted by the writer around October, 1988. In order to have some concrete information on which class discussions could be based, the writer asked 68 participants of a diploma program to list the common problems associated with the performance appraisal practice in their organizations both from their capacity as the appraisers and the appraisees. This question illuminates the perceived difficulties of the appraisers from two perspectives. The problem of lack of training on the part of the appraisers was mentioned by participants both in their capacity as the appraisers themselves and as the appraisees.

Ironically, from both perspectives, the respondents doubted the usefulness of the performance appraisal exercise, but for different reasons. It appeared that whereas the appraisers in this case tended to see performance appraisal as part of the formality which did not lead them anywhere, the appraisees tended to have high expectations of the outcome and were disappointed when a salary increase was not directly linked to the results of performance appraisal. From the viewpoint of the appraisees, there seemed to be communication problems between the two parties during the appraisal and the time allocated for the exercise was often insufficient. They were also upset by the fact that during the appraisal too much emphasis was given to their weaknesses rather than their strengths. As far as the appraisers were concerned, uselessness of the appraisal, insufficient time and preparation were all ranked equally high. While they also complained about the lack of an appropriate venue to conduct the appraisal exercise, they made no mention about their overemphasis on the weaknesses of the appraisees. Because of the nature of the sample, the results of this "opportunity" have to be viewed with caution; however, other research questions the usefulness of traditionally conducted performance appraisal (cf. Meyer, Kay, and French, 1965; Bernardin and Beatty, 1984).

Safety

The pragmatic attitudes of the Hong Kong people carry a price tag in the area of industrial safety (Poon, 1983). Basically, underlying industrial safety are the physical as well as psychological factors. The "I am the exception" mentality is by far the most difficult psychological factor to handle. When time is pressing, people often choose to take the easy way out, thinking that they can get away with it because of their expertise and experience, or even luck, for that matter.

This issue is certainly directly related to the psychological effects produced by factors such as company policies and the pay system. To the extent that people are paid by the piece-rate, or a bonus system is in operation, the behavior of people will be shaped in such a way that the consideration of industrial safety often becomes secondary. By way of illustration, workers in the garment industry were once asked to install a safety device when sewing. Eventually, it was the workers themselves who removed the device because their output was seriously affected by the equipment – so much so that they were virtually penalized by following the safety regulations. Ironically, their take-home pay was reduced if they produced less, thanks to the piece-rate system in operation.

The employers may also violate safety regulations by commission or omission. It is a well-known fact that the rent is high in Hong Kong. In order to cut costs, it is not unusual for employers to make use of the staircases in industrial buildings for the storage of their goods. If caught by the Fire Department, they are still better off because the fine is usually small when compared with the rent which they otherwise have to pay. On the other hand, there may be situations where there is very little the employers can do. When it comes to the layout of the plant, for instance, the shortage of space precludes the consideration for such things as clearly defined passageways and isolation of fire risk for the working area and so on. All in all, the preoccupation with success is often fulfilled at the expense of valuable human lives.

Training and Development

Last but not least, there has also been interesting development in the area of training and development. Due to its laissez-faire philosophy, the Hong Kong government has been doing what was only absolutely necessary to foster the growth of the local economy. Under most circumstances, it would like to leave the ball in the court of the capitalists. When Hong Kong was an entrepot, the ship repairing skills were in demand. Consequently, the shipyards themselves had to provide workers with their own training. During the early stage of industrialization, the need for training was almost nonexistent because cheap labor was the order of the day. During that period of time, however, the government did successfully update the education system, including the launch of industrial education to facilitate the growth of the textile industry.

Another achievement of the government was the establishment of the apprenticeship scheme which once and for all prevented unscrupulous employers from exploiting cheap labor in the name of a master-apprentice relationship. Under the new system, the period of apprenticeship must be clearly specified and the program registered with the government. The apprentices also have to undergo training in a technical institute. Whereas technical training has been taken care of for some time, supervisory and management training and development did not get off the ground until the 1980s. On the basis of a large-scale survey, five very serious management and supervisory problems were identified. They included (in order) poor communication, insufficient knowledge of management techniques, high turnover rate, lack of motivation and poor calibre (Committee on Management and Supervisory Training of the Hong Kong Training Council, 1980). As a result, the Hong Kong Management Development Centre (MDC) was established in 1984 to tackle the problems head-on.

The significance of the role of MDC has to be understood vis-à-vis the change which was taking place in Hong Kong. When China suddenly opened up to the outside world in the late 1970s, Hong Kong had in front of it a golden opportunity. Businessmen from Hong Kong and all over the world rushed to establish trading relationships with China, resulting in an economic boom in the region. As a consequence of the ten-year Cultural Revolution, there appeared to be a big gap in the development of China's education system. This gap, together with the communism which had been there for some 30 years, made it difficult for China to cope with the rapidly rising demand for managerial and supervisory staff. The expedient solution obviously lay in tapping Hong Kong's labor supply. In the hotel industry, for example, people with special training in all areas including management were widely recruited to China from Hong Kong. We can have some idea about the labor shortage problem in Hong Kong at that time when we add the number of people it needed for the expansion of its own business activities. The situation worsened when the uncertainty over Hong Kong's future developed in the early 1980s, causing people to begin to emigrate.

In connection with the initiative of the government in the area of training and development, the writer takes pride in the fact that he played a very active role in launching the first ever Diploma in Training Management program in 1982. As early as at the turn of the last decade, the writer was well aware of the potential of the training and development profession. His success in launching the Diploma program only confirmed that many companies saw eye to eye with him on their need for specialists to man their training and development functions. The program has been running uninterruptedly for the past ten years and has so far turned out more than 300 graduates. Most, if not all, of those who graduated in earlier years are now occupying managerial positions in the profession.

Another important change in training and development took place in 1992 when the government introduced the Employees' Retraining Bill to provide retraining to workers who were most vulnerable in the economic re-structuring process of the territory. Included in the consideration were workers who became unemployed, workers whose employment was at risk and even those who wanted to shift to jobs requiring new skills. Some critics argued that the government was doing this simply to appease those who opposed its imported labor program on grounds that our workers were not getting their fair share of our prosperity.

At any rate, the retraining program did not seem to be too successful in its initial stage. There were complaints that the retraining courses were launched without first identifying the training needs and that, with the small allowance given to the workers, there was no way for some of the workers to leave their jobs and attend the courses according to the specified schedules. There was also dissatisfaction about age discrimination. Women who were above 40 years of age felt particularly vulnerable because some of them were turned away even with newly acquired basic retail skills. The chairman of the Retail Management Association, however, denied the accusation of discrimination (Tam, 1992, p. 5). Learning from its own experience, the government has modified the original ideas and has recently launched the.On-the-Job Training Scheme. The major difference of the new scheme is that workers are now being offered employment at the sponsoring organizations before they start getting their training. In essence, as the chairman of the Employees' Retraining Board puts it, "trainees get properly paid, post-training placement is immediate and employers know their new staff are getting exactly the training they need" (*South China Morning Post*, 1993).

In sum, training and development are here to stay because Hong Kong, like most other developed countries, is experiencing the economic re-structuring process in addition to being under constant pressure to excel in its struggle against the competitors. Furthermore, the rapid change in China's economic system also makes the territory an attractive pasture for training and development professionals.

HRM in Smaller, Chinese-owned Companies

In the Hong Kong context, HR practices can be compared between organizations with Chinese and non-Chinese ownership, and they can also be examined in terms of types of business. In their attempt to determine how manpower planning was done in firms with Chinese and non-Chinese ownership, Graham and Tuan (1988) further dichotomized their sample into manufacturing and service sectors. Overall, they found that 65% of their respondents were of the opinion that manpower planning was "a combination of the staff and line function in their organizations" (Graham and Tuan, 1988, p. 23), raising the question of just how HR responsibility is to be shared. In terms of the components of manpower planning, forecasting was singled out as the most important item to be handled whereas "less attention (was) paid to manpower inventory and forecast of external supply at the administrative level, and to control/evaluation systems at the tactical level" (Graham and Tuan, 1988, p. 24).

Other interesting findings included the emphasis given by Chinese-owned firms to the review of monetary incentives and intangible advantages when forecasting the external supply; the reliance on job postings and help-wanted advertisements as the major sources of job candidates; and the tendency of most firms to periodically examine their evaluative systems (Graham and Tuan, 1988, pp. 24-25). In passing, the authors noted that internal promotion was the common practice of almost all respondents for filling managerial positions, and that the large Western companies, especially US multinationals, were most well-known for their manpower planning tasks (Graham and Tuan, 1988, pp. 24-25).

The Professionalization of HRM in Hong Kong

The history of human resource management as a profession in Hong Kong is relatively short. The industrial sector was the major driving force in the early stage of Hong Kong's development and it comprised mainly small factories. As late as 1978, some 80% of the manufacturing establishments employed less than twenty people (England and Rear, 1981, p. 43). Indeed, it makes more sense to talk about personnel management rather than human resource management in that context because the manager responsible for the function, if there was one, mainly handled the recruitment and payroll activities. It was not unusual, therefore, for line managers to take up these activities themselves. In the big British firms, the personnel manager sometimes had obtained his training from the military.

HKIPM (The Hong Kong Institute of Personnel Management) came into existence when the Articles of Association and Rules of the Hong Kong Institute of Personnel Management were approved at its first Annual General Meeting on February 10, 1977. Among the major objectives were the following:

- establish appropriate relationships with business and government;
- give attention to integration of Chinese-speaking personnel managers with IPM members;
- establish international relationships with other institutes in South East Asia;
- analyse change in business and personnel environment in South East Asia and respond accordingly to those which affect management of people (HKIPM *Newsletter*, May, 1977).

Of these objectives we need only comment on the one having to do with the Chinese-speaking personnel managers. As a matter of fact, the official language of HKIPM is English although many of its members are local people who are actually bilingual. At the time of HKIPM's formation, there were other personnel managers who had had similar organizations and they met regularly among themselves to exchange ideas and information on the personnel practice. In Kwun Tong, one of the major industrial zones, for example, the personnel managers of the factories formed their own group and they were quite happy about the informal atmosphere in which they met for their monthly gathering. Although it had been HKIPM's intention for some time to bring these people together to form a much more influential association, its efforts were by and large without avail. Today, the

Kwun Tong group comes under the name of Hong Kong Industrial Relations Association and, regardless of their ability to speak English fluently, its members still feel at ease when communicating in their mother tongue.

What differentiated HKIPM from its local counterparts was the aggressive approach which the former adopted. Simply put, HKIPM was not satisfied with being just an association in which people met informally and made friends. It wanted to make personnel management a bona fide profession and, in the process of doing that, tried to influence and shape the attitudes as well as behavior of the public at large and of its own members. Its mission was clearly spelled out in the early stage of its development.

HKIPM virtually started from scratch. Immediately after it was established, it began to approach the government and large corporations for subvention and donations. Initially, it also relied on the Hong Kong Management Association for financial and secretarial support. The association gradually became self-sufficient after successfully launching its programs. As early as 1978, it held its first conference on Contemporary Issues in Labor Relations in South East Asia with support from the International Labor Office. Other sources of income included the Pay Trend Survey reports, membership fees and subscriptions, and training and development programs. Currently, membership fees and subscriptions only account for one quarter of its revenue. HKIPM carried out its first salary survey in 1978 and was successful in selling 180 copies of the report. The project later evolved into the annual Pay Trend Survey and was met with increasing acceptance: in 1984, 82 companies each with at least 100 staff participated in the survey. In 1986, HKIPM was invited by the Standing Committee on Civil Service Salaries and Conditions of Service to join its Consultative Committee, further highlighting the Institute's influence on salary matters in the territory.

HKIPM was also active in information dissemination and public affairs associated with the personnel function. It sponsored research and survey activities to keep itself abreast of the needs of its members as well as the state of the art of the profession. It joined forces in 1983 with two other institutions of training and development to publish *Performance*, the first local journal on human resource matters. Today, the association publishes its own journal, titled *Hong Kong Staff*. Occasional lunch seminars and free consultative services on industrial relations matters have also proved to be great successes. The latter, in particular, constantly arouse personnel practitioner awareness of the increasingly complex environment in which they find themselves. Those who want to investigate general personnel practices or issues in Hong Kong can often learn more about these subjects by actively participating in the HKIPM events and talking to its members than by relying on traditional survey methods. Given the large number of teachers and students in the institutions of higher education who want to study such topics year after year and pretty well the same number of personnel managers who are constantly bombarded with questionnaires of one kind or another, it is understandable why survey response rates are usually low.

In facing critical issues or turbulence, reactions of HKIPM have generally been action-oriented. At the height of the labor shortage and brain drain, for example, it organized seminars and conferences to address the issues. It also set up an establishment to attract Hong Kong emigrants back from Canada, US and Australia. On the political front, HKIPM is actively seeking to be represented in the legislature. Its recent merger with the Hong Kong Society of Training and Development may result in a membership of around 2,400 people and help to move the institute one step closer to its ambition.

In the process of professionalization, a professional body usually tries to limit its membership to a selected group of people and to create the impression that the association is not for the average layman. HKIPM probably followed this strategy with the help of some of its members who were personnel managers of big corporations. For example, recruitment advertisements in the newspapers commonly stipulated that applicants should "preferably have IPM membership". When people are convinced that they stand to benefit from IPM membership, their motivation to join the institute is enhanced, hence giving HKIPM an advantageous edge in dominating the field.

With assets and annual revenues each exceeding two million Hong Kong dollars, HKIPM is currently a strong and growing institution. Its next priorities will most likely concentrate on two areas. Although not even remotely referred to in the early mission statements of HKIPM, China has practically emerged as a potential power in the region. Its influence and impact on Hong Kong simply cannot be taken lightly, particularly when 1997 is less than three years away. Indeed, HKIPM has already taken the initiative to approach China to see what role it can play to help streamline the personnel systems on the mainland. How successful HKIPM is in this area will depend on the extent personnel practices in Hong Kong and China can be integrated as personnel managers now frequently move between these two places to look after the operation of companies under the same umbrella structure.

In line with the philosophy which prevails in other parts of the world, HKIPM is contemplating whether the field of personnel management should now be more appropriately recognized as "human resource management". According to an influential personality in the territory, personnel management conveys the impression that people are just like machines and should therefore be handled in more or less the same way. On the other hand, human resource management tends to see human resources as valuable as, say, financial resources and advocates treating them with care and respect. At the end of the day, the ultimate challenge of human resource management is to create a system in which the human resource can flourish.

In the foreseeable future, HKIPM is definitely going to be the most powerful professional body to exert influence on matters concerning human resources in the territory. Whatever parameters it eventually decides to set for the profession will chart the course along which the state of the art will be directed.

Unionization and Hong Kong's Industrial Relations

In view of the union power in the West, it is conceivable that industrial relations tends to receive wider attention there. For example, in Britain, one of the institutions of higher learning once had a diploma program on Personnel Management. After completing the core courses in the first part, participants were allowed to choose as the elective either Industrial Relations or Training and Development. Such an arrangement gives people the impression that both topics are key components in their own right. The situation in Hong Kong, however, is rather unique due to the personality of the Chinese people and the special characteristics of the territory. In order to put things in perspective, it is important to first note the tolerance threshold of the Hong Kong workers. Given a chance, they tend to value peace and prefer harmony to confrontation. However, their attitudes can take a sharp turn if they are pressed too hard and the threshold is exceeded.

Hong Kong people are used to carrying their own weight and, due to the lack of unemployment insurance in the territory, they are less likely to press their points with strike action unless it is absolutely necessary. Indeed, the tight labor market and the proximity of one industrial zone to another would probably make it easier and more beneficial for them to shift jobs. The apathy of female married workers towards unionism is particularly obvious because, in addition to their employment in the factories, they still have to tend to their children and housework after work. For those who have to rely on others to look after their children during their absence, the urge to go home within the shortest possible period of time is totally understandable. Such attitudes can easily be explained in terms of the high degree of importance which the Chinese place on their families.

On a broader front, the union movement has been hindered by two major factors. First, the small size of the majority of Hong Kong companies and the high mobility of their workers make it difficult for unions to take root. Furthermore, the law which confines union membership to people "habitually engaged or employed in the relevant industry" results in different unions for different trades. This law, coupled with the ban on sympathetic strikes in support of workers outside one's own trade, greatly reduces the power base of the unions (Cheng, 1985, pp. 280-281).

The political polarization of two big unions is another unique characteristic of the local labor scene. Although the Communist Party successfully ousted the right-wing government to Taiwan in 1949, the influence of both regimes are still here. The Hong Kong Federation of Trade Unions (FTU) is sympathetic to the Beijing government and is the largest union in Hong Kong. With a membership of 214,848 in 1978 and another 69,922 being friendly to it, FTU could certainly be very powerful and aggressive if it so decided. However, it appears that in recent years FTU's efforts have been directed more to the recreational and social aspects rather than the traditional role of a typical union. It has been suggested that the situation might be the result of the policy which China has had for Hong

Kong. Since China derived tremendous benefit from the territory, there was every intention on its part to discourage the FTU from upsetting the apple cart (England and Rear, 1981).

The Hong Kong and Kowloon Trades Union Council (TUC) is a pro-Taiwan organization. During the 1960s, it was often used to counterbalance the growth of FTU. Indeed, there were companies which deliberately encouraged the co-existence of both unions within their organizations and played them off against each other to reduce their individual influence.

The reaction of employers to unionism is fairly typical. As a senior officer in a large banking corporation once told the writer, his company would try to forestall the formation of a union by its employees by doing whatever was necessary to reduce unionization incentives at the earliest stage. There is, however, a point beyond which many employers will not go. A case in point was the tough stance which a public transportation company took when its employees repeated the strike tactic which they used successfully in their first confrontation with the management. The company threatened to dismiss those who would not report for duties before a specified deadline and let it be known that, if the going got tough, they were well prepared to close down the system for six months and train up their new recruits within that period of time. The move proved successful. Few people, if any, would risk their own jobs for the cause of their group. After the confrontation was over, the company commissioned an expert from abroad to conduct a thorough attitude survey in an attempt to identify the actual reasons underlying the employees' grievances.

The "everyone for himself" mentality gives Hong Kong its dynamics to excel but it can also be a vital weakness of the labor movement. As recently as the end of last year, the management of Cathay Pacific Airline also made use of this weakness to squelch the wild-cat strike of its cabin crew.

At one time, the Labor Department was very keen in promoting the concept of Joint Consultation Committees (JCC). It encouraged companies to form JCCs comprising representatives of management and workers so that information and ideas could be exchanged to improve the internal communication of the organizations. The suggestion was met with lukewarm response, only to be gradually resisted when representatives of the workers found that they could not discuss in the meetings key issues such as salary increases and employee benefits.

Although Hong Kong has enjoyed relatively good industrial relations until now, changes are looming on the horizon. The white-collar workers have been gradually stealing the limelight from their blue-collar counterparts in recent years after forming their own unions. The civil servants and the school teachers are the typical examples of this trend. On the other hand, while the conventional unions are keeping a low profile, they may be the target of affiliation or collaboration in the wake of Hong Kong's political reform. In a couple of occasions, the British press has referred to Hong Kong as a political city. How the changing nature of the local political system will affect the industrial relations scene is certainly an interesting topic to pursue in days to come.

Conclusion

In view of space constraints, attempts were made to first outline the historical background of Hong Kong so that the stage was set for a discussion of the unique characteristics of local personnel practices. As is clear from what has been said above, no system exists in a vacuum. A system can be a sub-system of another larger system while containing its own sub-systems. The parameters which prevail in Hong Kong at present will certainly shape personnel practices here in the future although some will have greater impact than others.

It is believed that HKIPM will continue to help professionalize the art of personnel management in Hong Kong and that the prosperity and increasing sophistication of our community will gradually make the Western concept of HRM part of our routine practice in the course of time. HKIPM will also have an active role to play in bringing Hong Kong and China together in matters related to the utilization and management of human resources as more and more organizations set up their branches across the border. At a minimum, HKIPM must keep its members abreast of the state of the art in these two places so that the integration of personnel policies can be facilitated. Human resources management in China as a whole may eventually benefit from such linkages and exposure.

Whether the democratization of our political system will result in more conflict between management and labor is one of the interesting topics to pursue in the running up to 1997. With more and more representatives elected to the legislature, it is perhaps safe to predict that days are gone when the legislature was to perpetuate the interests of a selected group of the privileged.

On the domestic front, the challenge for the HRM professionals is likely to increase dramatically as 1997 draws near. Whereas some people are determined to stay in Hong Kong regardless of the 1997 issue, others are adopting a wait-and-see attitude. Still others may want to make as much money as possible before they leave in 1997. How to derive a personnel program which would cater to all these people is really a headache for many a HR manager, particularly against the background of a tight labor market. The challenge will call for innovative and proactive solutions on the part of HRM professionals. One solution which may suggest itself is to rely more on people outside Hong Kong either by bringing them in physically or by tapping their talent through telecommunications technology.

On the brighter side, given the unique culture and values of the Chinese people here, the Hong Kong work force will remain well educated and trained. If properly mobilized and explored, its high productivity can be continuously ensured. It goes without saying that productivity will be further improved if better coordination between the government and the private sector is fostered in areas such as retraining of workers and industrial safety. In this connection, the HRM professionals have to do their homework properly if they are to constructively contribute to new government policies in these areas.

HRM issues, such as the provident fund, which have been evaded in the past have again come into the limelight. Although people may have accepted the government's "positive non-intervention" policy in the past, a major concern at present is how to look after the "underdogs" of our community given our accumulated wealth.

Endnotes

1. Throughout the chapter, the terms "human resource management" and "personnel management" are used interchangeably unless specified otherwise.
2. A new method of representation and a new balance has been created by the Joint Declaration, but a new political system or structure has not.
3. The port and airport developments also aggravated the problem of inflation. At one time in 1991, for example, the ordinary savings account rate in Hong Kong was 4 percent; whereas the inflation rate was 12.7 percent, resulting in a negative interest rate of 8.7 percent. Unfortunately, since pegging the Hong Kong dollar to the greenback, the government has found it difficult to tackle inflation through its monetary policy. To illustrate, if the government tried to tackle inflation and speculation with interest rates, it might "put pressure on the Hong Kong rate against the US (because) capital (would move) from the US to Hong Kong dollars" (Perkin, 1991). Its hands were further tied when the economy of Hong Kong was running in exactly the opposite direction to that of the United States.

References

Asiaweek (1993a). "Vital Signs," April 21, p. 13.

Asiaweek (1993b). "Crossroads of the World - A Booming Economy Reverses the 'Brain Drain'", July 7, pp. 32-33

Bernardin, H.J. and R.W. Beatty (1984). *Performance Appraisal: Assessing Human Behavior at Work*. Boston: Kent Publishing.

Census and Statistics Department, Hong Kong (1990). *Living with Statistics*. Hong Kong.

Cheng, T.Y. (1985). *The Economy of Hong Kong*. Hong Kong: Far East Publications.

Committee on Management and Supervisory Training of the Hong Kong Training Council (1980). *Report on the First Survey on Training of Managers and Supervisors*. Hong Kong: Hong Kong Training Council.

Dessler, G. (1991).*Personnel/Human Resource Management* (5th. ed.). Englewood Cliffs, N.J.: Prentice-Hall.

Employment and Earnings Statistics Section, Census and Statistics Department, Hong Kong (1993). *Quarterly Report of Employment, Vacancies, and Payroll Statistics, March 1993*. Hong Kong Employment and Earnings Statistics Section.

England, J. and J. Rear (1975). *Chinese Labor under British Rule*. Hong Kong: Oxford University Press.

England, J. and J. Rear (1981). *Industrial Relations & Law in Hong Kong*. Hong Kong: Oxford University Press.

Francesco, A.M. (1981). "Recruitment and Selection of New Employees in Hong Kong: The Influence of Western Techniques." *The Hong Kong Manager*, 17, pp. 8-13.

Graham, R.G. and C. Tuan, C. (1988). "An Empirical Analysis of Manpower Planning in Hong Kong." *International Journal of Manpower*, 9, pp. 21-27.

Hong Kong Government Information Services (n.d.) *Hong Kong*. Hong Kong: Hong Kong Government Information Services.

Hong Kong Government (1973). *Hong Kong, 1973*. Hong Kong: Hong Kong Government Press.

Hong Kong Government (1990). *A General Guide to the British Nationality Selection Scheme*. Hong Kong: Government Printer.

Hong Kong Institute of Personnel Management (1977-1993). *Newsletter*. Various issues.

Industrial Production Statistics Section, Census Statistics Department, Hong Kong (1991). *1991 Survey of Industrial Production*. Hong Kong.

Kirkbride, P.S. and S.F.Y. Tang (1989). *The Present State of Personnel Management in Hong Kong*. Hong Kong: The Management Development Centre of Hong Kong.

Labor Department, Hong Kong (1991). *Labor and Employment in Hong Kong*. Hong Kong.

Marriage, P. (1991)."War Clouds Dampen Economic Hopes." *South China Sunday Morning Post Hong Kong Review*, p. 21.

Meyer, H.H., E. Kay, and J.R.P. French, Jr. (1965). "Split Roles in Performance Appraisal." *Harvard Business Review*, January-February, pp. 123-129.

Nyaw, M.K. (1993). *The Changing Environment of the Hong Kong Enterprises. The Management of Hong Kong Enterprises in Change*. Edited by M.K. Nyaw and S. Ho (in Chinese). Hong Kong: Joint Publishing.

Perkin, I.K. (1991). "US Dollar Peg Ties HK Government's Hand." *South China Morning Post Banking and Finance Review*, p. 23.

Penlington, V.A. (1978). *Law in Hong Kong*. Hong Kong: South China Morning Post Publication Division.

Poon W.K. (1983). "The Dilemma of the Safety Officer." *Performance*, 1, p. 13.

Poon W.K. (1989). "Proactive vs. Reactive – The Changing Role of the HRD Professionals." *Conference on Brain Drain and Human Resources Development – A New Scenario?*, September 18-19, 1989.

South China Morning Post (1989). "The Governor's Speech: Text." October 12, 1989, p. 15.

South China Morning Post (1993). "Labour for Everyone Guaranteed." May 24, 1993, p. 19.

Tam, B. (1992). "Workers Find Age a Barrier to Change." *South China Morning Post*. August 18, p. 5.

The Stock Exchange of Hong Kong Ltd. (1986). *Fact Book*. Hong Kong: The Stock Exchange of Hong Kong Ltd.

The Stock Exchange of Hong Kong Ltd. (1988). *Fact Book*. Hong Kong: The Stock Exchange of Hong Kong Ltd.

The Stock Exchange of Hong Kong Ltd. (1992). *Fact Book*. Hong Kong: The Stock Exchange of Hong Kong Ltd.

Waters, D. (1991). *21st Century Management: Keeping Ahead of the Japanese and Chinese*. Singapore: Prentice-Hall.

The Japanese Human Resource Management System: A Learning Bureaucracy

Motohiro Morishima

Introduction

Recently, there has been a change in the way we view Japanese human resource management and industrial relations (HRM/IR). Departing from simple descriptions of "lifetime" employment, seniority wage and promotion (*nenko* system), and enterprise unionism, observers have begun to emphasize how Japanese firms have been able to develop a motivated and skilled workforce that is willing to adapt to new changes, which, in turn, makes it possible for firms to utilize flexible operational technologies that rely heavily on human inputs. HRM practices such as broad job classifications, employee participation, extensive in-house training, and compensation practices that reward both employee performance and skill development are increasingly emphasized (for example, Koike, 1992). The embeddedness of these practices in labor-market institutions, such as long-term employment and enterprise unionism, is also stressed (for example, Aoki, 1988; Cole, 1992b).

Yet, what is less understood is how HRM/IR practices "hang together" as a coherent HRM/IR system. What is the relationship between work organization and extensive training? How do compensation and promotion practices influence the effectiveness of the training system? What are the hiring and staffing characteristics that are consistent with a career-long training emphasis? Finally, how does enterprise unionism fit in with the training, compensation, and staffing practices? Answers to such questions are not readily available. This chapter attempts to provide some answers to these questions.

Throughout the chapter, employee learning and skill/knowledge acquisition processes are explicitly discussed, whereby the Japanese HRM/IR system is described as a set of extensive organizational innovations aimed at enhancing the acquisition and sharing of knowledge, especially at the workplace level in factories and offices. Thus, the Japanese HRM/IR system is characterized as an employment bureaucracy whose basic principle is to enhance employee learning. It is an employment bureaucracy because codified rules and legitimized practices all work to rationalize Japanese employment and bring predictability and controllability to the behavior of the major actors, employees and employers. Yet, it is also an employment system into which the learning of new skills and acquisition of knowledge are explicitly designed, supported and encouraged by intra-firm assignment methods, compensation and promotion mechanisms, and enterprise unionism. The resulting high-skill, learning-motivated workforce makes it possible for large Japanese firms to employ production and organizational technologies that utilize employee inputs and involvement, and a decentralized decision making structure that taps on employee knowledge at the "front line". Taken together, the characterization that best fits the Japanese HRM/IR system is: a "learning bureaucracy".[1]

The chapter is divided into five sections. First, a brief history of the Japanese HRM/IR system is offered. Second, the design of the HRM/IR system in Japanese organizations is described, starting with the organization of work and followed by the four major HRM/IR functions: training, reward (compensation and promotion), staffing, and employee relations and conflict resolution. Work organization is placed at the beginning because of its theoretical importance in creating demands for human resources with certain qualities (see Kochan and Osterman, 1993, for example). Third, the chapter describes, to a limited degree, the role of HRM subunits in large Japanese firms. The discussion on the HRM/IR system and the role of HRM units is summarized in Table 1 shown at the end of the chapter.

Fourth, some of the institutional factors that contributed to the development of the Japanese work system are mentioned. Recent observers have stressed the importance of the institutional embeddedness of the Japanese HRM/IR system within not only labor-market institutions, but also corporations' governance structures (Aoki, 1988; Dore, 1992). Within the space limitations of this chapter, references will be made to the governance structure of the Japanese firm.

Finally, the chapter concludes with current and future trends, along with the potential difficulty this system might face, especially in its ability to adapt to future conditions in product and labor markets. There has been a tremendous amount of discussion in Japan and elsewhere regarding the degree of change in the Japanese HRM/IR system (Nihon Keizai Shimbunsha, 1993; Berggren, 1994). Based on the model presented here, some "theoretical" predictions are made on the difficulties which the Japanese HRM/IR system may face in the future.

One disclaimer is that the discussion of the HRM/IR system in this chapter is intended to apply mainly to production (blue-collar) and managerial/administrative (white-collar) workers of large Japanese manufacturing firms.[2] While it is generally believed that firms in other sectors of the economy (smaller firms and those in non-manufacturing industries) generally apply a similar set of HRM/IR policies and practices (see, for example, Koike, 1991a, 1993; Morishima, 1993), research has been scarce in these sectors.[3]

Historical Background

Pre-World War Two Legacies

The origins of the current Japanese HRM/IR system appeared around the turn of the 20th century when Japanese industrialization began to take off and economic and technological advances generated pressure for more effective employment arrangements (Gordon, 1985: chs. 2 and 3).[4] Government-owned firms and leading private sector firms in the heavy manufacturing industries, which were then the target industries of the Japanese government's industrialization strategies, were suffering from excessive turnover approaching 60% a year and were facing difficulties retaining skilled machine operators who could handle complex machinery imported from other nations (Shimada, 1968). In response, these firms began to offer such personnel practices as company-sponsored internal training programs and seniority-based pay increases and promotion, which were intended to train and retain highly qualified machine operators (Shimada, 1968). At the same time, to centralize and rationalize staffing practices, corporate HR departments were established which took direct responsibility over hiring, task assignment and firing. Up to this point, HR responsibilities, including hiring and firing, were in the hands of oyakata (foremen) who acted as labor brokers (Gordon, 1985: ch. 2).

Between 1910 and 1940, these "new" practices began to spread to other sectors of the economy due to a variety of organizational and institutional reasons. Most importantly, the surge of militancy in the labor movement in the *Taisho* era (1912-1926), the Great Depression in the 1930s, and the Japanese government's war mobilization efforts in the period leading up to and through World War II all accelerated the "rationalization" of employment in Japanese firms. Rationalization often meant the adoption of employment internalization practices.

Period Immediately Following World War II[5]

In the ten years after the end of World War II in 1945 marked an important era in the development of basic elements of the current Japanese HRM/IR system. The most important of these elements was the formation and rapid diffusion of enterprise unions. With the legalization of the labor movement by the Supreme Commander of the Allied Forces, unions were rapidly organized throughout the country, with the percentage of paid employees in organized labor unions climbing sharply from near zero to more than 46% in about two years. Up until the mid-1950s, however, the strategies chosen by these newly-born unions were far from peaceful and cooperative. The labor movement, often led by radical and militant unionists whose agenda centered around social revolution, frequently staged prolonged strikes. Work stoppages averaged 4.6 person-days lost per 10 employees per year in this period (Shimada, 1992).

After a decade of labor turmoil, however, the tide began to change, thanks largely to the efforts of employers led by the prominent Nikkeiren (the Japan Federation of Employers' Associations). Initially, these efforts were focused on replacing these politically-motivated labor leaders with unionists who embraced more business-oriented unionism. Efforts were also made to establish cooperative labor-management institutions such as joint consultation and workshop meetings.

Then, as labor relations became gradually pacified, the focus changed more to the development of a HRM/IR system that would subsequently help the Japanese economy plunge into its export-oriented phase. Specifically, by the end of the 1950s, Japanese corporations, especially those oriented toward exports, began to show increasing concern with improving firm productivity and product quality. Corporations recognized productivity enhancement and quality improvements as critical factors in the success of their products in the world market, and the government, which planned to use exports as the primary means for reconstructing the Japanese economy, supported corporate efforts to improve quality and productivity. In the manufacturing sector, these efforts led to the development of now-famous quality control activities, worker participation programs, the lean production system, and the like.

An important consequence of this campaign for quality improvement was that it required of employees both a fundamental grasp of technological knowledge and a recognition of the organizational implications of their contributions. This requirement prepared the groundwork for the development of an HRM/IR system based on continuous learning by employees, to be described in the following sections of this chapter. In addition, substantial energy was also expended to strengthen cooperative labor-management relations, which, firms considered, were the basis for productivity improvements.

Rapid Economic Growth up to the 1970s

The rapid economic growth period, spanning the late 1950s through the early 1970s, provided the right environment for large Japanese firms to strengthen their HRM/IR system based on long-term employment security and continuous learning. In particular, the rapid growth of the economy translated, in most cases, into rapid growth of the firms themselves. Thus, firms were able to reward their employees with promotions and substantial wage increases year after year. As will be discussed later, one of the major requirements of the HRM/IR system based on continuous employment and learning is that employees continue to be rewarded for their skill upgrading and that their motivation be kept high by hopes for better lives. Japanese firms, with their rapid expansion of sales both at home and abroad, were able to provide opportunities for promotion and annual wage increases that averaged 8% to 9% during this period. The growth convinced both employees and employers of the legitimacy of the HRM/IR system.

Oil Crises in the 1970s

Sustained rapid economic expansion and people's expectations for future growth were brought to a screeching halt by the first oil crisis in 1973. Yet, the economic recession triggered by this and the second oil crisis in 1979 worked to strengthen, not weaken, the HRM/IR system, since all the parties concerned utilized the system to its fullest extent in their efforts to ameliorate the impacts of the recession. Expressly, the system was used to facilitate reallocation of workers within and across firms to avoid layoffs and to convince workers to accept moderate wage increases and employers' cost-cutting measures. While the experience was certainly bitter, the belief in the HRM/IR system was even further reinforced, given the success of these operations.

Current Context

Thus, by the 1980s, the HRM/IR system, which we will see in this chapter, had come to occupy an important place in Japanese management. It has also become ingrained in Japanese people's values about employment relationships: "good" employers are those that commit to long-term employment security and offer systematized training programs and periodic opportunities for advancement in status and wages, and "good" employees are those who develop their careers within one firm and share interests and goals with their employers.

Equally important, over the course of this development, the Japanese HRM/IR system became closely tied to the vested interests of the participants as well as to the institutional rules of the society. Most important among these institutional rules is the legal framework which provides an enormous amount of employment security to employees and makes it almost impossible for firms to terminate their regular employees (see Koshiro, 1993 for a review of the legal foundations of Japanese employment security).

For this and many other reasons, the current system described in this chapter continues to be used by large Japanese firms, despite periodic calls for changes in the employment system. Calls for changes have always resulted in some modifications (see Morishima, 1992 for a review), but the main features of the system have remained untouched up to now.

The HRM/IR System

Organization of Work

One central idea in this chapter is that the work organization and production/organizational technologies demand high quality labor, and in response, it is the role of the Japanese HRM/IR system to supply these required human resources. By influencing how work is conducted and employee behavior controlled, the organization of work serves as one of the most critical influences on the HRM/IR system. It influences the type of human resources needed to staff the work organization, the methods of human resource development, and the HRM/IR practices that support the human resource development process. The strategic distinction of whether a firm competes on the basis of a low skill/high control system or a high skill/high commitment system often boils down to how work is organized in the firm (Walton, 1985; Kochan and Osterman, 1993). In large Japanese firms, the organization of work is characterized by: (a) the lack of rigidly defined job classifications and (b) the combination of decentralization in decision making and finely graded hierarchical structures.

Lack of rigidly defined job classifications. A long-standing theme in studies of Japanese work organization is that Japanese job classification is much simpler and broader, and that job assignments are much more fluid and flexible, compared to those in Western bureaucracies (Cole, 1979; Lincoln et al., 1986; Aoki, 1988). Employees are expected to perform a wide range of job functions and accept frequent assignment changes as part of their regular day-to-day operations (Lincoln et al., 1986). Relative to Western bureaucracies, individuals' roles have a lower degree of specialization and careers are structured around a general functional area or a product category, with specific assignments determined by the degree of employees' skill development and existing circumstances such as product demand. The lower degree of specialization in large Japanese firms has been reported in various case studies (Clark, 1979; Cole, 1979). A careful quantitative study conducted by Lincoln et al. (1986) also reports findings showing a lower degree of role specialization, relative to comparable U.S. firms. According to the Ministry of Labour's (hereafter, MOL) survey of approximately 6,000 firms with an employment size of 30 or larger, only about 3 out of 10 firms (31.5%) agreed with the statement that "in our company, division of tasks and responsibilities are clearly specified for each job". In contrast, the responses from foreign-owned firms operating in Japan show that almost 6 out of 10 firms (59.5%) specify their division of labor clearly (MOL, 1993a).

Specifically, the lack of rigidly defined job classifications refers to a formal division of labor that is typically based on broad job categories covering a wide variety of (related) tasks and responsibilities. It means that a person's area of responsibility is either designed very broadly to encompass a large number of related tasks or structured flexibly to effect changes in the contents of a person's work without wholesale redesigning. Moreover, as a corollary to having broad job classes, compensation and other rewards are not set according to the job which a person holds. Instead, employment conditions are determined on the basis of performance and skill evaluation (see the discussion on rewards below).

Staffing flexibility and high employee morale are often cited as benefits of broadly designed job classification and fluid job assignments (for example, Shi-

mada and MacDuffie, 1986). It is argued that the elimination of a rigid classification scheme enables all workers to accept most assignments needed to respond
to changes in technological needs. Also, from the workers' perspective, assignment flexibility has a secondary effect as a motivator. Some argue that broad job
classification has positive effects on work attitudes for production employees in
Japanese organizations since it allows them to learn new skills and knowledge
on the job, use skills and knowledge acquired on previous jobs, and break the
monotony of repetitive work (Lincoln and Kalleberg, 1990: ch. 4).

More importantly, however, broad job classification and flexible assignments
have an additional benefit: multi-skilling. Broadly defined jobs, which, by definition, contain a large variety of tasks, are characterized by much room for an
employee to learn new skills and improve upon old ones. As employees experience
a number of related tasks and duties, they are also more likely to be exposed to
the entire work process. To encourage multi-skilling, as Rohlen (1992) explicitly
stated, Japanese management "has consciously focused on the task of reducing
the vertical and horizontal barriers to ... learning" (p. 347). Japanese firms have
long been concerned about the possibility of strict standardization and narrow
specialization of employee skills, because of its negative effect on firm adaptability to changes in long-term business strategies and short-term market demand.
Multi-skilling, which refers to worker training in a variety of related tasks, was
one way to assure adaptability (Cole, 1992a).

*Decentralization of operational decision making and finely graded hierarchi-
cal structures.* Another common observation is that Japanese organizations often
show both advanced decentralization of decision making, an aspect often referred
to as employee participation or involvement, and a highly developed hierarchical
differentiation (Sullivan and Peterson, 1990; Lincoln et al., 1986). Involvement
by blue-collar workers through such means as quality control circles and team
production (Cole, 1979), and greater involvement of middle- to low-level managers in firms' strategic decision making (Nonaka, 1988b, 1991) are often cited
as examples of decentralization of decision making.

While employee involvement and participation are often discussed in terms of
motivational effects (Miller and Monge, 1986), the primary purpose of Japanese
decentralization practices is to make effective use of the information and knowledge possessed by employees directly involved in the operation (Aoki, 1988).
According to Aoki, participation increases firms' capabilities in problem solving
and decision making by increasing the total amount of information that the organization can utilize. He conjectured that this aspect of Japanese management
creates "information rent" which could be used to increase the value of the firm.
Decentralization in operational decision making allows lower-level employees to
introduce their own judgement into the work process and enables firms to capi-
talize on their relevant and concrete knowledge and information (Koike, 1992).[6]

For example, the production technologies that have come to be known as "the
Japanese production model" include aspects such as continuous improvement, in-

tegration of quality control into the production process, and teamwork, all of which rely heavily on the principle of using information and knowledge possessed by those directly involved in the operation. Continuous improvement (or *kaizen*) and integration of quality control into the production process are practices designed to use employee knowledge and input to remove defects in the production process and the product itself. Teamwork also requires careful coordination among functionally differentiated tasks and is made possible when employees autonomously attempt to coordinate their behavior without hierarchical intervention.

Similarly, what has often been described as consensus or collective decision making (such as the *ringi* system) in white-collar workplaces also takes advantage of information collected and possessed by individual employees, since it assures that the ideas created on the basis of information at lower levels of an organization find a way to upper level management. Also, as has been pointed out by a number of researchers (e.g., Pucik and Hatvany, 1983; Clark, 1979), white-collar workers are encouraged to engage in extensive information sharing among functionally separated positions.

One important consequence of decentralization in decision making is also skill-related. Decentralization requires a certain level of knowledge and information regarding the operational process. In order to make intelligent decisions, blue-collar workers must understand the technical and social nature of their work and acquire knowledge over a wide range of aspects including the position of their tasks in the overall production process. White-collar workers must learn a great deal about the products and services they handle, the customers they serve, and about their functions within the firm in order to make useful and effective decisions. Decentralization is an additional reason for enhancing learning and knowledge development in Japanese organizations.

In contrast, a finely graded hierarchy provides a mechanism for control in a decision-making structure that is largely decentralized. It is perhaps wrong to assume that Japanese employees are given total free-reign over the decisions they make. Instead, the delegation of decision-making power to lower hierarchical levels is often balanced by careful personal monitoring and assessment of employee behavior by managers (Aoki, 1988: ch. 2; Itoh, 1991). While (production) employees in Japanese workplaces are given opportunities to participate in important decision making from the early days of their careers, their performance in participation is always carefully monitored and assessed by their supervisors. This is an important difference which distinguishes Japanese participation from that in, for example, autonomous work groups in some European countries (Berggren, 1992). Finely graded authority differentiation, often observed in Japanese organizations (Azumi and McMillan, 1981; Lincoln et al., 1986), is one structural factor that enables personal control since it creates multiple layers of authority and smaller spans of control.[7] As a result, the accountability of employee behavior is increased to safeguard organizational interests against poor decision making and any self-serving behavior of lower-level employees.

Training and Human Resource Development

When learning is accepted as a legitimate component of job performance and decentralization requires lower-level employees to acquire high skills and knowledge about work processes, training and human resource development (HRD) is considered a pivotal HRM/IR function. A survey conducted by the MOL in 1991 (MOL, 1991), using a nationally representative sample of some 4,000 firms, estimates that Japanese firms with an employment size of 30 or more, spent an average of 24,000 yen per person per year (approximately U.S.$192 at 125 yen to a dollar). Large firms with an employment size of 1,000 or more spent approximately 31,000 yen. While an international comparison of these figures is difficult, one U.S. survey (quoted in Kochan and Osterman, 1993) shows that in 1985, only 6% of the Fortune 500 firms spent more than 100 dollars per person per year on training. Moreover, the Japanese figures (and perhaps U.S. figures as well) do not include expenses related to on-the-job training. Given the importance of OJT in Japanese firms, these figures underestimate Japanese firms' true expenditures for training.

Training in large Japanese firms usually takes advantage of both on-the-job-training (OJT) as well as off-the-job-training (Off-JT), although the emphasis is definitely on the former. There is already a large amount of literature on the prevalence of extensive internal training in Japanese organizations (Cole, 1979; Dore, 1987; Koike, 1988). In most large firms, internal training occurs as a combination of continuous OJT and periodic Off-JT throughout one's organizational career. For both production and white-collar workers, job rotation, the use of cross-functional teams, and coaching are the three main mechanisms of OJT, while Off-JT is usually offered as off-site, employer-provided classroom programs. In 1991, some type of Off-JT program was offered in 69.3% of the approximately 3,000 firms with an employment size of 30 or more, and 97.3% of the firms with an employment size of 1,000 or more.

However, what characterizes the Japanese training system most clearly is the systematic use of OJT and the content of employee learning on the job. Among the researchers that have focused on this aspect of the Japanese HRD system, Koike and his associates most convincingly show the contents and the process of skills/knowledge acquisition on the job in large Japanese firms (Koike, 1988, 1992; Koike and Inoki, 1991). According to their findings, most Japanese firms place a large amount of emphasis on problem solving and decision-making skills for routine, and especially non-routine, problems in the operation and systematically use OJT to train workers to handle progressively difficult non-routine operations.

In particular, acquiring skills and knowledge to handle non-routine problem-solving prepares workers both for planned adjustments arising from changes in the operation plans and for unexpected problems that occur due to factors in technology (e.g., machine malfunctioning) and environment (e.g., customer demands). Since skills and knowledge that enable workers to handle these "unusual operations" (Koike, 1991b: p. 2) are, by definition, difficult to standardize and build into the task procedures, workers have to be trained on the job through learning-by-doing by such means as supervisory and peer coaching, employee modeling, and interpersonal adjustments. Japanese firms encourage, through various means of incentives and norm-building, continuous on-the-job learning over the span of an employee's career. Since jobs are structured broadly and flexibly as noted earlier, there is much room for incremental learning on the job. Koike argues that in the end, workers are expected to acquire the ability to detect, diagnose and find solutions for problems, an ability which Koike calls "intellectual skills" (1991b: pp. 2-10).

According to Koike and Inoki (1991), training focused on intellectual skills has three benefits. First, training in intellectual skills creates a large cadre of skilled workers capable of making operational decisions. Thus, managers are freed from housekeeping issues such as attending to machine repairs and quality problems and are enabled to use their time for more difficult problems, and the organization-wide problem solving capability is upgraded. Second, it makes the content of learning much more organization- or plant-specific, thus increasing the relevance of the skills which workers learn. Since intellectual skills learned in OJT are based on supervisors' and peers' experiences, the contents are by design relevant to the concrete situations that exist at the workplace level. Third, since training is customized for an individual worker, his/her strengths and weaknesses can be taken into consideration.

Moreover, there is another important benefit in this type of training; it encourages and is encouraged by employee participation. As noted earlier, learning makes participation possible, but participation is an important mechanism for learning in Japanese organizations, a cycle which Rohlen (1992) calls the "learning-participation link" (p. 349). Supervisors often delegate decision making, not only for the purpose of delegation, but also for the purpose of training. Thus, learning and participation create an upwardly moving spiral in the process of increasing organizational decision making capability. While the previous discussion appears to apply mainly to production workers in the manufacturing sector, Koike (1991a, 1993) has recently expanded his analyses to white-collar workers. According to his findings, HRD for white-collar workers in large Japanese firms is quite similar, in principle, to that for blue-collar workers. Extensive OJT is used to train workers through learning-by-doing, while Off-JT is used to supplement this process with systematic and codified knowledge about the firm, industry and functions of which they are in charge. One major finding that is worth noting, however, is that for white-collar positions, training is a long process which might last up to 10 years, involving a number of assignments within a broadly defined specialization (Koike, 1993).

Specifically, Nakamura's (1993) study showed that the long formative years which characterize Japanese white-collar careers (Pucik, 1989; Wakabayashi and Graen, 1989) contain systematic job changes that are within what he calls a "career field" (pp. 68-69). Career fields are defined by either a function (e.g., marketing, finance, human resource management) or a product category (e.g., steel products, petrochemical products, agricultural products) or both, and consist of a set of interrelated jobs within a function or a product category.

Then, at intervals that are predictable by past practice, employees are systematically moved so that jobs employees hold touch upon the entire career field, thus resulting in what Koike (1993) calls "broad specialization". For example, a person who is assigned to the marketing and sales field (and is expected to develop a career in this field) might start with a job in charge of production control at a local plant to gain familiarity with a specific product category and the process of making these products, then move to a local branch sales office taking charge of sales of products in this category, and finally transfer to the sales and marketing department at the headquarters. Since moves are usually made every couple of years, three "formal" assignments cover the first five to seven years of one's career in a company. Nakamura (1993) also demonstrated that within each formal assignment (e.g., a sales position at a local branch office), there are a number of informal changes in duties that take advantage of broad and flexible jobs. A survey by the Japan Institute of Labour (hereafter, JIL) (1993a) of approximately 400 of the largest firms in Japan shows that HRD is the number one reason for formal assignment changes, followed by a more specific HRD reason, employee multi-skilling.

Moreover, frequent job assignment changes are also used to develop organizational skills which are required for coordination of work within a firm, across divisions, departments, teams, and individual workers. These skills are even more important in Japanese organizations, since, as noted earlier, broad job classification and decentralization assigns a vital role to "horizontal" coordination among individual employees (Aoki, 1988). Relationships that develop out of interpersonal contacts on previous assignments serve as a very important network resource for Japanese workers (Cole, 1992a). Communication and coordination skills are considered just as important as skills related to task execution (Kagono et al., 1985).

Finally, it must be noted that this heavy emphasis on internal training is embedded in the context of long-term employment practices (Cole, 1992b). With less of a threat of losing trained employees, employers are more willing to invest in skill development. Furthermore, as noted earlier, since constraints on inter-firm mobility are due not simply to economic gains, but to the institutionalized values created over the long history of Japanese employment practices, employees are not likely to move to other firms unless economic gains for doing so are overwhelming. Consequently, employers can actively engage in all kinds of training, even when the skills they are providing may not be firm specific, and hence, are valued by other firms.

Rewards: Compensation and Promotion

Even when learning is emphasized on the job and throughout an employee's career, without appropriate incentives, workers would not be willing to acquire intellectual and organizational skills. In large Japanese firms, both compensation and promotion provide such incentives. Seniority and supervisory assessments of performance and potential (called *satei* in Japanese) play a crucial role in the determination of both blue- and white-collar workers' pay and promotion (Endo, 1994).[8]

Compensation. If simplified, there are three components in Japanese employees' pay: base pay, skill-grade pay, and fringe benefits. Base pay and skill-grade pay make up an employee's cash take-home pay, with base pay accounting for approximately 60% of the total take-home pay on average and skill-grade pay the rest.

When an employee enters a firm, base pay is initially determined by a number of factors, including education, occupational category (blue- versus white-collar), previous experience and other qualifications. One characteristic of Japanese base pay is that, as employees accumulate tenure, base pay is usually increased annually by some amount. This practice of annual increases is the basis for so-called *nenko* (literally, contribution-by-tenure) compensation.

In most firms, however, the amount of these annual increases is not tied automatically to the seniority of an individual. According to a survey reported in Shirai (1992), in a sample of approximately 6,000 firms with an employment size of 30 or more, only 25.5% of the firms reported increasing base pay solely on the basis of employee seniority. In the rest of the firms, base pay is increased either strictly on the basis of supervisory assessments (21.4%) or using a combination of merit and seniority-tied increases (40.0%).[9]

When both merit and seniority are used, it is estimated that on average, the proportion of merit increase in the total increment may go up to 60% (Shirai, 1992). Endo (1994) also reports that in one firm he studied, the results of merit assessment could make a difference of up to 53% in the annual base pay increase. Other evidence also suggests that even in firms where simple seniority is applied to increase base pay, its proportion in the total increment declines as employees accumulate tenure, thus according a larger role to merit (for example, Mitani, 1992). It must be noted that these annual increases, merit- and seniority-based, are cumulative over an employee's career. Thus, even small differences due to performance appraisals could add up to make large differences in base pay across individuals in the later stages of their careers.

The second component of employee compensation that is affected by supervisory assessments is skill-grade pay or *shikakukyu*. A survey conducted by the MOL (1990a) shows that out of approximately 6,000 firms with employment size of 30 or larger, 79.6% used the skill-grade pay system to determine at least some portion of their employees' take-home pay. It is almost 100% for large firms with employment size of 1,000 or larger. Moreover, most firms use the skill-grade pay system to determine white-collar workers' pay as well as blue-collar workers' pay.

On the surface, the skill-grade system appears very similar to job-based pay with pay ranges such as the Hay system commonly in use in Western countries. The difference is, however, that the skill-grade pay system is based, not on the worth of the job a person performs, but on *the worth of the person him/herself* (Koike, 1991b). More specifically, using a set of very detailed criteria, each employee is assessed as to what he/she is capable of performing, not what he/she actually performs (Koike, 1991b). Figure 1 shows an example of a job grade system used in a large auto-manufacturer.

Thus, the skill-grade pay system is quite close to the system of skill-based pay or pay-for-knowledge that is becoming increasingly popular in Western countries (Lawler, 1990). Koike's (1991b) observation, however, suggests that, assisted by very broadly designed job classifications, there is a much larger number of skills to be learned in a Japanese skill grade, relative to those of a skill grade in, for example, a U.S. workplace. Typically, an employee spends three to four years completing a whole set of skills in a given grade before advancing to the next skill grade. Advancement to a higher skill grade is based mostly on supervisory assessment of an employee's learning and involves an increase in pay.

The skill-grade pay system encourages learning over a long span of one's career. Since there are on average seven to eight skill grades for an employee's occupational category and it takes a few years for an employee to complete a skill grade, advancing through the entire skill-grade hierarchy could take more than 25 years. Also, as Mitani (1992) found, in higher level grades, there are a number of employees who spend more than 10 years in a grade, thus creating large differences in pay between those who advance through grades quickly and those who do not. Moreover, since many firms require advancement to a certain skill grade as a precondition for promotion to managerial positions (that is, to be promoted to the position of, say, section head, one must be at least in grade, say, A5), this system takes on an added incentive value. Thus, skill-grade pay provides a strong incentive for Japanese employees to learn and improve their skills.

One consequence of having compensation determined as a combination of base pay (which is increased by small amounts annually) and job grade pay (which is increased on the basis of employees' skill and knowledge development) is that the differentials tend to be small among those employees with similar personal characteristics such as education, pre-employment training and, especially, firm tenure. Annual increases in base pay are usually kept modest since cumulative effects of large increments every year would place a substantial burden on the firm's labor cost, and increases in *shikakukyu* due to skill and knowledge acquisition also tend to be small since in the structured learning environment where the main method of teaching is OJT, employees do not have opportunities to try substantially different kinds of tasks in a short period of time. Thus, pay differentials are compressed

Grade	Grade Title	Qualifications
Production Employees		
P8	Foreman	Capable of performing all of the positions in the unit at the third level[1] Able, as a leader, to promote quality and productivity in the unit[4]
P7	Subforeman	Capable of performing most of the positions in the unit at the third level[1] Able, as a leader, to promote quality and productivity in the unit
P6	Group Leader	Capable of performing all of the positions in the subunit at the third level[1] Able, as a leader, to promote quality and productivity in the subunit
P5	Highly Skilled	Capable of performing most of the positions in the subunit at the third level[1] Capable of effectively advising during new production line starts
P4	Team Leader	Capable of performing all of the positions in the subunit at the second level[2] and some of the positions at the third level[1] Capable of dealing with problems
P3	Senior Worker	Capable of performing about $2/3$ of the positions in the subunit at the second level[2] Capable of being a leader of small group activities Capable of dealing with slightly difficult problems
P2	Second Class Worker	Capable of performing about $1/3$ of the positions in the subunit at the second level[2]
P1	Junior Worker	Capable of performing the assigned job at the first level
Managerial/Administrative Employees		
A8	Senior Managerial	Capable of evaluating strategic decisions that affect the entire corporation Capable of running a strategic business unit under the direction of the direction of the corporation's board of directors Capable of assisting the corporation's board of directors in the determination and execution of strategic business plans
A7	Junior Managerial	Capable of running a section in a strategic business unit under the direction of a manager responsible for the unit Capable of assisting the manager responsible for the strategic business unit in the determination and execution of business plans
A6	Senior Administrative	Capable of executing a project in a section of a strategic business unit by devising and executing an operational plan Capable of assisting the manager responisible for a section in a strategic business unit Capable of planning and executing a small-scale special project at the corporate level
A5	Junior Administrative	Capable of carrying out a segment of a project Capable of undertaking a small-scale special project at the business unit level
A4	Senior Clerical	Capable of dealing with complex and difficult "unexpected" problems Capable of devising day-to-day operational plans under the general guidance of a supervisor
A3	Middle Clerical	Capable of executing non-routine tasks Capable of carrying out day-to-day operation plans under the close direction of a supervisor
A2	Junior Clerical	Capable of executing routine day-to-day tasks under the close direction of a supervisor
A1	Trainee	Capable of assisting senior employees in the execution of routing day-to-day operation

1. "The third level" means that the worker can conduct the job skillfully enough so as to be able to instruct others.
2. "The second level" means that the worker can conduct the job by him-/herself without any help from others.
3. "The first level" means that the worker can conduct the job with help from an instructor.
4. A "unit" has a foreman and consists of several subunits which, in turn, have one subforeman in each.

Figure 1:   The Skill Grade System (adapted from the system used by a major automobile manufacturer) among employees who tend to be referents in pay comparisons, creating relative "equality" of pay in Japanese organizations. Moreover, the differentials are especially small for those employees who have not had many opportunities of annual and *shikakukyu* increases, i.e., those with relatively short firm tenure. Some have argued that compressed pay differentials in Japanese workplaces have positive productivity effects when work is organized to take advantage of cooperation among lower-level employees (Levine, 1991).[10]

Finally, as is true in many other industrialized nations, Japan also has a number of legislatively mandated benefits including health insurance, paid vacation, pension, unemployment insurance, and workers compensation insurance. Outside of these mandated benefits, however, large Japanese firms often offer additional benefits such as housing subsidies, supplements for non-working spouses and children, employee services programs (assistance for recreational and social activities and non-work related education), and retirement supplements (private pensions and retirement savings). Since the provision of most of these benefits is tied to employees' life stages and firm tenure, and benefit levels do not vary as a function of job classification, hierarchical positions or performance levels, the main purpose of these benefit programs is to increase attachment to firms. Little incentive value for better performance is found in Japanese benefit programs except to ease employees' concerns at different stages of life (Kurata, 1993). For these reasons, fringe benefit provisions are often called "welfare programs" in Japanese organizations.

Promotion. In addition to advancement in skill grades, promotion (here defined as movement up to a higher position in the authority hierarchy) provides another incentive for Japanese workers, especially for white-collar workers.[11] Generally, research has found that the white-collar promotion system in large Japanese firms follows what Rosenbaum (1984) described as the tournament system where only the winners of earlier competitions proceed to the next round of competition. Both Hanada (1987) and Pucik (1989) found this pattern to be dominant in Japanese firms (although Hanada added that there was a small but increasing number of firms where the competition was left open to those who had not made it in the previous round). In this sense, the role that promotions play in an incentive system does not appear to be different in the Japanese setting from that in Western workplaces (Rosenbaum, 1984).

Yet, a major difference exists in the speed with which tournament competitions occur. In general, among white-collar managerial candidates who started employment at a company at the same time in a given year (see the section on hiring for details), the first differentiation occurs after seven to ten years of employment (Hanada, 1987; Wakabayashi and Graen, 1989), and even then the differences in authority between those who were promoted and those who were not are minor. According to Pucik (1984, 1989), it takes a good 14 years of employment before promotions that involve a major increase in authority occur. Until then cohort members make career progress within firms without much differentiation in authority, a practice often identified as "slow progress" (Wakabayashi and Graen, 1989) or "late promotion" (Koike, 1993).[12]

From the firm's perspective, the positive side of this practice is its effects on employee learning. Specifically, competition over a long span encourages learning, since the degree and speed of learning and skill upgrading is an important criterion for future promotion. Also, since formal status differentiation does not become obvious until late in one's career, discouragement among those not chosen to advance is less likely to negatively affect employees' motivation.

Finally, in order to maintain the learning incentive value of promotions, Japanese firms rarely staff higher-level positions with external hires. The degree of commitment to internal staffing is, therefore, much stronger than, for example, in U.S. firms. For example, one survey finds that 46% of some 1,500 large firms report assigning even those who are only partially qualified to fill a vacancy, presumably, to maintain the vacancy chain and the internal promotion system (MOL, 1993b). The loss which a firm incurs while the new occupant of a position becomes qualified (learning process) is considered to be smaller than the loss of learning incentives among the remaining employees (Yashiro, 1991).

In the face of slow progress and little differentiation in the first decade or so of their careers, a natural question is why employees do not terminate employment at a given firm and move to a firm where promotion chances occur much earlier in one's career. Up to now, however, the lack of viable external labor markets for mid-career job changes has discouraged this behavior (Cole, 1992b). While the overall rate of voluntary labor mobility is not low by international standards in Japan (9.6% in 1991; MOL, 1993a), most changes involve moves to smaller size firms with relatively inferior employment conditions. One study estimates that in 1991, only about 10% of the total voluntary moves result in employment in firms with comparable or larger employment size (*Nikkei Business*, 1993). Moreover, the same study shows that even among those who succeed in landing jobs in firms with larger size, 56.7% end up receiving little or no pay increases. It is estimated that on average, a white-collar worker who moves from a large firm to a medium-sized firm between ages 30 and 35 loses more than 25% of his/her lifetime earnings (*Nikkei Business*, 1993). Mid-career changes carry a hefty penalty at least as measured by economic returns.

Staffing

Most models of HRM start their description of HRM functions with staffing (for example, Butler et al., 1991). Moreover, the topic is usually discussed as a combination of external (recruitment and selection) and internal (employee movements within the organization) staffing. In this chapter, external and internal staffing are separately placed, with internal staffing having been discussed in relation to job rotation and promotions. External staffing issues are placed here since, in order to appreciate the Japanese characteristics in this HRM function, work organization and employee training practices needed to be understood. At the end of this section, a brief reference is also made to *shukko*, because of its importance as a mechanism for large Japanese firms to adjust employment levels while maintaining the convention of long-term employment practices.[13]

Hiring for regular, full-time employees in Japanese organizations takes place in a way consistent with future learning in the firm. Two aspects are worth noting. First, while candidates are initially sorted by job category, educational qualification, and gender, important criteria for selection revolves around, not ability to execute tasks and duties, but trainability or ability to learn. In a survey reported in Fujiwara (1993), even for white-collar technical employees, fewer than 10% of the firms reported primarily emphasizing "technical expertise" for selection, with even smaller percentages for blue-collar workers and white-collar administrative employees. Instead, factors such as "ability to grasp new ideas" and "motivation to learn" are emphasized by more than 40% of the firms for all types of employees. Also, the potential to be good organizational citizens is also considered critical. Thus, hiring in Japan is based less on the match between individuals' qualifications and the requirements of a job, but more on the fit between employee characteristics and the organizational need for employees who are adaptable and trainable in the long-term employment context. Large Japanese firms use multi-rater sequential interviewing to assess these aspects, which, they believe, is the only way to assess learning potential (see JIL, 1993b).

The second important issue in hiring is the practice of cohort hiring. As noted by a number of previous researchers (e.g., Pucik, 1984), large Japanese organizations usually conduct recruitment and selection every year and hire a cohort of fresh school graduates annually in April, instead of conducting recruitment and selection throughout the year as vacancies arise. There is a separate cohort for each job category – blue-collar, white-collar administrative and white-collar technical – and the size of these cohorts varies from year to year, depending on the human resource needs of the firm in a given year.

The significance of having a cohort for career-long learning is that the members of a cohort (for a given job category) are used as reference points for evaluating employee progress. This is done both by employers and employees. Employers use cohort members to determine the relative standing of an employee within a group of employees who are in the same job category and have similar in-house experience and training. Employees also use their cohort members to judge their own relative progress, especially during the first seven to ten years of their career. As noted earlier, the tournament competition that results in observable differences occurs only after a long period of no differentiation. Until then, employees must rely on subtle differences between themselves and their cohort members to determine how they are judged by the firm. These social comparisons are expected to encourage competition, and consequently, learning (Itoh, 1991). An MOL survey (MOL, 1987) indicates that 85.0% of large Japanese firms plan to continue using the employee cohort as an important device in human resource management decisions.

Finally, the flexibility of large Japanese firms' staffing practices is, in part, sustained by *shukko*, which is a practice of transferring employees out of the parent firm to its subsidiaries and related companies, while maintaining them on the parent firm's payroll. Itoh (1993) reports that in the sample of approximately 1,500 large firms he surveyed, 97% engaged in some type of *shukko*. According to Fujiwara (1993), *shukko* may be used for employee training, for subsidiary assistance and monitoring, or for redundancy control. In the majority of cases, *shukko* is conducted as part of the parent firm's effort to monitor and assist subsidiaries' management. Itoh's (1993) survey reports that 56% of the firms used *shukko* for this purpose. In addition, the practice is sometimes used as a part of systematic job changes that companies provide to their employees for training purposes (Nakamura, 1993). Employees sent out of the parent firms in these types of *shukko* are usually called back within a few years.

However, an increasingly important use of *shukko* for large Japanese firms is employment level adjustment and redundancy control, especially with regard to older employees. Through this method, senior employees are transferred out of the parent firm before they reach retirement age, and are usually never called back to the parent firm. In most cases, they are kept on the parent firm's payroll for a few years, and later moved to the subsidiaries' payroll. Itoh (1993) reports that in his survey, 42% of the firms practiced *shukko* for controlling redundancy in the senior employee pool, a figure he estimates as being underreported due to social undesirability. In the case of a large steel manufacturer which employs approximately 52,000, every year six to seven hundred senior employees are transferred out to subsidiaries (Nihon Keizai Shimbunsha, 1993: pp. 55-56).

In an employment system where long-term employment is the norm and employee termination or layoff is uncommon, this type of *shukko* enables firms to reduce redundancy while partially fulfilling an implicit promise of "continuous" employment. To maintain the comparability of employment conditions, even after the transferred employees are permanently moved to the subsidiary's payroll, the parent firm often pays the difference in remuneration between the two firms. At the same time, since the practice is usually focused on senior employees, it opens up advancement opportunities for junior employees and enables firms to maintain the flow of long-term career and skill development within a firm. *Shukko* for senior employees has become an essential mechanism for large firms to maintain the system of long-term employment practices.[14]

Employee Relations and Conflict Resolution

Almost all employment relationships are mixed-motive situations where the interests of employers and employees partially coincide and partially conflict. Japanese employment relationships are no exception. While the cooperative nature of employee relations is often highlighted, Japanese employer-employee relations contain a number of conflicting interests that are resolved through a method that is common to those in workplaces in other countries: labor-management negotiations.

In labor-management negotiations of large firms, enterprise unionism still plays a very important role (Blanchflower and Freeman, 1992).[15] While the overall union density was just under 25% in 1992, within the large-firm sector (employment size of 1,000 or more), which often acts as the pattern-setter for the rest of the economy (Shimada, 1980), union coverage is still over 75%, thus making enterprise unionism a large-firm sector phenomenon. The membership of an enterprise union is usually restricted to regular-status (*joyo*) employees – both blue-collar and white-collar workers – to whom the foregoing descriptions of the Japanese HRM/IR system mainly apply. Part-time and temporary employees are excluded from membership. Thus, one important characteristic of Japanese enterprise unionism is that it mainly represents the interests of regular-status workers in large firms. Due to the occupational mix, however, a variety of interests are gathered under the same roof.

Some argue that this "company"-based union structure is precisely the reason for Japanese enterprise unions' cooperative attitudes toward management in large firms (Marsland and Beer, 1983). Other reasons are also cited, most notably that many union leaders return to management positions after serving in the enterprise union and that unions receive financial and in-kind assistance from employers (Shirai, 1992). These factors may explain some of the structural weaknesses which Japanese enterprise unions exhibit in their negotiations with management (see Turner, 1991: pp. 216-221). However, collaborative labor-management relations should not be understood simply in terms of unions' one-way dependence on management. Rather, its meaning needs to be understood through Japanese firms' highly structured internal labor markets and long-term employment practices, union membership that is limited to the employees of only one firm, and an HRM/IR system that fosters employee learning and decentralization of decision making (Shirai, 1983).

From the employer perspective, the Japanese production system, which relies heavily on employee involvement for efficacious operation, and the organization's decision making structure, which derives its vitality and adaptability from employee inputs, leave them highly defenseless to employee interruption. Without employee cooperation, the production system easily comes to a halt; in this sense, the Japanese system is "fragile" (Shimada and MacDuffie, 1986: pp. 27-29). White-collar workers have similar potential bargaining leverage because of the highly decentralized decision making structure and the role they play in carrying out firms' strategies (Nonaka, 1988b, 1991).

Similarly, from the employees' perspective, they have a stake in making sure that employers uphold the implicit understanding that organization-specific skills which employees have worked hard to acquire will be rewarded throughout the career. Their skills, both task-related and organizational, are not likely to be valued by other employers offering similar levels of employment conditions (i.e., other large employers). Thus, employees have a strong incentive to hold employers accountable to their promise of employment continuity and to keep the firm in business and profitable to maintain their employment status. Also, since the value of acquired skills depends largely on the technology used in the operation, employees have a strong interest in voicing their concerns in management's strategic and operational decision making. The introduction of new technologies might drastically alter the value of a skill downward. Therefore, this also becomes a primary concern for the employees and unions (Cole, 1992a).

Against this backdrop, what appears as a cooperative relationship between labor and management is embedded in a heavy interdependence between employers who rely on employees' skills and decision making ability on one hand, and employees who need continuity of employment to maintain the value of their hard-learned skills on the other. Thus, it is no wonder that bargaining in Japanese employee relations, regardless of whether employees are unionized or not,[16] is over employment continuity and the development of employee skills and decision making ability (Shirai, 1983).

Consequently, employers are likely to demand (and obtain) full control over the skill development process, including supervisory assessments of employee learning, frequent changes of assignment, and the use of the skill-grade system in compensation determination. Obviously, by taking almost exclusive control over these items, management gains strong power in the determination of employment conditions for individual employees. In return, however, employers tend to accede to employees' demands in two major areas: security of employment and partici-pation in firms' strategic decisions that potentially affect employment continuity. As Shirai (1983) notes, enterprise unions in large Japanese firms have always put employment security for their regular-status members – the core employees whose skills and decision making ability employers tend to rely on – as the top item on their bargaining agenda.

Wage negotiations, therefore, are not likely to generate overt conflicts within Japanese firm-level employee relations. In practice, through a mechanism called *Shunto* (the Spring Wage Offensive), wage negotiations have been taken out of the firm and put into coordinated industry-level bargaining between employers' as-sociations and union federations. *Shunto*, which occurs every spring to determine the average wage increases of regular-status workers, appears adversarial, but, in reality, has been remarkably successful in restraining wage increases and making them lag behind productivity increases (Shimada, 1983). In contrast, issues over employment security usually take on a much larger significance. Most of the bitter struggles in post-World War II Japanese industrial relations history have resulted from management's threat to employment security (Shimada, 1992).

In addition, employees and unions have demanded (and employers have given) participation in strategic decisions on such issues as introduction of new technology, redundancy handling, and changes in staffing plans. All of these issues have the potential of affecting employment continuity. MOL (1990b) shows that, when making decisions on these issues, more than 70% of large Japanese firms inform and solicit reactions from the labor side, and 30% seek to obtain union consent before proceeding to implement their plans. A mechanism often known as the joint consultation system is used for this purpose (Morishima, 1991a, 1991b). The joint consultation system is a form of representative participation in management decision making which serves the dual purpose of information sharing between labor and management and prior consultation by management before making strategic decisions. The joint consultation system existed in more than 70% of large firms in 1990 (MOL, 1990b).

Thus, enterprise unions have generally engaged in employment security/skill development bargaining whereby core employees win employment security in return for management's almost unilateral influence on the allocation of rewards and training opportunities to individual employees. Their strong insistence on employment security for firms' core employees precluded Japanese employers from competing on the basis of low wages and employment cuts, a policy which they attempted during the early 1950s (Gordon, 1985: ch. 10). Thus, by protecting employment continuity, union strategies have served as (and still are) a strong impetus for the development and maintenance of the Japanese HRM/IR system (see Table 1).

The Role of the HR Department

Because of the apparent heavy emphasis on human resources, the importance of HR departments in large Japanese firms has often been overestimated. Firms surveyed in one study rank the power attributed to HR departments in large manufacturing firms as fifth, following such departments as marketing, production, and research and development – exactly the same rank as HR departments hold in U.S. firms (Kagono et al., 1985: ch. 2).

More realistically, HR departments in large Japanese firms act as a central coordinating body for corporate-wide HRM activities. Three functions are most important. First, HR departments collect and file assessment and evaluation information on all core employees within firms. Such information is collected from supervisory assessments made on subordinates. Since employee development spans a long period with multiple assignments, moves both within and across sections and departments are commonplace, and create a need for some type of central information storage. Ratings from multiple raters are obtained and used for monitoring employee development.

Table 1:   Summary of the Japanese HRM/IR Systems

HRM Dimensions	Major Points
Organization of Work	• Flexibly and broadly defined job classification • Advanced decentralization in decision making • Finely graded hierarchical structure • Heavy reliance on employee participation for efficient operation
Training and Human Resource Development	• Mostly internal • Extensive OJT with intermittent Off-JT • Career-long skill development • Development of "broad specialization" • Emphasis on problem-solving, decision making and organizational/communication skills ("intellectual skills") • Heavy use of coaching and job rotation as training methods
Compensation and Promotion	• *Nenko* wage pattern due to annual increases • Reliance on supervisory assessment of skill development and trainability for employee appraisal • Almost universal use of skill-grade pay • Little use of job analysis and evaluation • Compressed wage dispersion and emphasis on relative equality • Tournament promotion (mostly white-collar) • Promotion competition as a strong motivator • Promotion decisions based on the degree of skill acquisition • Slow career progress/late selection (esp. junior workers)
Staffing, Hiring, Internal Staffing	• Prefer to hire fresh school graduates without work experience • Hiring a critical concern and large investment in selection • Cohort hiring to create basis for employee comparison • Emphasis on trainability and adaptability • Adherence to internal promotion and transfers • Frequent job rotation and assignment changes • *Shukko* as a method of redundancy control
Employee Relations and Conflict Resolution	• Labor unions organized on enterprise basis • Union insistence on employment continuity • Management's control over the skill development process • Employment security-skill development bargain
Role of HRM Units	• Coordination of corporate-wide personnel activities • Store career progress information on all core employees • Determine in-company personnel moves with line managers • Maintain consistency in personnel activities

Second, information collected on individual employees is used to make decisions on within-firm movements that have long-term implications for employees' career and skill development. Evidence suggests most personnel moves are determined jointly by corporate-level HR departments and managers in charge of the operation (Yashiro, 1992). HR departments oversee company-wide staffing in tandem with line managers who may otherwise attempt to maximize only their departments' interests by keeping the best.

Third, since employees frequently move and are rated by a number of supervisors, HR departments maintain consistency of performance and skill development assessments and integrity in decisions across divisions and subsections. Reward mechanisms such as the skill-grade system and promotion ladders are designed and executed centrally by corporate HR departments, leaving little room for line managers to influence reward levels for their own subordinates. In recent years, consistency has also been required to conform to government regulations and industry standards (Shirai, 1992).

Thus, the key word here is *coordination*. HR departments in large Japanese firms coordinate HR decisions and activities within the firm. In fact, most of the substantive activities in HRM/IR are conducted on the shopfloor and in offices by operating line managers – OJT, assessments, within-department job rotation, etc. As noted earlier, transfer and promotion decisions are made as joint decisions of operating managers and HR departments (JIL, 1993a). Kochan and Cappelli (1984) suggested that the importance of HR departments is derived from the degree to which they control the critical contingencies that are associated with the HRM/IR system. In large Japanese firms, the critical contingency is the development and maintenance of qualified human resources that match the level of production technologies and the decentralized decision making structure. In this sense, as Aoki (1988: p. 54) notes, HR departments in large Japanese firms play a "strategic" role.

Institutional Factors

The previous sections have stressed the interdependence between production technologies and organizational structure, among the components of the HRM/IR system, and between labor and management in bargaining over employment security and HRD. Yet, as recent theorists have suggested (Baron et al., 1988; Kochan et al., 1993), the system must also be seen as linked together in a coherent fashion to the institutional and contextual factors that support the existence of a particular type of HRM/IR system. Since complete coverage of these factors is beyond the scope of this chapter,[17] the focus will be on two factors that relate to the governance structure of the firm: 1) management's position in the corporate governance structure and 2) the role of the state.[18]

Management's Position in the Corporate Governance Structure

Management's position in the corporate governance structure is one of the most important institutional factors that helped Japanese firms develop and sustain their version of the HRM/IR system. More specifically, as suggested by recent researchers (Dore, 1992; Aoki, 1988), the financial market in which Japanese firms obtain resources does not place a heavy burden on Japanese managers to produce "quick and large" returns for their stockholders. Corporate financing is obtained mainly through bank loans and mutual equity holding among "friendly" firms within a corporate group. These banks and equity holders have generally been interested in firms' long-term stable growth in which, they considered, the development of a high-quality labor force plays a major role. Consequently, due to the lack of a strong principal-agent relationship between stockholders and managers, Japanese managers have been able to incorporate employees as one of the important stakeholders in their management activities (Dore, 1992; Aoki, 1988: ch. 4). Such coalition between employers and employees was considered necessary for utilization of production strategies and organizational structure that relies heavily on human inputs.

Role of the State

The second factor related to the corporate governance structure is the role of the state. In the post-Word War II development of the Japanese HRM/IR system, the government took an active role, not directly involving itself in firms' management of human resources, but by its macroeconomic policies regulating such factors as interest rates, financial markets, trade, and investment. Most importantly, the role of the Japanese government is seen as having provided a heavily controlled environment in which large firms were allowed to develop. By the use of industrial policies, the government directed investment and accumulation of capital into strategic sectors where large firms were carefully monitored for overindulgence in their market power, but shielded from fierce competition (Shimada, 1980). In these carefully monitored markets, large firms chose a long-term option of skill development and employment security. Firms that enjoy relatively good economy of scale and future probability of existence are in better position to utilize this type of human resource strategy (Kochan and Osterman, 1993).

In addition, the government also had an indirect role in defining the contents of the HRM/IR system that developed in the post-World War II period. By helping to create such organizations as the Japan Productivity Center, the Japanese Union of Scientists and Engineers, and the Japan Management Association, the government assisted in the introduction and diffusion of many of the techniques of the Japanese HRM/IR system, with two important effects. First, the endorsements by these organizations legitimized the techniques, thus creating a coercive force in the adoption and diffusion of the Japanese HRM/IR system. Second, as Cole (1989: pp. 40-48) notes, the introduction of techniques by these organizations lowered the cost for firms of developing and customizing the techniques to their own practices and technologies. While these organizations are not organs of the Japanese government by any means, the development of such national infrastructure was critical. These organizations acted to legitimate the Japanese HRM/IR system and lowered the cost of its diffusion.

The Future of the Japanese HRM/IR System

As we have seen in the foregoing discussion, the Japanese HRM/IR system is predicated on the interdependence among system elements, such as long-term development of employee skills, broad job classification, and determination of compensation and promotion based on a combination of nenko and skill development. These elements are structured in a coherent and mutually reinforcing manner to produce an employment bureaucracy focused on continuous learning by employees.

By most accounts (Cole, 1992b; Dore, 1992), this system has successfully produced the human resources required by production and organizational technologies that rely heavily on human inputs. Many researchers have also documented that this system has contributed particularly to Japanese manufacturers' ability to produce and sell in highly competitive foreign markets (Dore, 1986; Cole, 1992b; Shimada and MacDuffie, 1986). Currently, there is even discussion about the exportability of the Japanese production and HRM/IR systems (Florida and Kenney, 1991).

Yet, such "success" does not mean that the Japanese HRM/IR system is problem-free. Far from it, the system is currently under substantial attack by employers who must find ways to adopt more cost-conscious business strategies and employees whose quality of work life has not kept pace with the economic prosperity of large Japanese firms. Four areas stand out the most. First, protection and representation of employee interests and welfare need to be reconsidered, especially in issues such as quality of work life, shorter working hours, and employee autonomy (Shimada, 1992). These are especially important issues in Japan where enterprise unions have bargained away a large portion of the power to influence individual employees' conditions.

Second, the continued applicability of the Japanese HRM/IR system to white-collar and managerial employees is being seriously questioned (Nonaka, 1988a). Despite the noteworthy effectiveness of the HRM/IR system for production workers (Koike, 1988), the effectiveness of the white-collar HRM/IR system, in both manufacturing and nonmanufacturing, has not been established either by academic research or by practice. It is often alleged that this system, which depends so much on learning what already exists, is not suited for creating new ideas and innovations (Nonaka, 1988a).

The third issue is that because of the change in organizational demography – an aging workforce and an increasing proportion of middle-aged employees – Japanese firms are experiencing difficulties maintaining the motivational mechanisms to encourage learning (Kawakita, 1993). Higher-level positions are getting scarce relative to the number of employees competing in promotional tournaments. Learning-based compensation is becoming costly since older employees tend to have learned more and are entitled to receive higher pay. Yet, quick solutions to this problem, such as terminating or transferring (out to related companies) senior employees, might result in a loss of organizational knowledge and discourage those who are early in the career development process.

Finally, changes in employee values to seek more individual determination of their career development (Inagami, 1993; Kawakita, 1993) and in corporate structures to more decentralized and diversified forms (Nonaka, 1991) raise doubts about the viability of a centrally coordinated HRM/IR system. HRM/IR functions might also have to be decentralized to allow divisions and departments to make HRM decisions that are consistent with their own objectives. This may, however, result in the loss of corporate-wide consistency in HRM activities and in political strife between HRM staff and operating managers.

These and other issues will continue to put pressure on the Japanese HRM/IR system to change and to adapt to new conditions. But the system which large Japanese firms have created during the 40 some years of the post-Word War II period presents an alternative to other types of employment bureaucracies existing in other countries. What we must do is critically examine these alternative systems for their effectiveness.

Endnotes

1. Adler (1993) first coined this term. Some may argue that the "organic" structure of Japanese firms defies the description "bureaucracy". As Aoki's duality principle indicates (1988: ch. 3), it is, however, the centralized, bureaucratic nature of the HRM/IR system that makes it possible for Japanese firms to have organized work structures.
2. Large firms are usually defined in official Japanese statistics as those with 1,000 employees or more.
3. Employment conditions, especially compensation and benefit levels, tend to be significantly inferior in small and medium-sized firms (see Chalmers, 1989).
4. There is a school of thought which argues that the origin of the current Japanese HRM/IR system dates back to the employment practices found in merchant houses at the end of the *Tokugawa* feudal period, circa 1830 (for example, Hazama, 1978).
5. This section draws heavily on Shimada (1992: pp. 270-279).

6. See the discussion on rewards for the motivational mechanisms for employee participation.
7. By creating a finely-graded status hierarchy with little functional differentation, Japanese organizations also provide more promotion opportunities in an HRM/IR system that is based on long-term employment. An elaborate set of ranks means opportunities for regular advancement throughout the career, thus delaying discouragement due to career plateau.
8. As Koike (1988) notes, Japan is rather unique in that even unionized production workers are subject to merit assessments conducted by supervisors.
9. In this survey, 12.8% reported not increasing base pay annually. These firms are believed to have completely removed the *nenko* component from their base pay increases (Shirai, 1992).
10. The negative effects include the relative lack of reward for those who are capable of learning more quickly and of contributing more to the organization than others.
11. Although blue-collar workers advance through skill grades, they have fewer prospects of advancing through the ranks of hierarchy, relative to white-collar workers (Cole, 1979).
12. Wakabayashi and Graen (1989), however, reveal that during this period of apparently no differentiation, large amounts of data are accumulated on individual employees. These data are used to determine who will be chosen to advance in the firm in the later stages of careers.
13. Another important issue in staffing is the use of part-time and temporary workers who bear the cost of providing employment security to regular-status (core) workers. The issue of part-time and temporary workers is beyond the scope of this chapter; see Morishima (1993) for fuller discussion.
14. This practice, however, places a heavy burden on subsidiaries and related firms that must receive large firms' *shukko* employees.
15. Eighty-four percent of Japanese union members and 95% of unions are organized on an enterprise basis (MOL, 1993a).
16. Hiroki Sato, through personal communication, says that in his recent survey of about 300 non-union and union employees, no difference was observed in the proportion of firms (both around 70%) which agreed with a statement that "Management should always listen to employees' concerns in making decisions that affect their employment security."
17. Interested readers might refer to such publications as Gordon (1985), Shimada (1992), and Gerlach (1992).
18. Another important factor in the governance structure is union strategies (Kochan et al., 1993), which was discussed in the section on employee relations.

References

Adler, P. (1993). "The Learning Bureaucracy: New United Motor Manufacturing, Inc." In Larry L. Cummings and Barry M. Staw (eds.), *Research in Organizational Behavior*, Vol. 15. Greenwich, CT: JAI Press, pp. 111-194.

Aoki, M. (1988). *Information, Incentives, and Bargaining in the Japanese Economy*. New York: Cambridge University Press.

Azumi, K. and C. McMillan (1981). "Management Strategy and Organization Structure: A Japanese Comparative Study." In D.J. Hickson and C. McMillan (eds.), *Organization and Nation: The Aston Programme IV*. Westmead: Gower, pp. 155-172.

Baron, J.N., P.D. Jennings, and F.R. Dobbin (1988). "Mission Control? The Development of Personnel Systems in U.S. Industry." *American Sociological Review*, 53, pp. 497-514.

Berggren, C. (1992). *Alternatives to Lean Production: Work Organization in the Swedish Auto Industry*. Ithaca, NY: ILR Press.

Berggren, C. (1994). "Toward Normalization? Japanese Competitive Position and Employment Practices after the Heisei Boom." Paper presented at the Industrial Relations Research Association Meetings, Boston, Jan. 3-5.

Blanchflower, D.G. and R.B. Freeman (1992). "Unionism in the United States and Other Advanced OECD Nations." *Industrial Relations*, 31, pp. 56-79.

Butler, J.E., G.R. Ferris, and N.K. Napier (1991). *Strategy and Human Resources Management*. Cincinnati, OH: South-Western Publishing Co.

Chalmers, N.J. (1989). *Industrial Relations in Japan: The Peripheral Workforce*. London: Routledge.

Clark, R.C. (1979). *The Japanese Company*. New Haven: Yale University Press.

Cole, R.E. (1979). *Work, Mobility, and Participation: A Comparative Study of American and Japanese Industry*. Berkeley: University of California Press.

Cole, R.E. (1989). *Strategies for Learning: Small Group Activities in American, Japanese and Swedish Industry*. Berkeley: University of California Press.

Cole, R.E. (1992a). "Issues in Skill Formation in Japanese Approaches to Automation." In P.S. Adler (ed.), *Technology and the Future of Work*. New York: Oxford University Press, pp. 187-209.

Cole, R.E. (1992b). "Some Cultural and Social Bases of Japanese Innovation: Small-Group Activities in Comparative Perspective." In Shumpei Kumon and H. Rosovsky (eds.), *The Political Economy of Japan, Volume 3: Cultural and Social Dynamics*. Stanford: Stanford University Press, pp. 292-318.

Dore, R.P. (1986). *Flexible Rigidities: Industrial Policy and Structural Adjustment in the Japanese Economy, 1970-80*. London: Athlone Press.

Dore, R.P. (1987). *Taking Japan Seriously: A Confucian Perspective on Leading Economic Issues*. Stanford: Stanford University Press.

Dore, R.P. (1992). "Japan's Version of Managerial Capitalism." In T.A. Kochan and M. Useem (eds.), *Transforming Organizations*. New York: Oxford University Press, pp. 17-26.

Endo, K. (1994). "Satei (Personal Assessment) and Interworker Competition in Japanese Firms." *Industrial Relations*, 33 (1) pp. 70-82.

Florida, R. and M. Kenney (1991). "Transplanted Organizations: The Transfer of Japanese Industrial Organization to the U.S." *American Sociological Review*, 56, 381-398.

Fujiwara, M. (1993). "Hiring and Staffing." In Masumi Tsuda (ed.), *Personnel Management*. Tokyo: Minerva Publishing Co., pp. 107-120 (in Japanese).

Gerlach, M.L. (1992). *Alliance Capitalism: The Social Organization of Japanese Business*. Berkeley: University of California Press.

Gordon, A. (1985). *The Evolution of Labor Relations in Japan: Heavy Industry, 1853-1955*. Cambridge, MA: Harvard East Asian Monographs.

Hanada, M. (1987). "Tournament Mobility of Japanese Firms' Promotion Systems and Strategic Human Resource Management." *Organizational Science*, 21 (Summer), pp. 44-53 (in Japanese).

Hazama, H. (1978). *A Study on the History of Japanese Personnel Management*. Tokyo: Ochanomizu Shobo (in Japanese).

Inagami, T. (1993). "Individualization and the New Corporate Community." In Ministry of Labour (ed.), *Report on Human Resource Management in the 21st Century*. Tokyo: Ministry of Labour, pp. 143-165 (in Japanese).

Itoh, H. (1991). "Japanese Human Resource Management from the Viewpoint of Incentive Theory." *Ricerche Economiche*, 45, 345-376.

Itoh, H. (1993). "Use of *Shukko* in Personnel Management by Large Japanese Firms." In Ministry of Labour (ed.), *Human Resource Management in the 21st Century*. Tokyo: Ministry of Labour, pp. 69-77 (in Japanese).

Japan Institute of Labour (1993a). *Staffing and Promotion of White-Collar Workers in Large Firms*, JIL Research Report No. 37. Tokyo: Japan Institute of Labour (in Japanese).

Japan Institute of Labour (1993b). *Survey on the Career Management of White-Collar Workers*, JIL Research Report No. 44. Tokyo: Japan Institute of Labour (in Japanese).

Kagono, T., I. Nonaka, K. Sakakibara and H. Okumura (1985). *Strategic vs. Evolutionary Management*. Amsterdam: North Holland.

Kawakita, T. (1993). *Diversity and Human Resource Management in Japan*. Presented at Japan Institute of Labour-University of Illinois Institute of Labor and Industrial Relations Conference on "The Change of Employment Environment and Human Resource Management in the U.S. and Japanese Labor Markets." Tokyo, October 5.

Kochan, T.A., R. Batt and L. Dyer (1993). "International Human Resource Studies: A Framework for Future Research." In D. Lewin, O.S. Mitchell and P.D. Sherer (eds.), *Research Frontiers in Industrial Relations and Human Resources*. Madison, WI: Industrial Relations Research Association, pp. 309-337.

Kochan, T.A. and P. Cappelli (1984). "The Transformation of the Industrial Relations and Personnel Function." In P. Osterman (ed.), *Internal Labor Markets*. Cambridge, MA: MIT Press, pp. 133-161.

Kochan, T.A. and P. Osterman (1993). *Human Resource Development and Utilization: Is There Too Little in the U.S.?* MIT Industrial Liaison Program Report, No. 2-42-93.

Koike, K. (1988). *Understanding Industrial Relations in Modern Japan*. London: Macmillan.

Koike, K. ed. (1991a). *Human Resource Development of White-Collar Employees*. Tokyo: Toyo Keizai (in Japanese).

Koike, K. (1991b). "Learning and Incentive Systems in Japanese Industry." Mimeo. Tokyo: Hosei University.

Koike, K. (1992). "Human Resource Development and Labor-Management Relations." In Kozo Yamamura and Yasukichi Yasuba (eds.), *The Political Economy of Japan, Volume 1: The Domestic Transformation*. Stanford: Stanford University Press, pp. 289-330.

Koike, K. (1993). "Human Resource Development Among College Graduates in Sales and Marketing." In Kazuo Koike (ed.), *An International Comparison of Professionals and Managers*, JIL Report No. 2. Tokyo: Japan Institute of Labour, pp. 42-64.

Koike, K. and T. Inoki (1991). *Skill Formation in Japan and Southeast Asia*. Tokyo: University of Tokyo Press.

Koshiro, K. (1993). "Comment on 'Aging Population and Human Resource Management by M. Ito'." Presented at Japan Institute of Labour-University of Illinois Institute of Labor and Industrial Relations Conference on "The Change of Employment Environment and Human Resource Management in the U.S. and Japanese Labor Markets." Tokyo, October 5.

Kurata, Y. (1993). "Employee Welfare." In Masumi Tsuda (ed.), *Personnel Management.* Tokyo: Minerva Publishing Co., pp. 263-274 (in Japanese).

Lawler, E.E. III. (1990). *Strategic Pay.* San Francisco: Jossey-Bass.

Levine, D.I. (1991). "Cohesiveness, Productivity, and Wage Dispersion." *Journal of Economic Behavior and Organization,* 15, 237-255.

Lincoln, J.R., M. Hanada and K. McBride (1986). "Organizational Structure in Japanese and U.S. Manufacturing." *Administrative Science Quarterly,* 31, 338-364.

Lincoln, J.R. and A.L. Kalleberg (1990). *Culture, Control and Commitment: A Study of Work Organization and Work Attitudes in the United States and Japan.* New York: Cambridge University Press.

Marsland, S. and M. Beer (1983). "The Evolution of Japanese Management: Lessons for U.S. Managers." *Organizational Dynamics,* 11 (Winter), 49-67.

Miller, K.I. and P.R. Monge (1986). "Participation, Satisfaction, and Productivity: A Meta-Analytic Review." *Academy of Management Journal,* 29, 727-753.

Ministry of Labour (1987). *Prospects on Changes in Japanese Employment Practices: Survey Report.* Tokyo: Ministry of Finance Printing Office (in Japanese).

Ministry of Labour (1990a). *Comprehensive Survey on Pay and Working Hours.* Tokyo: Ministry of Finance Printing Office (in Japanese).

Ministry of Labour (1990b). *Status of Labor-Management Communication.* Tokyo: Ministry of Finance Printing Office (in Japanese).

Ministry of Labour (1991). "An Outline of the Survey on In-House Training Programs in the Private Sector." *Vocational Development Journal,* 33 (8), 22-27 (in Japanese).

Ministry of Labour (1993a). *1993 White Paper on Labour.* Tokyo: Japan Institute of Labour (in Japanese).

Ministry of Labour (ed.) (1993b). *Human Resource Management in the 21st Century.* Tokyo: Ministry of Labour (in Japanese).

Mitani, N. (1992). "Job- and Ability-based Pay Structure." In Toshiaki Tachibanaki (ed.), Assessment, *Promotions and Pay Determination.* Tokyo: Yuhikaku Publishing, pp. 109-136 (in Japanese).

Morishima, M. (1991a). "Information Sharing and Firm Performance in Japan." *Industrial Relations,* 30, 37-61.

Morishima, M. (1991b). "Information Sharing and Collective Bargaining in Japan: Effects on Wage Negotiation." *Industrial and Labor Relations Review,* 44, 469-475.

Morishima, M. (1992). "Japanese Employees' Attitudes Toward Changes in Traditional Employment Practices." *Industrial Relations,* 31, 433-454.

Morishima, M. (1993). "Externalization of Employment as a Response to Internal Labor Market Constraints: The Case of Japanese Food Service Establishments." Mimeo. Faculty of Policy Management, Keio University.

Nakamura, M. (1993). "Career Structure of College Graduates in Japanese Manufacturing." In Kazuo Koike (ed.), *An International Comparison of Professionals and Managers,* JIL Report No. 2. Tokyo: Japan Institute of Labour, pp. 67-85.

Nihon Keizai Shimbunsha (ed.) (1993). *Japanese-Type Personnel Management is No More.* Tokyo: Nihon Keizai Shimbunsha (in Japanese).

Nikkei Business (1993). "Price for Long-Term Employment." No. 710 (Oct. 11 Issue), 10-23 (in Japanese).

Nonaka, I. (1988a). "Self-Renewal of the Japanese Firm and the Human Resource Strategy." *Human Resource Management*, 27, 45-62.

Nonaka, I. (1988b). "Toward Middle-Up-Down Management: Accelerating Information Creation." *Sloan Management Review*, 29, 9-18.

Nonaka, I. (1991). *A Theory of Organizational Knowledge Creation.* Tokyo: Nihon Keizai Shimbunsha (in Japanese).

Pucik, V. (1984). "White Collar Human Resource Management in Large Japanese Manufacturing Firms." *Human Resource Management*, 23, pp. 257-276.

Pucik, V. (1989). "Managerial Career Progress in Large Japanese Manufacturing Firms." In A. Nedd, G.R. Ferris and K.M. Rowland (eds.), *Research in Personnel and Human Resources Management*, Suppl. 1. Greenwich, CT: JAI Press, pp. 257-276.

Pucik, V. and N. Hatvany. (1983). "Management Practices in Japan and Their Impact on Business Strategy." In R. Lamb (ed.), *Advances in Strategic Management*, Vol. 1. Greenwich, CT: JAI Press, pp. 103-131.

Rohlen, T.P. (1992). "Learning: The Mobilization of Knowledge in the Japanese Political Economy." In Shumpei Kumon and H. Rosovsky (eds.), *The Political Economy of Japan, Volume 3: Cultural and Social Dynamics.* Stanford: Stanford University Press, pp. 321-363.

Rosenbaum, J.E. (1984). *Career Mobility in a Corporate Hierarchy.* Orlando, FL: Academic Press.

Shimada, H. (1968). "Historical Formation of the Lifetime Commitment System: A Case Study of the Yawata Basic Steel Corporation, 1896-1934." *Mita Keizai Zasshi*, 61(3), 40-75 (in Japanese).

Shimada, H. (1980). *Japanese Employment System.* Tokyo: Japan Institute of Labour.

Shimada, H. (1983). "Wage Determination and Information Sharing: An Alternative to Incomes Policy?" The *Journal of Industrial Relations*, 25, pp. 177-200.

Shimada, H. (1992). "Japan's Industrial Culture and Labor-Management Relations." In Shumpei Kumon and H. Rosovsky (eds.), *The Political Economy of Japan, Volume 3: Cultural and Social Dynamics.* Stanford: Stanford University Press, pp. 267-291.

Shimada, H. and J.P. MacDuffie (1986). *Industrial Relations and "Human Ware": Japanese Investments in Automobile Manufacturing in the United States.* Working Paper No. 1855-86, Sloan School of Management, MIT.

Shirai, T. (1983). "A Theory of Enterprise Unionism." In T. Shirai (ed.), *Contemporary Industrial Relations in Japan.* Madison, WI: University of Wisconsin Press, pp. 117-143.

Shirai, T. (1992). *Personnel Management in Contemporary Japan* (2nd. ed.). Tokyo: Toyo Keizai (in Japanese).

Sullivan, J.J. and R.B. Peterson (1990). "The Japanese Lifetime Employment System: Whither it Goest?" In S.B. Prasad (ed.), *Advances in International Comparative Management*, Vol. 5. Greenwich, CT: JAI Press, pp. 169-194.

Turner, L. (1991). *Democracy At Work: Changing World Markets and the Future of Labor Unions.* Ithaca, NY: Cornell University Press.

Wakabayashi, M. and G. Graen (1989). "Human Resource Development of Japanese Managers: Leadership and Career Investment." In A. Nedd, G.R. Ferris and K.M. Rowland (eds.), *Research in Personnel and Human Resources Management*, Suppl. 1. Greenwich, CT: JAI Press, pp. 235-256.

Walton, R.B. (1985). "From Control to Commitment." *Harvard Business Review*, 63 (March-April), 76-84.

Yashiro, A. (1991). "Changes in the Structure of Intra-Company Promotion Systems." In Kazuo Kikuno and Takehisa Hirao (eds.), *New Visions of Employment Management*. Tokyo: Chuo Keizai, pp. 137-158 (in Japanese).

Yashiro, A. (1992). "The Organization and Function of Personnel Departments in Large Japanese Companies." *The Studies of the Japan Institute of Labour*, 4, pp. 13-24 (in Japanese).

Human Resource Management in New Zealand

Alan Geare and Ralph Stablein

Background

New Zealand is a nation state of 3.4 million people located on two main islands in the far South Pacific. Historically, human habitation is a relatively recent phenomenon. The indigenous Maori arrived in a series of migrations from Eastern Polynesia starting in the 10th century. The islands materialized on Western maps with the visit by Abel Tasman in 1642, who christened them in honour of his homeland. Western contact was established by Captain Cook in 1769, but for the next half century Western settlement was limited to whalers and missionaries. In 1840 the British entered into the Treaty of Waitangi with the Maori people. The Treaty recognised the traditional rights of Maori, and accepted them as citizens. Although in recent years there have been increasing claims from Maori that their traditional rights have been violated, it is indisputable that New Zealand Maori were treated considerably better, and afforded considerably more respect than were Australian Aborigines or Native Americans in Canada or the United States. Notwithstanding, with increasing migration from Britain, the Maori suffered population decline, land alienation and cultural malaise. In 1841, New Zealand became a British colony and was granted representative government in 1852. The second half of the 19th century saw rapidly increasing British migration, coupled with population decline for the Maori people largely as a result of epidemics. In this century, the Maori population has recovered and currently is growing at a faster rate than the *Pakeha* (i.e. non-Maori) population. Since World War II there has been significant migration from various Pacific Islands. After the Vietnam War, New Zealand accepted significant numbers of Kampuchean refugees.

Though formally independent from 1907, the country served as a loyal colony. Wool, meat and butter were exported to Britain in return for British manufactured goods and capital. In times of war, New Zealand, along with Australia and Canada, supplied quality troops for the British front lines. World War II and its aftermath changed New Zealand's position in the world. During the war, New Zealand had served as a staging area for the United States in its Pacific theatre operations. New Zealand began to look more to the United States and less to Britain.

Table 1:   Population Figures 1840-1986

	Predominantly European	Maori	Others (Predominantly Pacific Islander)	
1840	15,000	100–125,000	—	(Estimates)
1857–1858	59,413	56,043	—	(Census)
1896	697,196	42,113	3,905	(Census)
1961	2,220,452	167,086	27,446	(Census)
1986	2,877,421	295,659	134,004	(Census)

Source: *New Zealand Official Yearbook 1990*

Table 2:   Exports from New Zealand (in percentages)

	1951	1971	1991
Britain	57.6	34.4	6.6
Europe (other than Britain)	19.0	12.3	12.3
USA	11.7	17.3	13.3
Canada	3.5	2.9	1.5
Australia	2.1	8.7	18.9
Japan	1.6	9.2	16.8
Asia (other than Japan)	0.5	2.1	14.5
Oceania	0.0	1.1	3.5
Other	5.0	12.0	13.6

Economic

For a brief moment following WWII, New Zealand was wildly prosperous on the strength of its undamaged agricultural sector, enjoying arguably the highest standard of living in the world. However, post-war recovery and worldwide protectionist agricultural policies gradually eroded the terms of trade and New Zealand incomes.

As mentioned earlier, the Second World War caused New Zealand to start looking at countries other than Britain. Britain's entry into the EEC and its subsequent effect on New Zealand's trade finally made New Zealand realise it was no longer a "farm for Britain". Table 2 below graphically illustrates the move from dependence to independence.

Internal politics and massive overseas borrowing slowed recognition of, and response to, the decline. Finally, in 1984, a change in government provided the opportunity for reaction. Ironically, the new Labour government implemented a series of Thatcherite-Friedmanite experiments in taxation, deregulation and privatisation which placed New Zealand among the world's "freest" economies.

Table 3:   Working Age Population and Unemployment Rate by Ethnic Group
            (September quarter of each year)

	1991		1992		1993	
	('000)	(%)	('000)	(%)	('000)	(%)
European/'Pakeha'	2,125	8.2	2,177	7.8	2,176	6.7
NZ Maori	235	25.6	232	25.2	244	22.7
Pacific Islander	88	30.6	99	25.2	113	25.2
Other	110	14.1	78	13.8	80	12.0

Source: Household Labour Force Survey, September 1993 Quarter

To balance this economic policy, the new government declared independence from American nuclear hegemony by refusing to accept the "neither confirm nor deny" policy of the U.S. Navy, the only Western-bloc nation to do so.

The post-1984 economic reforms were truly radical. They involved a complete rupture with the fifty-year old programme of Keynesian macroeconomics and international protectionism favouring import substitution of manufactured goods. A number of commentators have described these changes in detail (Bollard and Buckle, 1987; Easton, 1989).

Today, New Zealand is in recession with over 10% unemployment and little prospect for rapid recovery. The economy continues to supply primary goods (meat, dairy, wool, timber) in return for imports of manufactured goods. The bulk of trade is divided between Japan, North America, the EEC and Australia in roughly equal proportions.

The structure of the New Zealand labour force is similar to that of other Western economies. Recent trends include increased labour force participation rates for women, and reduced manufacturing employment with proportionately more service sector employment. The impact of high unemployment is uneven. Minority groups (Maori and Pacific Islander) suffer unemployment rates that are more than three times higher than the European rate as shown in Table 3.

New Zealand's work force differs from the leading economies in several respects. There is more primary sector employment (10% of 1987 employment), more self-employment (17.8% of 1990 labour force), a lower retirement age (60) and a lower level of educational qualification in the workforce (27% of the 1991 labour force have no qualification).

Political

New Zealand has a one-house parliamentary system with the Queen as head of state (represented in New Zealand by the Governor General). Governance is very centralized. The central government has responsibility for a cradle-to-grave welfare system, including education, public health provision, police, etc. It raises revenues from a three-tiered income tax (maximum rate: 33.3%) and a value added tax of 12.5% on all goods and services. Local government has responsibility for the provision of local services and can raise revenue from rates (property tax). Various regional bodies have existed from time to time but these have limited mandates and powers.

A two-party system has evolved with regular attempts to establish a third party. The dominant party over the last 40 years has been the National Party, a conservative party with strong farmer and small business support. The National Party is currently the government. The opposition party is the Labour Party, which in the past had strong ties to the trade union movement. Labour was government from 1984-1990 and introduced reforms traditionally considered conservative. The ties with the union movement were severely strained, if not broken. Various populist parties (e.g., Social Credit, the New Zealand Party) in past elections have received significant proportions of the popular vote but few seats in the winner-takes-all system. A 1992 referendum on proportional voting systems revealed an overwhelming majority in favour of a mixed member proportional system. The 1993 General Election included a binding referendum which favoured a mixed member proportional system. The election also returned the National government, but with a paper thin majority.

HRM – Personnel Management and Industrial Relations

In recognition of reality in New Zealand – which clearly differentiates HRM/Personnel and Industrial Relations and affords industrial relations separate study, this chapter will consider the topics separately.

The HRM Setting in New Zealand

While the term "Human Resource Management" (HRM) is starting to enjoy more popular usage in New Zealand, it tends to be favoured by the more trendy academics and professionals, and rejected by the more traditional or conservative. The terms in more common usage are "Personnel Management" or "Personnel/Industrial Relations". There has never been agreement as to what is to be assumed by the term "Personnel Management". On occasion it is taken to mean *all* aspects of work relationship with employees – job design, job descriptions, selection, training, compensation, discipline, dismissals, collective bargaining, etc. – while at other times it is assumed to mean all the above aspects *except* those deemed to be "industrial relations". In New Zealand, industrial relations is usually accorded much higher status than personnel management. Consequently, industrial relations academics and practitioners tend to define "personnel management" as "personnel other than industrial relations", while personnel management academics and practitioners try to increase their status by subsuming industrial relations *into* personnel management. HRM is generally taken as being all embracing – personnel management together with industrial relations. Thus Boxall (1989) claims that HRM: "ranges from what some would call the 'soft' aspects of 'human resource development' to what others would call the 'hard' aspects of industrial relations" (p. 58).

The Industrial Relations Setting in New Zealand

Although historians report a number of incidents in the 1840s that can be taken as evidence of traditional "industrial relations", in general the shortage of labour, particularly skilled labour, resulted in good wages and conditions and little union activity. From the 1860s, however, conditions worsened and the New Zealand union movement really began. The real surge came later, and Roth claims that the number of unionists swelled from "an estimated 3,000 in 1889 to more than 40,000 ... late in 1890" (1978, p. 23). A central organisation, the "Maritime Council" was established.

At the same time, a general campaign started against the evils of "sweated labour", the atrocious working conditions, and low to zero wages, in factory employment. A series of sermons by a Dunedin minister backed by editorials in the local newspaper, the *Otago Daily Times*, eventually led to a Royal Commission being established in 1890. The Commission's report was strongly in praise of trade unions as a means of preventing exploitation. Late in 1890 occurred the so-called Maritime Strike which had spread from Australia. This proved disastrous for the established unions, which all suffered a major defeat. Although defeated industrially, unions had increasing political power with universal male franchise. The December, 1890 election was won by the Liberal Party, with a core of union-endorsed candidates. A series of labour laws was passed, but by far the most significant for industrial relations was the Industrial Conciliation and Arbitration Act 1894 (ICA Act 1894).

ICA legislation (and its numerous amendments and six re-enactments) remained in force until replaced in 1974, by the Industrial Relations Act 1973 (IR Act). However, as stated by a former Secretary of Labour, the IR Act offered "little more than the old pattern revamped" (Woods, 1974, p. 39). It was not until the *Labour Relations Act* 1987 (LR Act) that there was a significant redirection. The LR Act was the end of the "arbitration" era and signalled the start of a "collective bargaining" era. It gave support both to unions and the process of collective bargaining. The LR Act in turn was repealed by the *Employment Contracts Act* 1991 (EC Act), which introduced a third drastically different philosophy and industrial relations system. The EC Act basically is a *laissez-faire* Act, giving no support

to unions or collective bargaining. The result is that many significant features of
New Zealand industrial relations have been radically altered in the last few years.

The behaviour, beliefs and attitudes of participants in any industrial relations
systems are influenced not only by current laws and practices but also by the
past. The impact of the provisions of the Employment Contracts Act can only be
appreciated with some understanding of how it differs from past laws. The following discussion will briefly highlight notable issues in New Zealand industrial
relations, tracing changes from ICA legislation days to the present. For a more
detailed discussion of the ICA Acts, see Woods (1963), the IR Act see Seidman
(1974), and the LR Act see Geare (1988, 1989).

Sectors

The original ICA Act separated the private and public sectors, so that both operated in different systems. The ICA legislation applied only to the private sector.
In the public sector wages and conditions were set primarily by "relativity" arguments – comparisons ideally with similar groups in the private sector, otherwise
with others in the public sector – but also on recruitment and retention. In periods of inflation, this dual system with cross-comparisons would always fuel
any inflationary fires. Since the Great Depression the public sector has also been
used as a way both of relieving unemployment, through large scale public works
schemes, and concealing unemployment through overmanning in such organisations as railways and the Post Office. The State Sector Act in 1988 brought the
two sectors together by making the provisions of the LR Act 1987 applicable to
the public sector as well as the private.

Unions

The original ICA Act 1894 was partially entitled "an act to encourage the formation of unions", and this indeed reflected the initial attitude of the legislation.
Unions could register under the Act, and having done so were protected from
competition, as they were deemed the only organisation with the right to represent those workers. The initial number of workers required for a union to register
was small (7-15 minimum) and so New Zealand had a number of very small
unions. The monopoly power *allowed* small unions to exist – but the law also
caused the numbers to be great as it was not until 1936 that a union could cover
more than one of the eight "industrial districts" into which New Zealand had been
divided.

Until 1964, a Court ruling from 1917 restricted the activities of unions to the
negotiation of wages and terms of employment. When the restriction was lifted
in 1964, unions had been conditioned to this limited role, and union members

Table 4:   Number and Size of Unions 1985/1986 for Private and (State)

Size	Number		% Total		Workers Represented		% Total	
<1,000	136	(8)	62.4	(38.1)	37,722	(3,082)	11.4	(1.6)
1,000+	82	(13)	37.6	(61.9)	452,041	(185,961)	88.6	(98.4)

Source: Department of Labour Report, 1987, Public Service Association Journal,
v.72(3), 1985

had been conditioned to paying relatively low subscriptions (up to one percent of wages, but usually around half a percent).

In 1936, if there was a registered union in the worker's industrial district, covering his or her trade or occupation, then membership was compulsory by law. While this had a negligible effect on strong unions, it had a tremendous effect on weak unions with some having increases of 300-400% from 1935-1937. The overall increase in union membership was 188% (Geare, 1988, p.107). In 1961 the law was altered, but not the effect. The new law allowed the equivalent of a post-entry closed shop if there was agreement between union and employers or a majority vote in favour by the workers. However, agreement was always reached. Although the National (Conservative) Party always opposed compulsory unionism as part of their ideology, they did nothing significant while employers were clearly not interested in voluntary unionism by law. After steadily increasing unemployment since 1977, some employers, but more particularly the central body, the Employers' Federation, and the Business Round Table (CEOs of the largest organisations) called for voluntary unionism by law. This was introduced briefly in 1984-1985, then reintroduced by the EC Act 1991.

When combined with scattered communities and difficulties in communication, protection of registered unions and compulsory unionism meant that New Zealand had a large number of unions, some very small, and also a much higher percentage of workers in unions. Notwithstanding the *theoretical* compulsory unionism (if a union existed), some workers will always slip the net. It has been estimated (Geare, 1988) that in 1981, 63.7% of wage and salary earners were in unions. Of the remaining 370,000 some were exempt (because of salary level), some were in non-unionised areas (agriculture) but around 100,000 had avoided joining up.

Concern was frequently expressed over the large number and small size of unions. The LR Act 1987 required unions to have a minimum membership of 1,000 to remain registered. The SS Act 1988 made this a requirement as well for state unions. However, Table 4 shows that although at the time there was a significant percentage of small unions they only represented a very small percentage of *workers*.

By 1990, there were only 103 private and state unions combined. Presumably all had 1,000+ members.

The EC Act 1991 has radically affected unions. The Act in fact pretends "unions" no longer exist and refers only to "employee organisations". There is no longer any protection through registration and New Zealand may now enjoy the benefits and suffer the costs of union infighting for membership. The law requires voluntary membership regardless of the wishes of the employers and the majority of employees. Any closed-shop (pre- or post-entry) arrangement is illegal.

The outcome for the union movement and union structure will not be apparent for some time. The objective of the Business Round Table and the Employers' Federation in pushing for this Act seems to have been to create company unions, or possibly to destroy unions altogether. The strong unions, however, will in all probability *gain* some strength and will certainly not all disappear. It is also possible under this legislation for there to be a myriad of small, company and indeed part-company, unions. Whether new company unions will include workers from traditionally weak unions (for example, cleaners, clerical workers) remains to be seen. It is certainly apparent that in the meantime those weaker unions have been further disadvantaged by the new legislation.

Interest Dispute Settlement

An outstanding feature of industrial relations in New Zealand (and Australia) has been the acceptance of interest dispute arbitration in the private sector. While arbitration has been widely accepted for rights disputes in other Western countries, it is usually only in the *public sector* that arbitration has been acceptable to settle interest disputes.

Arbitration was seen by the supporters of the ICA Act 1894 as a better alternative than strikes. However, the intention was always for settlement to be by negotiation, if possible. "Conciliation" in the New Zealand setting differs from the American practice, as it was in effect *formalised* collective bargaining. The conciliator acted as chairman for the collective bargaining process and could help the parties reach a settlement in any way desired, but was not accepted (or allowed) to arbitrate. The conciliator process was used, in particular, for area or national negotiations covering a number of employers. Alternatively, parties could negotiate a settlement totally outside the system.

In practice, arbitration was not used very frequently. Over the last ten years of the ICA legislation (1965-1974) only 4.2 percent of disputes of interest went to arbitration, and approximately the same percentage went to arbitration from 1975-1987 (Geare, 1988). The vast percentage of disputes were settled by bargaining, independently of the system, or in a formalised setting (conciliation). On the few occasions a dispute did go to arbitration, usually only one or two (out of possibly 50) *items* needed arbitration. The other 48 to 49 would have been settled. However, this can understate the influence of arbitration. The fact that an arbitral body (known variously over time as Court of Arbitration, Industrial Commission,

Arbitration Court, Arbitration Commission) had the power to make a settlement will clearly influence negotiators. The anticipated "probable" decision of the arbitral body would be a bottom line.

From 1894-1984 interest arbitration (except for a brief period in the 1930s) was available if disputes would not otherwise be settled. From 1984-1991 arbitration could still be provided by the Arbitration Commission but only with the consent of *both* parties. This enabled the stronger party to refuse to go to arbitration, ensuring non-settlement or the *status quo*. The EC Act 1991, abolished the arbitral body and made no statutory provision for interest-arbitration at all (except for the police). Thus, what has been probably *the* significant peculiarity of the industrial relations system came to an end in May, 1991.

Union-Management Agreements

Prior to the recent EC Act 1991, there were two main types of union-management agreements. The first, similar to agreements in the United States or Canada, was called over the years an "industrial agreement" and later a "collective agreement" and relates to a single employer and a union. The agreement was reached by ordinary collective bargaining. The second type was more peculiar to New Zealand and was termed an "award". This occasionally was the result of arbitration, but more usually was reached by conciliation (formalised collective bargaining). What made "awards" significant was the provision in the legislation known as the "blanket clause". The significance of this was that the award coverage could be extended to any employer in that industry or occupation working in that industrial district (or districts). The New Zealand Plumbers Award, for example, would cover those employers who participated in its negotiation – *plus* every other plumbing firm in the country who had not negotiated an independent agreement. This system had advantages for workers, unions and employers (a minimum level of conditions, an efficient method of settlement without a multitude of negotiations, and an approximate knowledge of competitors' labour costs) but was subject to criticism. The major criticism was that the award system failed to take into account the particular need of an individual employer. This criticism failed to acknowledge that employers always had flexibility to negotiate or provide *better* conditions than the award or they could, with support of the union, negotiate independently. The criticism also failed to acknowledge that many small- to medium-sized employers were quite satisfied with the award system (McAndrew and Hursthouse, 1990). Notwithstanding, the EC Act 1991, while not making awards illegal, has removed all provisions which in the past encouraged their negotiation.

Table 5: Comparison of Working Days Lost per 1,000 Wage and Salary Earners – for
Five Countries

Years	N.Z.	Britain	Australia	Canada	USA
(a) Average 1947–51	541	98	571	462	883
(b) Average 1952–59	43	175	309	466	689
(c) Average 1960–68	90	143	199	425	378
(d) Average 1976–85	415	464	462	674	268
(e) Excluded	public sector	—	communications sector	—	strikes with fewer than 1,000 workers

Source: Geare (1988, p. 274)

Rights Dispute

While the New Zealand system has recognised rights-type disputes, these have
only been explicitly referred to in the legislation since 1973 and personal
grievances only since 1970. With some modifications the principles have been
maintained right through the IR Act 1973, the LR Act 1987 and the current EC
Act 1991.

Procedures are available to settle both rights disputes (over the interpretation
application or operation of the document – award, agreement or currently "employment contract") and personal grievances. If the original parties cannot settle,
the matter goes before the Employment Tribunal (previously a committee) where
the Tribunal member may arbitrate. On appeal the matter can go to the Employment Court. Strikes have, in the past and currently, been illegal over rights disputes
and personal grievances.

Strikes

In theory, the system provided by the ICA Acts did away with the need for strikes,
and indeed New Zealand was "strike free" from 1894 to 1906. This encouraged
extravagant claims to be made about the success of the system. Certainly this
system provided an alternative to strikes – but a more significant reason for the
lack of strikes were the weakened condition of the established, better organised
unions and the underdeveloped state of the new unions. Thus from 1906 to the
present day, strike incidence – as elsewhere – has had peaks and troughs. This is
illustrated in Table 5, for the post-war period.

Over this century, strike prone industries have tended to be those identified
nearly forty years ago by Clark Kerr and Abraham Siegel (1954) – meat freezing,
coal mining, seamen, waterside workers.

Up until 1987, strikes in most situations were explicitly illegal and subject to penalty, and in addition unions could be deregistered and have their assets frozen for striking, or even threatening to strike. However, the deregistration penalty was only rarely imposed. "Strikes", under New Zealand legislation, covers most forms of group action – not only work stoppages, but also "go-slows", work to rule, refusal to work normal overtime, and refusal to work at normal bonus incentive rates.

From 1987, strikes have been made explicitly lawful and not subject to penalty or court action by employers in specific circumstances. The LR Act 1987 allowed strikes over the negotiation of an interest dispute in the period up to 60 days before expiry of the previous agreement. The EC Act 1991 now allows strikes – but only in relation to the negotiation of a collective employment contract after the expiry of the previous document. Strikes over rights disputes are illegal.

Managerial Prerogatives

The issue of managerial prerogatives has been dealt with over this century in a somewhat oblique fashion. The legislation up until the LR Act 1987 only allowed unions to negotiate what were deemed "industrial matters". These were "matters relating to work done or to be done by workers ... and the rights, privileges and duties of employers, workers ... and union officials".

The interpretation of "industrial matters" both in New Zealand and in Australia varied over the years depending on the particular judges looking at issues. While some interpreted the definition in a broad fashion, many took a very narrow definition ruling, for example, at various times that the following were *not* "industrial matters" (and hence could not form part of any union management agreement):

(a) hours worked by the employer or members of the employer's family after normal working hours (regardless of the impact this had on the work available for employees),
(b) pensions,
(c) the introduction of new technology,
(d) the removal of employer initiated perks (low interest loans for bank workers) (see Geare, 1988, pp. 131-135).

From 1987, however, all issues may now be negotiated and form part of the employment contract. Ironically, the economic climate has meant that although workers and union are now legally able to negotiate over a wide spectrum, their bargaining power is now so weak with high unemployment that simply preserving the status quo is to many work groups an impossible target.

The Ideology of the Legislation

There have been significant ideological shifts in the principal legislation. The original ICA Act 1894 was fundamentally paternalistic and supportive of unions. During the period to 1987, the legislation became increasingly unitarist in sentiment, with strikes being increasingly prohibited and managerial prerogatives supported. In 1987, however, there was a radical swing in underlying ideology to pluralism, with strikes becoming legal and managerial prerogatives removed.[1]

The current legislation governing New Zealand industrial relations is the Employment Contracts Act 1991. This piece of legislation has radically redefined the system around completely voluntary contracts between an employer and an employee or group of employees. The intent of the legislation is to encourage establishment-level contracts with company unions or no unions at all (Geare, 1991).

Specifically the Act:

(a) removes all legislatively imposed rights and powers from unions,
(b) abolishes the concept of state provided arbitration for interest-type disputes,
(c) places individual bargaining and individual employment contracts on an equal basis to collective bargaining and collective contracts.

The Employment Contracts Act 1991 purports to be neutral, providing a level playing field. This it does, and on the surface it can be described as "neutral" or "laissez-faire". "Neutral" legislation is arguably fair when the parties have approximately equal bargain ing power. When the bargaining power is clearly not equal – as between unskilled, immigrant female cleaners and multinational employing companies – the effect of changing legislation from that which favours workers and unions to that which is neutral is in reality to allow employer power to dominate and determine to a great extent wages and conditions.

IR in the Near Future

Over the next few years, there will almost certainly be a widening gap between the "haves" and the "have-littles" in the workforce and between the "have-littles" and the unemployed. While some employers may use their increased power to introduce desirable improvements in efficiency, many will take the easier option of forcing down labour costs with a lack of concern for long term workforce productivity. Reduction in penal rates for overtime and weekend work is reasonably common. Reduction in basic wages is occurring not infrequently.

Unions will be variously affected. Those unions currently concerned with the low paid will be most affected. This will involve a disproportionate number of young, women and Polynesians. As Brosnan and Wilkinson (1989) point out in a case study of the low paid, the current strength of the cleaners' unions "owes much to the national award system and compulsory unionism" (p. 86). Under the EC Act 1991 the two foundations have disappeared. Stronger unions, such as the meat workers or electricians, have already been significantly affected by the economy over the last ten years (and last five in particular) and the legislative changes resulting from the Act may have relatively little impact.

The impact on employers will again be varied. Many small- to medium-sized employers will just be irritated and inconvenienced. Many were happy with the national award system (McAndrew and Hursthouse, 1990) and will try to get something similar with as little pain as possible. For many it will be an additional cost – paying someone to sign up a document for which they will have been no more involved than under the award system. A few may take the opportunity to negotiate genuine and innovative productivity deals. A proportion will take the opportunity to, if not "exploit" their workers, at least demand a lot more from them in exchange for the same or for less in return.

The question remains whether that nebulous concept "New Zealand as a whole" will benefit or not. Again, the effect will not be uniform. This writer does not believe that benefits will be significant. Innovative productivity deals could have been and were negotiated under the Labour Relations Act or its predecessors. Employers that really wanted to negotiate such agreements were able to achieve such deals. Hence there is little likelihood of a boom in growth. New Zealand will become a much less congenial society, even for those fortunate enough not to be in the bottom segment of the dual labour market. As history has shown, those who can really profit from exploitation are very satisfied and happy for it to continue. Many other sections of society, even if not directly exploited, will probably find life becoming less congenial.

In a recent monograph, Wright (1991, p. 1) claims that in Australia "the role of the personnel manager remains largely unexamined". Unfortunately, this is largely true for New Zealand, with the exception of the survey conducted in 1958, 1968, 1978 and 1989 discussed later in this chapter. However, very little academic research has been done on *any* aspects of personnel management (other than industrial relations). Thompson and Sibbald's (1990) bibliography of over 1,100 entries reveals that only a very tiny percentage of the publications are in academic journals. Likewise, only a tiny percentage are on aspects of *New Zealand* personnel management as opposed to general articles on, for example, "selection" published in a New Zealand professional journal.

The institutional setting within which HRM operates in New Zealand is dominated by the industrial relations scene. Thus we have devoted a considerable portion of the chapter to it. In addition, various governments over time have had an influence on HRM practice through specific legislation. The legislation has provided minimum conditions of work through, for example: Minimum Wage Act 1983 and Holidays Act 1981. It has attempted to reduce discrimination through: Smoke-free Environment Act 1990, Health and Safety in Employment

Act 1992, Parental Leave and Employment Protection Act 1987, Equal Pay Act 1972, Human Rights Commission Act 1977 and Race Relations Act 1971.

Within the public sector, HRM has been given a significant boost by the State Sector Act 1988 which required employers to be demonstrably "good" employers. This was interpreted, and reinforced, by requirements for professionalism in personnel matters. Thus, for example, formal performance appraisal has been encouraged along with equal employment opportunity policies.

HRM in New Zealand as a whole could see an upsurge in significance following the passing of the Employment Contracts Act 1991, as it creates an environment where organisations can "keep out" unions, by emulating such organisations as IBM, which provide an environment where unions are not seen as necessary. However, the state of the economy is such that some organisations may rely on the fear of unemployment rather than the provision of first class HRM in order to achieve their goals.

The Present State of New Zealand HRM

The description of the current state of New Zealand HRM in this chapter is primarily based on a 1990 survey of all New Zealand establishments with more than 100 employees. There was a response rate of 39% of the 1,100 questionnaires posted. Twenty-nine questionnaires were from establishments with less than 100 employees and another 29 respondents did not complete the questionnaire, yielding a total of 369 usable responses from establishments. Additional data regarding HRM managers is available from a 1987 survey (Gilbertson, Fogelberg and Boswell, 1987) conducted for the New Zealand Institute of Personnel Management. This 1987 survey first identified New Zealand private organisations employing more than 100 employees which employed personnel staff. Of the 777 organisations identified as having more than 100 employees, 649 responded, with 230 (35%) claiming to have personnel staff. The survey achieved a 74.5% response rate from the 781 personnel staff working at the 230 New Zealand private organisations.

Historical data is provided by three earlier surveys of New Zealand personnel practices in 1958 (Personnel Group, 1958), 1968 (Personnel Management Association, 1968), and 1978 (New Zealand Institute of Personnel Management [NZIPM], 1979). The 1958 survey achieved a response rate of 35% of the 150 questionnaires distributed with 39 usable responses. The sampling frame was all private sector firms with more than 150 employees. The 1968 survey achieved a 54% response rate of the 372 questionnaires with 195 usable responses. The sampling frame was identical to 1958. The 1978 survey achieved a 68.5% response rate of the 622 questionnaires sent with 348 usable responses. The sampling frame was expanded to include both private and public sector employers believed to have more than 150 employees.

All surveys asked the respondents to identify which activities (from a list) were performed by the HRM department. Each survey expanded the number of activities on the list. The 1958 and 1968 surveys asked whether these same activities were performed by another department. In the results reported, no distinction was made between single or joint departmental responsibility for the performance of the activity. In the 1978 and 1990 surveys respondents were asked to distinguish for each activity whether HRM had sole responsibility, another department had sole responsibility, there was joint departmental responsibility, or the activity was not performed.

Unfortunately, the surveys do not provide detailed data on any of the activities. Thus, for example, we know that a firm claims to have job descriptions, but we do not know if these are "good" ones. We do not know about the state of practice in the ten to twelve year gaps between snapshots. However, the 1978 survey explicitly considered the volatility of practice issue. Very few organisations reported abandoning a practice once it was adopted (NZIPM, 1979, p. 35).

We discuss the current state of New Zealand HRM under three broad headings: HRM practices, the HRM manager and the HRM profession.

HRM Practices

Our description of current HRM practice in New Zealand is based on a number of scales constructed from the 1990 survey responses. Using cluster analyses, factor analyses and reliability analyses, the activities have been grouped into ten categories: Employment; Salary Administration; Management Development, Health and Safety; Welfare; Productivity and Participation; Incentive Programmes; External Relations; EEO; and Planning and Research. EEO activities are further split into Women's Issues and Bi-/Multi-culturalism subgroups. Appendix 1 lists the activities which are represented on each scale. Table 6 provides the number of specific activities that constitute each scale, and Cronbach's alpha for each scale. The fifteen-page survey was not completely comprehensive in its coverage of all possible HRM activities. In particular, few items related to labour relations were included due to the impending changes in New Zealand's industrial relations legislation.

The "Mean % performed" column of Table 6 reports the percentage of respondents whose organisation perform the specific HRM activity, averaged over all the activities of that type. The next three columns describe the distribution of responsibility for each activity type across the various departments of the organisation. The three columns taken together add to 100%. In interpreting the distribution of performance percentages, keep in mind that 15% of the responding establishments did not have a fulltime HR staff member. Thus 85% is the highest possible percentage of performance by the HR department alone.

Table 6: HRM Activities

Class of Activity*	No. of Activities	Alpha	Mean % Performed	Where activity was performed, the performance was responsibility of:		
				HR only	Joint HR & others	Other than HR
Employment	27	0.71	89	24	45	31
Salary Administration	12	0.78	90	43	32	25
Management Development	6	0.75	65	34	44	22
Health and Safety	18	0.78	68	31	34	35
Welfare	14	0.69	61	33	30	37
Productivity and Participation	8	0.79	48	12	58	30
Incentive Programmes	9	0.72	34	28	45	27
External Relations	5	0.66	71	42	27	1
EEO	13	0.80	65	44	40	16
Women's Issues	11	0.74	68	43	40	17
Bi-/Multi-culturalism	3	0.75	57	52	36	12
Planning and Research	15	0.85	88	41	43	16

* The full range of activities for each class is given in Appendix 1

Table 7 provides a breakout of HRM activity performance by industrial group. The industrial categories follow the New Zealand Standard Industrial Classification. Sample sizes are too small to report the results for Division 1 (agriculture, hunting, forestry and fishing), Division 2 (mining and quarrying), Division 4 (electricity, gas and water) and Division 5 (construction). A further 5 respondents were classified as multi-industry. In total, 20 respondents are not represented in Table 7.

Major differences in HRM practice within the Division 9 (community, social and personal services) require separate reporting for four relatively homogeneous groups. Three of these groupings follow the NZSIC system: Group 9101 (central government administration and defense), Group 9102 (local government administration), and group 933 (medical, dental, other health and veterinary services). Finally, the remaining group is a combination of establishments in the 93 (social

Table 7: HRM Activities by Industry (Mean % Performed)

	Total	Manufacture	Wholesale	Transport	Financial	Central Administration	Local Administration	Health	Other Services
Number	(370)	(118)	(36)	(38)	(44)	(37)	(17)	(25)	(35)
Employment	89	89	88	92	92	89	86	91	81
Salary administration	89	92	93	92	90	83	96	87	76
Management development	64	62	73	68	75	64	62	67	52
Health and safety	68	73	64	71	61	67	66	75	58
Welfare	60	66	56	63	57	66	53	71	48
Incentive programmes	33	37	42	35	44	26	25	20	18
External relations	71	77	74	78	74	49	78	62	53
EEO	64	53	49	63	68	86	73	91	73
Women's issues	66	57	53	67	72	83	75	90	73
Bi-/Multi-culturalism	56	42	35	53	54	97	69	96	73
Planning and Research	87	86	90	90	92	90	87	88	80

and related community services) and the 94 (recreational and cultural services) groups.

In the following sections the findings for each activity type will be discussed briefly under the appropriate heading. In addition, historical comparisons for individual activities will be highlighted when appropriate. Additional commentary from other sources and the open-ended comments of the 1990 respondents will be offered, as well.

Employment

Employment is the largest class of activity included in the survey. Nearly all large New Zealand organisations perform the standard HRM employment activities.

The most important shift in employment activity for New Zealand HRM has been the reduction in employment ("redundancies") in many organisations due to recessionary pressures, restructuring through merger and acquisition in the 1980s and the state's corporatisation and privatisation programs. These reductions have been accomplished primarily by reverse seniority redundancies and self-selection, motivated by various redundancy incentives. Many respondents commented on the importance of un-employment as opposed to employment in dominating their recent HRM activity.

Industrial variation in employment practices is limited. Only the "other services" group stands out as significantly lower than the remaining industrial groups.

Salary Administration

Salary administration activities are also widely practised by responding organisations. Responsibility for these activities are more centralized in the HR department than the employment activities.

The local government division reports the performance of the highest number of wage and salary administration activities. The central government and other services establishments report the lowest level. Note the importance of disaggregating the service sector to get a more accurate picture of HRM activity. The remaining industrial groupings are very similar in this area.

Management Training and Development

New Zealand organisations appear to take a consistent view of management development as opposed to the training of other employees. Only the management-oriented activities clustered together in the 1990 survey. The mean performance of management development activities, 65%, appears to be rather low in large

New Zealand organisations. New Zealand managers have traditionally learned on the job and come up through the ranks. There is a growing awareness of the utility of university education for managerial positions, reflected in the qualifications of younger cohorts (Gilbertson, Fogelberg and Boswell, 1987). The number of respondent organisations (54%) with management trainee programmes for university graduates is pleasantly surprising in this respect.

In general, New Zealand organisations are not big spenders when it comes to investing in human resources. For example, a 1989 survey by the Employers Federation set the national average spent on in-house training at 2.16% (*National Business Review*, 1991). A national decline in formal apprentice and cadet programmes has been recognized as a national problem. For the large New Zealand firms represented in the 1990 survey 59% reported involvement in apprentice training as opposed to 74% in 1978. The government has passed new legislation, the Industry Training Act 1992, to partially fund and stimulate training. The act creates industry-based training organisations which will act as the sole purchaser of apprentice training for the industry. To date, fourteen industrial training organisations have been recognized. Early developments point to a rationalisation and centralisation of training provision. Thus while industrial relations legislation heavily emphasises the individual workplace, the industrial training legislation is reverting to an industry focus.

Management development is another area of HRM practice that reveals the dangers in broad generalisations about the services sector. Note that the highest (business/finance) and lowest performers (other services) of management development activities are service providers.

Health and Safety

The level of organisational involvement in health and safety matters, an average of 68% of large New Zealand organisations, may surprise overseas readers. In New Zealand, the state plays a major role in the health and safety area. The primary vehicle of state intervention is the Accident Compensation Corporation, which administers and funds all payments for accidental injury. Both organisations and employees are levied. There is industrial variation in levies according to risk and "safety incentive bonuses", which have just been introduced for the first time. There is as yet no indication if the bonuses are sufficient to prompt a change in behaviour in those organisations who were not safety conscious in the first place. While there is some legislation and regulation of workplace conditions, the standards and enforcement levels are minimal relative to OSHA activities in the United States.

Looking at the historical data, one sees increased health and safety activity relative to 1978 and earlier. However, the responsibility for these activities has seen a significant shift from sole HR department responsibility to a responsibility shared with other units.

As one might expect, health services and manufacturing establishments report more activity in the health and safety area than service establishments (business/finance sector and other services). Within the manufacturing division, group 32 (textile, apparel and leathergoods) reported significantly fewer health and safety activities.

Since the 1990 survey, two significant pieces of workplace health legislation have been passed. First, the Smoke-free Environment Act 1990 became law. The act requires employers to develop, implement, and maintain a policy, in consultation with employees, that provides a smoke-free workplace for all who desire one. Second, on April 1, 1993 the Health and Safety in Employment Act 1992 came into force. This Act replaces the Factories and Commercial Premises Act 1983. The new act requires employers to practice health and safety management, and provides for the approval of codes of practice. The new act will increase the level of monitoring and reporting in the health and safety area, but it is too soon to tell if improved outcomes will result.

Welfare

New Zealanders are proud to have led the world with the first welfare state. This has reduced the need for New Zealand organisations to provide welfare benefits such as insurance and pensions. However, a degree of paternalism expressed in welfare activities has existed in the workplace in line with the British influence on New Zealand manage ment. Since 1984, there has been a shift to libertarian social ideology and an erosion of the welfare state (Roper and Rudd, 1993; Shannon, 1991; Jesson, Ryan and Spoonley, 1988). Compared to 1978, the 1990 data show reductions in welfare activities, reflecting both hard economic times and a shift to New Right social ideology. The only services which have increased are the provision of child care facilities, industrial chaplaincy, and retirement preparation. For those activities which are performed there is evidence of a shift away from sole HR responsibility toward joint responsibility for the services.

There is industrial variation in the provision of welfare services. Health services, central government, manufacturing and transport, storage and communication establishments report significantly more welfare activities than those establishments in the other services group.

Productivity and Participation, and Incentive Programmes

Despite occasional government promotion, employee participation initiatives have never caught on in New Zealand (Boxall, Rudman and Taylor, 1986). Perhaps this reflects paternalism in the workplace. HRM departments have played a minimal role in these activities. Recent economic conditions and the changes in the industrial relations climate appear to have resulted in more employer efforts on cutting labour costs (e.g., removal of penal rates) than on pioneering productivity-enhancing innovations. The Department of Labour reported in November, 1992, that 40% of all enterprises surveyed had reduced or abolished weekend pay rates and overtime. There is less participation/productivity activity reported in the 1990 survey than in the 1978 data. There have been a few well-publicised, innovative workplace agreements at Fortex, Nissan, Comalco and Dominion Breweries. In the public sector, there is a substantial amount of rhetoric, but little action devoted to productivity-based wage agreements. Another innovative scheme gaining quite a bit of attention today is Total Quality Management (TQM). In 1990, there was no item directly assessing TQM, but 39% of the responding establishments reported quality circle activity. Productivity and participation is the only activity cluster for which there are no reliable differences between industries.

A modest average of 34% of establishments report the use of various incentive and merit programs. This figure actually represents a decline from the 1978 survey data. This would seem to go against the overseas popularity of pay-for-performance. It likely reflects the difficult economic climate and labour market conditions. The business/finance and wholesale/retail sectors report the greatest use of incentives. Government, health and other services report the least usage.

External Relations

The HRM department often plays a major external relations role in New Zealand organisations. The 1990 survey reveals that the HR department is the major functional area to take on external relations activities for the organisation, such as representing the organisation or employer associations. However, HR departments are less likely to represent the organisation than in the past. Here, too, joint responsibility is on the increase. Central government and, to a smaller extent, health services and other services report less external relations activity than establishments in other industrial groups.

EEO, Women's Issues, and Bi-/Multi-culturalism

Equal opportunity in employment is a relatively recent consideration in New Zealand. Prior to the 1990 survey, questions on activities related to EEO have not been included in the surveys administered by HR professionals. Presumably, these issues were not even on the agenda of the specialist HR profession. Table 7 indicates that most establishments now recognize their significance. In the open-ended comments, no one listed these concerns as a declining area of HRM activity.

However, only 11 establishments recorded EEO as a major growth area. It would appear that within the organisation, the HR function is taking a leading role here. Overall, it would be fair to conclude that these concerns are now on the agenda for NZ HRM but are considered less prominent than in other Western economies.

Within the public sector, EEO issues have a high level of salience. The State Sector Act 1988 requires that the Chief Executive of a Department "operate a personnel policy that complies with the principle of being a good employer" (section 56). This section goes on to define a good employer as one who operates a policy requiring:

(a) good and safe working conditions;
(b) an equal employment opportunities programme;
(c) the impartial selection of suitably qualified persons for appointment;
(d) recognition of

(i)   the aims and aspirations of the Maori people;
(ii)   the employment requirements of the Maori people;
(iii) the need for greater involvement of the Maori people in the Public Service;

(e) opportunities for the enhancement of the abilities of individual employees;
(f) recognition of the aims and aspirations, and the cultural differences, of ethnic or minority groups;
(g) recognition of the employment requirements of women; and
(h) recognition of the employment requirements of persons with disabilities.

This has prompted a number of actions which have been variously considered: "tokenism", "a step in the right direction", "hypocrisy", "a waste of money", "a sincere effort to redress wrongs". There is now widespread use of the Maori title for departments, ("Te Tari Taake" for Department of Inland Revenue); job advertisements are sometimes printed in both English and Maori, and EEO policies and EEO officers are legion.

Overt discrimination on the basis of race (or sex) has actually been illegal for a number of years under the Race Relations Act 1971, the Human Rights Commission Act 1977, the Equal Pay Act 1972, and also industrial relations legislation – the Labour Relations Act 1987 and currently the Employment Contracts Act 1991. Moreover, New Zealand has declared itself a bicultural society. The two cultures are Maori and "pakeha". Pakeha refers to the Western, mainly British, cultural heritage.

A resurgence of Maori pride and population and government commitment has increased the salience of biculturalism in the workplace. It is not primarily an issue of language as virtually all Maori are English speakers. The issue is one of respecting, and developing ways to include, Maori cultural practices in the organisation. References to multiculturalism are common, as well. Multiculturalism usually refers to the cultures of the various Pacific Islander immigrant groups and more recent Asian immigrants – Cambodian refugees, and the Chinese from Hong Kong.

Nevertheless, there is greater industrial variation in EEO activity than in any other HRM area surveyed in 1990. As one would expect from the review of current legislation above, the health sector and central government are the most heavily involved in EEO activities. Wholesale/retail and manufacturing establishments reported the least performance of these activities. Comparing the women's and bi-/multi-culturalism subsets of the EEO items reveals two findings. First, the level of performance of women-related activities is higher. Second, the difference between the public sector and the private sector is even more extreme with respect to bi-/multicultural activities.

Planning and Research

Open-ended comments on the 1990 survey indicated that this was a major area of concern and activity for the HR department. The quantitative data reported in Table 4 reveal the same message. Compared to earlier surveys, two points are clear: first, there has been an increase in policy and planning related activities, second, there has been a shift from HR departmental policy making toward shared policy responsibility with others in the organisation.

The public sector has experienced a tremendous restructuring. Some portions have been privatised. Other units have been corporatised. The remaining have been mandated to perform as "good employers" by the State Sector Act 1988. In the private sector a wave of mergers and acquisitions and the economic climate have motivated substantial restructuring, as well. Deregulation has had significant effects in the transport and finance sectors. All in all, the entire economy has been under pressure to change, resulting in an almost uniformly high level of HRM planning activities. While there is a marginally significant difference between industrial groups, no one sector stands out.

This cluster of activity includes the record-keeping HRM tasks. Restructuring has created a need for establishing, coordinating and integrating record-keeping systems. In doing this, utilisation of new technology has been a factor that a number of respondents mentioned in open-ended comments.

HR Managers

The 'most probable' profile of the HR manager in New Zealand is that the manager is a married man in his 40s, a New Zealander of British descent. He is a non-graduate but has had a fair amount of HRM training. Although he has had over 10 years experience in management, only around five years have been in the HR department. His job title is 'Personnel Manager', and he is on a salary in excess of

$NZ50,000. The description of course fails to acknowledge the *range* of profiles which is illustrated by Table 8, or changes over time.

Probably the most notable differences between the ranges shown in Table 8 and the "most probable" profile are the fact that while the majority of HR managers are non-graduates, there are now a significant proportion of graduates (37%) and likewise there are also a significant proportion of women (31%). In both cases the proportions are significantly different to those reported by Gilbertson, Fogelberg and Boswell in 1987. In their survey graduates comprised only 17% of the sample and women only 19%.

HRM Profession

Compared to the major Western economies, New Zealand has only recently recognized HRM as a distinct body of professional knowledge and practice. Prior to World War II there was little evidence of any attention to HRM as a functional area of organisational management, other than in industrial relations (and wage settlement in particular). In this area, Employers' Associations have a long history. Rudman (1974) reported that the inaugural meetings of the Otago and Canterbury Associations took place in 1890 with Auckland and Wellington following on soon after. Hare (1946) makes two passing references to the state of HRM management in his comprehensive, 400-page treatise on New Zealand industrial relations. The personnel movement began through the welfare side with the appointment of industrial nurses. By 1946 Hare had observed "a growing movement to employ industrial nurses... There are now approximately 38 industrial nurses in New Zealand..." (p. 160). However, personnel officers were still extremely scarce. Hare noted: "the absence of trained personnel officers and the lack of differentiation of function in the management of business" (p.155). He went on to give the impression that he was acquainted with every personnel practitioner in the country:

a few of the largest firms are beginning to employ male personnel officers... not more than two or three examples of this policy can be found and in each case the person appointed has usually had no formal training in personnel management (p. 161).

Indeed, there was no opportunity to obtain HRM training in New Zealand. Historically, the university curriculum in business was devoted to the training of professional accountants. The earliest formal training in HRM was offered at relatively low status polytechnic institutions in the 1960s. University training lagged. At the University of Otago, for example, substantial HRM content entered the curriculum in the late 1970s.

The post-war years exhibit a growing recognition of the profession. One evidence of this is increased resource allocation within organisations for personnel with specific HRM responsibility. In 1958, the first survey of New Zealand per-

Table 8:   Profile of HR Managers

	%		%
1.Title		7. Ethnic Origin	
Personnel	72	N.Z. (British descent)	72
HRM	37	N.Z. (Maori descent)	3
Industrial Relations	28	N.Z. (Other)	11
Training	46	British	11
		Other	3
2. Sex		8. Salary	
Male	69	$ 20,000 < $ 40,000	18
Female	31	$ 40,000 < $ 60,000	48
		$ 60,000 < $ 80,000	28
		$ 80,000 < $ 100,000	3
		$ 100,000 +	3
3. Age		9.Benefits	
25 < 30	9	None	56
30 < 40	32	< $ 5,000	27
40 < 50	42	5,000 < 10,000	8
50 < 60	16	10,000 < 20,000	6
		20,000 < 30,000	3
4. Marital Status		10. Years in Management	
Single	13	< 1 year	4
Married	78	1 < 5 years	21
Other	9	5 < 10 years	26
		10 < 20 years	35
		20 + years	14
5. Education/Training		11. Years in HRM	
University degree			
No	63	< 1 year	10
Yes	37	1 < 5 years	33
		5 < 10 years	28
		10 < 20 years	24
		20 + years	5

6. HRM Training	In-company	Outside
None	10	13
Little	30	24
Fair	41	51
Extensive	19	12

sonnel practice was administered. Only four of the managers surveyed were appointed before 1945. After 1945, growth was gradual with an additional 33 managers appointed over the 1945-1958 period. In 1968, 24% of responding organisations (all with more than 150 employees) employed someone with "wholly or predominantly" HRM responsibility. By 1978, this proportion had jumped to 60% of responding organisations. In 1990 this had risen to 88% of responding establishments of the same size.

The survey data reveal a modest increase in the professionalism of employment practices over the 1978 survey. This is indicated by higher rates of performance of "modern" HRM activities. Of greater magnitude is the shift away from unilateral HR department responsibility. A number of respondents mentioned a movement toward handing over or sharing responsibility with line staff. A look at individual activities reveals slight increases in the professionalism of practice since 1978, e.g., the use of job evaluation. One difference in the 1978-1990 responses is striking and unexpected. This is the reduced use of wage and salary surveys.

Despite the increasing number of specialist HR employees, other evidence points to a low level of development of HR as a profession. Campbell-Hunt, Harper and Hamilton (1993) develop a rather negative evaluation based on their review of contemporary research. Gilbertson, Fogelberg and Boswell (1987) conducted a survey of 582 HR staff from 230 organisations. They concluded that:

Professionalism does not exist for many companies' people and in many firms personnel and industrial relations work is not regarded as an area of activity requiring specialist knowledge, skills, and experience (p. 47).

However, they go on to suggest that New Zealand should not attempt to build an HRM profession. Instead they suggest that the professional body should attempt to provide training and diagnostic services for general managers who rotate through the HRM functional positions in organisations.

In the 1990 survey we asked New Zealand HR staff for their views on the profession. The results are displayed on Table 9. All but one of the items were answered on a 5-point scale, where "5" indicated "strong agreement" with the statement and "1" indicated "strong disagreement". The exception was the item which asked respondents to rate the prestige of the HR department relative to other functional areas within the unit as "high (1)", "medium (2)" or "low (3)". (The mean of 1.84 indicates moderate prestige.)

To assess the degree to which HR managers in New Zealand believe that they constitute a profession, the professionalism items developed by Moore and Robinson (1989) were used. Both the current state and desirable state of the profession were assessed. On average, the HR personnel surveyed reported moderate professionalization (3.08, where "5" indicates highly professionalised). Unlike Gilbertson, Fogelberg and Boswell (1987), these practitioners preferred an increased, but not extreme, level of professionalization (4.13).

Table 9:   HR Managers' Opinions

Opinion	No. of Items	Alpha	Mean	SD
Influence of the HRM Department	4	.75	3.86	.72
Current Professionalisation of HRM	6	.74	3.08	.64
Ideal Professionalisation of HRM	6	.82	4.13	.63
Expected Growth of HRM	3	.77	3.74	.75
HRM Prestige within own organisation	1		1.84	.63
Expected contracting out HRM	1		2.84	1.04

Given the late development of personnel management as a profession, the establishment of professional societies has been quite rapid. The New Zealand Institute of Management (NZIM) was founded in 1945. From the beginning it concentrated much of its efforts in HRM areas seeing its role to provide training and development to managers. Specific "Personnel Groups" within NZIM were formed in 1956 (see Gilbertson and Burgess, 1990, for a detailed chronicle of the Wellington group's activities). The work of such groups included the 1958 survey (by the Wellington group) and the 1968 survey (by the Auckland group) referred to earlier in this review. In 1969, the first properly constituted body of HR specialists was founded with the establishment of the New Zealand Institute of Personnel Management, an organisation still under the umbrella of the NZIM. This organisation published a journal for some years, organised national conferences and encouraged regular meetings of personnel managers, and others interested in HRM, in the main centres. The organisation lost impetus in the early 1980s and was replaced in 1985 by the existing organisation, renamed the Institute of Personnel Management New Zealand Inc. or IPMNZ, which is independent of the NZIM.

The IPMNZ began with a membership of 220. It has subsequently grown to 1,085. It conducts numerous seminars and workshops both nationally and at branch level and holds an annual national conference. It cooperates with the Australian Human Resources Institute in publishing the *Asia Pacific Journal of Human Resources*.

The IPMNZ is a young, growing and rather fragile organisation. The newly adopted constitution establishes three classes of membership: general, certificate, and fellowship. Of particular interest is the certificate classification as this is the first attempt at professional HRM certification in New Zealand. The criteria for certificate membership are currently being developed.

In summary, the specialist HR profession in New Zealand is at a critical juncture. Almost all large New Zealand organisations recognize the need to hire HR staff. These staff are not well-trained or well-organised as a profession. However, the decision in favour of a strong professional system has been taken. The next years will determine the credibility and acceptance of the HR profession in New Zealand.

The Future of HRM

We have tried to provide a descriptive overview of the HRM practice of medium-to large-size organisations in New Zealand. The tables provide data on the incidence and distribution of responsibility for a large number of individual HRM activities. In the text, contextual information and open-ended responses have been summarized to direct and aid interpretation of the quantitative results.

In looking at these results, there are two conclusions worth highlighting. First, New Zealand HRM practice is professional. Key practices are nearly universal in adoption. Despite concerns, there has been an active professional organisation for over 30 years. There is certainly room for improvement. In particular, the training of HRM staff could be upgraded. Nearly half of staff have no post-secondary school qualification (Gilbertson, Fogelberg and Boswell, 1987).

Second, the 1990 data show a clear shift in responsibility away from sole HRM department responsibility to other departments. Often, the responsibility is shared with the HRM department. This shift is mainly a shift onto line management of partial or full responsibility for HRM activities.

Across the various sections in this report we have attempted to identify factors which influence New Zealand HRM. We suggest that the three most significant factors in terms of direct and indirect influence on HRM practice are: (1) economic conditions affecting the power balance between employers and employees, (2) government measures since 1984 to deregulate the economy, and (3) specific pieces of government legislation notably the State Sector Act 1988 and the Employment Contracts Act 1991.

Since 1978, economic conditions in New Zealand have resulted in levels of unemployment unheard of since World War Two. Indeed for most of the post-war period up to 1978 unemployment was virtually non-existent. While it took some years for the labour market realities of plant closures, redundancies and long-term unemployment to have noticeable affect in attitudes and behaviour, over the last few years significant numbers of employees and unions have accepted their weaker position and been more receptive to employer initiatives. When employers are interested in introducing progressive HRM practices they usually face a much more receptive workforce who are much less inclined to reject change out of hand, and are usually not in a position to successfully reject change anyway. Despite an improved economic outlook for New Zealand, no significant reduction in the unemployment rate is foreseen for several years.

The 1984 Labour government deregulated much of the economy, removing much of the protection previously afforded New Zealand industry. This increased competition therefore forced employers into considering changes, including change in HRM practice, as necessary for survival. Moves toward further deregulation continue, especially in the agricultural sector. For example, the Apple and Pear Board has recently lost its monopoly over domestic apple sales. Roger Douglas, the Finance Minister in 1984 and the architect of New Zealand deregulation, now heads a lobby group that may become a minor political party. He calls for continued privatisation of state sector activities such as education. However, he no longer attracts wide public support.

The third area mentioned was legislation. The State Sector Act 1988 required public sector employers to operate personnel policies that compelled with the principle of being a "good employer". Amongst other features, the Act presumes a "good employer" to operate an EEO programme. A number of HRM practices were therefore directly required by that Act, and many more were required indirectly. For example, improved selection procedures, performance appraisal and promotion schemes are commonly required to be able to demonstrate that EEO is being practised.

The Employment Contracts Act 1991 has further tipped the power balance in favour of employers and has resulted in a significantly weakened union movement, which has lost sole bargaining rights, compulsory union membership, and its system of area-wide and nation-wide agreements ("awards"). A return to strong pro-union legislation is unlikely, even if Labour returns to power in 1996.

Thus, overall, the economy and government action has resulted in:

(a) a weakened union movement,
(b) an apprehensive and weakened workforce receptive to change,
(c) employers in some cases required by law to bring about changes to HRM practice,
(d) employers with an incentive to change HRM practice to bring about efficiency, productivity and survival.

Some employers have responded to this situation predominantly by cost cutting alone. They have quite frequently reduced penal rates for overtime and weekend work and, admittedly much less frequently reduced basic rates. Other employers have responded very differently and have set about increasing productivity, profitability and growth by improving efficiency and increasing the "output" part of the productivity formula, rather than simply reducing the "input" (i.e., unit labour costs). Yet again, some employers respond to legislative requirements by tokenism, the appointment of EEO officers, and introduction of schemes without any real commitment or desire. Others have responded in a genuine fashion, have seen the situation as an opportunity, and have produced quite startling changes.

The small, centralized political system of New Zealand means that government is in a pivotal position to affect HRM. The next government of New Zealand will be selected via a mixed member proportional system like Germany's rather than the first-past-the-post system. Thus future governments may well be coalitions or minority governments. Fewer and less radical changes in legislation are likely.

New voices, such as the Alliance Party (a grouping of old-style Labour, greens and Maori) will gain political influence. The future impact on HRM is unclear.

The varied nature of the driving forces to change and the varied responses to the forces makes any prediction of the future very hazardous. It is probable that HRM practice and activities will continue to grow. The extent to which change is real as opposed to token and the extent to which change is for long-term, universal benefit as opposed to short-term, selfish gain is, unfortunately, an imponderable.

Endnote

1. The terms unitarism and pluralism are as commonly understood in industrial relations writings (see Fox 1966, 1974).

Appendix 1: Description of activities outlined in Table 6

Employment includes the following activities:
  Job analysis
  Time and/or motion studies
  Writing job descriptions
  Internal recruiting
  Advertising for staff
  Use of employment agencies
  Selection tests
  Contract of engagement
  Engagement (final decision)
  Induction to organisation and rules
  Follow-up interviewing
  Performance appraisals and rating
  Performance counselling
  Promotions – managerial
  Promotions – non-managerial
  Transfers
  Dismissals (final decision)
  Policy over voluntary resignations
  Exit interviews
  Discretionary time off work
  Control of absenteeism
  Approval of overtime
  Changes in hours of work
  Approval of annual holidays
  Approval of special leaves

Early retirement programme
Redundancy policies

Salary Administration includes the following activities:
Design of salary structure
Design of wage structure
Maintenance of salary structure
Maintenance of wage structure
Review of individual salary rate changes
Review of individual wage rate changes
Fringe benefits
Wage comparison surveys
Salary comparison surveys
Authorization of deductions from wages
Above award payment
Pension or superannuation funds

Management Development includes the following activities:
Management trainee programmes – graduate entry (primarily)
Management trainee programmes – non graduate entry (primarily)
In-company executive development
External executive development in New Zealand
Overseas executive development
Career planning/counselling

Health and Safety includes the following activities:
Provision of statutory requirements on health
Professional medical services
Surgery services
First-aid services
Cleaning staff/contract
Health scheme (e.g., Southern Cross)
Dental services
Executive routine medical examinations
Smoking policy/services
Alcohol rehabilitation
Drug testing
Drug rehabilitation
Provision of statutory requirements on safety
Promotion of accident prevention
Fire prevention and fire drills
Traffic control
Accident statistics and reports
Attendance on safety committee

Welfare includes the following activities:
  Canteen administration
  Social clubs and credit unions
  Sick benefit scheme
  Advice on personal problems
  Laundry services
  Accommodation
  Employee commuter transport
  Employee insurance
  Employee buying privileges
  Industrial chaplaincy service
  Retirement preparation programmes
  Welfare committee
  Canteen committee
  General educational programmes

Labour Relations includes the following activities:
  Trade union negotiations
  Investigation of complaints
  Attendance at external meetings on IR matters
  Establish disciplinary code
  Control of disciplinary procedure
  Operation of grievance procedure – for union members

Productivity and Participation includes the following activities:
  Quality circles
  Job enrichment
  Job enlargement
  Autonomous/semi-autonomous work groups
  Works council
  Staff suggestion scheme
  Job design change
  Team building

Incentive Programmes includes the following activities:
  Individual incentive schemes (e.g., piece rate)
  Group incentive schemes (part-department up to plant wide)
  Merit bonuses
  Profit sharing
  Staff share purchase scheme
  Self selection management remuneration package
  Production/productivity committee
  Bonus/incentive scheme committee
  Employee recognition programs

External Relations includes the following activities:
   Company participation in employers association
   Company or industry participation in training or other employment related
      bodies
   Company membership in New Zealand Institute of Management
   Company membership in Institute of Personnel Management, New Zealand
   Promoting company views to local bodies, media, or other interest groups

EEO includes the following activities:
   Affirmative action/EEO
   Job sharing provisions
   Flexitime options
   Job evaluation – managerial/supervisory
   Job evaluation – non-managerial jobs
   Pay equity
   Operation of grievance procedure – for union members
   Women and minority employment statistics
   Child care facilities
   Bicultural/multicultural programmes
   Appeal system (appointments)
   Review and monitor organisational practices for discriminatory impact
   Bi-/multicultural sensitive policies

Women's Issues includes the following activities:
   Affirmative action/EEO
   Job sharing provisions
   Flexitime options
   Job evaluation: managerial/supervisory; non-managerial jobs
   Pay equity
   Operation of grievance procedure – for managerial staff
   Women and minority employment statistics
   Child care facilities
   Appeal system (appointments)
   Review and monitor organisational practices for discriminatory impact

Bi-/Multi-Culturalism includes the following activities:
   Bi-cultural/multi-cultural programmes
   Review and monitor organisational practices for discriminatory impact
   Bi-/multi-cultural sensitive policies

Planning and Research includes the following activities:
   Participate in developing human resource policy/strategy
   Initiate new human resource programmes
   Participate in overall organizational strategic planning
   Identifying innovative HRM practices in New Zealand

Identifying innovative HRM practices overseas
Succession planning
HR planning (manpower planning)
Staff planning (budgets)
Engagement of consultants
Organisational structure
Organisational review/development
HR research
Employee surveys
Employee records
Labour turnover statistics

References

Baron, J.N., P.D. Jennings, and F.R. Dobbin (1988). "Mission Control? The Development of Personnel Systems in U.S. Industry." *American Sociological Review*, 53, 497-514.

Bollard, A. and T. Buckle (eds.) (1987). *Economic Liberalisation in New Zealand*. Wellington.

Boxall, P. (1989). "Where is Human Resource Management in New Zealand Heading? Key Issues for the 1990s." *Asia Pacific HRM*, 27(2) 58-70.

Boxall, P., R. Rudman, and R. Taylor (1986). *Personnel Practice*. Auckland: Longman Paul.

Brosnan, P. and F. Wilkinson (1989). "Low Pay and Industrial Relations: The Case of Contract Cleaning." *New Zealand Journal of Industrial Relations*, 14(1) 83-90.

Campbell-Hunt, C., D.A. Harper, with R.T. Hamilton (1993). *Islands of Excellence? A Study of Management in New Zealand*. Research Monograph 59. Wellington: NZ Institute of Economic Research.

Easton, B. (ed.) (1989). *The Making of Rogernomics*. Auckland: Auckland University Press.

Fox, A. (1966). *Industrial Sociology and Industrial Relations*, Research Papers 3. London: HMSO.

Fox, A. (1974). *Beyond Contract: Work, Power and Trust Relations*. London: Faber.

Geare, A.J. (1988). *The System of Industrial Relations in New Zealand*. (2nd revised ed.) Wellington: Butterworths.

Geare, A.J. (1989). "New Directions in New Zealand Labour Legislation." *International Labour Review*, 128(2) 213-228.

Geare, A.J. (1991). *Employment Contracts Act 1991*, Research Centre for Industrial Relations and Labour Studies, Working Paper 9101.

Geare, A.J. (1993). "Review of the New Zealand Employment Contracts Act 1991." Dunedin: Firre.

Gilbertson, D. and S. Burgess (1990). "'Professionalization' and the Emergence of Specialist Personnel Management Bodies in New Zealand." In P. Boxall (ed.), *Function in Search of a Future*. Auckland: Longman Paul.

Gilbertson, D., G. Fogelberg and C. Boswell (1987). *Personnel and Industrial Relations Staff in New Zealand*. Wellington: New Zealand Institute for Personnel Management.

Harbridge, R. (ed.) (1993). *Employment Contracts: New Zealand Experiences*. Wellington: Victoria University Press.

Hare, A.E.C. (1946). *Report on Industrial Relations in New Zealand*. Wellington: Victoria University.

Jesson, B., A. Ryan, and P. Spoonley (1988). *Revival of the Right: New Zealand Politics in the 1980s*. Auckland: Heinemann-Reed.

Kerr, C. and A. Siegel (1954). "The Interindustry Propensity to Strike – An International Comparison." In A. Kornhauser, R. Dubin and A. Ross (eds.), *Industrial Conflict*. New York: McGraw Hill.

Kirkbride, P. and S. Tang (1989)."Personnel Management in Hong Kong: A Review of Current Issues." *Asia Pacific HRM*, 27(2) 43-57.

McAndrew, I. and P. Hursthouse (1990). "Southern Employers On Enterprise Bargaining." *New Zealand Journal of Industrial Relations*, 15(2) 117-128.

Moore, L.F. and N. Bu (1990). "Human Resource Planning in Canada: A Perspective." *Asia Pacific HRM*, 28(1) 5-23.

Moore, L.F. and S. Robinson (1989). "Human Resource Management Present and Future: Highlights from a Western Canadian Survey of Practitioner Perceptions." In A. Petit and A.V. Subbarau (eds.), *Proceedings of the Administrative Science Association of Canada*. Montreal: McGill University.

National Business Review (1991). "Government Gets Cracking On Tomorrow's Skills." December 20, 1991.

New Zealand Institute of Personnel Management, Wellington Branch (1979). *Personnel Management, 1978*. Wellington: NZIPM.

New Zealand Official Yearbook 1990 (1990). Wellington: Department of Statistics.

Personnel Group of the New Zealand Institute of Management, Wellington Division (1958). *The Scope of Personnel Management in New Zealand*. Wellington: Personnel Group of the New Zealand Institute of Management.

Personnel Management Association of the New Zealand Institute of Management, Auckland Division (1968). *Personnel Practices in New Zealand*. Auckland: Personnel Management Association of the New Zealand Institute of Management.

Roper, B. and C. Rudd (eds.) (1993). *State and Economy in New Zealand*. New York: Oxford University Press.

Roth, H. (1978). "The Historical Framework." In J. Deeks, (ed.) *Industrial Relations in New Zealand*. Wellington: Methner

Rudman, R.S. (1974). "Employer Organisations: Their Development and Role in Industrial Relations." In J.M. Howells and F.W. Young (eds.), *Labour and Industrial Relations in New Zealand*, Carlton, Vic: Pitman Pacific.

Seidman, J. (1974). "New Zealand's Industrial Relations Act, 1973." *International Labour Review*, 110(6) 515-538.

Shannon, P. (1991). *Social Policy*. Auckland: Oxford University Press.

Thompson, V. and A. Sibbald (1990). "Personnel Management in New Zealand: A Bibliography 1941-1989." *Research Centre for Industrial Relations and Labour Studies*, University of Otago. Discussion Paper, No.9001, 50.

Woods, N.S. (1963). *Industrial Conciliation and Arbitration in New Zealand*, Wellington: Government Printer.

Woods, N.S. (1974). *The Industrial Relations Act 1973*, Occasional Papers 11. Wellington: Victoria University.

Wright, Chris (1991). "The Origins of Australian Personnel Management," *ACIRRT Working Paper No. 8*, University of Sydney.

Human Resource Management in the People's Republic of China

Mee-Kau Nyaw

An Overview of Political-Economic Developments

China is one of the largest countries in the world with a total area of 9.6 million square kilometres, which is equivalent to that of continental Europe, and a total population of 1.16 billion in 1991 (*China Statistical Yearbook*, 1992). The People's Republic of China (PRC) was founded in 1949 after the Communist Party of China (CPC) led by Mao Zedong defeated the Nationalist Party (Kuomintang) and took control of the entire mainland. Chiang Kai Shek led his loyalists and fled to Taiwan.

The recent economic history of PRC can be divided into the following periods: Economic rehabilitation (1949-52), the first Five-Year Plan (1953-57), the Great Leap Forward (1958-60), economic recovery (1961-65), the Cultural Revolution (1966-76), and the post-Mao period after 1976. Basically, the different periods were characterized by ideological oscillation between moderation/pragmatism and radicalism. The economic rehabilitation period following peace in 1949 was a transitional period characterized by experimentation, pragmatism and diversity. During this period, the leadership's overriding concern was to consolidate its political power. Enterprises with clear connections to Chiang Kai Shek and the Kuomintang regime were nationalized while other enterprises were allowed to remain partially private. Impressive economic progress was achieved during this period (see Table 1). The high growth rates of GNP and industrial production were partially due to the very low base of the economy.

The first Five-Year Plan (1953-57) was also a period of substantial industrial growth, though not without problems of industrial management. The management system was in a large part copied from the Stalinist centrally-planned model in place in the USSR. Industrial morale was reported to be high during this period and structural problems were not yet obvious because basic levels of plant utilization had only just begun to recover their normal levels (Yu, 1985, p. 32). The Soviet Union's Stalinist system of industrial management was subsequently modified in response to changing economic and political conditions, and the basic elements remained unchanged until the industrial reforms promulgated in 1979 began to filter through into practice.

Characterized by extreme leftist policies, the Great Leap Forward (1958-61) was a disastrous period. The second Five-Year Plan (1958-62) was practically abandoned in favour of a Maoist development strategy to accelerate economic

Table 1:   Development Periods, Policy Orientations and Economic Growth, 1949-1991

Periods	Policy Orientations	Annual GNP Growth-rates (%)*	Annual Indus-trial Growth-rates (%)*
Economic Rehabilitation (1949-1952)	moderation/pragmatism	22.1	35.6
First Five-Year Plan (1953-1957)	moderation/pragmatism	6.7	9.3
Great Leap Forward (1958-1961)	extremism	−6.6	−18.2
Economic Recovery (1961-1965)	moderation/pragmatism	8.1	15.1
Cultural Revolution (1966-1968) (1969-1976)	extremism	−2.5 6.1	−11.0 7.2
Post-Mao Periods (1977-1983) (1984-1991)	moderation/pragmatism	10.7 16.7**	9.3 26.1

* Compound annual growth-rates. Calculation was based on current market prices; real
    growth rates should be lower as there were close to 12–15% inflation rates in late
    1980s and early 1990s.
** 1985–91.

Sources: Computed from State Statistical Bureau, (1984); *China Statistical Yearbook*
           (various years).

growth without considering its objective constraints. Politics was in command
during the Great Leap Forward period. As a result, both GNP and industrial
output plunged (see Table 1).

Liu Shaoqi assumed responsibility for reconstructing the economy when Mao
sidestepped into the "second line" in 1961, after the collapse of the Great Leap
Forward. Liu initiated an economic recovery programme which was characterized
by ideological moderation, the restoration of the bonus system, and a host of other
measures to revitalize the economy. Political campaigns were sharply reduced,
and there was renewed industrial progress during the recovery period (1962-65).
Annual industrial growth was estimated to be 15.1 percent.

In spite of rapid industrial growth under Liu's leadership, China reverted to
ideological extremism in 1966 when Mao emerged from the "second line" to
launch the Great Cultural Revolution (1966-76). Subsequently Liu was purged.

Politics was again in command. The "Gang of Four" and other Mao loyalists believed that "spirit is all-powerful" and that intensive political education was therefore the most socially efficient way of stimulating industrial production. Like the Great Leap Forward, the Cultural Revolution brought the nation's economy to near-collapse.

After wavering for two years following the death of Mao and the downfall of the "Gang of Four" in 1976, the Chinese Communist Party finally resolved to carry out economic reforms and to adopt open-door policies at the crucial Third Plenary Session of the 11th Party Congress of the CPC in December 1978 under the leadership of Deng Xiaoping. Economic reform programmes introduced in the industrial sector over the years included greater emphasis on the efficiency of production, a freeing of centrally-set prices, reducing subsidies, adopting a contract responsibility system, introducing share-holding companies, and giving more freedom to factory directors. Given the shortage of domestic funds, Deng and his group advocated an open-door policy, aiming to attract foreign investment from other countries and to increase exports to finance imports of technology. Five Special Economic Zones (Shenzhen, Zhuhai, Santou, Xiamen and Hainan) were established after 1979. Fourteen coastal cities, various development areas and many inland cities were subsequently opened to foreign investors. During 1979-92, China attracted US$110 billion of direct foreign investment in terms of contractual value, principally from Hong Kong, Taiwan, U.S., Japan, Western Europe and Southeast Asian nations (Nyaw, 1993). Trade between China and other Pacific Rim countries has been increasing very rapidly in the last decade.

The PRC moved one critical step ahead in its reform programmes when the Third Plenary Session of the 14th Party Congress of the CPC held in November, 1993, officially affirmed that the country will henceforth be adopting a socialist market economic system. This signals a departure from the past as "market economy" was a taboo in China's official documents for the past forty odd years. Marketization processes in the Chinese economy are expected to accelerate, which will have a bearing on human resource management practices in China.

In the following sections we will focus our discussion mainly on the HRM system of state-owned enterprises. We will also briefly highlight the HRM practices of international joint ventures which are distinctively different from state enterprises.

The Industrial Relations Setting

The industrial relations system in a socialist country like the PRC plays a very different role compared to its counterparts in the West. In China, the trade union plays a supporting role rather than an adversarial role. The communist ideology dictates that workers are "masters of the house". Therefore, worker participation in management takes place in most communist countries (the same was true for former Soviet-bloc countries), although it varies in form. The workers' partic-ipation in Chinese state-owned enterprises is carried out through the workers' congress.

The Chinese workers' congress system under the leadership of the Communist Party was promulgated in the 8th CPC Congress in 1956. Workers' congresses were established to encourage workers' participation in management through making proposals to management. However, the Congress had no executive au-thority since it had no power to make decisions binding on the factory director. During the Cultural Revolution, enterprise Party committees were dismantled and were replaced by revolutionary committees. Workers' congresses and trade unions also disappeared. When the Cultural Revolution officially ended in 1976 with the arrest of the "Gang of Four", the enterprise Party committee, the trade union and the workers' congress were reinstated in their former roles.

There was some confusion about the exact status of the workers' congress until the publication of an important economic reform programme entitled "Reform of the Economic Structure" adopted at the Third Plenary Session of the 12th Central Committee of the CPC in October 1984 (hereafter referred to as the *1984 Reform Document*). In June, 1981, the Central Committee released a document on workers' congresses entitled "Provisional Regulations Concerning Congresses of Workers and Staff Members in State-owned Industrial Enterprises". According to this document the workers' congress was to become an "organ of power" in the enterprise and this gave rise to some speculation that China was about to embark on a more active form of worker participation than had occurred in the past. However, this never seemed particularly likely given that one of the first major policy declarations by Deng stressed the importance of developing a proper responsibility system in which managerial authority prevailed over others in enterprise management.

The 1984 Reform Document of the CPC seems to recognize the contradiction of expecting enterprise directors to take overall responsibility for an enterprise while denying them the ultimate responsibility for decision-making. Thus the document states categorically that the director must assume "full responsibility". Why the Central Committee felt obliged to issue the directive of June, 1981, is not quite clear, but the directive would seem to reflect concern about appearing to move too rapidly towards an autonomous state enterprise system with excessive "capitalistic" powers. The June, 1981, document now appears to have been an interim measure designed to dilute the power of the enterprise Party secretary in preparation for full transfer of power to the factory director while developing the workers' congress as an enterprise-oriented check on the factory director's performance. The major responsibilities of the workers' congress are summarized in Table 2.

Among other things, the workers' congress has the power to examine and adopt resolutions on production and budget plans prepared by the director, to decide welfare funds for workers and staff, to discuss and pass resolutions relating to wage adjustment and workers' training, and to elect factory directors subject to approval by higher authority. The delegates of the workers' congress also generally include workshop directors, section chiefs and group heads; but workers should constitute not less than 60% of the total number of representatives. The revival of the workers' congress represents a step towards organisational democracy which gives some additional rights to workers; in particular, it requires top management to report on its activities on a regular basis. However, the factory director has the authority to return a resolution to the workers' congress for reconsideration. Should this fail, the dispute may be referred to a higher authority in the state apparatus who will make the final ruling.

In summary, the workers' congress represents a consultative forum that imposes limited obligations on top management. Like most representative bodies in capitalist economies, workers' congresses tend to be dominated by more skilled workers and supervisors. When not in session, decisions of the congress are handled by standing committees that draw on specialists with knowledge of the problems concerned. There seems to be no uniform pattern as to whether the trade union or the Party services these committees. However, since the Party Secretary is the final arbiter in disputes with management his influence tends to be pervasive.

The trade union is another important pillar in the decision-making structure of state-owned enterprises in the PRC. Although the trade union movement has had a somewhat chequered history since 1949 (Harper, 1971; Henley-Chen, 1981; Littler-Lockett, 1983; Warner, 1990), it presently plays an important role in the political education of the workforce. According to Lenin's doctrine, the trade union is the "transmission belt" linking up the Party with the masses and its primary function is to inculcate in workers the virtues of diligence and hard work. It has been argued by some that the trade union committee is an unnecessary organization and its role was ridiculed as *pao loong tau* (a body to fill any temporary or available vacancies). However, its role as a functioning body or working organ has been stressed by Deng Xiaoping: "The trade union in an enterprise will be the functioning body between workers' congress and general membership meetings. Therefore it is no longer an unnecessary organization as some believed" (Deng, 1984, p. 127). Other functions of the trade union committee in a state enterprise are given in Table 2.

The re-allocation of duties and responsibilities for the enterprise has done little to reduce the considerable overlap in the roles of the trade union and the Party committee. Both have always been concerned with political education but in the past the trade union was placed in a lower position in the hierarchy of power and its functions were more mundane; that is, centred on matters of labour productivity, worker morale and welfare rather than with the interpretation of national policy. With much greater emphasis now being placed on economic efficiency and restrictions on the powers of the Party committee, we may expect the status of the trade union in the enterprise hierarchy to improve. In particular, the reliance presently being put on the "collective contract" system and various forms

Table 2:   Major Functions, Authorities and Responsibilities of Workers' Congress and
Trade Union Committees in China's State-owned Enterprise since 1984

Workers' Congress (or Assembly)	Trade Union Committee
(1) an agency of power in the enterprise (not merely an advisory organization);	(1) act as an agent to help implement the decisions made by the workers congress;
(2) has the power to: (a) examine and adopt resolutions submitted by the factory director on production plans, budgets, etc; (b) discuss and decide on the use of funds (for labour protection, welfare, bonus etc.), regulations for awarding or penalizing workers and staff, allocation of housing for workers and staff; (c) approve reforms of management structure, wage adjustments and vocational training; (d) recommend leading cadres for commendation or promotion, propose to higher authority criticisms, punishment, or removal of negligent or irresponsible cadres; (e) elect administrators (cadres) subject to approval and appointment by appropriate higher authorities;	(2) protect workers' rights and material interests; (3) linking the party with the masses;as a school of communism and a 'transmission belt'; (4) as a school of management for workers; (5) to co-operate with enterprise managers in carrying out state decrees concerning workers' interests and welfare; (6) organize workers in running the enterprise as 'masters of the house';
(3) support the factory director in the discharge of his functions and powers and defend the authority of the chain of command in production matters;	(7) prepare for the convocation of the workers' congress, elect delegates, sort out proposals, deal with workers' appeals, canvass reactions, etc.
(4) educate workers and staff to act responsibly to observe labour discipline, and carry out the responsibilities for production and technical matters;	(8) serve as an executive body the implementation of congress resolutions.
(5) may disagree with decisions or directives of higher authority. However, if the latter upholds its original decision after deliberation, the workers' congress must abide by it.	

Sources: 'Provisional regulations concerning congresses of workers and staff in state owned industrial enterprises', *Beijing Review*, 7 September 1981, 24, 36, 16-19; also in *Renmin Ribao* (*People's Daily*), 20 June 1981; *Gonghui Gongsuo Wonda* (*Questions and Answers on Union Work*), Congren Chubanshe (Workers' Publishing House), Beijing, 1981; All-China's Trade Union Federation Constitution 1983, passed at the 10th National Congress in October 1983; *Decision of the Central Committee of the Communist Party of China on Reform of the Economic Structure*, adopted at 12th Central Committee of the Communist Party of China, 3rd Plenary Session, 20 October 1984.

of "economic responsibility" for individuals implies a strong "productionist" role for the trade union. Under the collective contract system an agreement is signed between management and the trade union specifying the kind of tasks the workers are responsible for and how and when they are to be accomplished. For example, the Chengdu Machine Cutting and Tools Plant has had a comprehensive contract system since 1979 which is based on the "four fixes" (*fix* labour, machines, man hours per unit of output and output volumes) and the "three ensures" (*ensure* product types, quality and profit) (Zhang et al., 1982, p. 24). The contact may also specify targets for departments within the enterprise. As the Reform Document states:

Enterprises must specify in explicit terms the requirements for each work post and the duties of each worker and staff member must establish various forms of the economic responsibility system with contracted jobs as the main content so as to invigorate the urban enterprises, raise the sense of responsibility of the workers and staff members and bring into full play their initiative, enthusiasm and creativeness (Reform Document, 1984, p. 21).

This, however, does not mean that the state is introducing an adversarial system of collective bargaining between management and workers as Littler and Lockett seem to suggest, since the trade union movement is officially committed to working with management and the Party committee to solve problems (Littler and Lockett, 1983, p. 38). The key objective in the Chinese system of employee relations remains to arrive at a consensus that satisfies all parties involved. Moreover, the trade union is barred from taking up workers' grievances for it is the responsibility of the Party committee to deal with complaints against management. Only the Party secretary has official access to higher authority within the state apparatus, and this is what ultimately counts because it is the state that appoints the factory director who has "full responsibility" for the enterprise.

HRM Practices Under the Reform Programmes

China's human resource management practices, like the industrial relations system, have been shaped and influenced by a host of ideological, historical, political and economic factors. The locus of control of HRM was and continues to be in the hands of the state. Under the existing reform programmes, the influence of the state is still very considerable, although some market forces are introduced into the HRM system.

Employment

Before the latest economic reform programme was launched in 1979, there was tight control by the Ministry of Labour over labour allocation. Workers and staff were assigned to particular jobs in a unit (such as an enterprise) by the local labour bureau within an overall quota set by the Ministry of Labour. Neither workers nor enterprises had any say in the allocation process but had to accept whatever jobs or manpower were given. Workers could not quit their jobs and were ensured lifetime employment unless they committed a very serious offence or got into trouble in politics. Job swaps for family reunions or other personal reasons were allowed but permission was difficult to obtain. The recruitment function was practically nonexistent in a state enterprise. This system results in a mismatching of talents and jobs and a misallocation of labour resources in state-owned enterprises.

After 1979 the labour control system loosened up somewhat. On top of a host of enlarged powers enjoyed by experimental state-owned enterprises, such as freedom to engage in foreign trade etc. (Henley and Nyaw, 1986), an enterprise could recruit workers on the basis of merit, decide on the size of the labour force, and discharge workers in case of a serious violation of law and discipline. This practice should have provided greater incentive to achieve greater economic efficiency by getting rid of inefficient and redundant labour. However, for a number of years, hiring workers on the basis of merit or firing of workers by state-owned enterprise was not widely practiced. Many considered it to be socially unacceptable given the high level of youth unemployment in China. The Chinese preferred to call unemployment "waiting employment" in the past as it was argued that there was no unemployment in a socialist country. China now formally admits that, like other market economies, unemployment does exist.

In 1988, the "State-owned Enterprise Law" was promulgated. This law officially stipulates that state-owned enterprise has the right to recruit and dismiss workers and staff as well as the authority to decide its own staffing plan. In addition, the enterprise can reject assignment of labour by the labour bureau. The "Regulations of Transforming Operating Mechanism on State-owned Enterprise" adopted in 1992 (hereafter called the 1992 Enterprise Transforming Regulations) further stipulates that an enterprise can recruit technical and managerial personnel from overseas with the approval of the relevant government agency (Clause 18). This is a strategic shift from central allocation to marketization of the labour force in China. But the legacy from the past cannot be easily dispensed with overnight.

In China the lifetime employment system (the so-called iron rice bowl system) has gradually been replaced by a "labour contract system" which applies to all workers and staff who first entered into the labour force after 1986 (see Provisional Regulations on Labour Contract System in State-owned Enterprises, 1986). The labour contract specifies terms and conditions of employment, and rights and responsibilities between workers and employers. It can be signed by an individual or on a collective basis, and the contract period may vary from a specified time period to unspecified period, depending on the nature of jobs (Clause 17, *1992 Enterprise Transforming Regulations*). Although this practice is now written into law, layoff of redundant workers is still uncommon as there is strong "unofficial" opposition from the state security unit for fear of social unrest if workers are thrown out of jobs into the streets.

Wage System

Basic wage. The Chinese Communist Party has for a long time pursued a policy of combining both material and non-material incentives (or "moral encouragement") to stimulate productivity towards growth. Material incentives have been developed according to the socialist principle of "from each according to his ability and to each according to his work". In practice this means payment of a basic wage according to national scales plus an incentive bonus, developed at the plant level. Moral encouragement has relied on a variety of different campaigns designed to strengthen the political and ideological education of workers so that they recognize their moral obligations to work hard for the benefit of the nation since, under socialism, they are "the master of the house". Historically, material incentives were emphasized during periods of political moderation and industrial growth while moral incentives were stressed during periods of political extremism and low growth (see Table 1).

In China, the principal forms of material incentives include basic wages (time-work or piece-work), subsidized commodities, bonuses, and welfare benefits such as privileged access to public housing. We shall first focus on the wage system with special reference to basic wages.

The industrial wage system in China is highly complicated. The current system, which was partially copied from the Soviet system practised in the 1930s, was established through the wage reforms of 1956, 1963 and 1985. Wage scales vary among different branches of industry, trades, enterprises, types of work and regions. At present, there are literally hundreds of wage scales and more than one thousand wage grades (Feng and Zhao, 1984, p. 607). For simplicity, the Chinese industrial wage system can be roughly broken down into three sub-systems: (1) the system of wage brackets for workers; (2) the post or job-type wage system; and (3) the system of wage brackets for cadres.

Under system (1), industrial workers are allocated to grades which are differentiated according to variations in the level of skill required of the job-holder. The majority of workers, such as those employed in the machinery and the chemical industries, were paid according to an eight-grade wage system before 1985. In 1985 the eight-grade wage system was broken down into 15 grades which are further sub-divided into eleven wage regions.

From Table 3 it can be seen that the standard monthly wage for unskilled labour (grade 1) is set at ¥33 (approximately US$10.60) in wage area 1, whereas a highly-skilled worker (grade 15) receives ¥99 per month after 1985. As the standard monthly wage varies between each industrial sector as well as between enterprises of the same sector in different geographical regions, wage payments for ostensibly similar jobs requiring identical levels of skill may be different. Thus, workers in heavy industry are generally paid better than their counterparts in light industry, even though the content of their jobs is the same in every respect.

Under system (2), industrial workers are paid according to the job-type they hold in the enterprise. The system is usually adopted in those industries or enterprises where skills are less complicated, job differences small, and the division of labour highly developed. Production workers in the textile or chemical industries are typically paid according to job-type (Jiang and Shen, 1985, p. 335).

Under the third system, remuneration for cadres (factory directors, other managers and technical staff) is governed by the system of wage brackets which was first implemented in 1956. The system was simplified and consolidated in 1963 and 1985 respectively. Under the system, China is divided into nine groups in eleven regions, and within each region an industry is assigned to one of nine groups according to its importance. At present the minimum number of grades for cadres is seventeen with several grades further sub-divided into two sub-grades (see Table 4).

The variation in the Chinese system of wage brackets and posts reflects the principle of "to each according to his work". The motivational interpretation of this principle was given by Lenin who argued that wages were the primary means of stimulating workers to labour diligently until their social consciousness had progressed to a higher, Communist stage. Apart from the large number of wage scales and grades, China has in the past officially adhered to a "rational low-wage policy", where wage increases were infrequent, occurring at intervals of several years. For practical purposes, a real wage increase requires promotion to a higher grade.

A number of problems have been found with the wage system and current wage reforms are now targeted at these. The chief problem has been identified as the overwhelmingly egalitarian nature of the wage system. For example, wages and bonuses of workers and staff were unrelated to the performance of the enterprise and were paid irrespective of how well or how poorly the enterprise was managed. The way in which an individual performed also made little difference to the level of pay. This practice, now officially derided as "eating from the same big pot", still operates in many state-owned enterprises. It is argued that egalitarianism has gone too far and has seriously reduced the initiative and motivation of good workers. As the 1984 Reform Document admits:

The [egalitarianism] has resulted in … the practice of 'eating from the same big pot' prevailing in the relations of the enterprises of the state and in those of the workers and staff members to their enterprises. The enthusiasm, initiative and creativeness of enterprises and workers and staff members have, as a result, been seriously dampened and the socialist economy is bereft of much of the vitality it should possess (p. 5).

A second major criticism has been that wage grades are often complicated and difficult to justify using economic criteria. For example, the system of setting

Table 3: Grade Patterns of Workers in Large and Medium-scale State-owned Enterprises (Unit: Yuan)

Before 1985

Wage Grade	1	2	3	4	5	6	7	8
Standard Monthly Wage (¥)	33	39	46	54	64	74	85	99.5

Since 1985

Wage Grade	1	2	3	4	5	6	7	8	9	10	11	12	13	14	15
Wage Regions (range from 1 to 11) 1	33	36	40	44	48	52	56	61	66	71	76	81	87	93	99
8	40	44	48	53	58	63	68	73	79	85	91	98	105	112	120
11	43	47	51	56	61	66	72	78	84	91	98	105	113	121	129

Sources: Guoying (1985); Weiyi (1991, p. 117)

198   Mee-Kau Nyaw

Table 4:   Patterns of Standard Wage for Cadres in State-owned Enterprises

		Wage Regions (9 groups in 11 regions)								
		1	2	3	4	5	6	7	8	9
Wage Grade	1	248	255	263	270	277	285	292	299	306
(ranges from 1 to 17)	10	102	105	108	111	114	117	120	123	126
	17	34	35	36	37	38	39	40	41	42

Source: Weiyi (1991, pp. 118-119)

wage norms according to the relative importance and administrative affiliation of the enterprise produces arbitrary distinctions. Thus, wage norms in heavy industry are generally set higher than those in light industry, yet much of so-called light industrial work is heavy in practice and is also of strategic and economic importance. In addition, the rewards for managerial and technical work compared with manual work are meagre indeed. According to data published in 1979, university graduates of 1959 were being paid around 25 percent less than workers who entered the labour force in 1951 with only junior high school certificates (both groups were of the same age). There have also been cases reported where workers have been reluctant to be promoted to cadres, or have asked to remain on manual wage scales (Zhao and Pan, 1984, p. 163).

A third complaint, voiced at the enterprise level in particular, has been that there is over-centralization of wage management, and enterprises have no autonomy in setting wage rates. Increases in rates were controlled centrally, regardless of local conditions. In spite of centralization, many enterprises have no work norms or measures for assessing productivity. Some enterprises have also resorted to improper ways of funding bonus payments (Feng and Zhao, 1984, p. 160).

Recognition of the limitations and arbitrariness of the wage system as outlined above has forced Party leaders to promote a series of wage reforms. Indeed, wage reform is now an integral part of the more general economic reform programme officially announced in the 1984 Reform Document, and the latter draws on the experience of a number of experiments carried out since 1978. The guiding principle of the current wage reform, "to each according to his work" is laid down in the 1984 Reform Document (p. 24). Deng, the architect and prime mover behind the reform programme, has explicitly elaborated the principle:

(It) calls for distribution according to the quantity and quality of an individual's work ... a person's grade on the pay scale is determined mainly by his performance on the job, his technical level and his actual contribution (Deng, 1984, p. 117).

The most salient feature of the current Chinese economic reform programme compared with past reforms is that enterprises are now being given more autonomy in the decision-making process which, among other things, includes decision-making power over wages and rewards. This is a significant departure from the two major wage reforms of 1956 and 1963. Although there are wide variations in wage reform programmes among different experimental enterprises, they all aim "to better link wages and bonuses with the improved enterprise performance" (1984 Reform Document). A brief description of some of the more important pilot experiments seems warranted:

1. Many enterprises adopted the floating wage system. Under this system part (usually less than 50 percent) of a worker's standard wage and bonus (sometimes including part of the profit at the disposal of the enterprise) becomes a "floating wage" which is then paid to workers on the basis of their performance. This seems to be a very popular wage reform to date.
2. Some enterprises have introduced a "floating" promotion system financed from part of the wage and bonus fund. This has enabled enterprises to promote a greater number of the more capable workers and technical staff than was possible under the rigid wage increase system normally operating.
3. Other enterprises have adopted what is termed the "structural wage system". Under this system wages are broken down into four parts: a base wage, a seniority wage, a position wage and a flexible wage. The base wage is supposed to ensure that a worker's basic needs are met so that, although the basic wage remains relatively stable over time, it may be adjusted according to the inflation rate if it is deemed necessary. The seniority wage is based on years of working experience but is subject to performance appraisal. The position wage is a responsibility payment to cadres, technical staff or highly-skilled workers. Finally, the flexible wage is based on a measure of the enterprise's performance and of the contribution of individual workers. In general, it consists of a floating wage, bonus and subsidized benefits.

The bonus. The bonus has a long history as an important component of the Chinese wage system. The current reform programme aims to restore the bonus element in an industrial worker's wages to something like its original significance. In the past, state-owned enterprises were restricted to paying no more than two months' basic wages as an annual bonus. Since the replacement of "profit delivery" by taxes in October, 1984, enterprises now pay a contracted tax rather than handing over any surplus (or loss) to the state ("the contracted responsibility system"). In connection with this reform, enterprises can now "decide on the amount of bonuses for their workers and staff members according to the results of enterprise operation while the state only collects an appropriate amount of tax on the above-norm bonus from enterprises" (1984 Reform Document, p. 23). With the new ruling, bonus limits were lifted so that tax only became payable on bonuses of over four months' basic wages. According to a statement by Vice-Premier Tian (1986, p. 10), most industrial enterprises paid a four months' bonus in 1985. On the other hand, based on the contracted responsibility system, "enterprises which have failed to fulfil their quotas and paid less taxes and earned less profits must reduce or stop bonuses, or even withhold portions of their employees' wages"

(Jin, 1984, p. 4). This would seem to suggest that there is still some way to go before enterprise bonus levels reflect real profits or efficiency.

The success or failure of the wage reform in China is likely to have a far-reaching effect on the economy. At present, the wage level in China is still very low. Monthly pay for a skilled worker at grade eight is slightly over ¥100 (US$32). Deng anticipates that, as production expands, there will be more promotions to higher grades and increases in standard wages of each grade (Deng, 1984, p. 117). However, because of the low base wage and the ambitious development programme of the state, China is likely to remain a low-wage economy for a fairly long time. Another problem facing wage reformers is how to widen differentials for higher-level technical and managerial manpower to reflect more accurately supply-and-demand conditions in the labour market. In addition, imbalances in differentials between skilled trades that do not reflect marginal productivity have yet to be resolved. What is not in doubt is the intention of the Chinese leadership.

Another critical issue in wage reform is the linkage between wages and prices. Because of the irrationality of official prices that do not reflect relative scarcity, the profit performance of enterprises is blurred. How to link wages with the economic performance of the enterprise remains an unsolved problem and further experiments have been abandoned pending wider reform of prices generally (Tian, 1986, p. 10). From a worker's point of view, the key issue is maintenance of one's real wage in the face of changes in hitherto state-controlled commodity prices nearer to true market values.

The lifting of bonus limits is a bold and significant development. Enterprise management now has the ability to reward the good and diligent and punish the lax and unproductive. This ought to enhance the motivation of workers and technical staff, but in order to have any effect income differences must increase.

Subsidies and other supplementary benefits. On top of the standard (basic) wage, the position wage, and the bonus, the subsidy is another important form of payment received by a worker or staff in a state-owned enterprise. Although China underwent a structural reform of its wage system in 1985, the levels of standard wages remain unchanged as compared to 1956. On the other hand, the cost of living has increased substantially during the period. Periodically, the state provides price subsidies to cushion the effects of inflation. The amount of subsidy varies in different regions. During 1979-87 the price subsidies for workers and staff was about ¥20 (in Beijing, price subsidy was ¥5 in 1979, ¥7.5 in 1985 and ¥10 in 1987) (*Special Study Group of Workers' Wage*, 1991, p. 87). Nevertheless, the subsidies could not totally offset price increases. Some enterprises have had to explore other means to generating income not directly related to their normal business activities. The income is then distributed among workers and staff to supplement their meager wages.

Apart from price subsidies, there are other subsidies, such as the hardship allowance, for people working in remote locations or unfavourable conditions, as well as a years-of-service subsidy, special and duty allowances, etc. All subsidies taken together constitute a significant portion of the total wage payment to workers. The basic wage component in the total wage payment declined from 85.7% in 1978 to only 54.3% in 1989 whereas the share of subsidy increased from 6.5% to 23.1% in 1989 (*Special Study Group of Workers' Wage*, 1991, p. 85). This practice of a low basic wage with many subsidies is unique in China; a paradox which has yet to be resolved. Apparently, China is reluctant to make a fundamental change to this wage system, preferring to take a piece-meal approach for fear of upsetting the existing social balance for the huge number of workers and staff in the nation.

In addition to the above subsidies, there are other supplementary benefits provided to workers and staff in the state-owned enterprises such as free medical treatment, low-cost housing, retirement pensions, child-care, etc. Workers and staff are taken care of from "cradle to grave". This social support system drains substantial resources from the enterprises, and over the years has become a great burden to them. The existing practice is now a target for reform. The state is expected to play a more important role in providing social security to workers and staff.

Performance Appraisal

Performance appraisal of workers and staff has been widely practiced in the state-owned enterprises of China. It is used for promotion, training, rewards, transfer and demotion, etc. (Chen, 1985; Su and Chu, 1992), and is carried out either monthly, quarterly, semi-annually or annually, depending on the nature of jobs. For example, production workers are appraised both monthly and quarterly (Chen, 1985).

One unique feature of the appraisal system in China is that it places great emphasis on the "moral" aspect such as political attitude of workers and staff (Chen, 1985, p. 74; Liao, 1991, p. 235; Su and Chu, 1992, p. 162, 510). It considers that political consciousness, (i.e. support of the CPC line) and other personal attributes such as patriotism, team spirit and diligent work for the motherland are important attributes that workers and staff of a socialist country should possess. Other factors that have been taken into consideration in the performance appraisal system include (1) capability; (2) initiative, discipline, responsibility and seriousness of work; (3) output performance such as quantity and quality of work, and (4) physical fitness such as adaptability and resourcefulness (Su and Chu, 1992, pp. 162-163); Liao, 1991, p. 235). Table 5 shows the performance appraisal system used by the Xiamen Arts and Crafts Production Company for the promotion of its managers and non-managerial staff. Although political attitude is not shown in the table, it usually predominates over others. A worker or staff member who has been branded as a political trouble maker can never be promoted. Therefore, performance appraisal can be subject to abuse by superiors who could deny the promotion opportunity of a capable managerial staff member simply by branding him/her as "politically unreliable". A political burden is sometimes inherited from one's family background such as he/she was born into a family considered to be the "class enemy" of the communist state. Although family background has been somewhat downplayed in the last few years or so, political background is still a major factor used for appraisal. It is highly unlikely that it will be dropped in the foreseeable future.

Another unique feature of the appraisal system in China is that the performance of senior factory cadres is sometimes assessed by subordinates through the public opinion survey method. Usually a cadre is rated on one of the following five scales: "outstanding", "good", "average", "barely acceptable", or "poor". Although such a system has some merits, those cadres who are considered "nice" but not necessarily "capable" are usually given high scores whereas those who are capable and very demanding are given low scores. In addition, the performance appraisal system in China is also faulted for its subjectivity and static rather than forward-looking attitude (Chen, 1989, p. 142).

Training and Management Development

The quality of China's labour force is significantly lower compared to that of other industrialized countries. For example, at the technical level, the ratios of senior technicians, middle technicians and junior technicians are 0.02, 0.24 and 0.74 respectively in China; whereas in Japan, the ratios are 0.32, 0.43 and 0.25 respectively in 1987. At the educational levels, the comparison between China and Japan is as follows: the ratio of Chinese workers and staff with post-secondary levels and above is 0.03 (Japan: 0.33); the ratio for high-school level is 0.16 (Japan: 0.57); and the ratio for medium-school level and below is 0.81 (Japan: 0.10) (Liao, 1991: 140). Recognizing the importance of worker education and industrial training in the reform programme, *The Decision Concerning Strengthening the Task of Worker Education* promulgated by the State Council in 1981 states that "Worker education is the important route to developing the nation's human resources and strengthening their intellectual capabilities. It is a dependable safeguard to help sustain the continuous growth of the nation's economy. It is closely related to the success at constructing the country to become a modern one."

Given the tradition of centrally allocating labour, there is a consistently high degree of State involvement in the provision and regulation of manpower training resources at the enterprise levels in China. Jurisdiction over worker education and training rests mainly with the State Education Commission and the Bureau of Training and Employment under the Labour Ministry. The All-China Federation of Trade Unions (ACFTU) also oversees and coordinates manpower and vocational training in the enterprise. At the state level, the government runs the two-year vocational/technical training schools which prepare secondary school graduates

Table 5:   Performance Appraisal of the Xiamen Arts & Crafts Co.

Factors for Evaluation	Weights (%)	
	Managers	Non-managerial Staff
Attitude of Work		
Discipline	6	7
Coordination	6	7
Responsiveness	6	7
Responsibility	6	7
Initiative	6	7
Sub-total	30	35
Performance-related Results		
Quality	5	15
Quantity	5	15
Instruction	7	—
Innovation, improvement	8	—
Sub-total	25	30
Capability		
Intellectual	5	5
Physical	5	5
Personality	5	5
Knowledge	5	5
Skills	5	5
Judgement	5	5
Expression, negotiation	5	5
Supervision	5	—
Applicability	5	—
Sub-total	45	35
Total	100	100

Score is assigned to each sub-factors ranging from 2 to 10 where 2 denotes "poor", 4 "relatively poor", 6 "average", 8 "relatively good" and 10 "outstanding".

Source: Liao (1991, pp. 257-258)

Table 6:   A Typical Worker Education and Training in a State Enterprise

Training Routes	Training Schemes for Shopfloor Workers and Staff
Secondment Training in Other Plants	Short-term Training Class
Technical Schools	Job-specific Training
Vocational Schools	Workgroup Leadership and Supervisory Training
Workers and Staff University	
Correspondence University (Open University)	Various Technical Trainings
	Skills Development
Television University	Technical Performance Training
Evening University	Basic Skill Training
Post-secondary Colleges and Institutes	
Enterprise Management College	
Training Abroad	

for technical work. After 1979, the Bureau also designated to labour service companies the role of training unemployed youths with basic vocational skills for a duration of three months to one year in preparation for placement with various units. Most state-owned enterprises also run their own vocational and technical schools. Apprentice training takes place largely in the workplace and is organized by the individual factory.

Worker education basically consists of two parts: political courses and cultural-scientific subjects (Luk, 1990, p. 257). The former is aimed to indoctrinate workers and staff with communist ideology, patriotism and moral values; whereas the latter is to equip them with basic knowledge of various subjects relevant to daily life and work. This form of worker education usually takes place after work. For industrial training, there are basically three forms: (1) one-the-job training; (2) special short-term training courses relating to new technology; and (3) longer-term training courses with leave from the enterprise. Workers can be sent back to universities or abroad for training relevant to their work (Liao, 1991, pp. 137-138). At each enterprise there is usually an education committee to staff and oversee the worker education and industrial training function. A network of multiple-training routes and training schemes for a typical state enterprise is presented in Table 6.

In order to promote the standards of technical personnel and continue to upgrade the education level, the state further introduced a contingent of administrative directives and regulations at the enterprise level, which among others include the following provisions:

(1) training centres are to be established by the big enterprises within their own plants; (2) the capital costs for building and constructing the training facilities can be borne from the enterprise's investment and re-investment funds; (3) each enterprise is to be required to set aside a minimum 1.5 percent of its total wage bill as the recurrent fund for worker

education – defrayed in the same manner as costs of production, and covering such items as scholarship for training abroad, training outlays on technological transfer, updating and development; (4) the trade union organization at the enterprise is to mobilize 25 to 37.5 percent of the union funds assigned from the enterprise for spending on worker education, and (5) a reservoir of full-time and part-time teachers ... be recruited and enlisted in enterprises at the manning scale of 3 to 5 in every thousand (Lansbury and Ng, 1989, pp. 12-13).

While training for technical staff has been emphasized since the reform programme was launched in 1979, training for cadres or managers ("management development") has been carried out with equal vigour. It has been recognized that training of a core of managers is the key to successfully implementating the nation's modernization programmes. This view is in great contrast to the Cultural Revolution years (1966-76), during which management as a subject of study was abolished by the 35 tertiary institutions which offered the programme modelled after the Soviet Union. Since 1978, management training has been resumed and expanded (Warner, 1985, 1986a, 1988). In March 1979, the China Enterprise Management Association (CEMA), a professional organization with nation-wide networks created jointly by the State Economic Commission and industrial enterprises, was established to promote and diffuse modern management techniques. In conducting executive training programmes, China also received help from EEC countries and Japan, Canada, United States, Hong Kong, as well as from professional associations and international consulting firms. Hundreds of management books and scores of management journals/magazines have been published in the past ten years or so. Many training manuals have also been written and published. As a result, modern management concepts such as PERT, critical path analysis, network analysis, value analysis and value engineering, total quality control (TQC), management by objectives (MBO) and systems analysis, have become widely known to managers. The techniques are now beginning to enter practice in some enterprises, though with varying degrees of success. Even Western behavioural psychology, which at one time would have been considered totally incompatible with Chinese socialism, is widely discussed if not openly practiced.

Managers are trained both by enterprises themselves as well as universities and finance/economics colleges. Since 1979, most leading universities have established management schools offering both undergraduate and graduate (Master's and Ph.D.) programmes. Management courses have a heavy emphasis towards quantitative methods such as production engineering, quality control, operations research, statistics, and so on. Qualitative courses such as HRM, marketing and skill developments are rather weak. This is a legacy inherited from the now-discarded Soviet model which looked at management merely as technical problem-solving. In recent years, universities have found it difficult to place their fresh management graduates, as enterprises prefer their own in-house managers who have years of managerial experience. China now faces a dilemma: while there is an acute shortage of managers on the one hand, enterprises are reluctant to recruit management graduates. In 1991, the State Education Commission selected nine key universities to offer the first-ever MBA programmes in China, roughly modelled after the Western countries. Although China's State Planning Commission and EEC jointly launched an MBA programme in Beijing a few years ago, it is not taught by local academics. It has been reported that the initial response to MBAs was less than satisfactory. The traditional Master's Degree in Management continues to be preferred by applicants (Xu, 1993). The future success of the new MBA will largely depend on the extent of backing by enterprises which are willing to recruit the new MBA graduates on a large scale. Of course, programmes offered need to meet the needs of enterprises in order to win their support.

Promotion System

For a long time the promotion system in Chinese state-owned enterprises has been based on seniority of workers and staff rather than on performance. There is also a "theory" which argues that a cadre who "contributes" relatively more in his present position should be promoted. This "theory" has in fact been practiced. It implies that cadres holding important positions generally have better opportunities for promotion than those who do not hold such positions, as it is claimed that the former play more important roles in an enterprise. This theory can be faulted because achievement of an enterprise can be attributable to a number of factors such as the wisdom and efforts of a number of colleagues rather than one single senior cadre alone.

"*Guangxi*" (or "connection") is another major factor in determining who should be promoted. Workers and staff who have special "*guangxi*" with the superiors in power, either through family connections or forming special cliques, normally get promoted over others lacking the connections. The above various malpractices deny many capable workers and staff the chance for promotion to higher ranks. Furthermore, a cadre can also be known to be "sitting on an iron chair" while enjoying an "iron rice bowl"; i.e. he can be promoted to senior ranks but cannot be demoted regardless of his capability or performance. This has resulted in a phenomenon where there are too many high-ranking officials with too few rank-and-file staff, and there is over-staffing with too few staff actually performing work (Chen, 1989, p. 101). Although the reform programme since 1979 attempts to rectify such practices, there are a number of obstacles which make it difficult to implement: (1) due to low wage levels, senior cadres are unwilling to step down from their positions of influence as doing so would imply that they would lose their many concomitant privileges which they are used to enjoying; (2) the lack of a rigorous performance appraisal system in place; and (3) the lack of implementable and enforceable regulations. However, based on a survey of six Chinese state-owned enterprises conducted in 1984, there is evidence that promotion is increasingly based on ability (Warner, 1986b).

Other HRM Practices

Labour disputes and arbitration. With the adoption of "the labour contract system" in 1986 and the bankruptcy law of state-owned enterprises in 1985, labour could be laid-off or made redundant. Laid-off workers can request improved terms and conditions of service in a new labour contract. Sometimes disputes do arise. In 1987 the State Council adopted the "Provisional Regulations for Settlement of Labour Disputes in State-owned Enterprises", which sets up various arbitration channels for solving disputes. When a contract-related labour dispute occurs, it is first referred to an arbitration committee at the enterprise level for arbitration. If solution cannot be achieved, the dispute is then referred to a governmental arbitration council. Issues relating to dismissals or firing of workers for violation of discipline can be referred directly to the latter body for arbitration. If one side disagrees with the arbitration result, it can appeal to the People's Court for final arbitration. This is the first step taken in China to protect the rights of both the enterprise and its workers and staff. However, little is known about how many cases of labour disputes are actually handled by arbitration since no such data are published.

Retirement. There is uniformity in the retirement systems for all workers and staff of all governmental units including state-owned enterprises in China. Basically, there are three forms of retirement schemes in existence: (1) the *tui xiu* or retirement scheme; (2) the *li xiu* or retirement for old "revolutionary cadres" scheme; and (3) the *tui zhi* scheme. Retirement schemes apply to workers and staff who have reached retirement age (normally age 60 for males and age 55 for females) and have worked for ten consecutive years. Early retirement is allowed for workers and staff with poor health. Under this scheme, a pensioner can enjoy three types of benefits: (1) a retirement allowance of 60%-80% of monthly wage depending on one's years of service; (2) medical benefits equivalent to that of the same level of existing workers and staff; and (3) a special subsidy for those who move to other places (i.e. home town, etc.) for retirement.

The *li xiu* scheme is a new scheme adopted in 1981. It applies only to cadres and workers joining the communist revolution before the founding of the PRC, i.e. November 30, 1949, who have reached the ages of 60 to 70; and it is dependent on their ranks. On top of enjoying the same benefits as those in the first *tui xiu* scheme, workers and staff under this scheme can receive additional wages equivalent to two-month's pay as subsidy per annum plus other benefits such as allowances for visiting relatives and building a new home in one's home town.

The third scheme, *tui zhi*, applies to workers and staff who do not qualify for the first two retirement schemes, but who have to quit work due to poor health or incapacity. They can draw 40% of the standard wage per month for their living. Medical and other benefits are identical to the first two groups of pensioners.

Each enterprise is responsible for disbursement of all benefits to the foregoing three groups of pensioners. This responsibility constitutes a heavy burden to the enterprise both financially and administratively as the payrolls become larger and longer. Enterprises which suffer from continued loss are particularly hard hit and have to rely on the state to bail them out.

Contract workers employed after 1986, are requested to purchase labour insurance from a social labour insurance company located in their work place. They can draw pension benefits after retirement. Moving toward a social security system for workers and staff is the current trend in China. However, it covers only a small portion of the population, i.e. level of "socialization" is still low (Kui, 1993, p. 87).

HRM Practices of Joint Ventures

Since 1979, China has adopted an "open-door policy" and has opened up its economy to foreign investment. Five types of foreign investment can be identified inside China, namely, processing and assembly, compensation trade, equity joint ventures, wholly foreign-owned enterprises and cooperative ventures. In official policy, equity joint ventures are assigned a crucial role in achieving the two main objectives of the open-door policy; namely, facilitating the transfer of technology and management techniques, and increasing foreign exchange earnings. Joint ventures are of considerable importance in terms of the number of establishments and value of direct foreign investment (Nyaw, 1993). In this section we shall briefly highlight some salient features of joint venture HRM practices in China.

Joint ventures in China are mainly governed by the "Law of the PRC on Chinese-Foreign Joint Ventures" (hereafter called the Joint Ventures Law) and the "Regulations for the Implementation of the Law of the PRC on Chinese-Foreign Joint Ventures" (hereafter called the Joint Ventures Implementation Regulations) which were promulgated in 1979 and 1983 respectively. According to the Joint Ventures Law, there is no upper limit to foreign investment in a joint venture, but the law sets a minimum of 25 percent for investment by foreign party or parties (Article 4, Joint Ventures Law, 1979).

The Joint Ventures Law further stipulates that the board of directors shall be the highest organ of authority. Initially, the law required that the chairman of the board be appointed by the Chinese partner, and the vice-chairman (or vice-chairmen) by the foreign partner (Articles 33, 34, Joint Ventures Implementation Regulations). However, on April 4, 1990, a crucial amendment to the Joint Ventures Law was made by the Chinese government; i.e. chairmanship of the board of directors will be subject to negotiation by both the Chinese partner and the foreign investor, or by election at the board meeting. Should the chairmanship go to a person from one side, the deputy chairmanship will then be a person from the other partner. This change could be interpreted as a major concession from China. The relaxation of the stipulation of chairmanship of the board of directors is in line with the generally accepted practice of international joint ventures in most countries. The responsibility for day-to-day operations and management rests with the general manager, who "within the scope authorized by the board of directors ... represents the joint venture in external matters and, within the venture, appoints and dismisses subordinate personnel, and exercises the other powers conferred upon him by the board of directors" (Article 39, Joint Ventures Implementation Regulations). In other words, the general manager is the chief executive of the joint venture and has full autonomy within the policy guidelines established by the board.

Unlike state-owned enterprises, there is no provision for workers' congresses in joint ventures in China. However, as stipulated in the Constitution of the Trade Unions of the PRC, trade union organizations in joint ventures are an integral part of the All-China Federation of Trade Unions (ACFTU), but "provisions dealing with the special problems of trade unions in such enterprises are stipulated separately by the ACFTU" (Article 35, Constitution of the Trade Unions of the PRC, 1983). Unfortunately, ACFTU to date has no provision dealing specifically with trade unions of joint ventures. Instead, provisions dealing with the joint ventures in China are contained in two separate sources. In the "Provisions for Trade Unions of Special Economic Zone Enterprises in Guangdong Province", it is stipulated that trade unions in such enterprises (including joint ventures) are legal entities and the chairmen of trade unions are their representatives (Article 3). On the other hand, the Joint Ventures Law stipulates that a joint venture is a limited-liability company (Article 4, Joint Ventures Law). Trade unions are therefore not appendages of the joint venture. Trade unions have been formed in most joint ventures in the PRC in accordance with the Joint Ventures Law. However, they are not mandatory. Ninety-two percent of foreign or foreign participating firms had their trade unions set up in Shenzhen in 1987 (*Shenzhen SEZ Daily*, April 16, 1987). Although there is no workers' congress in a joint venture, the "Joint Ventures Implementation Regulations" stipulates that there is a need for the enterprise "to heed the opinions" of staff and workers, particularly on labour-related issues. However, the extent of worker participation in management is far less than in state-owned enterprises.

Unlike its counterpart in the West, the "management" of a joint venture is supposed to "positively support" the work and activities of its trade union (Chen and Li, 1987, p. 87). Union representatives have the right to sit in the board of director's meeting to air workers' opinions, although they do not have the right to vote.

China considers that it is the political right of staff and workers to join a trade union in the joint venture. The trade union of a joint venture, like its counterpart of any enterprise in China, is a member of the local union for a particular industry or the local trade union council. Theoretically, the general objectives of the joint ventures are in line with that of the trade unions, i.e. to make the venture a success. A successful joint venture benefits both the foreign investors (in the form of "profit") and the nation (in the form of technology transfer and foreign-exchange earnings). However, it is emphasized that the trade union of a joint venture has a duty to represent the interests of the staff and workers, and "shall have the right to represent them in signing labour contracts with the joint venture and supervising the implementation of such contracts" (Article 96, Joint Ventures Implementation Regulations).

One unique aspect of the trade unions of joint ventures in China is that they deal directly with foreign partners or their representatives with regards to labour disputes or grievance. They are not dealing with the joint ventures *per se* as the latter are owned partly by the state. Unions are a transmission belt between the Party and the masses. They are not supposed to "negotiate" with the Party-controlled state. In dealing with foreign investors, union representatives need considerable skills in negotiation, which they tend to lack. The Chinese emphasize "consultation" rather than "confrontation" in dealing with most matters. Should a labour dispute such as a worker's dismissal not be resolved through consultation, one or both parties can request arbitration of the local government, in accordance with the Provision for Labour Management in Chinese-Foreign Joint Ventures (Article 4). However, arbitration seems to be rare in Chinese joint ventures. In contrast to the adversarial roles of many trade unions in Western countries, the Chinese partners emphasize that the trade unions of joint ventures in China are cooperative and conciliatory. Among other things, they organize vocational, scientific, and technical studies, and they educate the workers to observe labour discipline and to fulfil the economic task of the enterprise. Joint ventures have to allot a sum equal to two percent of the actual wages of all staff and workers as union funds to finance these activities (Articles 98-99, Implementation Regulations).

We now turn to other issues of labour management such as the employment and wage system. As a joint venture in China involves two or more partners from different value structures and socioeconomic systems, its personnel system becomes more complex. As indicated in preceeding sections, Chinese state-owned enterprises have little control over the employment of the workers and staff. Although labour-management reform has been introduced in the last few years, it is carried out only on a limited scale. In contrast to state enterprises, the workers and staff of joint ventures are principally hired by the enterprise through the labour service company with approval from the labour bureau, or through advertisements. Successful candidates may undergo a three-to-six-month probation period, a practice commonly found in a market economy. Theoretically, the joint ventures will have priority to recruit qualified workers and staff previously engaged in other units. However, because of the lack of an effective labour market in China, the firms have to "consult" with the units concerned – the success rates of which are known to be low as the latter are usually reluctant to release their workers and staff unless they themselves are partners of the joint ventures.

A joint venture has the right to lay off staff and workers whose employment is considered redundant (Provisions of PRC for Labour Management in Chinese-Foreign Joint Venture, 1986). It can also fire undisciplined workers or those who have committed serious offenses. This has in fact taken place. China Hewlett-Packard Ltd. has fired nine workers since its inception to 1987 (*Hong Kong Economic Journal*, June 28, 1987), and a successful Hong Kong-Chinese joint venture manufacturer of matchbox toys in Shanghai has dismissed eleven workers from 1980 to 1986 (Koo, 1987). None had encountered opposition from the trade unions. On the contrary, they had the latter's support since reasons for dismissals were justified.

As far as salaries and wages, bonus, welfare benefits, and labour insurance for workers and staff in the joint ventures are concerned, it is stipulated that a joint venture's salary and wages and bonus system should adhere to the principles of "to each according to his work", and "more pay for more work" (Article 39, Joint Ventures Implementation Regulations). The distribution principles are analogous to that of the Chinese state-owned enterprises which subscribe to the "socialist" principle of "from each according to his ability and to each according to his work" after China launched its economic reform programme in 1979. In fact, there is little difference between China and other market economies as far as this particular principle is concerned. What matters is the actual pay practices of the enterprises.

Article 8 of the Provisions for Labour Management in Sino-Foreign Joint Ventures in 1980 stipulates that the wage levels of the local staff and workers "shall be fixed at 120 to 150 percent of the real wages of the staff and workers of state enterprises in the locality in the same line of business." Apparently, the higher wage levels are intended to attract competent staff and workers to work in the joint venture enterprises. However, it does not take efficiency and work intensity into special consideration as the latter is, in general, higher than 20-50 percent as compared to that of state-owned enterprises. In addition, staff and workers are younger and have brighter ideas as they are generally recruited from the labour market rather than "being assigned". They are also willing to work harder. The fixing of wage levels at 20-50 percent higher, therefore, is not entirely justifiable as it lacks flexibility.

The wage fund of a joint venture is derived from its "labour service fees" allotted by the enterprise. Labour service fees paid to local staff and workers include wages, labour insurance, medical welfare, and subsidies of various kinds. According to a survey, wages of staff and workers account for about 70 percent of total labour service fees of joint ventures. It also varies from different localities (Lin, 1992, p. 117). The amounts of these fees are decided at the board level each year.

The foreign partners consider that workers and staff of a joint venture do not enjoy all the fruits of labour services fees paid by the joint ventures. This may have a negative impact on the workers' motivation to work. The Chinese side argues that benefits and various government subsidies currently enjoyed by staff and workers are, in fact, paid by the government. Therefore, joint venture enterprises have to pay back the Chinese side for its contribution in accordance with the standards for state enterprises. However, various subsidies are difficult to calculate especially as price in China is mainly an "administered price" which does not reflect scarcity of resources.

There is no single "model" of wage payment to staff and workers of joint ventures in China. Instead there emerges a variety of wage patterns. In general, the wage level can be broken down into the following five components: basic wage, floating wage, position wage, piece-rate wage, and bonus. The basic wage is the wage which guarantees that workers and staff can meet daily basic needs, whereas the position wage is a remuneration for holding a certain position. When a position changes, the position wage will change accordingly. The floating wage refers to the system whereby workers' wages may float fully or partially, the levels of which depend on the profitability of the enterprise in different periods.

According to a survey of 38 joint ventures conducted in Shenzhen SEZ, there are as many as 13 combinations of the wage components for firms in the survey differing by industry, location, or class of workers (Nyaw and Lin, 1990). For production workers, the "wage + bonus" model is more common. The bonus is generally linked to workers' efficiency. The different wage patterns are in line with the Provisions for Labour Management which stipulate that the system of wage standards, type of wages, bonuses, etc., are at the discretion of the board of directors (Article 9). A joint venture has autonomy in deciding which wage pattern suits them best. The survey results in Shenzhen show that workers and staff of joint ventures were generally satisfied with the amount of wages they received. The satisfaction levels were as follows: "extremely satisfactory" (5.3 percent), "satisfactory" (47.4 percent) and "moderately satisfactory" (4.2 percent). Only about five percent of workers and staff were not satisfied (Nyaw and Lin, 1990). This can be explained by the fact that workers and staff receive higher wages than their counterparts in state-owned enterprises. It can also be justified by the fact that efficiency of joint venture enterprises is higher vis-à-vis state-owned enterprises in China. This may also indicate that financial reward is an effective means to elicit greater efforts from staff and workers.

The foregoing discussion focusses on compensation for staff and workers from the Chinese side. As far as expatriates are concerned, their remuneration is based on a contract signed between the employees and the joint ventures subject to approval by the board of directors. Expatriates usually hold managerial or supervisory positions or serve as consultants. In general, foreign employees receive a comparable wage which they would otherwise receive in their own countries plus hardship allowances and other benefits. The term "hardship allowance" is not used in China as it is sensitive to the Chinese partners. The general practices are to include them in an "other benefits" item.

Conclusion

China has encountered formidable problems in managing its labour force in its quest for national modernization. Both unemployment and "disguised unemployment" (i.e. overstaffing where marginal productivity of labour is equal to zero) are known to be high although no official statistics are ever published regarding the level of unemployment rates where the figure is considered to be "sensitive". On the other hand, there is a vast pool of unskilled labour which badly needs training. Retraining of existing workers and managers under the reform programme is also a pressing need because either their skills are obsolete or lacking completely – particularly the managerial skills.

In China there is a high degree of state control over human resources in the industrial sector. Under the centrally-planned system, there was an extensive and elaborate set of laws, rules and regulations in guiding allocation of human, financial and material resources. State-owned enterprises had little or no autonomy in deciding the use of human resources, which had thus stifled their invigoration and initiatives. Unlike Russia which adopted the "shock therapy" approach in its economic reforms in the early 1990s, China has followed a step-by-step method which is characterized by a Chinese generic term "crossing the river by touching the stone beneath it". Market forces have been gradually introduced into the industrial management system since 1979 (Henley and Nyaw, 1986). Although the marketization process has accelerated since 1992, it still maintains certain elements of socialism such as the socialist principle of distribution in its wage system as well as its welfare structure and retirement benefits. The "market socialism" evolving in China is characterized as "Socialism with Chinese Characteristics" by Deng Xiaoping. The latter term is vague and has not been clearly articulated. The evolving marketization process of China's reform programme until now clearly demonstrates that the state continues to have a high degree of involvement in setting various new rules and regulations. This is certainly true of human resource management of state-owned enterprises as discussed in this chapter.

The HRM policy and practices of the Chinese state enterprises are in a state of flux under the reform programme. New HRM policies and regulations had been constantly introduced or promulgated in the last decade or so. It is expected that more new schemes will be introduced in the foreseeable future. For example, it was revealed to this author by a high-ranking cadre of the Labour Bureau in Yantai that the state is now drafting a minimum-wage law for workers in various regions or localities for implementation in 1994. A collective bargaining mechanism relating to wage determination is also to be introduced in protecting workers' rights in the foreign-funded enterprises which is expected to take effect in 1994 (personal interview, October, 1993). Despite these changes, the HRM practices in state-owned enterprises in China have not yet reached the levels of sophistication comparable to those of established firms in developed countries. For example, job analysis and job evaluation are practically non-existent in state enterprises. After surveying a dozen textbooks on HRM in China, the author found that none has covered these two important topics on HRM. Lack of proper job evaluation has meant that wage levels are more or less arbitrarily determined by state bureaucrats for all Chinese state-owned enterprises. Under China's existing marketization scheme, there is a growing similarity between HRM practices in China and other Asian market economies at the conceptual level. In essence though, these practices usually have different meanings than are generally understood in a market economy. For example, new policy permits "mobility" of workers and staff. However, given that a mature and sophisticated labour has not yet emerged, labour mobility among state enterprises exists in name only, if an enterprise does not allow its workers or staff to transfer to another unit; or if it does allow the transfer, it demands the recruiting firm to "compensate" for the past "training costs" involved, the amount of which is arbitrarily determined. This practice is not acceptable in a market economy. Another notable example is that "subsidy" to workers and staff in Chinese state enterprises is, in fact, part of the wage payment rather than a form of "fringe benefits" as it is generally understood.

Prior to the economic reform in 1979, labour and personnel management was an insignificant function in state-owned enterprises. The human resource has never been considered as a strategic element in the enterprise management. Consequently, the professional status of personnel cadres are far lower than that of engineers and accountants. Personnel managers are, in fact, not professionally trained. They are merely policy implementators rather than strategic decision-makers. As a result, most human resource managers in Chinese state-owned enterprises to date cannot deal with a wide range of complex human resource issues in the ever-changing macro environment. Although the importance of human resources has been recognized, the professionalism of human resource managers needs to be upgraded. As a first step to revamping the HRM structure, it is necessary to design a set of uniquely tailor-made professional courses for HR managers. Such courses are presently lacking in China. Over time, it is expected that due recognition will be given to professional human resource managers as the Chinese economic system moves closer to a market system.

References

Chen, Kuotai (1989). *Personnel Management*. Beijing: China People's University Press (in Chinese).
Chen, S.F. and P.K. Li (eds.) (1987). *The Management of Chinese-Foreign Joint Venture*. Kexue Puji Publisher (in Chinese).
Chen, Suo (ed.) (1985). *Comprehensive Labour and Personnel Management in Enterprises*. Shanghai: Shanghai Science and Technology Press (in Chinese).
Deng, Xiaoping (1984). *Selected Essays of Deng Xiaoping (1975-1983)*. Beijing: Remin Chubanshe.

Feng, Lanrui and Zhao Lukkuan (1984). "Urban Employment and Wages." In Yu Guangyuan (ed.) *China's Socialist Modernization*. Beijing: Foreign Languages Press, 567-617 (in Chinese).

Harper, P. (1971). "Workers' Participation in Management in Communist China." *Studies in Comparative Commission*, July-October, 111-140.

Henley, J.S. and P. Chen (1981). "A Note on the Appearance, Disappearance and Reappearance of Dual Functioning Trade Unions in PRC." *British Journal of Industrial Relations*, XXI(1), 87-93.

Henley, J.S. and M.K. Nyaw (1986). "Introducing Market Forces into Managerial Decision-making in Chinese Industrial Enterprises." *Journal of Management Studies*, 23(6), 635-656.

Jiang, Xiwei and Shen Hungsen (1985). *Industrial Enterprise Management*. Beijing: Economic Management Press. (in Chinese).

Jin, Qi (1984). "New Bonus System Lifts Limits." *Beijing Review*, 27(26), June 25.

Koo, S.K. (1987). "Understanding Business Relationships Between China and Hong Kong." Speech presented to a seminar organized by the Chinese Executives Club, Hong Kong Management Association, December 12 (in Chinese).

Kui, Shiyung (1993). *The Development and Management of Market System in China*. Beijing: China Planning Press (in Chinese).

Lansbury, R. and Ng Sek Hong (1989). "Manpower Development in China: A Cursory Note." Paper presented at the Symposium on Labour-Management Relations in the Asia Pacific Region, Centre of Asian Studies, University of Hong Kong, August 28-30.

Liao, Chuenwen (1991). *Human Resource Management*. Shanghai: Tungchi University Press (in Chinese).

Lin, Gongshi and H.P. Chou (1992). *An Introduction to Joint Ventures: Investment, Establishment, Organization and Management*. Beijing: Tsinhua University Press (in Chinese).

Littler, C.R. and M. Lockett (1983). "The Significance of Trade Unions in China." *Industrial Relations Journal*, 14(4), 31-42.

Luk, H. (ed.) (1990). *Enterprise Labour Management*. Beijing: Labour Personnel Press (in Chinese).

Nyaw, Mee-Kau and G.S. Lin (1990). "Wage Models of Joint Ventures in China: A Preliminary Study," unpublished mimeograph (in Chinese).

Nyaw, Mee-Kau (1993). "Direct Foreign Investment in China: Trends, Performance, Policies and Prospects." In J.Y.S. Cheng and M. Brosseau (eds.) *China Review 1993*. Hong Kong: The Chinese University Press, 16.1-16.38.

Reform Document (1984). *Reform of the Economic Structure*, Party document adopted at the Third Plenary Session of the 12th Central Committee of the Chinese Communist Party, Beijing, October.

Special Study Group of Workers' Wage (1991). "Staff Income Composition and Corresponding Policy Research." *Management World*, 3, May, 85-90 (in Chinese).

State Statistical Bureau (1984). *Glorious 35 Years, 1949-1984*. Beijing: China Statistics Publication.

Su, T.L. and Chu Chinfang (eds.) (1992). *Ren Shi Xue Dao Lun (Fundamentals of Personnel)*, Beijing: Beijing Normal College Press (in Chinese).

Tian, Jiyun (1986). "On the Present Economic Situation and Restructuring the Economy." *Beijing Review*, 29(6 and 7), February 10.

Warner, M. (1985). "Training China's Managers." *Journal of General Management*, 11(2), 12-26.

Warner, M. (1986a). "The Long March of Chinese Management Education." *China Quarterly*, (106), 326-42.

Warner, M. (1986b). "Managing Human Resources in China: An Empirical Study." *Organization Studies*, 7(4), 353-356.

Warner, M. (1988). "China's Management Training at the Crossroads." *Journal of General Management*, 14(1), 78-91.

Warner, M. (1990). "Chinese Trade Unions: Structure and Function in a Decade of Economic Reform, 1979-1989." Management Studies Research Paper No. 8/90, Cambridge University, U.K.

Weiji, L. (1991). *Wage System in China*. Beijing: China Labour Publishing Press (in Chinese).

Xu, Kuohua (1993). "China's MBA: Current Status and Future Prospects." Paper presented to the Conference on Management Education in PRC, Hong Kong and Taiwan, Hong Kong, May (in Chinese).

Yu, Guangyuan (1985). "Reform During Socialist Construction in Terms of World and Chinese History." *Social Sciences in China*, 3, 23-38.

Zhang, Ku (1982). "Chengdu Machine Cutting and Tools System Reform." *Jinji Guanli*, 18, 22-26 (in Chinese).

Zhao, Limin (ed.) (1990). *Enterprise's Labour and Personnel Management*. Tienjen: Tienjen Science and Technology Press (in Chinese).

Zhao, Lukuan and Pan Jingwa (1984). *Labour Economics and Labour Management*. Beijing: Beijing Press (in Chinese).

Human Resource Management in South Korea

Marianne Koch, Sang H. Nam, and Richard M. Steers

Recently, both management and economic researchers have focused increased attention on the unparalleled growth and development of the Korean economy. However we measure it, Korea has indeed been an economic success story, emerging from the ashes of both World War II and the Korean War to become the seventeenth largest economy and the twelfth largest trading partner in the world. Its gross domestic product has risen an average of 8.7% per year over the past thirty years, surpassing even the growth rate of Japan and Germany. While much has been written about the economic foundations of such growth and some has been written about the general subject of business and management, very little is known about Korean human resource management (HRM) practices.

In this paper, we attempt to redress this omission by examining the cultural interplay between corporations and their employees as they attempt to achieve a suitable employment relationship. In particular, we consider recent trends in HRM and industrial relations as they affect employee behavior and corporate performance in Korea. This paper is divided into six parts: 1) a geo-political overview of the country; 2) the context surrounding HRM/industrial relations activities; 3) an overview of Korea's human resources as a nation; 4) a specific examination of Korean HRM policies and practices; 5) the Korean HR manager as a professional; and 6) the future of HR practices in Korea. Throughout, we will examine how cultural influences helped shape the management of human resources in this East Asian country.

Geo-political Overview Of South Korea

The Land

The Republic of Korea (South Korea) occupies the southern half of the Korean peninsula. Its only land boundary is with the Democratic People's Republic of Korea to the north. South Korea is approximately 966 kilometers (600 miles) long and 217 kilometers (135 miles) wide and covers a land mass of 99,117 square kilometers (38,925 square miles). Thus, the country is about the same size of

Indiana in the United States. China is to the far north, bordering North Korea, and Japan lies 193 kilometers (120 miles) to the east.

Most of Korea (approximately 80%) consists of rugged, mountainous terrain. Historically, this has helped Koreans defend themselves from various invasions and to preserve traditional Korean culture. At the same time, however, it makes both commerce and agriculture more difficult. Land suitable for planting is in limited supply and transportation is difficult although major progress has been made in recent years.

The People

South Korea today consists of over 42 million people. Approximately 80 percent of the people live in urban areas. The capital, Seoul, consists of over 10 million people and represents the commercial and political hub of the country. The next largest cities (Pusan and Taegu, with populations of 3.4 million and 2.0 million respectively) are pale in comparison to Seoul in terms of importance. A fact about the capital that is repeatedly pointed out to visitors is that it lies only about 45 kilometers (or "30 seconds by missile") from the border with North Korea. Needless to say, Koreans from all walks of life are continually aware of possible security threats from the north.

The Koreans are believed to be decendents of several Mongolian tribal groups that migrated from Manchuria in pre historic times. Over time, they became a distinct homogeneous race quite apart from either the Chinese or the Japanese. Their language belongs to the Ural-altaic family and originally had more in common with Turkish, Finnish, Mongolian, and Hungarian than Chinese. However, over time and as a result of Chinese influence, the language increasingly assumed a Chinese flavor and until the mid-15th century all writing consisted of Chinese characters. In 1446, King Sejong, perhaps the most respected leader in Korean history, introduced the *han-gul* alphabet as a means of better representing the Korean language sounds. Through this de velopment, Korea and the Koreans took one more step forward in the development of a national identity.

Korean Values and Beliefs

While traditional Confucian values characterize much of what we now see in Korea, their impact on society is blended in a curious way with a series of more contemporary or modern values that significantly influence how business is done. Many of these newer values result from the significant changes Korea has had to undergo during the past several decades. The Japanese occupation prior to the Second World War, for instance, introduced significant changes in the administrative, legal, and educational fields (Rhee, 1985). The extent of this influence was somewhat limited, however, by the restrictions placed by the Japanese on Korean participation in economic planning and management. Since World War II and the Korean War, with the concomitant rise in Western involvement in Korean affairs, many so-called Western values have begun to become more prevalent in the society. Democratic values, combined with increasing urbanization and globalization, have put the Koreans in ever-increasing contact with the peoples of the world. More and more young people are being educated in the West, particularly the United States, and they have tended to take new ideas back home to blend them with their own. And for those Koreans who never leave the country, there is the continual presence of the American military as a further influence on social patterns.

As a result of this blending of new and old, we see the emergence of a people who place high value on achievement, individualism (compared to the Japanese if not the Americans), perseverance, loyalty, optimism, and a nationalism approaching xenophobia (Hurst, 1984; Hofstede and Bond, 1988). Koreans also have a strong sense of national cohesiveness, due in part to their unitary ancestral roots. That is, Koreans are proud that they have maintained a single blood line throughout their 4,000 year history, despite repeated invasions over the centuries. These traditional values have been reinforced during the period of industrialization.

In addition, however, possibly because of the repeated patterns of invasion and occupation, there appears to be a strong sense of insecurity and preoccupation with survival that permeates much the political and economic environments (Kim, 1987). National security and business development are intimately interrelated and many of the government policies that made the growth and development of Korea's major business enterprises possible were the result of a pragmatic need to centralize both effort and limited resources to insure safe, timely, and predictable returns on investment. Thus, we can see that in the words of K.D. Kim (1987, p.15), "The distinctive nature of Korea's development stems from something even deeper than the secular orientation of Eastern religions. This may be a combination of the experiences of the Korean people throughout their history, and their adaptability to their changing environment, which together have produced the nation's current business success."

The Korean HRM/Industrial Relations Context

If we try to understand the context in which HRM and industrial relations activities occur within organizations, we must begin with an understanding of the role of Confucianism in Korean culture. Confucianism is a code of ethical behavior developed by a civil servant who lived in China around 500 B.C. The foundations of Confucianist beliefs are contained within the so-called *five cardinal virtues*: filial piety and respect, subservience of women to men, strict seniority, mutual trust between friends, and absolute loyalty to one's legitimate superiors. In other words, the fundamental nature of human relationships in Korea is not that of interactions among equals but rather interactions between unequals. "Correct" interpersonal behavior is determined by gender, age, and position in society and a breech in this social etiquette carries with it severe penalties.

Several characteristic behaviors of Korean workers can be traced to this Confucian tradition. For instance, there is a strong work ethic in South Korea, which is exemplified by long working hours that have continued to this day despite recent increases in wages and affluence (Oshima, 1988). Ancestor worship and the importance of family, another aspect of Confucianism, is also believed to influence Koreans' dedication to hard work and saving for the future, as well as emphasizing education and self-improvement as a means of sustaining one's clan.

Early Experiences in Industrial Relations

Because industrialization in South Korea has occurred relatively recently, the history of labor-management relations in South Korea is relatively brief. As in other industrialized countries, the industrial relations scene is dominated by three central players: unions, the government, and corporate management. What follows is a brief history of the relations between the three parties.

From the turn of the century through World War II, Korea was occupied by the Japanese and the economy was dominated by Japanese firms (Oshima, 1988). Korean language, culture, and history were suppressed by the Japanese rulers. All Koreans had to take Japanese names and Japanese became the official language of the country. As a result, the early vestiges of labor unions in Korea emerged as part of the resistance to Japanese colonialism. In fact, labor clashes were often seen as patriotic and received widespread support from the Korean people (Chung and Lie, 1989).

By the end of World War II and the division of Korea into North and South, Korean labor leaders, like the Korean people in general, were divided into philosophical camps of capitalism and communism. For a time, both communist-oriented and capitalist-oriented unions existed in the South. In 1949, South Korean President Syungman Rhee's government threw his support behind the Federation of Korean Trade Unions, or FKTU (similar to the AFL-CIO in the U.S.), and helped it defeat the pro-communist unions in South Korea (Chung and Lie, 1989). This was the beginning of strong governmental involvement in union activity in South Korea.

After the Korean War (1950-1953), the Trade Union Act was passed. This act was similar to the National Labor Relations Act of the United States, and gave workers the right to organize, bargain collectively, and engage in collective action. One important difference from the U.S. National Labor Relations Act, however, was the absence of an enforcement agency (like the National Labor Relations

Board) to protect rights of the newly created unions and their members. This lack of any enforcement mechanism made the rights of labor difficult to realize.

In reality, the government controlled the FKTU, and the enforcement of labor laws during the 1950s was minimal. Anti-government sentiments among unionists increased and in 1960, labor activists joined student demonstrations aimed at overthrowing the government of President Rhee. The government's response to this threat was to use government security forces to curb labor's new assertiveness. In fact, in some cases, government agents have been more aggressively anti-labor than companies (Kearney, 1991). Suppressing labor activity in the 1960s and 1970s was a government strategy to control labor costs, a key ingredient of the government's economic development plan (Chung and Lie, 1989). Or, as some observed, the position of the government was that strong labor unions were "conflictful, unproductive, and disruptive in the context of economic growth" (Choi, 1983, p. 282).

Enterprise Unions and Works Councils

Governmental pressure on labor relations intensified during the 1970s and early 1980s under President Park Chung-Hee. In 1971, the Korean government issued the Special Act on National Security; this Act required government approval to hold any labor negotiations. In 1980, the government banned industry-wide national unions altogether and replaced them with enterprise (or company) unions following the Japanese model, in which each union was wholly contained within an individual company. Enterprise unions were managed by labor-management works councils. Korean labor laws (especially the Labor-Management Council Act as revised in 1988) mandated that every company with over fifty employees create a "works council" (nosa hyeobeuihoe, in Korean) designed much along the lines of those found in Western Europe. These councils were seen by the government as a substitute for labor unions in handling labor-management relations.

In theory, these works councils provided for equal labor and management representation and such bodies were to serve as a means of democratizing the work place and providing for labor-management cooperation and productivity enhancement. In actual practice, however, management typically controlled the works councils and they lost their potential as an agent for real change in the workplace. The selection of the labor representatives was frequently influenced by management, which often acted on its own behalf. Moreover, the councils were inexperienced in negotiating, owing in part to the Special Act on National Security and, thus, during disputes government officials were called in by management to settle differences. The government policy of "growth first, distribution later" typically led to pro-management contract settlements (Chung and Lie, 1989).

An example of how these works councils functioned can be seen in the case of Hyundai Motor Company (Bae, 1987). At Hyundai, the council consisted of twelve management representatives (including the factory's chief executive officer, the personnel director, and ten members selected by the CEO) and twelve members elected annually by the workers. The council was required to meet at least once every three months but could meet more often if it wished. Agenda items that could be discussed at the council were clearly specified: 1) how to improve productivity and efficiency at work; 2) how to educate and train workers; 3) how to prevent labor-management disputes; 4) how to handle workers' grievances; 5) how to promote workers' interests; 6) how to increase safety and improve the work environment; and 7) how to increase labor-management cooperation.

Regulations governing the council at Hyundai also stipulated that: 1) the purpose of the council is to foster labor-management cooperation and industrial peace; 2) members of the council should not engage in any behavior that might encourage a labor-management dispute or break the industrial peace; and 3) the council cannot be used for collective bargaining.

In actual practice, many workers felt that these regulations put them in an impossible situation. The law governing works councils required that all worker demands had to be channelled through the works councils, yet real collective bargaining was proscribed. Hence, all the workers at Hyundai could do was to express their grievances to management; they had no mechanism to require management to agree with their demands. Even so, this system continued to function throughout most of the 1980s.

In the early 1980s, union membership hovered around 800,000 in South Korea. The revocation of the Special Act on National Security in 1981 revived labor rights and increased labor organizing. Union membership began to increase sharply in 1985, and grew to over 1,600,000 union members by 1989 (Clifford, 1990). By 1991, 2.1 million Koreans belonged to unions.

The 1987 Reforms and Beyond

The rapid rise of unionism was aided by the political reform declaration of President Roh Tae Woo on June 29, 1987. Roh's declaration reduced government intervention in labor-management relations and served to revitalize unionization rights. For example, under the reform, union shops were now allowed if more than two-thirds of the employees in an establishment were union members. National unions were again permitted. New amendments to the Trade Union Act identified unfair labor practices by management for the first time, including: 1) dismissal of, or discrimination against, workers who join or attempt to organize a union; 2) rejection of a collective bargaining agreement; and 3) interference with workers in the formation and operation of a trade union (Chung and Lie, 1989).

Workers, with their new-found rights but without bargaining experience, took their grievances concerning wages and working conditions to the public for support. As Korean companies and the country as a whole became more prosperous, workers and unions began a concerted drive to improve both wages and working conditions. The number of strikes rose from 300 in 1986 to over 4,000 in 1987 and continued into 1988 and 1989. Behind these strikes was a widespread feeling by workers that the Korean economic miracle was not being shared equally throughout the country. Many felt that the miracle itself had occurred only as a result of the sacrifice of the Korean workforce and that the time had come for a return on that investment. In fact, real wages in Korea had fallen substantially behind the nation's Gross Domestic Product. Moreover, real wages also lagged far behind industry-wide productivity gains and workers decided it was finally time for change (Steers et al., 1989). An era of real collective bargaining had begun.

Whatever the cause, the strikes were hard fought and cost the Korean economy dearly. Results of the strikes led to major pay increases across broad segments of the workforce. In 1987, the average pay increase in the industrial sector was 22 percent. This was followed in 1988 by an additional 15 percent average pay raise. Hence, in two years, wage rates – and labor costs – rose 37 percent even before considering fringe benefits (Steers et al., 1989). Korea was no longer a cheap labor country, and Korean companies began almost at once to look for cheaper sites offshore (most notably China, Indonesia, Malaysia, Thailand and, most recently, North Korea) for their production and manufacturing needs.

In spite of the renewed rights of labor unions since 1987, there remain a number of ways in which labor activity continues to be constrained. For instance, unions still have no national contracts, there are still no shop-steward networks, and third-party interventions are not allowed under current law (Clifford, 1991). Overall, the Korean government has been less involved with labor-management relations since 1987. Moreover, the number of strikes has subsided in the past few years as wages and working conditions continue to improve (Clifford, 1991). The government's *laissez-faire* attitude is not complete, however; where it serves its political or economic purpose, the government continues to intervene and support either labor or management – predominantly the latter.

An Overview of Human Resources in Korea

The configuration that an HRM system takes on in organizations and society typically depends in large part on the types and characteristics of the people for which it is responsible. In the case of Korea, this system has been built on a foundation characterized by an abundance of human resources and a scarcity of natural resources. The Koreans are indeed rich in human resources: 98% of South Koreans can read and write; 80% graduate from high school, and the majority of high school graduates get some sort of college or vocational training after high school (Chang, 1989). Koreans are a highly-educated people, and have been since the beginning of their history (Oshima, 1988; Kearney 1991).

The general lack of natural resources has only served to intensify the need to develop the country's human resources. Korea must import most of the natural resources required to manufacture their products and exports. "Manufacturing and service industries are human resource intensive and the poverty of natural resources requires, therefore, that human resources be developed in order to be able to export" (Oshima, 1988, p. 111).

Another labor force characteristic that Korea shares with the rest of the industrialized world is an increase in the labor force participation of women – a phenomenon that traditionally did not occur due to Confucian tradition. Korean women are entering the labor force in increasing numbers: among women 15 years and older, 40.7 percent worked in 1984, and 47.2 percent worked in 1990 (Clifford, 1991). Korean women in managerial or executive positions is quite rare, however; they typically hold low-level jobs and they only make between 50 and 80 percent of what Korean men do for the same work (Clifford, 1991).

Korean HRM policy makers also face the issue of the current shortage of new entrants into the labor force. Twenty-seven percent of the 42.9 million South Koreans are currently in school, from elementary school through graduate school (Jameson, 1991). The shortage of workers is one factor precipitating the entrance of women into the workforce. Some companies are even hiring foreign workers to fill low level jobs.

Finally, it is important to note that lifetime employment and internal labor markets occur much less frequently in Korea than in Japan. In fact, South Korea workers are more mobile and change jobs more frequently than their Japanese counterparts, although such changes are less frequent than are found in the U.S. (Lie, 1990).

HRM Policies and Practices in Korea: Examples from the Field

In view of the current trends in human resources in Korea, it is important to know the extent to which such trends are reflected in the HRM policies and practices of contemporary Korean corporations. In this section, we go beyond corporate personnel policy statements and examine the actual practices of several major companies to see what can be learned about how human resources are "managed" in Korea.[1]

Korean HRM practices have resulted largely from two forces. The earliest – and perhaps still the most pronounced – influence emerges from the Confucian tradition that permeates so much of Korean society. As noted above, here we see the origins of corporate concern for such values as hard work, dedication, seniority, and absolute loyalty to the company. Paternalistic leadership and top-down decision making are characteristics of the prevailing management style in Korean businesses. As noted by Lee and Yoo (1987, p.75), "The distinguishing characteristics of Korean management ... can be summarized as follows: clan management;

top-down decision making; flexible lifetime employment; high mobility of workers; Confucian work ethic; paternalistic leadership; loyalty; compensation based on seniority and merit rating; bureaucratic conflict resolution; highly bureaucratic and yet less degree of formality and a standardized system; close government-business relationship within the company." This management style extends to the management of human resources as well.

The second and more recent influence on HRM practices is the more contemporary push to utilize "modern" (typically Western) approaches to management and personnel development. Here, companies are concerned with making improvements in such practices as employee recruitment, employee training, performance appraisals, and so forth. This increasing tendency toward newer approaches has been facilitated by executive decisions to make their personnel policies more "scientific". These decisions, in turn, have been encouraged by changes in the economic, social, technological, and political environments surrounding the corporations.

Whatever the cause, changes are indeed emerging as corporations begin moving away from the traditional approach toward a more professional approach to management. In this section, we review the general trends in HRM policies and practices in Korean firms. Included here are the following: 1) recruitment and selection; 2) training and development; 3) compensation and benefits; 4) performance appraisal and promotion; and 5) terminations, lay-offs, and retirement.

Recruitment and Selection

Recruiting methods of Korean firms vary considerably according to such factors as company size and the positions for which they are recruiting. As we might expect, smaller companies tend to rely less on open recruitment and testing and more on personal connections in recruiting blue-collar employees. This is also true of companies located in the more rural areas of Korea. For the major corporations, however, trends in both white-collar and blue-collar recruitment are discernable.

White-collar employees: Becoming a salaryman. For white-collar jobs, applicants are often actively recruited from the better-known universities. Most applicants must pass company-sponsored entrance examinations that typically include English-language proficiency in addition to knowledge both in a major field and in general abilities or common sense. Moreover, applicants must pass through extensive interviews (sometimes including one with the Chairman of the company) and reference checks. New college graduates are preferred to people with experience and, once hired, the new employees are typically assigned to such core departments as planning, finance, and accounting after a relatively short training and indoctrination period. This contrasts with the typical American recruiting practice where previous work experience is more valued and where new employees are typically assigned to a functional department based on their specialty. It also contrasts somewhat with Japanese companies in that new employees in Japan are more likely to begin their jobs in the field, rather than at corporate headquarters.

A recent study by Steers et al. (1989) sought to identify how the major Korean companies describe the "ideal manager". What, in other words, are the keys to managerial success and how do companies identify these characteristics when hiring new employees? Results across companies like Lucky-Goldstar, Samsung, Daewoo, Doosan, Sunkyong, Kumho, and others yielded similar results. The ideal young candidate for most companies was both smart and highly-motivated. He exhibited a strong work ethic and a positive attitude toward hard work for company and country.[2] Personal initiative was important here. He had a good character and background and was willing to learn. And, finally, he presented himself well and was comfortable to be around. Some companies also indicated that the ideal candidate was a risk-taker who had the capacity to make rapid and incisive decisions under pressure.

Consider the example of the Samsung Group, which hires between 3,000 and 4,000 people per year and has a selection ratio of about 4:1. In examining management potential, Samsung considers native intelligence as the first prerequisite. Initial screening for this is made based on written tests. Following this is a series of interviews, in which company officials examine more interpersonal factors, such as initiative, personal responsibility, and interpersonal style. At times, two candidates are put into a debate with each other to see how they perform under pressure. Throughout the process, the company tries to select those candidates with the greatest potential to develop into long-term, committed, and useful employees for Samsung.

Similarly, consider the application and screening process for salarymen – the term used in Korea to refer to white collar employees – at the Sunkyong Group. Sunkyong is a diversified corporation that now ranks as the fifth largest concern in Korea. The company attributes its success to a combination of high technology and human resources. Sunkyong has been an industry leader in the development of highly-sophisticated personnel policies that are designed to secure the best possible employees. Referred to as the "Sunkyong Management System" (or SKMS), Sunkyong has taken a systematic approach to management that incorporates the traditional management functions with a dynamic concern for developing employees to their fullest. Central to this model is the notion of *eui-yok* management, which is defined as providing the conditions under which individuals and groups can draw satisfaction from and take pride in their work.

Since it is often identified in surveys as one of Korea's most preferred employers, Sunkyong can afford to be highly selective in its new hires. In their policy manuals, the company identifies six primary criteria for selection (Office of the Chairman for Management and Planning, Sunkyong Group, 1986, 1987): 1) *paegie*, meaning "the spirit to get the job done and win the business"; 2) business knowledge; 3) business-related knowledge, such as foreign language expertise or practical science knowledge; 4) social attitudes and interpersonal skills; 5) home management, including having a stable home life; and 6) health management, including physical and mental well-being. Within the company, these six criteria are referred at the principles of "SK-manship".

When selecting new employees, information concerning these six criteria are collected from screening documents, aptitude tests, personality tests, interviews, and physical examinations. Letters of recommendation are requested from outsiders and reviewers are asked to rate the candidate's "positive thinking", "progressive action", "responsibility", and "social attitude". Finally, applicants are asked to complete an extensive self-report inventory that includes demographic data plus a self-appraisal on such variables as leadership, sociability, ambition, responsibility, and self-control. All of this information is then reviewed and assigned points by the professional personnel staff to decide who to hire. Throughout the process, the aim is to secure a small number of highly-skilled and highly-motivated employees who can fit into the company's culture and make a long-term commitment to develop and grow with the company.

Blue-collar employees: Back door and open recruitment. At the blue-collar level, corporate approaches to recruitment are quite different. It has been estimated that a large though unspecified number of blue-collar jobs are filled through what has been termed "back door recruitment", or what in the West is called an employee referral (de Mente, 1988). This involves hiring someone either because he is recommended by a friend or relative who is already employed by the firm or at the very least hiring someone who heard about the job through such channels. It is often felt that such techniques lead to good employees, since the company already has someone on the payroll who will vouch for the sincerity and dedication of the candidate.

In addition, many jobs are filled through "open recruitment", where prospective job candidates hear about openings through public announcements or through direct inquiries. And about ten percent of blue-collar hires come from vocational school placements. Graduates of technical high schools and vocational training institutes must obtain a skill-test certificate from the National Skill Testing Agency, while graduates of other high schools usually must pass company entrance examinations or have the support of a strong connection within the company. Some of the largest corporations, such as Hyundai and Samsung, manage their own vocational training institutes to insure a steady supply of well-trained workers.

Training and Development

Like their Japanese counterparts, Korean companies consider human resources to be the central building block for long-term corporate success. Considerable effort goes into the development of employees at all levels. With the increasing competitiveness of the early 1990s, this developmental trend continues.

Management training and the "all-around man". At the managerial level, the objectives and methods of corporate training and development are somewhat different that those found in the West. Here, the focus is not so much on gaining new job-related knowledge or skills as it is on molding current and future managers to fit into the company's corporate culture. Emphasis is placed on developing positive attitudes over professional skills under the assumption that loyalty, dedication, and team spirit are more important than current job skills. As the companies see it, their aim is to develop what is often called the "all-around man". The all-around man possesses general abilities; he is not a specialist. His commitment to the company and his coworkers is unquestioned and above all he fits into the group. Training is seen as one means of insuring this across the corporation.

To see how this works, consider the managerial training methods at Daewoo Group. Organizationally, the Education and Training Department reports directly to the Chairman's Office, in contrast to most Western companies. The Executive Director for Education and Training oversees and is responsible for all corporate developmental efforts. Many years ago, the company established a clear link between the development of employees and the development of the company. This can be seen in a recent statement of the basic principles for corporate training, where the company expressed the belief that its business philosophy and its business spirit (summarized by the motto, *creativity, challenge, and self-sacrifice*) are both directly influenced by the cultivation of Daewoo personnel. This, in turn, is influenced by the company's six training objectives (Education and Training Department, Daewoo Corporation, 1991):

- to implement the Daewoo business philosophy and business spirit;
- to develop managerial techniques and improve professional knowledge and specialized ability;
- to foster adaptability to meet changing business environments;
- to maximize organizational efficiency;
- to enhance the special identity of Daewoo employees;
- to motivate self-development.

A number of specific training programs are offered to facilitate these objectives (see Figure 1). We mention here four as illustrative of the variety and depth of such programs. At the entry level for new employees destined for managerial positions, Daewoo offers the Newcomers' Training Program. This program lasts eleven days and nights and include the following topics: 1) "Daewoo-manship" and the business philosophy; 2) an introduction to affiliated companies of the Daewoo Group; 3) a case study of job performance; 4) freshman's life planning; 5) a tour through affiliated companies; 6) a team demonstration; and 7) a videotaped speech by the Chairman.

Moving up the ladder, the Middle Manager's Training Program consists of fifteen days and focuses on improving managerial abilities, especially those relating to human resource management. Emphasis is also placed on understanding

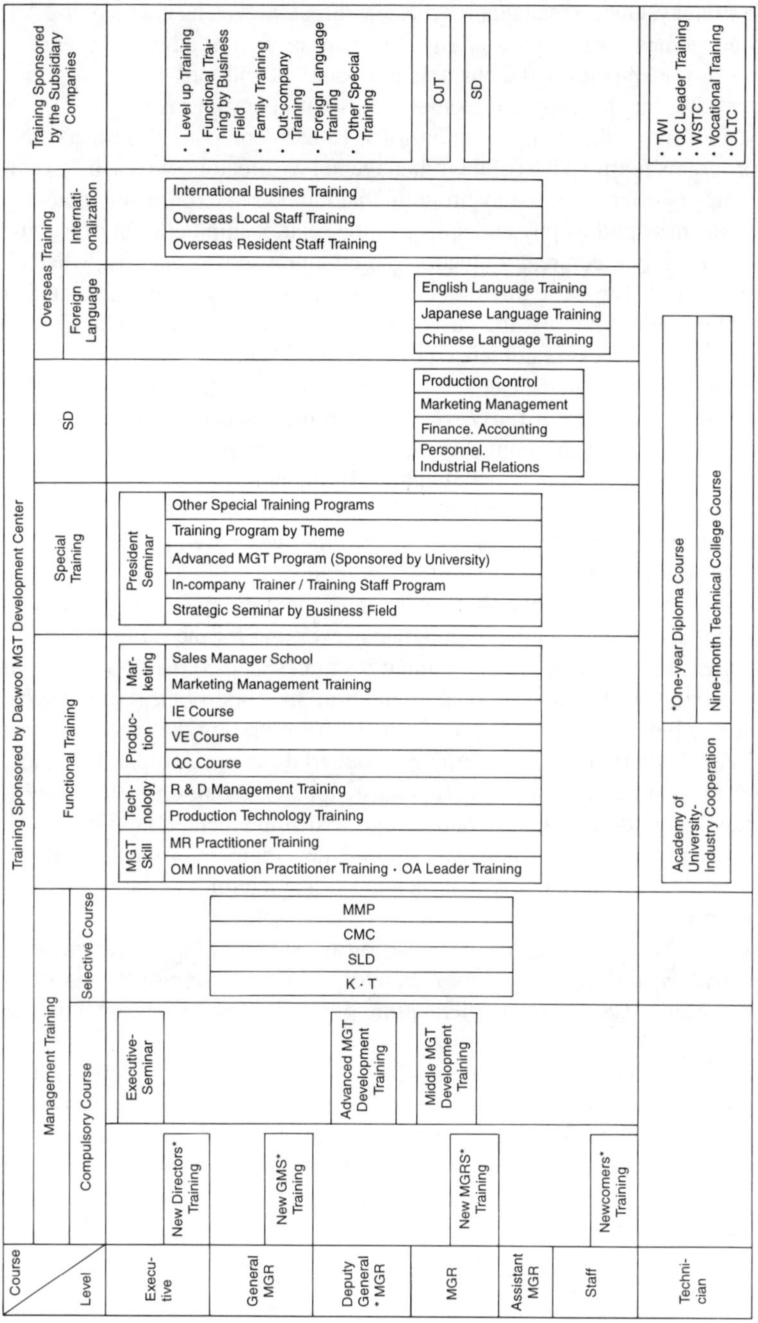

Training Sponsored by Dacwoo MGT Development Center

Management Training

Compulsory Course:
- New Directors* Training
- Executive-Seminar
- New GMS* Training
- Advanced MGT Development Training
- New MGRS* Training
- Middle MGT Development Training
- Newcomers* Training

Selective Course:
- MMP
- CMC
- SLD
- K · T

Functional Training

MGT Skill:
- OM Innovation Practitioner Training · OA Leader Training
- MR Practitioner Training

Tech-nology:
- Production Technology Training
- R & D Management Training

Produc-tion:
- QC Course
- VE Course
- IE Course

Mar-keting:
- Marketing Management Training
- Sales Manager School

Special Training

President Seminar:
- Strategic Seminar by Business Field
- In-company Trainer / Training Staff Program
- Advanced MGT Program (Sponsored by University)
- Training Program by Theme
- Other Special Training Programs

SD
- Personnel. Industrial Relations
- Finance. Accounting
- Marketing Management
- Production Control

Overseas Training

Foreign Language:
- Chinese Language Training
- Japanese Language Training
- English Language Training

Internati-onalization:
- Overseas Resident Staff Training
- Overseas Local Staff Training
- International Busines Training

Training Sponsored by the Subsidiary Companies
- Level up Training
- Functional Trai-ning by Business Field
- Family Training
- Out-company Training
- Foreign Language Training
- Other Special Training
- OJT
- SD
- TWI
- QC Leader Training
- WSTC
- Vocational Training
- OLTC

Academy of University-Industry Cooperation
- *One-year Diploma Course
- Nine-month Technical College Course

Course / Level:
- Execu-tive
- General MGR
- Deputy General *MGR
- MGR
- Assistant MGR
- Staff
- Techni-cian

Figure 1

corporate strategy. Once a manager reaches the director level, he is sent to the Advanced Management Training Program. This consists of four days and examines such topics as understanding the business environment and long-range corporate strategy. In addition, this program includes talks with the Chairman.

Finally, in a move that is uncommon for a Korean company, Daewoo offers training programs for the wives of their managers. For directors' wives, for example, the company offers a three-day program that includes the following topics: 1) Daewoo's business philosophy and spirit; 2) the relationship between office and home; 3) educational lectures; 4) "economic common sense"; and 5) "what's a happy home life?". The basic thrust of the wives' program is to demonstrate that the entire household – not just the husband – belongs to the Daewoo family and that the husband's success is influenced by a supportive homelife.

Thus, regardless of the level, Daewoo is committed to developing its managerial personnel through a series of fairly sophisticated programs tailored to the short and long-range goals of the company. A similar situation can be found in the management training procedures at Hyundai. Hyundai has as a matter of policy established the goal of having each of its 13,000 managers in the company visit the training institute a minimum of once every other year, even if only for a few days. Clearly, training is important for this company.

The general philosophy that underlies much of the training efforts at Hyundai consists of three concepts: 1) the importance of working for the further development of Korea; 2) the importance of human resources; and 3) the importance of international relationships and a global orientation. In support of this philosophy, three training objectives have been set forth: 1) incorporating the Hyundai spirit in the manager's daily life; 2) developing managerial skills and capabilities; and 3) strengthening international competitiveness. Finally, on an operational level, three principles guide actual program design and implementation. Thus, each program includes components relating to: 1) the development of managerial and technical skills; 2) the development of mental skills, including a heavy emphasis on what is termed "oriental values" such as creativity, positive thinking, tenacity, fraternity, devotion to company, and industriousness; and 3) the development of one's physical capabilities, including mandatory physical exercise beginning at 6:30 each morning. These three implementing principles aim to develop what the company refers to as the "Hyundai man".

Hyundai offers five kinds of programs for managers. These programs include top management executive training, mid-level managers programs, professional courses (e.g., accounting, job skills), language training, and rather unique courses to train trainers. Courses for top and middle managers cover different topics each year and a typical course lasts three to four days. Teaching methods are diverse and include lectures, case analyses, experiential exercises and in-basket techniques. Instructors come both from the company staff and from the more prestigious university business schools.

Training industrial workers. By contrast, at the blue-collar level, the primary instructional methods involve on-the-job training aimed at improving job-related skills and correct attitudes toward the company. As these employees gain experience, the focus of training shifts to the development of future first-line supervisors for the company. Hence, at this level, the approach to training is not unlike that found in many industrialized countries of the world.

Compensation and Benefits

The topic of employee compensation is always a difficult one to examine. Information is often confidential and what is public is often incomplete or misleading. Moreover, given the current volatile labor situation in Korea today, any specific data available would be subject to rather dramatic changes. Even so, we shall attempt within these limitations to provide a general description of the compensation and benefit policies of the largest Korean firms. As a starting point, it must be recognized that even with the recent sizable pay raises given to Korean workers, the average Korean employee – both blue-collar and white-collar – works longer hours than his or her counterparts in most other countries (including the newly industrialized countries) and often receives less money for doing so (Steers et al., 1989; Chung and Lie, 1989). Wage and salary determination in Korea consists of three factors: 1) basic wages; 2) allowances; 3) and bonuses.

Basic wage. The basic wage is clearly the largest and most important part of the wage package and consists of the employee's starting wage plus annual increments and cost-of-living adjustments. Starting salaries are determined largely by one's educational level and initial point of entry into the company. This, in turn, is influenced at least to some extent by external market rates (e.g., university graduates with science or technical backgrounds generally receive a higher starting salary that those with business degrees). Currently, high school graduates begin at salaries that are approximately 85 percent of those received by college graduates, compared to 70 percent in the U.S. and 80 percent in Japan.

Annual salary increases are determined largely by seniority and, to a lesser degree, merit. The concept of "pay for performance" or merit compensation is largely avoided except at the highest managerial levels since it is felt that a seniority system contributes more toward the maintenance of group harmony. Thus, over time, employee salaries tend to progress slowly upward for everyone as a group. The one exception to this is among production workers, who often see real pay *decreases* after the age of fifty due presumably to their reduced physical contribution to the company.

Allowances. The second component of the wage package consists of a set of allowances granted to employees. Allowances can take several forms. For example, the Korean Labor Standards Act requires employers to pay one-and-one-half times regular pay for each additional hour worked beyond eight hours per day (Kim, 1987). For white-collar employees, an overtime allowance of two hours per day is typically automatically added to one's pay. One-and-one-half times the base wage is also paid to employees working from 10:00 p.m. to 6:00 a.m. Employers are also required to provide workers with eight days paid leave for one full year's service without absence; each absence is subtracted from this total. Employees also typically receive one day of paid vacation per year for each year of tenure (e.g., five days annual paid vacation after five years of service), and after twenty vacation days are accumulated employees can take the extra days in wages instead of time off. In most Korean companies, like their Japanese counterparts, few employees actually take all the vacation time to which they are entitled for fear of appearing to show disloyalty toward the company.

Female employees are entitled to one day's paid leave per month and sixty days paid leave for pregnancy. Beyond what is required by law for both males and females, many companies offer additional allowances for such things as being assigned to a remote area, having an official skills certificate, possessing skills that are in short supply, and having a large number of dependents. Housing and car allowances are also common. In case of death, it is customary for the company to provide 1,000 days of wages plus funeral expenses to the family. All told, allowances often constitute about 30 percent of the employee's pay package.

The complexity of factors that comprise the Korean pay system has led many companies to employ a rather unique approach to the calculation of actual compensation. This is called the "Reverse Calculation System" (RCS). Under RCS, the employer pays employees a fixed monthly amount that is based on a formula estimate of all the expenses associated with the employee's allowances. This is preferred because of its simplicity over having to calculate each benefit for each employee on a monthly basis and the Korean government has generally held that such an approach is within the statutes of the Korean Labor Standards Act.

Employee bonuses. Finally, the third part of the wage package consists of employee bonuses. While not required by law and while ostensibly based on company performance, bonuses have come to be an expected part of the compensation system, in part because of the relatively low salaries paid to employees. The typical large company pays annual bonuses amounting to about four to six months' gross salary (referred to as a "400 percent" or a "600 percent" bonus); smaller companies typically pay somewhat less than this. Bonuses are usually paid out four times per year (to coincide with New Year's Day, the beginning of summer vacation, Korean Thanksgiving Day, and Christmas). The majority of companies provide bonuses in equal amounts according to one's level in the hierarchy. Even those companies that give differential bonuses (that is, giving different bonus amounts to employees at the same level) typically give 90 percent of the employees on each level the same amount. Most managers believe that in view of the cooperative nature of work it is simply not possible to differentiate performance levels between employees with any degree of accuracy (except at the higher levels of management). It also disturbs the harmony among employees.

While the amount of the bonus can vary depending upon business conditions, some companies continue to pay the bonus even during difficult economic times in order to show goodwill and maintain harmony within their workforce.

Performance Appraisal and Promotion

All large Korean companies (and many smaller ones) use some form of an annual performance appraisal system. At the blue-collar and lower managerial levels, the primary emphasis in such evaluations is on employee development, since promotion is largely based on seniority. (For salarymen, the first promotion usually comes after three to four years of employment.) Even so, companies take these evaluations very seriously since they represent a part of the human resource management process. Managers feel a special responsibility to help develop employees below them in exchange for employee loyalty to the company and its leaders. Throughout this process, evaluators look carefully at the "whole man" such that factors like sincerity, loyalty, proper attitude, and initiative receive as much attention as actual job performance in the evaluation.

At the higher levels of management, more emphasis may be placed on actual performance and contribution to the company (instead of seniority) as a determining factor in promotions. In some companies – particularly those involved in high technology – we even see the emergence of "star players", who move on a fast track toward the top. Even so, seniority still plays an important role in determining who gets ahead even at these higher echelons.

One of the more comprehensive performance appraisal systems can be found at Sunkyong. Like other companies, Sunkyong's approach places heavy emphasis on employee development. The goals set forth for the evaluation process include the identification of employee inadequacies or weaknesses in need of correction, the development of managerial capabilities, and the enhancement of the company's HRM process. Sunkyong's system begins with an extensive self-assessment by the employee. Employees are asked to complete this inventory accurately and sincerely, evaluating themselves on such factors as "SK-manship", managerial capacity, communication, coordination, and their adequacy for and satisfaction with their present assignment. For each factor, employees are asked to identify anything that may be obstructing their improvement on that factor. Employees are also asked to describe how their job performance has contributed to company well-being, as well as their feelings about general company administration.

This inventory, then, becomes input for interviews (and written reports) first by one's immediate supervisor and later by the supervisor's supervisor. Peer assessments from co-workers are also sought. Through extensive discussions, efforts are made to reach agreement concerning the employee's strengths and weaknesses and a plan of action for self-improvement. Ultimately, the written materials go to the corporate HRM department for final disposition and approval.

Throughout, emphasis is placed on developing the employee's long-term potential as a Sunkyong manager. In order to accomplish this, considerable effort is devoted to developing a trusting relationship between superiors and subordinates and insuring shared mutual expectations for the future of the company.

Terminations, Lay-offs, and Retirement

Under the Korean Labor Standards Act, termination of employees is legal so long as the company can show just cause. Under such circumstances, the employer must provide either thirty days' notice or one month's salary. In addition, severance pay equivalent to one month's salary for each year of continuous service must be paid.

In contrast to Japan, lay-offs are not uncommon in Korea and the concept of "lifetime" employment is rarely seen in practice. Instead, companies typically rely on a strategy of continued corporate growth and expansion to insure fairly stable employment. When lay-offs are necessary, companies often encourage older workers or female employees of marriageable age to leave, providing extra financial incentives in the process. Given Korea's extended family system, in which the incomes of all family members are often pooled, such laid-off employees are frequently absorbed back into the family and provided for.

Retirement is mandatory in most cases at age 55. Retiring employees typically receive a lump sum payment equal to one month's salary for each year of service. Few employees are offered part-time work or consulting work with the company after retirement, as is the case in Japan.

Professionalism and the Role of the Korean HR Manager

The development of the HRM profession in Korea is perhaps best described as just emerging from its nascent stage. The reason for this is that, in general, Korean management is still characterized by family management. Family members frequently hold top level jobs, as opposed to externally-hired specialists and professionals in the functional areas. These family members are not typically trained in human resource management and thus real innovation in HRM practices may be more difficult to carry out. There is some movement toward replacing or augmenting family member managers with professional managers, however. For example, at Lucky-Goldstar (one of Korea's largest firms), owners and founders established an executive committee in 1991 to plan and organize Lucky-Goldstar's human resource policies for the future (Nakarmi, 1991). Primary emphasis was to be given to developing entrepreneurial professional managers to oversee the future growth and development of the company.

To examine the nature and extent of these emerging changes, we had an opportunity in the summer of 1991 to conduct a survey of Korean HRM managers. Our aim was to replicate the Moore and Robinson (1989) study among Canadian HR managers to determine any differences between the two cultures with respect to their perceptions of the respect and importance of their field, the extent to which the input of HR managers was sought in making key personnel decisions, and the extent to which HR managers in Korea we viewed as an identifiable profession.

To accomplish this, we made use of the HRM questionnaire developed by Moore (Moore and Robinson, 1989). The questionnaire was translated to and back-translated from Korean, and all responses were anonymous. (As we report the findings below, we will compare the results with an equivalent sample of 426 Canadian HR managers using the same questionnaire; see Moore and Robinson, 1989.) Useable questionnaires were received from eighty-eight HR managers for a 76% response rate. For the sample, the average age was 36, and 87% of the sample had bachelors degrees. Of these, 44% of the degrees were in business, 18% in economics, and 13% in law, with the remaining degrees in various arts and sciences. The average tenure with the organization was nine years. Fifty-four percent worked for public corporations (with broad stock ownership), 25% for family-held companies, 9% for a government agency, and 7% for a government-owned corporation. The remaining 5% reported that they worked for employee-owned companies.

Our first interest in these data focused on how Korean HR managers see their role within the organization. As can be seen in Table 1, Korean HR managers tend to see their role in the organization quite differently than their Canadian counterparts. In particular, when compared with the Canadian sample, Koreans felt that they had more organizational support for their activities, provided greater leadership in hiring and promoting the best candidates, were less insular, knew more about operations than they were given credit for, actually practiced what they preached about personnel practices, and felt their primary responsibility was more to the employees as a whole than to management. Many of these findings can be explained by the Confucian traditions found in Korean organizations. For example, "good" Korean managers are expected to be a part of the entire group (not some small clique), be ideal role models for their subordinates (that is, practice what they preach), and stand up for correct moral principles (for example, selecting the best possible employees). Moreover, the Korean practice of extensive job rotation may explain why Korean HR managers report higher job knowledge than given credit for. Thus, the questionnaire results are consistent with expected Korean role behavior for HR practitioners.

Next, we examined the extent of the involvement of the HR department in important personnel decisions within the organization. As shown in Table 2, Korean HR managers described their level of involvement in such issues as research and planning, contract negotiations, training and development, and promotions and transfers as being significantly higher than that of their Canadian counterparts.

Table 1:   How Korean HR Managers See their Role

Items	Percent Agreement[#]	
	Korea	Canada
Supervisors outside the personnel office view personnel as a nuisance, not an aid	22	35*
Most personnel people keep up with recent developments in the field	67	64
Personnel people provide vigorous leadership needed to support merit principles in such actions as selection and promotion	74	58**
Personnel people stick together too much – speaking their own language and remaining aloof from those outside the field	21	33*
Personnel people usually know more about the operating programs they service than line managers give them credit for	88	68***
Few personnel people actually practice with their staffs what they preach to operating officials	3	43***
Most personnel people are prone to hide behind rules and regulations as an excuse for a lack of positive action	33	27
Most personnel programs have the respect of employees in the organizations they serve	61	55
The primary responsibility of the personnel office is to management rather than to employees	15	41***

N = 88 and 426, respectively, for the Korean and Canadian managers.
[#] Following Moore and Robinson's (1989) methodology, percent agreement is defined as the number of respondents who either agree or strongly agree with the item on a five point scale. Canadian data from Moore and Robinson are reported here for purposes of comparison.
  * Differences in percentages significant at .05.
 ** Differences in percentages significant at .01.
*** Differences in percentages significant at .001.

However, the Canadians saw their involvement in handling grievances, involuntary separations, and safety as being higher than that of the Koreans. Such differences may reflect the different emphases placed on the various HR functions in the two countries. For example, safety is a far more sensitive social – and legal – issue in Canada (and the U.S.) than it is in Korea, as witnessed by the plethora of health and safety regulations that exist in Canada. On the other hand, the majority of Korean companies see employee training and development as crucial to long-term competitiveness in view of the tendency toward *de facto* lifetime employment. Similarly, the Korean emphasis on HR planning and research and on promotion

Table 2:   Extent of HR Department Involvement in Personnel Decisions
            (rank order by level of involvement)

Personnel Decisions	Percent Reporting High Involvement[#]	
	Korea	Canada
Recruitment & selection	87	79
HR research	81	55***
HR planning	79	60***
Benefits	74	70
Contract negotiation	74	62*
Training and development	70	53**
Compensation	67	73
Human resource policy	64	71
Promotion	62	36***
Control/discipline	60	50
Performance appraisal	57	57
Transfer	56	36***
Counselling	55	56
Grievances	51	67**
Affirmative action/EEO	48	39
Involuntary separation	45	78***
Voluntary separation	40	44
Job design	37	35
Incentive payment	37	34
Safety	21	42***

[#]   Data are reported in percentage agreement using the method reported in Moore and
     Robinson (1989). Items are rank-ordered in terms of the relative influence of the
     Korean HR managers in each decision. Canadian data from Moore and Robinson are
     reported here for comparative purposes.
 *   Differences in percentages significant at .05.
 ** Differences in percentages significant at .01.
 *** Differences in percentages significant at .001.

and transfer also reflects the centrality of employees as a fixed cost and a key corporate resource, compared to the Canadian (and American) view that employees
are a variable cost of doing business.

Finally, we turned our attention to the extent to which HR managers were seen
in Korea as belonging to a distinct profession. As can be seen in Table 3, the
results point to the conclusion that Korean HR managers do not see themselves
as representing a distinct profession, while their Canadian counterparts do. In

Table 3:   Degree of Professionalism of HR in Korea

Professional Dimension	Percent Agreeing that Dimension is Highly Descriptive of HR Managers[#]	
	Korea	Canada
A body of specialized knowledge including standardized terminology	14	87***
Widely recognized certification based on standardized qualifications	18	31*
Code of ethics	31	55***
Members oriented towards a service objective	2	85***
Recognized by the general public as a profession	18	60***
Limited access to the field, based upon acquisition of standard skills/knowledge	26	63***
A professional society or association which, among other things, represents and gives voice to the entire field	22	61***
Practitioners are licensed	15	8*
Close collegiality among practitioners	31	73***

[#] Results for the Korean sample were scored according to the procedure outlined in Moore and Robinson (1989). Canadian data from Moore and Robinson are included for purposes of comparison.
  * Differences in percentages significant at .05.
 ** Differences in percentages significant at .01.
*** Differences in percentages significant at .001.

view of the similar nature of their respective responsibilities, this significant perceptual difference highlights not only a cultural difference in attitudes, but also the temporal definition of the profession. What is seen as a distinct and identifiable profession in one culture is viewed as just one more area of managerial responsibility in another. This phenomenon is consistent with the Confucian-influenced norms of considering managers as an integral part of the corporate family, instead of as members of a separate or distinct group. Family members do whatever is necessary for the family. They fit in; they do not stand out.

Summary and Future Considerations

The industrial landscape of Korea is indeed changing at a rapid pace. We have tried to summarize the nature and origins of these developments as they relate to the management of human resources. The next several years will witness even more developments as Korean firms continue to try to find their place in the global marketplace. Within this dynamic environment, predictions concerning the implications for HRM in Korea are at best problematic. However, we offer here several observations that seem to represent emergent trends in the "New Korea".

First, consider the prevailing social norms and mores of industrial Korea. Within the corporate environment, it is unclear at present how those social norms espoused by traditional Confucianism will be affected by the continued rise in unionism. On the one hand, the emphasis on hard work, self-improvement, and education suggests that workers might be willing to stand up to management in order to improve themselves, their working conditions, and their skills. Indeed, the labor movement has made significant strides in confronting management on behalf of industrialized workers. On the other hand, the Confucian tradition favors regimentation, authoritarianism, and social harmony; thus, there are still great pressures on Korean workers to not push too hard to improve their working conditions for fear of jeopardizing the balance of nature (Kearney, 1991). Achieving a workable balance between these two opposing forces represents a sizeable challenge for management and labor alike.

Next, consider the future state of industrial relations in Korea. Two issues will more than likely to predominate in the near future. First, both labor and management will have to develop improved skills in collective bargaining and dispute resolution. Government intervention in labor relations over the last five decades has not allowed management and labor parties to develop the skills and knowledge necessary for collective bargaining to succeed (Chung and Lie, 1989). Only time and repeated interactions can teach both parties how to work through their differences by themselves.

The second issue in South Korean industrial relations is that management will have to learn how to deal with a more vocal and powerful workforce. As a result of the growth in unionism, employees' demands for better wages and working conditions have become a reality for Korean workers since the late 1980s. Indeed, over the past five years, wages in Korea were among the fastest rising in the world. As worker demands continue to increase, issues emerge concerning how Korean companies will be able to meet such demands without losing further ground in the increasing competitiveness that characterizes the global manufacturing sector.

Finally, consider the future of HRM. In our view, the field of human resource management will continue to rise in importance in Korea as union activity remains high. Some have argued that proficiency in human resource management is now necessitated as a means of avoiding union organizing. Indeed, some *chaebols*, like Samsung, continue to practice union avoidance by paying high wages and offering generous benefits.

Developments in Korean HRM will depend in part upon the future political landscape of Korea's government. Because of the traditionally strong links between business and government, major shifts in governmental policy – such as those we are currently witnessing with President Y.S. Kim – will have a direct impact on how businesses are organized and managed. Enhanced government support of workers' rights and of ethical codes of corporate conduct are currently serving to constrain the way in which Korean firms approach employee relations. As a result, firms are having to enhance their HR expertise in order to lessen the threat of increased unionization and industrial action.

Korean firms will also face an increasing challenge from female workers. Korean traditions have blocked women from achieving most positions of importance in corporations. However, the emergence of an organized Korea women's movement – plus the need for more skilled employees – is beginning to bring pressure to bear on Korean firms to open up their managerial ranks to female employees. This movement, if successful, will serve to bring new challenges and opportunities in the Korean HR arena and, indeed, may represent a major challenge to the fundamental Confucian traditions of the country.

In summary, current evidence suggests that the HR function in Korean firms will continue to rise in importance due to the limited skilled human capital available in Korea to meet the new global realities. As Korea continues to be squeezed by Japan and the United States on technological frontiers, contemporary HR practices represents one avenue for Korean companies to pursue as they try to continually upgrade their employees. It has been noted that Korea stands now in a "sandwich economy;" that is, the technological giants are increasingly refraining from sharing breakthrough technologies with Korean companies for fear of the competition. At the same time, however, Korea has lost its traditional position as a cheap labor country. As a result, increasingly, Korean firms lag in both technological innovation and price competitiveness, with a resulting loss of market share in several key industries. Contemporary HR practices may help alleviate this squeeze by maximizing the contribution of available human resources to industrial competitiveness.

Endnotes

1. The data reported in this section are based upon the research reported by Steers, Shin, and Ungson (1989), as updated by the current authors.
2. In this section, we use the masculine pronoun exclusively to reflect the fact that, with few exceptions, males hold the dominant positions in South Korean corporate management. In point of fact, there is no "gender revolution" or serious societal move toward advancing women into managerial ranks in Korea at the present time.

References

Bae, K. (1987). *Automobile Workers in Korea*. Seoul: Seoul National University Press.

Chang, C.S. (1989). "Human Resource Management in Korea." In K.H. Chung and H.C. Lee,(eds.), *Korean Managerial Dynamics*. New York: Praeger.

Choi, J.J. (1983). "Interest Conflict and Political Control in South Korea: A Study of Labor Unions in Manufacturing Industries: 1961-1980." University of Chicago, Ph.D. Dissertation.

Choi, J.J. (1989). *Labor and the Authoritarian State: Labor Unions in South Korean Manufacturing Industries, 1961-1980*. Seoul: Korea University Press.

Chung, K.H. and H.K. Lie (1989). "Labor-Management Relations in Korea." In K.H. Chung and H.C. Lee, (eds.), *Korean Managerial Dynamics*. New York: Praeger.

Clifford, M. (1990). "Pre-emptive Strike." *Far Eastern Economic Review*, April 19, pp. 74-75.

Clifford, M. (1991). "Inoffensive Spring." *Far Eastern Economic Review*, May 23, pp. 28-31.

DeMente, B. (1988). *Korean Etiquette and Business Ethics*. Lincolnwood, Ill.: NTC Business Books.

Education and Training Department, Daewoo Corporation (1991). *Education and Training at Daewoo*. Seoul, Korea.

Hofstede, G. and M. Bond (1988). "The Confucian Connection: From Cultural Roots to Economic Growth." *Organizational Dynamics*, Spring, pp. 5-21.

Hurst, G.C. (1984). "Getting a Piece of the ROK: American Problems Doing Business in Korea." Hanover, N.H.: Universities Field Staff International Reports.

Jameson, S. (1991). "Soldiers to Help Ease Labor Pinch in South Korea." *Los Angeles Times*, July 8, p. D1.

Kearney, R.P. (1991). *The Warrior Worker: The Challenge of the Korean Way of Working*. New York: Henry Holt and Company.

Kim, S.J. (1987). "Labor and Employment." In A. Whitehill, (ed.), *Doing Business in Korea*. London: Croom, Helm.

Lee, S.M. and S. Yoo (1987). "The K-type Management: A Driving Force of Korean Prosperity." *Management International Review*, 27(4), pp. 68-77.

Lie, J. (1990). "Is Korean Management Just Like Japanese Management?" *Management International Review*, 30(2), pp. 113-118.

Moore, L.F. and S. Robinson (1989). "Human Resource Management Present and Past: Highlights from a Western Canadian Survey of Practitioner Perceptions." In A. Petit and A.V. Subbarau, (eds.), *Proceedings of the Administrative Sciences Association of Canada*. Montreal: Personnel and Human Resources Division, McGill University.

Nakarmi, L. (1991). "At Lucky-Goldstar the Koos Loosen the Reins." *Business Week*, February 18, pp. 72-73.

Nakarmi, L. (1993). "Is Korea Blowing its Big Chance?" *Business Week*, August 23, p. 42.

No author (1993). "Hyundai's Labor Strife: A Harbinger of Future Labor Movements." *Business Korea*, August, p.13.

Office of the Chairman for Management and Planning, Sunkyung Group (1986). *Sunkyung Management System*. Seoul: Sunkyung Group.

Office of the Chairman for Management and Planning, Sunkyung Group (1987). *Outline of Human Resources*. Seoul: Sunkyung Group.

Oshima, H.T. (1988). "Human Resources in East Asia's Secular Growth." In *Economic Development and Cultural Change*, Vol. 38 (Supplement), pp. 5103-5122.
Rhee, Y.S. (1985). "A Cross-Cultural Comparison of Korean and American Managerial Styles." In B.W. Kim, D.S. Bell, and C.B. Lee, (eds.), *Administrative Dynamics and Developments: The Korean Experience*. Seoul: Kyobo Publishing Company.
Sohn, J.A. (1993). "Samsung Group: Embracing Breathtaking Change." *Business Korea*, August, pp. 15-19.
Steers, R.M., Y.K. Shin, and G.R. Ungson (1989). *The Chaebol: Korea's New Industrial Might*. New York: Harper & Row.
White, G. (1991). "Asia's Shifting Search for Labor." *Los Angeles Times*, April 15, p. D2.

Human Resource Management Practices in Singapore

Yuen Chi-Ching and Yeo Keng-Choo

Introduction

Singapore is an island-nation situated at the tip of the Malay peninsula with a total land area of 640 square kilometres. It has a population of 2.7 million (1990 census) comprising 77.7% Chinese, 14.1% Malays, 7.1% Indians and 1.1% of other races. The country's economic activities are concentrated on manufacturing, services (finance, banking, transportation and communication) and commerce which together make up 87% of its gross domestic product. Although a small country, its achievements have often been described as remarkable.

As a newly-industrialised country, the double digit growth of its economy in the 1970s and 1980s has earned it a place among the "four tigers" of the Asia-Pacific region. Its per capita GNP, which was US$ 12,000 in 1992, is ranked second to Japan among countries in this region. Of a workforce of 1.55 million (1991), its labour force participation rate is 64.8% and unemployment rate is low at 1.9% (1991). For more than a decade, Singapore workers have been rated top by a US-based international consulting firm, BERI (Business Environmental Risk Intelligence) (National Productivity Board, 1992).

These achievements are not random events but deliberate efforts initiated by the government, drawing on the country's only resource – its people. The government's efforts are supported by employers and the labour movement. This tri-partite participation is a distinct feature in the growth of the country and has shaped many of the human resource management practices in Singapore.

Historical and Economic Development

Singapore was founded by the British as a trading outpost in 1819 and trade flourished, attracting migrants mainly from China and India to join the indigenous Malay population. Until World War II and the subsequent achievement of self-government status in 1959, the economy was rural and based on entrepot business.

The newly-elected government which took over from the British in 1959, was faced with a serious unemployment situation among other problems. It decided to industrialise and urbanise so as to create more employment and provide a basic standard of living for the population. Efforts to achieve these objectives began and the Economic Development Board (EDB) was established in 1961 to spearhead the industrialisation programme. The Board's work continued into the period of merger with Malaysia from 1963 to 1965. The separation from Malaysia in 1965 and the cessation of British protection in 1967 created greater impetus for economic planning.

Since foreign investment and know-how were key factors for the success of the industrialisation programme, the government worked at gaining workforce cooperation and acceptance of multi-national companies (MNCs). Labour laws were introduced to bring in line labour relations practices that are essential for good labour-management relations. Attention was given to the provision of efficient infrastructure for industry. The aim was to make Singapore attractive as a manufacturing centre for MNCs (Ariff & Tai, 1991).

By the end of the 1980s, foreign-owned companies had become prominent not only in manufacturing where they accounted for the bulk of the outputs and exports (about 70%), but also in the services sector including finance and business services. The evidence shows that MNCs are generally better managed and their overall business efficiency is higher. They also bring to the country modern business practices in various areas including human resource management.

Another important factor in the economic growth of Singapore is the management of its population growth. Until World War II, the population of Singapore had been increasing primarily through immigration. There was no large scale immigration in the post-war period but, consistent with the world-wide phenomenon experienced in developing countries, the rate of population increase accelerated because mortality had declined rapidly while fertility remained constant (Saw, 1991). The population growth rate in 1957 was 3.5%. As a result of controls on immigration and an intensive family planning programme, the growth rate fell to 1.8% in 1977 and reached a low of 1.4% in 1987. With jobs created through the industrialisation programme, full employment was attained in 1979. Meanwhile, the success of the family planning programme had resulted in a decreasing number of youths entering the labour market each year. A tight labour situation was thus experienced in the late 1970s. The emphasis of the economic strategy was then changed to inducing higher productivity and creating more value-added products. Instead of focusing on labour intensive industries, the EDB's efforts shifted to encouraging investments in high-technology industries.

Other than investments, there was much concern with increasing productivity through automation and the development of a highly skilled workforce. Since 1981, the productivity movement has increased in momentum under the National Productivity Board (NPB) which was set up in 1972. Besides promoting productivity concepts and practices, the NPB supports industries through training and consultancy.

The tight labour situation also brought problems of labour turnover. In a 1983 study of productivity in the manufacturing sector by the NPB (National Productivity Board, 1983), more than 50% of the respondents indicated that they had problems with high labour turnover. A task force on job-hopping appointed by the NPB found that the average resignation rate was 23% in 1987 and that the problem was more serious in the manufacturing and commerce sectors (National Productivity Board, 1988).

Government Initiatives in Human Resource Management

Industrial Relations

The government's efforts in the development of Singapore have had significant impact on many areas relevant to human resource management practices in the country. The first of these is in the area of industrial relations. Industrial strife was rampant in post-war Singapore. Organised labour worked with political parties in the national movement to obtain independence from colonial rule. With self-government in 1959, the newly-elected People's Action Party (PAP) introduced the Industrial Relations Act in 1960. This was the beginning of the legislative thrust which was to shape the industrial relations scene in Singapore.

The Act introduced the principle of conciliation by the Ministry of Labour when free collective bargaining breaks down and also imposed compulsory arbitration awards by an industrial arbitration court under certain circumstances. It also spelt out the managerial prerogatives in areas such as hiring, firing, retrenchment and assignment of work which cannot be included as items for negotiation by a trade union. Though seen by some as limiting union power, the major reasons stated at that time for the Act were the achievement of "industrial peace with justice" and the creation of better employment conditions through a less combative union stance (Ariff & Tai, 1991).

The industrial relations scene remained volatile in the early 1960s as unions were involved in political parties with differing ideologies. This volatility continued into 1963 when Singapore joined Malaysia and until 1965 when it was expelled. Throughout this period, the economy had stagnated. All these factors together with the announcement of a total British military withdrawal soon after created a sense of national crisis and served as a rallying point for the political leaders (Wan et al., 1989). One outcome was the amendment of The Trade Disputes Act in 1966 which served to make general and sympathy strikes illegal. As a result, there were fewer industrial disputes and those that arose were settled through collective bargaining, conciliation and/or arbitration.

Other legislation enacted or amended during the 1965-1969 period included The Regulation of Employment Act, 1965; The Employment Act, 1968; The Factories Act, 1969; The Workmen Compensation Act, 1969; and amendments to the Central Provident Fund Act (1968) to provide for home ownership for citizens. Among the issues covered in this legislation were working hours, overtime, medical leave eligibility, maternity benefits for female workers, earned annual leave, and notice of termination of contract. These laws established minimum standards for working conditions that employers must observe and provide, in particular to workers in manufacturing organisations. The laws also helped to establish norms of conduct of employers and employees. These initiatives in legislation have no doubt contributed to the peaceful industrial relations scene in the country. Notwithstanding the legislation, union membership reached a peak of 249,710 in 1979 out of a workforce of 1.1 million. Since then, it has levelled at around 215,000.

Tri-partism

After experiencing conflicts over nationalism and ideology in the 1950s and 1960s, the union movement began to stabilise. By 1969, most unions were affiliated with the National Trade Union Congress (NTUC) which had formed a "symbiotic" relation with the PAP, the ruling political party. PAP Members of Parliament elected to union offices have strengthened the ability of the government to monitor and sustain workers' aspirations. Since 1969, the union movement under the NTUC has resolved to work in cooperation with management. Thus began the practice of tri-partism in Singapore's industrial relations scene. The tri-partite philosophy emphasises the need for government, employers and labour to work closely to advance social and economic objectives of the country.

Tri-partite consultation now pervades many socio-economic activities in Singapore. Union and employer representatives are invited to sit on the boards of key government bodies and statutory boards and participate in their decision-making process. Even in parliament, a few seats are set aside for "Nominated Members of Parliament" (NMPs) who are individuals appointed through nominations (but not election) by the people to represent their views or interests. Similarly, organisations are encouraged to adopt a consultative approach and promote good labour-management relations. In the 1983 NPB study of manufacturing companies mentioned earlier (NPB, 1983), 66% of the companies indicated they had cooperative labour-management relations, 33% had relations of mutual tolerance while the remaining one percent had relations of conflict.

Wage Guidelines

An example of tri-partite practice was the formation of the National Wages Council (NWC) in 1972. This is a body with equal representation by labour, government and employers which meets in April to June every year to determine a national guideline for wage policies consistent with the state of economic development at the time. Although not obligatory, the NWC's recommendations are widely accepted and form the basis for most wage negotiations.

In the period 1972-1978, the NWC made recommendations for annual wage increments of between 6% to about 10%. When the economic strategy changed from labour-intensive manufacturing exports to skill and capital-intensive manufacturing exports, the NWC recommended a three-year "wage correction" policy to induce more efficient use of labour. This resulted in higher (as much as 20%) wage increases for subsequent years. The practice of high wage increases was subsequently revised in 1986 (in the face of a painful recession) to a "flexible wage" approach where wage increases would be determined by the firm's profitability or productivity gains. This meant that organisations had to re-examine their compensation systems to bring wages in line with company performance. Human resource management activities such as job analyses, job evaluation and performance appraisal began to be more widely accepted as standard practices in industry.

Education and Training

Besides legislation and institutional structures to regulate labour-management relations, government efforts were also focussed on education and training. Education was provided free at the primary and secondary levels resulting in an increase in the literacy rate from 56% in 1960 to 91% in 1991. In the 1960s and 1970s, in line with the industrialisation programme, emphasis was given to technical and vocational training at the secondary school level. Intakes to the tertiary institutions are regulated to match with the needs of industry. For the older workers (above 40 years of age) which form 30% (1991) of the workforce, courses in basic English are offered (BEST and WISE courses) to help them in their learning skills. Skills training for industry is also provided by the NPB and through a number of training institutions set up by the EDB and the NPB jointly with governments of developed countries and with multi-national companies.

To encourage wider participation of worker training, the Skills Development Fund was set up in 1979 with a levy on workers' wages (from 2% in 1979 to 4% in 1980 and reduced to 1% in 1986). This levy is payable by employers for every worker who earned less than S$750 per month. Organisations could seek approval for the use of the fund, which is currently administered by the NPB, for the training of their employees. Since then, training activities in organisations have flourished. A 1987 survey by the NPB (NPB, 1988) showed that 25% of the workforce had undergone training and that half of the companies surveyed spent less than 1% of their manpower costs on training. By 1990, the situation had improved. Twenty-nine percent of the workforce had undergone training and the companies had on average spent 2.4% of their payroll costs on training. The target of the NPB is to have 50% of workers undergo 35 hours of training each year and to have companies spend 4% of their payroll on training.

Labour Supply

To reverse the decreasing trend in population growth, the government provides a number of economic and social benefits and incentives (e.g. income tax, priorities in school admission, child care centres) to encourage marriage and larger families. Population growth, has, since 1986, increased to 2.1% in 1991. The higher rate of population growth will ease the supply of labour for industry in the future. In the meantime, to overcome the current shortage of labour, the government has taken initiative to increase the supply of labour from three sources: the female population, retirees and foreign workers.

The participation rate of females in the labour force has risen from 44.8% in 1981 to 50.5% in 1991 (*Yearbook of Statistics*, 1992). This is largely the result of many incentives provided and employment practices encouraged by the government (e.g. income tax, child care centres, imported domestic help, flexi-time, part-time employment) to encourage married women to remain in or rejoin the workforce. Notwithstanding the increased economic role, the domestic role traditionally expected of women has not been reduced. This creates dilemmas for women at work and has implications for organisations planning careers for women.

A consequence of the decreasing population trend is an increasing proportion of elderly people. In 1980, the number of persons above 50 years of age as a pro-portion of all persons above 15 years of age was 16.9% (*Yearbook of Statistics*, 1981). In 1991, this had increased to 21.9% (*Yearbook of Statistics*, 1992). How-ever, those in the same age group who were economically active as a proportion of the total economically active population above 15 years of age had increased by a smaller proportion from 10.8% in 1980 to 12.3% in 1991. To tap the potentials of the retiring population, the government had for many years exhorted employers to extend the retiring age from 50 or 55 to 60 and beyond. This culminated in the passing of the Retirement Age Act in 1993 which provides for a minimum retirement age of 60. It is expected that this minimum will be raised to 64 in 4 to 5 years and to 67 in 10 years. Contributions to the Central Provident Fund for the older workers have been reduced to encourage employers to retain older workers. While the availability of older workers may ease the labour supply situation to some extent, it also brings to employers issues such as re-training in new tech-nologies/work processes and adjustment of compensation levels commensurate with worker productivity. Also, for the professionals in organisations, peaking their careers too early (usually in their 40s) is likely to become an issue.

The tight labour supply situation has forced many industries to look beyond Singapore for the necessary employees. The hiring of foreign workers requires the approval of the government. Highly skilled and talented people are readily accepted for employment and offered permanent resident status. The employment of lesser skilled foreign workers are regulated through setting a "dependency ceiling" which limits the number (40% of total workforce for manufacturing sector and 20% for services sector) that can be employed in each company. A monthly levy is also imposed on each low-skilled foreign worker to discourage companies from using this alternative as a source of cheap labour. The restraint on this source of labour supply means that high wage levels for citizens are sustained. Also, the abundance of employment opportunities during periods of high economic growth gives rise to significant levels of job-hopping. Companies employing foreign workers also need to be concerned about the socialisation issues and the impact on the workplace.

Surveys on Personnel Management Practices in Singapore

In discussing the local personnel management practices, it is important to note the prevalence of small, service-oriented businesses which are heavily concentrated in the retail sector, personal/household services (e.g. beauty parlours, restaurants, provision shops, car repair, etc.), and business services (e.g. maintenance of estates). As most of these small businesses comprise sole proprietors, partners and/or family members (NPB, 1992), they usually do not have established personnel policies/practices.

Our discussion on the current personnel management practices in Singapore is based on two recent surveys: a survey conducted by the joint authors in 1988 and the 1990 survey jointly conducted by the National Productivity Board and the Singapore Institute of Personnel Management (NPB-SIPM, 1991). Before considering the findings of the two surveys, it must be mentioned that the two studies were not strictly comparable because of different sample characteristics. The 1990 survey involved a sample of 408 companies of which 41% (167) employed less than 50 persons and another 17%, between 50 and 99 employees. The sample therefore included a large number of small companies and this accounted for the large proportion (31%) of chief executive officers being in charge of the personnel function in that study. The 1988 survey involved a sample of 182 companies. A breakdown of the sample showed that it comprised a larger proportion of large companies with established personnel/human resource functions. Only 11.5% of the sample employed less than 50 persons (and of the 11.5%, 43% employed between 40-49 persons). The percentage of firms with 200-499 employees and that for firms with over 500 employees doubled those for the same categories in the 1990 survey. Another difference in sample characteristics is that the 1988 survey involved more manufacturing firms (48% versus 30% for the 1990 survey), while the 1990 survey included more commercial firms (26% versus 18% for the 1988 study) and firms providing personal/household services (10% versus 0.6% in the 1988 survey).

In terms of the distribution of companies by employment size, the 1990 sample was fairly representative of the profile of local companies. The 1990 survey would therefore provide a better picture of the overall practices of the local companies.

On the other hand, the 1988 survey provides a better picture of human resource practices in larger companies.

Current Practices

In the 1988 study, managers in charge of the personnel/ human resource function were asked to rate on 7-point Likert scales, 36 personnel activity items on the extent the activities were practised in their company, and on their perceptions of the importance of the activities in the industry in the next five years. Table 1 presents the ratings and standard deviations of the activity items. An analysis of the most extensively practised items showed "bread and butter" personnel administration (including personnel record keeping, vacation and leave administration, wage and salary administration, and benefits administration) to be the most extensively practised category. This was followed by recruitment and selection, welfare, personnel policy formulation, performance appraisal, and the house-keeping tasks of discipline and grievances handling. Among the moderately practised items were promotion, training and development and a number of employee-oriented activities such as social recreational activities, employee orientation, building morale and satisfaction.

Based on the findings, the personnel practices of Singaporean companies can be summarised as follows:

a. The overall emphasis was still on the traditional personnel functions of personnel administration, recruitment, welfare, discipline and grievance handling.
b. At the same time, corporate personnel practices also reflected the influences of the local environment. While the high rating given to recruitment reflected the tight labour supply situation, the need for proper selection was not neglected. The latter can be attributed to the government's continued emphasis that human resources, properly selected and trained, can be a major source of added value in the production process. The widespread practice of performance appraisal among the companies surveyed can be linked to the stance of the National Wage Council (NWC) that wage should be tied to performance, and to the efforts of the National Productivity Board in promoting performance appraisal in organizations.
c. Companies in Singapore can also be described as moderately employee-oriented. This can be seen from the moderately high rankings given to training and development, and to employee relations items such as social recreational activities, employee orientation and building morale and satisfaction. With the emphasis the government placed on productivity and human resource development, and with the establishment of the Skills Development Fund (SDF), one would have expected training & development to be more extensively prac-

Table 1:   Descriptive Statistics on HRM Activities

Activity Items	Singapore (n=60)		U.S. (n=31)	
	Mean	SD	Mean	SD
Wages & salary administration	5.81	1.51	6.03	1.02
Benefits administration	5.69	1.53	6.06	1.06
Safety/occupational health				
Administration	4.28	1.69	5.48	1.46
Employee orientation	4.91	1.58	5.42	1.50
Industrial relations	5.13	2.34	3.17	2.88
Contract/wage negotiation	5.03	2.21	2.97	2.64
Job counselling	4.02	1.59	4.84	1.55
Employee career counselling/planning	3.46	1.50	4.42	1.65
Performance appraisal	5.43	1.56	5.97	1.35
Job analysis and specification	4.28	1.62	4.81	1.68
Human resource planning	4.32	1.58	4.77	1.61
Labour market & wage surveys	4.31	1.85	5.71	1.37
Recruitment	6.19	1.17	6.39	1.12
Selection & placement	6.04	1.20	6.06	1.15
Personnel record keeping	6.54	.77	6.68	0.70
Grievances	5.20	1.55	5.87	1.06
Public relations	3.52	1.79	4.42	2.03
Social recreational activities	4.70	1.54	5.58	1.61
Training & development	4.88	1.62	5.74	1.39
Cultivating corporate culture	3.49	1.74	4.65	1.62
Building morale/satisfaction	4.31	1.65	5.61	1.17
Selection testing & other personnel research	3.26	1.87	3.68	1.89
Morale (opinion) research	2.89	1.71	3.90	1.90
Personnel policy formulation	5.46	1.73	6.03	1.40
Discipline	5.48	1.34	5.58	1.54
Discharge/layoffs/retirement	4.38	2.25	4.81	2.37
Vacation/leave administration	6.11	1.02	6.19	1.25
Cultivation of corporate image	3.72	1.67	4.13	1.69
Employee welfare	5.61	1.19	6.23	1.02
Employee newsletter	3.85	2.33	4.23	2.63
Job design	3.61	1.48	4.26	1.79
Introducing incentive-merit programs	4.31	1.63	4.42	1.93
Retirement counselling	2.31	1.60	2.33	2.01
Job evaluation & pay structure	4.21	1.79	5.20	1.92
Transfer	5.00	1.66	5.42	1.69
Promotion	5.22	1.34	5.71	1.55

tised. However, the high labour mobility rate could have been a deterrent to corporate efforts in providing long-term training for the employees.

On current personnel practices, the findings of the 1988 and 1990 surveys showed broad agreement. The 1990 study reported that the five most commonly performed human resource functions in companies were in order of ranking: recruitment and selection, welfare and benefits administration, wage administration, performance appraisal, and employee communication. These were followed by training & development and HR policy formulation. The major differences between the two studies were the higher rankings given to personnel policy formulation, discipline and grievance handling in the 1988 study which can probably be attributed to the fact that the sample included more large companies.

Comparing Singaporean and American Practices

Data from the 1988 survey were further broken down to enable a comparison of the practices of Singaporean and American companies (respectively 33% and 17% of the firms surveyed). Overall, American companies with an overall average score (across 36 activity items) of 5.08 (on a 7-point scale), practised personnel activities more extensively than the local companies which had an average overall score of 4.62.

Using the non-parametric Kruskal-Wallis one-way analysis of variance test, the ratings of US and local companies on the 36 activity items were compared. Fourteen items were found to be significantly different at the .05 level. Of these, American companies scored higher on twelve items. Table 2 shows the relative ratings of the items which showed significant difference.

The findings showed that companies of American origin practised IR and IR-related activities (Contract & Wage Negotiation) significantly less than the local companies. On the other hand, US companies practised the following three types of activities more extensively:

a. Wage Determination

   – Labour Market & Wage Survey
   – Job Evaluation and Pay Structure Design

b. Employee Welfare and Development

   – Safety and Health Administration
   – Job Counselling
   – Employee Career Counselling/Planning
   – Employee Welfare
   – Training & Development
   – Job Design

Table 2:   Personnel Activities Ratings of Significantly Different Items

Items rated higher by U.S. companies	Singapore	U.S.	Signif.
Safety and health administration	4.30	5.48	.001
Job counselling	3.98	4.84	.017
Employee career planning/counselling	3.45	4.42	.005
Labour market and wage survey	4.31	5.71	.001
Social recreational activities	4.68	5.58	.011
Training & development	4.82	5.74	.009
Cultivating corporate culture	3.45	4.65	.002
Building morale and satisfaction	4.43	5.61	.001
Morale research	2.98	3.90	.021
Employee welfare	5.68	6.23	.032
Job design	3.53	4.26	.040
Job evaluation & pay structure design	4.15	5.20	.006
Items rated higher by Singaporean companies			
Industrial relations	5.00	3.17	.016
Contract & wage negotiation	4.88	2.90	.007

c. Morale and Corporate Culture

  − Social Recreational Activities
  − Building Morale and Satisfaction
  − Cultivating Corporate Culture
  − Morale Research

To a large extent, the above differences reflected an American approach to personnel/ human resource management. The American human resource system has been described as being based on a labour-market model (McMillan, 1985). Employment relations tend to be contractual in nature and wage levels fluctuate with the supply and demand of labour. In the light of this, the concern of American companies with labour market and wage surveys as well as job evaluation and pay structure design can be understood. Furthermore, as a result of the confrontational relationship between management and labour, American companies tend to adopt a union-avoidance strategy. In the 1988 study, this was reflected in the low ratings given to industrial relations and contract & wage negotiation by the local subsidiaries of American companies.

It has been suggested that the emphasis US companies place on employee morale and satisfaction is part of an attempt to reconcile workers to the harsh realities of labour under the capitalist mode of production (Braverman, 1974), and to pre-empt employees from being drawn to the labour movement or becoming militant. This results in conscious management attempts to strengthen the

Table 3:   Average Ratings of Personnel Activities
            American and Local Companies by Size of Workforce

Head-office Location Size	Singapore		U. S.	
	No. (%)	Mean	No. (%)	Mean
less than 100	12 (20.0%)	3.91	11 (35.5%)	4.79
100–399 employees	23 (38.3%)	4.55	12 (38.7%)	5.22
over 400 employees	25 (41.7%)	5.04	8 (25.8%)	5.44
Total	60 (100.0%)		31 (100.0%)	

relationship between labour and management and to de-emphasise that between employees and trade unions. This characteristic of American companies appears to have influenced the personnel practices of American subsidiaries in Singapore which practised to a significantly greater extent employee welfare and development items, as well as items aimed at building employee morale and corporate culture.

In Singapore, due to the history of tri-partism, employers do not have a "phobia" about trade unions. The IR function was given moderate attention as was reflected in its 19th ranking. (IR was also ranked 19th in the personnel managers' perceived importance of various personnel activities.) It appears that managers in local companies neither avoided such activities nor found them sensitive enough to devote much time and effort on them.

Size, Bureaucratization and Personnel Practices

To analyze the extent personnel practices were bureaucratized and the relation between bureaucratization and organizational size (size of workforce), the American and local sub-samples were further divided into three size categories: small, medium and large. Table 3 presents a breakdown of American and local companies by size, and the overall average rating (across 36 items) for each category.

As can be seen from the overall ratings in Table 3, as size of employment increased, the extent personnel activities were practised also increased. When the ratings of American and local companies on individual items were compared with size controlled (using the non-parametric Kruskal-Wallis Test), more items

Table 4:   Comparative Ratings of Personnel Activities Items Showing Significant Difference

Items	Small		Large	
	Local	US	Local	US
# Wage & salary administration	4.81	6.14	6.28	5.87
# Benefits administration	4.19	6.21	6.32	5.87
# Labour market & wage surveys	3.25	3.50	4.96	5.62
# Training & development	3.69	5.36	5.96	6.37
# Selection testing & personnel research	2.37	3.93	3.48	3.12
# Discharge/layoff/retirement	3.06	4.79	5.28	3.87
# Cultivating corporate image	2.56	4.00	4.17	5.00
# Employee welfare	4.94	5.93	6.00	6.37
# Employee newsletter	1.44	3.07	5.22	5.50
# Job evaluation and pay-structure design	3.44	5.21	4.48	5.29
#* Building morale & satisfaction	4.44	5.36	4.52	6.12
* Morale research	2.94	4.14	3.04	4.50
* Grievances handling	4.75	5.29	5.24	6.37
* Employee career counselling/planning	3.19	4.14	3.84	5.12

\# Items showing significant difference between small US and local companies.
* Items showing significant difference between large US and local companies.

showed significant difference between small local and small American companies than between their large (over 400 employees) counterparts.

Table 4 provides the ratings of American and local companies on items which showed significant difference. Between *small* US and *small* local companies, significant differences were observed for eleven items which can be grouped into the following five categories. It is interesting to note that for all the eleven items, American ratings were higher than the local ratings:

a. *administrative items*: Wage and salary administration, benefits administration, discharge/layoff/retirement;
b. *wage determination*: Labour market and wage surveys, job evaluation and pay structure design;
c. *employee-oriented items*: Newsletter, building morale and satisfaction, employee welfare;
d. *training and development*;
e. *others*: Cultivating corporate image, selection testing and personnel research.

When the ratings of *large* local and *large* US companies were compared, only four items were significantly different: building morale and satisfaction, morale research, grievances handling, and employee career counselling/planning. Once again, American companies rated all the four items higher. Based on the above findings, the following comments can be made about American and local personnel practices. As the local companies increased in size, they caught up with the American companies to the extent "bread and butter" administrative activities were practised (such "bread and butter" administrative items included wage determination activities, employee welfare, training & development, and employee newsletter). In other words, as the local companies increased in size, they adopted more standardised administrative procedures, more formal wage determination processes, became more welfare and image conscious, and more concerned about training. Hence, between large local and large American companies, differences in these activities were no longer significant. There were only four items showing significant difference between large local and large American companies and of these, three were related to employee morale. Large American companies are thus characterised by their attention to employee morale and satisfaction.

As is common in many Asian societies, small local firms tend to be family businesses and, as such, often operate without standardised personnel policies and procedures. While this could have contributed to the large number of differences between *small* local and US firms, it is also possible that with the tendency of American personnel management practices being more formal and bureaucratic, small American subsidiaries in Singapore could have adopted personnel practices that were more formal than was necessary for their size.

Perceived Future Importance of Personnel Activities

In the 1990 survey, in addition to current practices, responding companies were asked to indicate the importance of various personnel activities then, and "over the next three years". Three items showed considerable change when their ratings for current practice, perceived importance in 1990, and "over the next three years" were compared. Training & development, which ranked sixth in current practice, was rated the second most important item in 1990 and the most important activity for "the next three years". Manpower planning was ninth in current practice, but its importance increased from sixth in 1990 to fourth "in the next three years". On the other hand, while employee communication received the fifth ranking in current practice, it was perceived to be eighth in importance and remained so for "the next three years".

In the 1988 study, responding companies were asked to indicate their perceived importance of the activities items over the next five years (current importance was not included in the survey). A major difference between the two surveys involved training and development. While the item was considered the most important personnel activity "in the next three years" in the 1990 study, it ranked behind administrative activities (wage and salary administration, personnel policy formulation, personnel record keeping, and benefits administration), recruitment and selection, performance appraisal and welfare in the 1988 survey. The difference can probably be explained by the fact that smaller local companies, with less attractive wage and benefit packages, usually engaged less "qualified" employees and therefore felt a greater need to upgrade employee skills through training.

Another difference involved personnel policy formulation which in the 1988 study was ranked second in importance among 36 activities, but was rated only tenth among thirteen activities in the 1990 study. The difference in importance attached to policy formulation can be attributed to difference in organizational size between the two samples (larger companies are more likely to feel the need for standardised personnel practices).

How Personnel Activities are Carried out

Bearing in mind that managers may not actually carry out the activities the way they indicated in questionnaires, this section will look at actual personnel practices using performance appraisal, a key personnel activity, as the example.

Performance Appraisal Practices in Singapore

As performance appraisal is not part of the traditional local management practice, its development in Singapore has been affected by two factors: the practices of MNCs operating locally and the local wage system. While the former accounted for the limited introduction of performance appraisal to selected local subsidiaries of MNCs and provided role models, it was the local wage system which accounted for the proliferation of performance appraisal in Singapore.

With the government's adoption of a high-wage policy in 1979, the need to link reward to performance was emphasized. In May, 1980, the NWC recommended a two-tier wage increase system under which normal annual increment was to be awarded to average performers while an additional 3% (increased to 10% in 1981) was to be given to the above-average workers only. The identification of the "above-average workers" thus required some form of performance appraisal which, according to a survey conducted by the NPB in 1981, was practised only by a small number of companies. As the absence of performance appraisal systems would impede the implementation of the two-tier wage guidelines, the government, through the NPB, made a concerted effort to introduce performance appraisal to both public and private sector organizations. This resulted in the rapid proliferation of performance appraisal within a relatively short time.

Most companies in Singapore, when asked whether performance appraisal is practised or not, will answer in the affirmative and can pull out a performance appraisal form to substantiate their claim. According to Wee (1982) and Shaw et al. (1987), 82% and 88% respectively of the companies surveyed operated some kind of performance appraisal scheme. However, with the momentum coming from the government and with its rapid proliferation, performance appraisal systems in Singapore face a number of problems:

a. The PA schemes in many companies may not be vigilantly carried out. Due to a tight labour market, many companies find it difficult to recruit and retain their workers. Hence, some employers avoid creating an additional source of discontent by implementing differential bonus payment. Workers may still be appraised as a formality, but the second-tier bonus is often paid to all employees.

b. Performance appraisal systems are operated more for compensation and wage administration than for developmental purposes. In fact, with the high turnover rate experienced by organizations, employers may find it difficult to develop long-term plans for the training and development of their workers.

c. PA schemes may be installed without a clear understanding of what HRD is about or the acceptance of the philosophy behind it. A good PA system requires top management commitment, the existence of a climate of trust and openness and mutual respect between the management and the workers. It requires skills and training on the part of the appraisers as well as a supporting HRD system. In short, without ensuring the existing of these ingredients, a PA system runs the risk of being superficial.

d. The Implementation of PA at the level of skilled and unskilled workers is difficult. Manual workers in Singapore, especially the older ones are not well educated and some can only communicate in dialects. It is difficult to engage in performance discussions with them. Furthermore, the workers may not appreciate the fine distinction between constructive feedback and criticism.

e. Most appraisal systems in Singapore are closed. In an oriental culture where concern for "face" and traditional authority prevail, open appraisal is still sensitive and therefore rare.

f. According to both the 1987 and 1990 surveys, the primary form of performance appraisal was rating scales focussing heavily on traits and personality variables. The authors suggested that it would be "more appropriate to rate observable behaviours or performance outcomes" (Shaw et al., 1987)

While there are still many teething problems, performance appraisal is widely implemented in Singapore. With continual education, PA systems in organizations are likely to become more refined. However, due to influences of the local culture, the wholesale adoption of the western model is unlikely. In a culture in which personal trust and relationships (guan-xi) remain important, the stress on traits and personality variables in performance appraisal is likely to continue. Furthermore, with the concern for "face", it is hard to envisage the widespread adoption of open appraisal in the near future.

Differences between Personnel and Line Perceptions of Importance

Another way to explore differences between actual personnel practices and personnel practices as reported by personnel managers is to compare personnel and line managers' perceptions of the importance of various personnel activities. In the implementation of personnel policies, personnel managers need the cooperation of line managers. Hence, perceptual differences between personnel and line managers would suggest that personnel managers might experience problems in implementing a policy.

In the 1988 survey, line managers working in the same companies as the responding personnel managers, were asked to rate the importance of the 36 personnel activity items for their organization over the next five years. Using the nonparametric Kruskal-Wallis test, the ratings of personnel and line managers were compared. Of the 36 items, significant differences at the .05 level were observed for the following items:

a. *Items rated higher by line managers*:

  - labour market and wage surveys
  - public relations
  - morale research
  - discharge/layoff/retirement
  - vacation/leave administration (marginal .057)
  - cultivating corporate image
  - retirement counselling;

b. *items rated higher by personnel managers*:

  - recruiting
  - selection and placement.

Regarding the importance of key personnel functions, it appears that line and personnel managers were, with the exception of recruitment and selection, broadly in agreement. (Line managers perceived recruitment and selection to be less important activities than did personnel managers.) This suggests the absence of serious conflicts between personnel and line perceptions. On the other hand, compared with personnel managers, line managers attached significantly greater importance to 7 activity items. An analysis of the items shows that five of them (public relations, cultivating corporate image, labour market and wage surveys, discharge/layoff/retirement, and retirement counselling) pertain to managing the boundary between the external environment (labour market) and the organization as an employer. Line managers also expected personnel managers to provide relevant information regarding the labour market, wage levels, and employee morale.

With the exception of those working in high-technology companies, the involvement of human resource managers in strategic decision making in the organization appeared to be limited. Due to the tight labour market and the shortage of skilled labour, HR managers in high-technology firms tended to play an important role manpower planning, succession planning, and in the training, development and retention of the employees. Not only were they more involved in strategic decision making, they also enjoyed a higher status in the organization.

The findings suggest that line managers perceived the personnel function as a broad, supporting one, encompassing not only the management of employment relations within the organization, but relations with the workforce and the general public as well. Since local human resource managers tended to focus on bread-and-butter personnel issues like recruitment, selection, personnel record keeping, wage and salary administration, and regarded activities such as public relations, cultivating corporate image as peripheral ones, the difference in perceptions between human resource and line managers can be a potential source of conflict between them.

Professionalization of Human Resource Management

The respondents to the 1990 survey were "persons in overall charge of the organisation's HR functions". About one third of the 408 respondents were chief executive officers, one quarter were HR managers, one tenth were HR executives and the remaining one third were administrative/finance managers, executives or junior executives, secretaries etc. The HR managers were mainly between 31-40 years old, had been with their current organisation for an average of five years, and had an average of 9 years of experience in HR functions. About three fifths of them had a university degree.

About half of the companies surveyed indicated a degree as the minimum academic qualification required for the post of HR or Personnel Manager while 38% specified a diploma qualification. The five major areas of skills or knowledge needed most by HR practitioners to enhance professionalism in the next three years were identified as: effective communication; training and development; employment act and industrial relations; computer technology; recruitment and selection.

Despite the fact that human resource management is one of the key factors in the growth of the country, the survey shows a lack of specialised training and qualification among those responsible for HRM. The problem may be the short supply of qualified personnel and this reflects the transitionary stage of development which the human resource professionals are undergoing. The attempt to raise the professional standing of the personnel management function began with the establishment of the Singapore Institute of Personnel Management (SIPM) in 1965. Membership has grown slowly over the years, the number of ordinary members was 497 in 1991. Only 19% of the respondents to the 1990 survey were SIPM members. In the early years, the SIPM had been concerned with the issue of qualifications and criteria for membership. The main activities were organising training and discussion sessions and providing certificate and diploma courses in Personnel Management. In April, 1993, members voted for the name of the organisation to be changed to Singapore Institute of Human Resource Manangement (SIHRM). This change reflected its new vision of "raising the quality of worklife in Singapore through the promulgation of sound, effective and appropriate human resource practices". In the discussion among members preceding the name change, it was recognised that there was a need for "personnel specialists to integrate their long term strategies with the business goals of their organisations" and to be "seen as strategic top management players" (SIPM, 1993). With this thrust, the professionalisation of the human resource function can be expected to develop further.

Conclusion

The industrial relations system in Singapore is rather unique. It is based on the philosophy of tri-partism and the government plays an important role in management-labour relations. Singapore has occasionally come under the criticism of western observers that the country's labour movement is government-controlled, tame and non-confrontational. However, unions are known to have challenged unreasonable demands by employers. Furthermore, if one considers that the major objective of the labour movement to be improving the lot of the workers vis-à-vis that of the employers, then Singaporean workers have fared fairly well. While the country's GNP and per capita income have been continually on the rise since the mid-1960s, its public housing program is highly acclaimed. To date, over 80% of its population own their residences. The government's policies on workers' benefits and training are also fairly progressive. Contribution to the workers' provident fund (the Central Provident Fund) is targeted at 40% of the worker's annual salary, and the government has been playing a delicate balancing act in adjusting the ratio of employer/employee contributions to the 40% (currently employers contribute 17.5% and employees, 22.5%). The dual objectives of monitoring the ratio of employer/employee contributions are to upgrade the workers' standard of living and at the same time, to retain the attractiveness of Singapore to foreign investors. When the economy was booming in the 1970s and early 1980s and companies were generally doing well, employers' contribution was set at 22.5%. However, during the recession years of 1985-1987, the employers' contribution was reduced to 10%, and subsequently raised to 17.5% as the economic climate improved. It is worth noting that the workers can use their provident fund to purchase private/public residential properties, to pay for their medical expenses and the educational expenses of their children, and to invest in selected stocks.

The same policy was applied to the Skills Development Fund. Employers' contribution to the fund was compulsory but fluctuated between 4% and 1% depending on the economic condition.

Turning to human resource management practices, there is considerable diversity in the microcosm due to the influences of local traditions (Chinese, Indian and Malay), the presence of a large number of MNCs from different countries, and the mix of small family businesses and large public enterprises. By and large, the emphasis of most corporate human resource systems is still on the traditional functions of personnel administration, recruitment, welfare, discipline and grievances handling. The attention given to proper selection, performance appraisal, compensation, and training and development can be attributed to government interventions which had both positive and negative effects on local human resource management practices. On the positive side, awareness of the importance of proper human resource management practices has increased and certain human resource management practices (for example, performance appraisal and training & development) have proliferated in a matter of 12-13 years. However, with many companies being induced to adopt such practices, the lack of commitment of senior corporate executives and other line managers has at times resulted in badly implemented practices. When such practices fail, the public may come to question their relevance and usefulness.

Comparing the human resource practices of the local companies and American subsidiaries in Singapore, American subsidiaries practised to a greater extent activities that are related to wage determination, employee welfare & development, employee morale, and corporate culture. However, they placed significantly less emphasis on industrial relations and wage & contract negotiation. The findings are consistent with the literature on American human resource system which is based on a labour-market model. While large American and large local companies were differentiated only by the extent they emphasized employee morale and satisfaction, small American companies were found to be significantly more bureaucratic and formal in their personnel practices.

Singapore is a rapidly developing nation with a history of only 28 years. This, coupled with the paucity of vigorous research on the local culture, makes it premature to discuss human resource management practices in the context of local values and culture. However, over the years, certain images of the country and its people did emerge in the popular press. Singapore has come to be viewed as an orderly and efficient society with the government not only guiding its social, economic policies, but involved in the management of various aspects of its people's life as well. Singaporeans are generally perceived as efficient, competitive (the popular local term for this is "kiasu"), and on the whole, being able to accept authority and regulations. The development of human resource management has reflected the influence of these cultural characteristics. The industrial relations system evolves around the concept of tri-parte cooperation, and when this fails, it is backed by an efficient industrial arbitration system. The nation has been strike free since 1978 except for a two day strike in 1986 which involved 61 workers and a loss of 122 man-days (Ong, 1989). The government makes strategic plans and uses a combination of policy interventions, public education programs, and economic incentives (for example, policies on wages, labour supply, automation, immigration, education, training, and productivity) to shape the development of the nation's industrial relations and human resource systems and to gear them to the economic and social developments of the nation.

With the PAP firmly in power and with the economic success of the nation, the present trend is likely to continue. In a recent ministerial speech (Straits Time, 16 August, 1993), the Prime Minister identified education and training of the workforce as the prime objective of the nation in the coming years. It was reasoned that as the nation moves towards the "developed nation" status, it would no longer be able to compete with developing nations for jobs at lower skill levels. It is important therefore that the nation upgrades the quality of its workforce. Indeed it has always been stressed that being a small nation with little natural resources, the nation's competitive advantage has to come from its human resources. The upgrading of the education and skills of the workforce is to be accompanied by selective immigration practices aimed at giving preference to professional and technical immigrants of Asian origin.

In the past years, as organizations had to deal with industrial arbitration and administer government labour policies, the employment of professional personnel/human resource managers became common in large organizations. With the recent emphasis on training and development, and with the continual shift towards higher value-added industries and high-technology manufacturing, human resource managers are likely to play an increasingly important role in organizations. Human resource professionals are likely to attain higher status as well.

References

Ariff, M. and S. Tai. (1991). "Singapore Human Resource – Industrial Relations Policies and International Competitiveness." Paper presented at the International Conference on the Future of Human Resource Management, Singapore.

Braverman, H. (1974). *Labour and Monopoly Capital*. New York, London: Monthly Review Press.

McMillan, C.J. (1985). *The Japanese Industrial System* (2nd ed.). Berlin, New York: de Gruyter.

National Productivity Board (1983). *Survey on Factors Affecting Productivity in the Manufacturing Section*. Singapore: NPB.

National Productivity Board (1988, 1992). *Productivity Statement*. Singapore: NPB.

NPB-SIPM (National Productivity Board – Singapore Institute of Personnel Management) (1991).*1990 Survey on Human Resource Management-Practices in Singapore*. Singapore: NPB-SIPM.

1990 Census (1990). Singapore: Department of Statistics.

Ong, Y.H. (1989). Industrial Relations in the 1990s. *Productivity Digest*. Singapore: NPB.

Saw, S.H. (1991). *Demographic Changes & Their Relevance to Employment Opportunities, 30 Years On*. Singapore: National Trade Unions Congress.

Shaw J.B., C.D. Fisher, and I. Chew (1987). *A Survey of Personnel Practices in Singapore*. Singapore: Singapore Institute of Personnel Management.

Singapore Institute of Personnel Management (1993). *Review* 3(4).

Wan, D., T. Wyatt, A. Tseng, and H.B. Chia (1988). "Human Resource Management in Singapore – An Overview." *Asia Pacific Human Resource Management*, 27(2).

Wee, L.D. (1982). "A Survey of Performance Appraisal Practices in the Private Sector." Unpublished BBA thesis, National University of Singapore.

Yearbook of Statistics (1981, 1992). Singapore: Department of Statistics.

Human Resource Management in Taiwan, The Republic of China

Jiing-Lih (Larry) Farh

This chapter reviews current human resource management (HRM) practices in Taiwan. Because these practices reflect the country's culture and evolve as the society develops, a brief review of Taiwan's social-economic and political developments is in order. This general review is followed by a description of current HRM practices in Taiwan.

The Country and The Economy: Historical Background and Present Configuration

Introduction

Taiwan is an island centrally situated in the arc of islands that flank the Western Pacific. It is the largest body of land in the chain between Japan and the Philippines. It is about 90 miles off the southeastern coast of China, with a total area of 36,000 sq. km., or 18,000 sq. mi. (about the size of the Netherlands or the state of New Jersey).

Taiwan's present population stands at about 21 million. Although there was a small aboriginal population (less than 2% of the current population), the Chinese in Taiwan came primarily from the mainland, especially from the provinces of Kuangtung and Fukien. Although Taiwan appeared in Chinese historical records dating before the Han Dynasty (206 B.C.-A.D. 221), it was not until the 17th century that large groups of Chinese began to cross the Taiwan straits to settle the island. Because the great majority of people on Taiwan are descendants of mainland immigrants, Taiwanese customs, lifestyles, and artistic tradition were all brought from the mainland. In both outward appearance and inner spirit, the Taiwanese reflect their mainland heritage.

Taiwan was made a province of China in 1886. At that time, it had a population of 2.5 million. At the end of the first Sino-Japanese War in 1895, Taiwan was ceded to Japan. The defeat of Japan in World War II brought the return of Taiwan to China after 50 years of Japanese occupation. In 1949, because of the civil war between the Nationalists and the Communists, China was divided into two countries, the People's Republic of China (also known as Communist China) on the mainland, and the Republic of China (also known as Free China) on Taiwan. The seat of the central government of the Republic of China (ROC) was moved from the mainland to Taipei, Taiwan, in December, 1949. In this chapter, Taiwan and ROC are used interchangeably, both referring to the political economic entity located on Taiwan.

Economic Development

Taiwan, one of the four mini-dragons in East Asia, has enjoyed an impressive economic growth in the last four decades. The average GNP growth for this period was 10%, among the highest of all countries in the world. As recently as 1960, Taiwan was a relatively poor country with a per capita GNP around $200 (U.S.). By 1990, per capita GNP had risen to $7,997 (U.S.). With a GNP at $161.7 billion (U.S.) in 1990, Taiwan was the 21st largest economy in the world.

Export expansion has for decades been the driving force behind ROC's economic growth. Over the years, the government instituted a series of export promotion programs such as export processing zones and tax rebates on exportable industrial commodities. Since 1971, ROC has maintained a trade surplus every year except in the oil crisis years of 1974 and 1975. In 1990, total two-way trade volume reached $121.9 billion (U.S.), the 13th largest in the world.

As the economy has grown over the years, there has been a rapid and profound shift in the industrial structure. For example, the share of agriculture in the gross domestic product (GDP) has steadily declined, from 36% in 1952 to 4.95% in 1989, with a corresponding increase in industry's share from 18% in 1952 to 43.56% in 1989. There has been little change in the service sector's share of GDP, accounting for 46% in 1952 and 51.49% in 1989. Two decades ago, major exports of the ROC were agriculture and textile products with low added value. Today, machinery, electronics, and electrical appliances are becoming the top export items (China, 1990).

The emergence of the ROC on Taiwan as one of the Newly Industrialized Countries (NIC) has received much attention (Borthwick, 1992; Kuo, 1983; Li, 1991). The general success story has been labeled "Taiwan Experience", and is widely attributed to the following factors:

1. *U.S. aid*. U.S. aid started in 1951 and ended in 1965. Because other foreign investment was very rare during that period, U.S. aid provided ROC with precious capital to repair and expand its war-torn infrastructure, including electricity, transportation, and communications (Kuo, 1983). In addition to the aid, the U.S. government opened up its giant domestic market for Taiwanese products, which later fueled Taiwan's export-driven economy.

2. *Successful land reform program.* This program was carried out during the 1950s. Its success led to a mass transfer of land from landlords to tenants, which provided economic incentives for high agricultural productivity.
3. *State-guided capitalism.* The basic policy of the country has been a state-controlled market economy. Although the overall direction of economic development has been led by centralized government planning, the island's able planners have always had a deep respect for private initiative and the free market. Administrative controls were rarely used to replace market forces (Li, 1991). Through a series of government-directed economic plans, the country has successfully built an advanced infrastructure for further industrialization.
4. *Political stability.* From 1949 to 1987, late President Chiang Kai-shek and his son Chiang Chin-kuo dominated the island's political scene without any serious opposition.
5. *Confucian ideology.* With its strong emphasis on mutual obligations, stable hierarchical relationships, education, self-control, discipline, diligence, and frugality, Confucianism is the most widely adopted value system in Taiwan. The values embodied in Confucianism are highly conducive to entrepreneurship and have been found to be associated with fast economic growth in East Asian countries, once other political and economic conditions necessary for development are set in place (Hofstede & Bond, 1988; Rozman, 1992).
6. *High domestic savings rate.* The ratio of savings to GNP was 19.5% in 1965 and about 25% in the 1970s. This high savings rate helps the country accumulate needed capital for industrialization.
7. *Excellent education system.* Taiwan's school system is noted for its relentless demand on students from kindergarten through high school. The country also has an excellent university system, especially in the areas of science and technology.

Despite Taiwan's success in economic development in the past, the country's future development is threatened by several problems common to many newly industrialized nations (China, 1990).

1. *Rising labor costs.* In recent years, labor costs have been rising at a faster rate than the gain in productivity. Part of the reason for this sharp increase is a shortage of labor (especially unskilled labor in the construction industries), skyrocketing real estate prices, and burgeoning union movements among workers.
2. *Management and labor disputes.* As the country moved rapidly toward political liberalization and democratization, blue-collar workers became increasingly cognizant of their employment rights, and organized labor also began to gain strength.
3. *Environmental protection awareness.* In the pursuit of economic development, government and industry neglected many environmental issues. As a result, the

country is suffering from serious industrial pollution. The ROC government is now having to redirect efforts to control environmental pollution.

4. *Appreciation of the new Taiwan dollars.* Because of the huge trade surplus in the 1970s and 1980s, the ROC has been under pressure to strengthen its New Taiwan (NT) dollars. Since 1985, the NT has appreciated by more than 60%. This, coupled with increasing competition from other developing nations such as PRC, puts many of the country's labor-intensive industries under high stress.

5. *Increasing rents for industrial real estate.* In recent years, real estate prices in Taiwan have skyrocketed as a result of speculation. Resulting difficulties in acquiring land for industrial development have caused many local enterprises to move their factories to foreign countries.

6. *Public disorder.* Rapid modernization in the last four decades has shaken the roots of traditional Chinese society. The ensuing urbanization and liberalization have brought a steady increase in political protests, crime, and corruption.

In addition, recent democratization and liberalization have led to political instability, which has resulted in lower domestic investment and capital flight.

Democratization and Liberalization

On the political front, Taiwan is undergoing a rapid transformation from a one-party-dominated political system to a democratic and competitive party system. Kuomintang (KMT, the Nationalist Party), led by late presidents Chiang Kai-shek and his son Chiang Ching-kuo, dominated the island's politics from 1949 until the late 1970s. In the late 1960s and early 1970s, a new generation of young Taiwanese entered electoral politics. The tangwai (which is translated literally as "outside the party") emerged in the 1972 election and won an unexpectedly large number of seats in the 1977 election. In 1986, those associated with tangwai finally formed the Democratic Progressive Party (DPP), a genuine opposition political party (China, 1990). In the parliamentary election in December 1992, DPP received about 36% of the votes, compared to 62% for KMT and 2% for the independents. Within KMT, a division has also emerged between those who are supported by 'native' Taiwanese (who have lived there for several generations) and the mainlanders and their descendants who came to Taiwan after the defeat of the Nationalists in 1949.

Under pressure from the DPP and the Taiwanese people, the country's political system has been gradually democratized (expanded participation) and liberalized (increased competition). Recent major political reforms include the following:

1. A series of liberalization measures endorsed by President Chiang Ching-kuo prior to his death in 1988 was carried out in 1987 through 1989, including: lifting the 38-year Emergency Decree; enacting the Law on Assembly and

   Parades; guaranteeing the right of peaceful demonstration; allowing Taiwan's residents to visit relatives on the mainland; dropping the restrictions on new newspaper registrations and limitations on the number of pages permitted; and revising the Law on Civic Organizations to legitimize the formation of new political parties.

2. All senior members in the three representative bodies, who were elected on the mainland in 1947 and had retained office since then, retired in 1991.
3. "The Temporary Provisions Effective During the Period of Communist Rebellion", which suspends certain articles of the republic's Constitution and greatly enlarges the power of the President, was abolished in 1991.

Industrial Relations and Employment Legislation

Industrial Relations

Every country's industrial relations system is different because it evolves from the interplay of historical, social, economic, and political forces shaping that society. Taiwan is no exception. To understand industrial relations in Taiwan, one has to re-examine events that happened in mainland China before 1949. In that tumultuous period, the ROC government controlled the mainland China and held military superiority over its bitter rival – the Communists. In the prolonged and bloody civil war between the Nationalists and the Communists, organized labor sided with the Communists and staged a series of strikes, demonstrations, and work stoppages that helped cripple the nation's economy and eventually turn the tide in communism's favor.

   Because of that painful experience, the ROC government has a deep-seated fear of labor unrest. After fleeing to Taiwan in 1949, the ROC made national security and economic development its top goals. The ROC government adopted a policy that placed organized labor under strict government control. This policy was implemented through a three-pronged approach.

   First, the government has maintained a strong influence on the Chinese Federation of Labor (CFL), the only national trade union center authorized by the Labor Union Law. In 1990, the CFL and its affiliates comprised 2,500+ unions with a combined membership of more than 2 million. The CFL essentially represents the entire official union movement in ROC. Government influence on the CFL is reflected in the fact that Kuomingtang party membership still appears to be a prerequisite for upward mobility in the CFL and its affiliates (Moore, 1988).

   Second, the union movement was kept in check by the government through restrictive labor laws. Taiwan has an impressive array of laws on the books that regulate many aspects of the management-labor relationship, although these laws are not always strictly enforced. They include the Labor Union Law, the Collective Agreement Law, the Settlement of Labor Disputes Law, and the Labor Standards

Table 1:   Selected Provisions in the Collective Bargaining Law that Discourage the
            Development of a Bilateral Bargaining Relationship

Article 4 – Every collective agreement must be approved by the government before it
             takes effect. The government has the right to cancel or amend any of its provi-
             sions if the government finds that any provision of the collective agreement is
             contrary to laws or regulations or incompatible with the progress of the
             employer's business or is not suited to ensure the maintenance of the work-
             ers' normal standards of living.

Article 11 – Settlements for overtime work and holiday pay cannot exceed the maximums
             established by law.

Article 13 – An agreement may not place any restrictions on the introduction of new tech-
             nology.

Article 28 – Agreements may be annulled by the government in case of serious economic
             changes after the conclusion of a collective agreement.

Source: Council of Labor Affairs (1990a)

Act. Several of these contain provisions that virtually deny workers' rights to strike
and discourage the development of a bilateral bargaining relationship. Table 1 lists
a number of those provisions in ROC's labor laws that restrict union activities.

And third, the ROC government – confronted in the 1980s by the sweeping
demand for democratization and the increasing awareness of workers concerning
their rights – responded by passing worker-friendly labor laws that mandate
generous benefits for workers. The strategy of the government is to use these
laws to ensure industrial peace by preempting the need for bilateral collective
bargaining over divisive interest issues. The centerpiece of this policy is the
Labor Standards Act enacted in 1985. This statute is discussed in the next section
of this chapter.

Under this three-pronged policy, the role of official unions in Taiwan is being
transformed from representation of worker interests to the provision of member
services. The major functions of the unions have been to enforce worker discipline, conduct training programs, improve productivity, influence government
policy, and administer worker services. The government's dominance in the union
movement has led some researchers to conclude that the union movement in Taiwan until 1985 was merely an administrative arm of the government (Lee, 1988).
Unions were thought to be pawns used to promote economic development and,
to varying degrees, the social and political agenda of the government as well
(Kleingartner and Peng, 1991).

After martial law was lifted in 1987, Taiwan's labor relations entered a new
stage. The ensuing political democratization and liberalization have increased
workers' awareness of their rights and profound dissatisfaction with the lack
of independence of the official union movement. Scores of demonstrations and

wildcat strikes by worker groups erupted after 1987. These protests were led by the unofficial union movement, consisting of enterprise-centered organizations that rise in response to a specific incident or set of grievances. After the initial surge, however, the number of demonstrations and strikes subsided, and by the end of 1991, had virtually ceased. It is doubtful that this union movement will grow and emerge as a major force in ROC's future labor movement for two reasons: (a) most enterprises in Taiwan are small (see "Types of Enterprises"); and (b) there are often extensive social ties among owners, managers, and workers based on relationships such as kinship, teacher-student, and friendship. These factors make it difficult for Taiwanese workers to organize and develop powerful enterprise-based unions.

Employment Legislation

As mentioned earlier, contemporary ROC employment legislation centers on the Labor Standards Act (LSA) adopted by the Legislature Yuan in 1984. The law has its origin in 14 outdated labor laws, many of which were enacted before 1949. The purpose of LSA is threefold: (a) to provide minimum standards of labor conditions to protect workers' rights and interests; (b) to strengthen the labor-management relationship; and (c) to promote social and economic development. The law covers most basic industries as well as many classes in Taiwan's large civil service workforce. Industries not covered include banking, hotels, restaurants, travel agencies, and education. In 1988, the LSA covered 3.5 million workers, approximately 41% of the labor force (Directorate General, 1989, p. 13).

The LSA regulates virtually every aspect of the employment relationship, including: labor contracts, minimum wage, overtime pay, work hours, time off, leave of absence, child workers and women workers, retirement age and pensions, compensation for occupational accidents, work rules, supervision and inspection, and worker and management conferences. The law goes much beyond what is typically covered in labor standards laws in other industrialized nations. Many of the law's provisions, however, are typically included in a Western union-management contract. Table 2 highlights some of the provisions of the LSA.

The law underscores the government's policy to maintain an active role in managing labor-management relations. Instead of serving as a referee who defines and enforces a legal framework in which labor and management freely interact and compete, the government has come off the bench and ironed out a standard contract on behalf of all workers and all employers. This law, therefore, is said to be an example of state-mandated enterprise paternalism (Deyo, 1989).

Immediately after passage of the LSA, the number of work disputes increased sharply. The law has taught workers concerning their employment rights. Many employers, who had paid little attention to the LSA prior to its passage, suddenly found themselves unwilling, sometimes financially unable, to abide by the law.

Table 2:   Selected Provisions of ROC's Labor Standards Act

Separation fee

When an employer terminates a labor contract..., he shall pay separation fee to the worker... Separation fee equivalent to one-month's average wage shall be paid to the worker who has continuously worked in the business entity of the same employer for each full year (Article 17).

Wage liability during bankruptcy

In case an employer winds up his business, liquidates, or is adjudicated bankrupt, his workers shall have top-priority right in receiving wages which are payable under labor contracts and overdue for a period of less than six months (Article 28).

Year-end bonus

After the closing of books at the end of the business year, a business entity shall, after having paid income taxes, covered losses and set aside stock dividends and provident funds, pay allowances or bonuses out of the balance of profits, if any, to workers who have committed no misconduct in the preceding year (Article 29).

Sick leave and miscellaneous leave

A worker may take time off because of marriage, bereavement, sickness or other proper reasons. The permissible number of days off and the minimum rate of wage payment for other leaves than casual leave shall be prescribed by the central competent authority (Article 43). (In a separate document entitled : "Rules on Leave-taking by Workers", the government prescribed detailed rules for leaves. For example, article 2 of the document states: "On wedding day, a worker shall be entitled to 8 days of wedding leave with pay.")

Annual leave

When a worker continues to work for one and the same employer or business entity for a certain period of time, he shall be granted special leave on an annual basis on the following scale:

1. seven days for the service of more than one year but less than three.
2. ten days for the service of more than three years but less than five.
3. fourteen days for the service of more than five years but less than ten.
4. one additional day for each year of service over ten years up to a maximum of thirty days (Article 38).

Overtime work

An employer shall not compel a worker to do work besides regular work hours which hecannot do on account of health or other suitable reasons (Article 42).

Nighttime work for female workers

No female worker shall be permitted to work between ten o'clock in the afternoon and six o'clock in the following morning, unless any of the following situations prevails and the consent of the labor union or worker has been obtained, the three-shift system is in operation, the safety and health installations are good and suitable, dormitories for women workers are available, ... (Article 49).

Maternity leave
A female shall be granted maternity leave before and after childbirth for a combined period of eight weeks. ... Where the female worker ... has been in service for more than six months, she shall be paid wages for the maternity leave; if her service has been less than six months, she shall be paid wages at half her regular rate (Article 50).

Breast feeding
When a female worker is required to breastfeed her baby of less than one year of age, the employer shall permit her to do so twice a day, each for thirty minutes, besides the break period prescribed in Article 35 (Article 52).

Retirement benefits
A worker who is in any of the following situations may apply for voluntary retirement:
1. When the worker attains the age of 55 and has worked for 15 years.
2. When the worker has worked for more than 25 years(Article 53).
... According to the years of service: a payment of two units for each year of service, provided, however, that it shall be one unit per year after the completion of the fifteenth year, and that the total units shall not exceed 45. ... Each unit of retirement payment ... shall be computed as the average wage at the time of approved retirement (Article 55).

Labor-management conference
A business entity shall convene labor-management conference to coordinate the relationship and promote cooperation between management and labor as well as to increase work efficiency... (Article 83). (The detailed rules about the nature and the structure of such conference are described in "Convocation Rules of the Labor-management Conference".)

Work rules
An employer who hires over 30 workers shall establish work rules, and shall report them tolocal competent authority within 30 days for registration. The same applies for changes to such rules. The competent authority may, if necessary, notify an employer for making changes to such rules (Article 37 of the Enforcement Rules for the Labor Standards Act).

Source: Council of Labor Affairs (1990a)

The government, surprised by the turmoil resulting from the law, was slow to respond and lenient in its enforcement. As a result, four years after the passage of the law, a government study found that more than 50% of employers were not abiding by some of the provisions of the law (Huang, 1990). The ROC government is now revising the law to loosen some of the overly restrictive provisions (such as work hours rule) and to sharpen the language so as to avoid confusion. Coverage will also be extended to include most of the service industries.

Labor Market Characteristics

At the end of 1990, Taiwan had a population of 20.36 million. Over the last 30 years, the population growth rate has dropped sharply – from an average of over 3% during the 1960s, to 2% during the 1970s and 1.3% during the 1980s.

Table 3:   Distribution of Population in Taiwan by Age Group (1960–1990)

End of year	Total population (millions)	Percentage of Population			
		Under age 20	Age 20-34	Age 35-54	Age 55 & above
1960	10.79	54.1	21.3	18.0	6.6
1965	12.63	54.4	19.8	18.7	7.1
1970	14.68	51.6	20.7	19.8	7.9
1975	16.15	47.2	23.9	20.0	8.9
1980	17.81	43.3	27.1	19.2	10.4
1985	19.26	39.5	29.1	19.2	12.2
1990	20.36	35.9	28.2	22.5	13.6

Source: Statistics were compiled using data from the Council for Economic Planning and
Development (1991).

As a result of the decline in population growth rate and the gradual rise in life
expectancy, the ROC population as a whole has aged with many now entering
middle age. (Table 3 presents selected population statistics.) In 1970, more than
half of the population was under age 20, and less than 8% was over age 55. By
1990, however, the percentage of population under age 20 had decreased to 35.9%,
and the percentage over age 55 had risen to 13.6%. This shift in demographics
has caused a shortage of young workers for the entry-level jobs, especially in
construction-related industries (Wu & Huang, 1990).

The selected labor force statistics in Table 4 reveal several patterns. The percentage of total labor force increase has slowed significantly since 1985. For
example, from 1980 to 1985, the total labor force increased by 13.1%. From 1985
to 1990, however, the total labor force increased by only 6%, less than half that
of the previous period. In addition to the passing of the baby boom generation,
the lower labor force participation rate (LFPR) after 1987 also contributed to the
slow increase in total labor force. Historically, the LFPR for males was high and
relatively stable. Since 1980, the LFPR for males has been on the decline at a
relatively gradual pace, probably accounted for by the aging of the population. It
is the sharp increase in the female LFPR during the last two decades that really
provided the extra labor force needed in a fast-growing economy. The female
LFPR peaked and began to inch downward afterwards. With a decreasing young
worker population and a decreasing LFPR, the ROC is likely to face continued
labor shortages in the future.

Table 4 also presents data on labor force distribution by industry type. Primary
industry – including agriculture, forestry, fishing, and animal husbandry – has
declined steadily over the years. In 1990, it employed less than 13% of the
labor force. In contrast, tertiary industry (service industry) has steadily gained

Table 4:   Selected Labor Force Statistics for Taiwan (1960–1990)

Year	Labor Force (in millions)	Unemployment Rate (%)	LaborForce Participation Rate (%)			Employment by Industry (%)		
			Male	Female	Combined	Primary	Secondary	Tertiary
1960	3.62	2.5	87.2	36.4	62.4	50.2	20.5	29.3
1965	3.89	1.9	82.6	33.1	58.2	46.5	22.3	31.2
1970	4.65	1.0	78.9	35.5	57.4	36.7	28.0	35.3
1975	5.66	1.4	77.6	38.6	58.2	30.4	34.9	34.7
1980	6.63	0.7	77.1	39.3	58.3	19.5	42.4	38.1
1981	6.76	0.8	76.8	38.8	57.8	18.8	42.2	39.0
1982	6.96	1.2	76.5	39.3	57.9	18.9	41.2	39.9
1983	7.27	1.6	76.4	42.1	59.3	18.6	41.1	40.3
1984	7.49	1.5	76.1	43.3	59.7	17.6	42.3	40.1
1985	7.65	1.7	75.5	43.5	59.5	17.5	41.4	41.1
1986	7.95	1.6	75.2	45.5	60.4	17.0	41.5	41.5
1987	8.18	1.2	75.2	46.5	60.9	15.3	42.7	42.0
1988	8.25	1	74.8	45.6	60.2	13.7	42.6	43.7
1989	8.39	0.9	74.8	45.4	60.1	12.9	42.2	44.9
1990	8.43	1.0	74.0	44.5	59.2	12.9	40.9	46.3

"Primary industry" includes agriculture, forestry, fishing, and animal husbandry. "Secondary industry" includes mining, manufacturing, construction. "Tertiary industry" includes commerce and utilities, transport, storage, and communications, financing and business services, public administration, and social and personal services.

Sources: Council for Economic Planning and Development (1991);
             Directorate General (1990).

employment. In 1988, tertiary industry started to employ more workers than secondary industry (manufacturing-based industry). After decades of growth, the share of the labor force employed by secondary industry peaked in 1987 and began to slip after that.

In terms of labor force quality, Taiwan's workers are well-educated. Foreseeing the need for a well-educated labor force, the ROC government extended compulsory education to nine years in 1968. In 1990, more than a quarter of the island's population was in school, and 99.9% of school-aged children were enrolled in elementary school. Nearly 11% of the population at or over the age of six has a college education, and 46% has a secondary education. The illiterate rate for the population at or over the age six was less than 7% in 1990. The country has also sent more than 85,000 students abroad to pursue advanced studies in the last three decades.

Taiwan's schools are known for their "pressure-cooker" teaching philosophy. Not only do they have more school days than schools in other industrialized nations, they also have exceedingly high expectations for the academic performance of their students. All this hard work has not gone unnoticed. Using standardized tests, recent studies (e.g., Stevenson, 1992) have shown that Taiwanese students from kindergarten to senior high school compared favorably with students from other nations, especially in the areas of science and mathematics. A side benefit of such schooling is that it helps cultivate a well-disciplined work force.

Human Resource Practices in Taiwan[1]

Human resource management (HRM) as a basic management function exists in any Taiwanese firm that employs human resources. In Taiwan, companies can be grouped into five distinct types. Each type operates under different environmental constraints and has different goals and strategies. Over the years, each group has developed its own cultural and management practices. The general characteristics of these five types are presented next, before proceeding to a review of specific HRM issues.

Types of Enterprises

Small, family-owned companies. Among the largest of the five types is small, family-owned companies, which employ 1 to 99 persons. In 1986, 63.6% of the companies in ROC's manufacturing sector employ 1-9 employees, 27.7% employ 10-49 employees, 4.7% employ 50-99 employees, and only 4% employ more than 100 employees (Liu, 1992). In 1986, small companies accounted for 62.5% of ROC's total export as compared to 12.7% for South Korea and 35.2% for Japan (Liu, 1992).

To further understand the dominance of small, family-owned companies, let us examine the composition of the island's employed labor force. Of the 8.2 million employed persons in 1990, 4.9% were employers; 18.6%, own-account workers; 8.3%, unpaid family workers; 11.35%, government workers; and 56.9%, workers hired by private enterprises (Directorate General, 1991). In other words, about one-third of the island's labor force worked either in their own businesses or businesses founded by their family members. Together, these small, family-owned companies employ about two-thirds of the country's labor force and account for at least two-thirds of the country's economy. This unprecedented family entrepreneurship is the hallmark of Taiwan's economic growth.

In most cases, the owner of the small, family owned company is its managing director as well. Because of the heavy influence of familism, key positions in the company are nearly monopolized by the close relatives of the owner (Cheng, 1991; Redding, 1990). As Rozman (1992) aptly observed, these small employers rely not only on family labor but also on the entrepreneurial aspirations of workers eager to earn start-up capital for their own future firms.

The greatest challenge facing these companies is survival. Because of their small size and their lack of resources to cope with environmental uncertainty, the key to success for these companies is their capability to adapt quickly to environmental changes. The pragmatic company owner usually keeps a tight reign on company decisions, especially in the areas affecting company finances. Because personnel decisions directly affect a company's labor costs, the owner is usually involved in every aspect of such decisions, with little need and help from professional personnel staff.

Subsidiaries of Western multinational enterprises. In the last three decades, a large number of Western multinational enterprises (MNE), especially those from the U.S., were attracted to Taiwan to set up foreign subsidiaries. These companies came to Taiwan primarily because of the island's cheap, yet highly disciplined and educated, labor force. Sensing a need for foreign capital and technology, the ROC government has implemented a series of policies to encourage foreign direct investment; for example, favorable tax policies and export processing zones. Originally, Western investments in Taiwan were usually offshore assembly operations, in which product components were shipped from overseas to Taiwan for assembly, and finished products were then shipped out to serve the home country or other industrialized nations (Grosse & Kujawa, 1992). As Taiwan's economy grew, its domestic market rapidly expanded. More and more MNEs came to Taiwan to set up operations in order to compete in the island's domestic market.

When the Western MNEs came to Taiwan, many held an ethnocentric view about subsidiary management. On a wholesale basis, they transplanted the management practices of their parent companies to their overseas subsidiaries. A host of U.S. developed HRM practices such as job evaluation, merit pay, management by objectives, performance appraisal, equal pay for equal work, and management development and training were thus introduced to Taiwan. Some of these concepts and practices became the target of emulation by locally owned Taiwanese companies as well as state-controlled enterprises.

Subsidiaries of Japanese multinational enterprises. The Taiwanese, by and large, have had an ambivalent relationship with Japan. Prior to World War II, Taiwan was occupied by Japan for 50 years (1895-1945). During the war, Japan invaded China, starting an eight-year bloody struggle that ended with Japan's defeat. After the war, Taiwan was returned to the ROC. Despite the war, the two countries have maintained a close economic relationship. During the last four decades, Japan has remained the second largest trading partner of Taiwan, second only to the U.S. Taiwan's trade relationship with Japan, however, is very different from that with the U.S. Unlike the U.S. which opens its markets for Taiwanese products and generously shares its technology, Japan closely guards its domestic market as well as its technology. The relationship between Taiwan and Japan manifests itself in the bilateral trade between the two countries. While Taiwan has maintained a trade surplus with the U.S. ($9.1 billion in U.S. dollars in 1990) and other major industrialized countries, Taiwan has a large and growing trade deficit with Japan ($7.7 billion in U.S. dollars in 1990) (Council for Economic Planning and Development, 1991). The deficit is due mainly to Taiwan's heavy dependence on Japan for key product components and advanced machinery and electrical equipment.

When wages in Japan rose sharply during the 1970s, many Japanese manufacturers migrated to Taiwan to set up production facilities to take advantage of the island's cheap and abundant labor. To many Japanese, Taiwan must seem more like home than other less developed nations, except Korea. After all, the two countries share important cultural heritages such as language, Confucian ideology, and religion. After 50 years of Japanese occupation, many Taiwanese, especially the older generation, are fluent in Japanese and are often enthralled by Japan's economic success.

Japan's influence on Taiwan's HRM practices is more profound and widespread than is Western management thought. In a study that compared management practices of local Taiwanese firms to those of American and Japanese subsidiaries in Taiwan, Yeh (1991) found that the management practices adopted by local Taiwanese firms were a mixture of those of the American and Japanese subsidiaries. A close examination of Yeh's data shows, however, that local Taiwanese firms were distinctively more similar to Japanese subsidiaries than to U.S. subsidiaries in terms of HRM practices. This is hardly surprising in view of the common cultural heritages, similar geography, and the resource-poor economy between Taiwan and Japan. Taiwanese executives found that Japanese HRM techniques are more compatible with the island's culture and could thus be more easily adapted and assimilated.

Moderate-to-large private enterprises. The large companies locally owned and run by Taiwanese represent a significant growing segment of Taiwan's economy. These companies grew from small enterprises to their present stature when the island's economy blossomed in the 1970s and 1980s. A good example is Formosa Plastics Company, a giant in the chemical industry. The company, founded in 1954, had world wide sales over 4 billion in U.S. dollars in 1991. Like many successful companies, these Taiwanese companies have established a distinct corporate culture. Their management style usually includes a heavy influence of Confucian values (e.g., familism), mixed with traces of Japanese and Western management practices.

The pervasive influence of familism in the management of large Taiwanese companies can be seen from two recent studies. Peng (1989) examined the relationship between chairman and president (i.e. chief-executive-officer) in the largest 200 privately-owned manufacturing companies in Taiwan. He found that in 25.8% of the cases, the chairman is also the president of the company; in another 27.4% of the cases, the chairman and the president are close relatives (e.g., father and son, brothers). Cheng (1992) surveyed personnel managers of the largest 800 private manufacturers in Taiwan. He asked them to indicate how many of their company's top five executives were relatives of the owner of the company. The result shows that in 54% of the companies, two or more of their top five executives were relatives of the owner. The above results demonstrate the significance of familism in the management of large Taiwanese enterprises.

It is worth noting that founders of many of these large companies have either retired or are quickly approaching retirement age. These companies will soon be taken over by their sons (in most cases) and daughters, many of whom have had Western management education, such as the MBA.

Government-owned or -controlled enterprises. As is the case in many less developed countries, the ROC government is actively involved in the island's business life. In 1990, state-controlled enterprises produced 19% of the total industrial production and employed 16.6% of all paid employees on the island (Council for Economic Planning and Development, 1991). These state-controlled enterprises are by far the largest companies on the island. These companies by government regulation, dominate certain sectors of the economy such as banking, airlines, mining, steel production, shipbuilding, oil and gas, telephone and telecommunications, railroad, utilities, tobacco, and postal service. These companies are highly formalized. All major personnel policies such as hiring, retirement benefits, salary structure, and promotion are controlled by rigid, written policy statements. For example, to be hired by one of the companies, one must pass a tough entrance examination. In addition to meeting a state-mandated profit goal, these companies also seek to provide stable employment for their labor force. For this reason, layoffs by these companies are unheard of. Most employees work for the companies until their retirement. Following a wave of privatization in the world, the country is currently pursuing an active policy to transfer state ownership of these enterprises to the private sector. Recently, the government has also opened up industry sectors such as banking and insurance to allow for private competition.

Development of HRM in Taiwan

The introduction of modern human resource management practices to Taiwan
began with state-owned enterprises (Huang, 1992). In 1952, Civil Air Transport
Corporation was the first company in Taiwan to establish an American style
personnel department responsible for personnel matters. From 1952 to 1956, the
Taiwan Fertilizer Corporation commissioned psychologists at National Taiwan
University and National Normal University to revise American psychological
tests to meet its staffing needs. Job analysis and job evaluation systems were
introduced to state-owned enterprises in 1963.

Beginning around 1960, large U.S. multinationals such as IBM, General Instrument, RCA, and Texas Instruments, and large Japanese multinationals such
as Matsushita and Mitsubishi came to Taiwan to establish operations to take
advantage of the island's abundant, cheap labor. These companies brought with
them their home-country personnel management practices. The personnel chiefs
of each group of companies met regularly with their counterparts to exchange
personnel information. Although many of the personnel practices they brought
with them needed adaptation to fit the local culture, these multi-nationals sowed
the seeds for modern personnel management in Taiwan.

During the 1970s, a group of Taiwanese professional personnel managers
emerged on the scene. These managers held bachelor's degrees in a variety of related disciplines such as business administration, public administration, psychology, and labor administration. They formed several professional groups, which
met regularly to exchange personnel information and promote friendship.

Today, the largest personnel professional organization in ROC is the Human
Resources Management and Development Committee (HRMDC), which is affiliated with the Chinese Management Association. It has a membership of more
than 600. HRMDC organizes and sponsors a number of activities to promote
modern personnel practices. Major activities include seminars on selected personnel issues, personnel consulting services, personnel training workshops, and
publication of HRM books and videotapes. In 1987, a group of academicians and
practitioners founded another organization, the Human Resources Development
Association (HRDA). HRDA has a membership of about 500. Its functions and
activities are similar to those of HRMDC.

Selected Human Resource Functions

The following section reviews current HRM practices in Taiwan, focusing on privately owned enterprises, large and small, rather than state-controlled enterprises
or subsidiaries of foreign MNEs. Since very few systematic surveys have been
conducted on HRM practices, the review is based on impressionistic observation
as well as empirical evidence. Since the late 1980s, the Council of Labor Affairs

of the ROC has published a series of survey results on the status of the island's labor force. These publications were used extensively in the review.

Compensation practices. In a recent survey of workers, engineers, and managers employed in computer and electronics industries in Taiwan, compensation and benefits were considered the most important factors in influencing the quality of work life (Chan & Farh, 1992). Other studies using samples from traditional industries also show that compensation and benefits are the primary concern of workers in Taiwan.

From the employer's perspective, compensation and benefits determine labor costs. In the last three decades, economic growth in Taiwan has been based on export growth. The competitive advantage for Taiwanese firms lies in low labor costs. Cost leadership has therefore been the dominant strategy pursued by Taiwanese firms in international competition (Porter, 1985). From 1986 to 1989, despite management efforts to control labor costs, wages have risen at an average rate of 13% a year, far out-stripping the average growth rate of labor productivity for the same period, which was about 7% a year (Directorate-General, 1990). The sharp increase in wage rates was due largely to the shortage of labor, which was discussed earlier. During the same period, the New Taiwan dollar appreciated about 33% against the U.S. dollar. These factors together impose tremendous pressure on the companies to contain labor costs.

The compensation systems used by private companies in Taiwan have the following characteristics:

1. *Extensive use of the bonus.* There is a general attempt by management to keep the base wage low and to supplement it with various types of bonuses. The most popular type of bonus is the year-end bonus. Based on a recent study by ROC's Council of Labor Affairs (1990b), the year-end bonus as a share of annual wage averaged about 10.4% in 1986, 11.1% in 1987, and 12.3% in 1988. Among some 355,014 business establishments in the Taiwan area in 1988, 89.1% paid a year-end bonus. Among firms that have a workforce of 500 or more, virtually all firms (over 99%) paid a year-end bonus. According to employers surveyed, the most important factor in determining the size of the bonus was business performance, followed by compliance with market practice and change in cost of living standards. More than 70% of the bonus-paying firms used the total monthly payroll multiplied by a fixed percentage as a formula to calculate the total amount of the bonus. The method used most commonly to calculate the year-end bonus for an individual employee was to multiply the employee's monthly wage by a fixed factor (45%). About 43% of employers also considered the individual's rank and position, performance evaluation, and attendance record in distributing the year-end bonus. Less than 7% of employers paid a fixed-dollar bonus to their employees.

   Using a bonus as a form of compensation has two major advantages. First, unlike the base wage, which is a fixed labor cost, bonus payments are variable, rising and falling with company performance. This flexibility makes companies more competitive. The second advantage is lower benefit costs. Current ROC labor laws tie a company's contribution to labor insurance, retirement pension, and severance pay to average wage, which is defined as the average wage for six months preceding the day on which a matter of computation occurs. All types of bonuses, including the year-end bonus, are not considered regular payment according to the law, and are thus excluded from the calculation of average wage.

In addition to the year-end bonus, Taiwanese firms also use a variety of performance bonuses to encourage worker productivity. These bonuses are usually paid biweekly, monthly, or quarterly. They may be based on individual or group performance (such as piece-rates and meeting specific production or sales quotas), attendance, and years of service. Workers in general are used to the various types of bonus programs. According to the study conducted by Yeh (1991), total annual bonus as a percentage of total wage (12 months) averaged around 21%, with a standard deviation of 15.9% for large, local Taiwanese firms.

2. *Emphasis on external competitiveness.* Most local firms in Taiwan do not use job evaluation systems to price job structure. This is not surprising. Job evaluation systems established in the U.S. focus on the internal consistency of pay relationships in organizations (Milkovich & Newman, 1993). This practice has been criticized as highly bureaucratic and placing undue restriction on management flexibility (Lawler, 1990). Unlike large firms in developed countries, Taiwanese firms are relatively small and compete heavily in international markets based on low labor costs. The shortage of labor and high turnover rates force companies to direct their attention to the external competitiveness aspect of their pay policies rather than focus on internal consistency. To keep abreast of the market pay movement, personnel managers from firms of competing industries often meet regularly to exchange wage and salary information. This is not to say that internal consistency issues are totally neglected. It is common that companies use a variety of allowances to adjust worker pay, based on different job situations, such as work hazards premiums, shift differentials, tenure, holiday pay, etc.

3. *Employee benefits.* Benefits are generally considered part of total compensation. They are treated as a separate topic because they represent a significant portion of worker compensation. In most industrialized countries, benefits constitute more than 30% of take-home pay, and several major forms of benefits are required by law. For example, in the U.S., employers are required to provide payments for social security (including retirement benefits, survivor's or death benefits, and disability payments), unemployment compensation, and worker's compensation. In less developed countries, government-mandated benefits are less comprehensive.

Two major laws mandate benefits for workers in the ROC.

1. *The Employee Welfare Fund Law*. This law requires factory, mine, and other undertakings that employ 50 or more persons to set aside a sum of money for the welfare fund. The sources of the fund include: (a) 1% to 5% of the total amount of capital at the time of the establishment; (b) 0.05% to 0.15% of the entire monthly business income; (c) 0.5% of the monthly salary or wage of each employee; and (d) 20% to 40% of proceeds from sale of wastes at the time of each sale. The law also requires formation of an employee welfare committee, consisting of worker and management representatives, to be responsible for custody and use of the welfare fund.

   According to a recent survey by Council of Labor Affairs (1991), about 73% of the employers who are required by law to set up a welfare fund had done so by 1988. The average expenditure per employee is equal to 14% of the annual base salary. The type of benefits provided by the fund varies by company, depending on workers' desire. Among the most popular benefits are company-sponsored cafeterias, mutual assistance and consolation funds, toilet and bathroom supplies, transportation expenses, arts funds, on-site library, company infirmary, picnics and recreation activities, etc.

2. *The Labor Insurance Act (as amended in 1988)*. This law is designed to protect workers' livelihood and promote social security. Labor insurance coverage consists of two types: (a) ordinary injury insurance, which provides seven kinds of benefits; i.e., maternity, injury and sickness, medical-care, disability, unemployment, old-age, and death; and (b) occupational injury insurance, which provides four kinds of benefits; i.e., injury and sickness, medical care, disability, and death. In the case of ordinary injury insurance, 20% of the premium, currently set at 7% of worker's monthly wage, is paid by the insured worker and 80% by his/her employer. The premium of occupational injury is contributed by the employer entirely.

Although the coverage of labor insurance is broad, its benefits are often inadequate. The problem is twofold. First, many employers deliberately underreport the worker's monthly insurance salary in order to save premium (Huang, 1990). Since most of the insurance benefits are cash payments, which are computed on the basis of a worker's average monthly insurance salary, workers are often underinsured by their employers. Second, some of the benefits provided by labor insurance are highly restrictive. For example, the medical care insurance provides benefits for workers only, excluding their spouses and children. In addition, the law specifically excludes medical care benefits for conditions such as legally declared epidemics, leprosy, narcotic conditions, child delivery, miscarriage, etc.

In the last decade, the government has gradually broaden the social insurance coverage to other groups of citizens (e.g., retirees, civil service personnel, peasants). Today, national health insurance covers about one-third of the labor force. The government plans to expand its coverage to the entire population in the mid-1990s.

It is interesting to note that when the ROC government expands insurance coverage for a target group, they place higher priority on spouses and parents of the insured persons over their children. A case in point is the civil service workers. These servants were first insured in 1958, the coverage was extended to their spouses and parents in 1982, and only recently the children were included in the coverage. This government policy reflects a Chinese cultural value that one's first and foremost responsibility is to take care his elderly parents.

Employee staffing: recruitment and selection. In many developed countries, job candidates are recruited from a variety of sources, including advertisements, employee referrals, campus recruiting, private and public employment services, walk-ins, and write-ins. In the ROC, job candidates are recruited differently. Table 5 lists the percentage of employed persons, by educational attainment, who found their present job using one of the methods listed. Note that, overall, more than 58% of employed persons in the ROC found their present jobs through referrals by relatives or friends. This percentage is highest among workers of low education and decreases as the worker's educational level rises. But even among college graduates, more than one-third (33.3%) found their employment through referrals. The second most widely used approach to finding a job is employment advertisements in newspapers or magazines (28.3% of employed persons). About 9% of employed persons found their jobs through government examination and placement. Note that these are jobs in civil service and government-controlled enterprises, which often require that all candidates pass a tough entrance examination. The other sources – including public and private employment services – together accounting for less than 5% of employment opportunities.

Typical selection procedures include completion of an application form, educational qualifications, background check, recommendation letters, physical exam, interview, and testing. Different types of organizations place different emphasis on the various procedures. For state-owned enterprises, the tradition of examination is strictly followed. Candidates who meet the minimum requirements of the job (e.g., educational credentials) are selected solely on the basis of exam performance. Examination is used not because of its proven validity to select the most qualified applicant, but because of tradition and the public's demand for objectivity and fairness.

In the private sector, all kinds of selection procedures are used. According to Huang (1992), the interview is used most frequently and weighted most heavily among the procedures used. This is not surprising in view of the strong emphasis by the Chinese culture on interpersonal harmony. An interview is the most practical method to assess the fit of potential job candidates to a corporate environment. In general, testing is used infrequently in selection. Its limited use may be attributed to a shortage of validated tests and a low level of awareness of their potential utility among personnel practitioners.

Table 5:   Methods Used by Employed Persons to Find Present Job*

Person's Educational Attainment	Percentage of Employed Persons Using Method					
	Public Employment Service	Private Employment Service	Government Examination and Placement	Advertisements	Referrals (Relatives or Friends)	Others
Primary School or Under	1.4	0.8	0.8	18.9	75.8	2.3
Junior High	0.7	1.6	1.5	26.5	68.1	1.6
Senior High	2.0	1.0	10.9	31.4	52.9	1.8
Vocational	1.6	0.8	8.3	35.7	52.4	1.2
Junior College	2.3	0.7	26.0	33.1	36.0	1.9
College & Graduate School	2.8	0.6	29.4	31.1	33.3	2.8
Overall	1.5	1.0	8.9	28.3	58.5	1.8

* Excludes self-employed individuals and those who were transferred or promoted into their present jobs.

Source: Adapted from Directorate-General (1991, p. 37).

Two other characteristics of staffing practices should be noted.

1. Because of a shortage of skilled technical employees, many employers in Taiwan obtain experienced personnel by hiring them away from competitors. This practice is widespread because small to medium companies, which dominate the island's economy, do not have sufficient resources to invest in and develop their own employees. The wide use of this practice leads to high turnover rates among technical employees. High turnover, then, is an impediment for companies wishing to upgrade their technology.
2. Familism plays a central role in staffing in many companies in Taiwan. As in other East Asia NICs, family is the single most important social institution in Taiwan (cf. Oh, 1991). Private companies are usually owned and operated by close family members (Cheng, 1991; Peng, 1989). Non-family employees of family-owned firms are often distrusted and permanently excluded from the inner family circle, where the ultimate decision making power resides. The strong tendency for family-owned firms to hire relatives and their friends explains the high percentage of employed persons who find their jobs through referrals from relatives and friends.

Training and development. The effort to train and develop human resources takes place at two levels.

1. *Governmental level*. Because of the large number of small-to medium- sized companies in Taiwan, which have very limited resources for training, the ROC government has long adopted a policy of active involvement to ensure a plentiful supply of human resources for economic development. The focus of this manpower development policy is twofold:

   a. Over the years, the government has built a vast educational system to train high school graduates to meet the needs of economic development. This system consists of vocational schools, junior colleges, and universities. The highly centralized educational system allows the government to take a decisive role in meeting industry needs. For example, a strong demand for engineers in manufacturing has led to an educational policy that places strong emphasis on engineering-related disciplines. In the 1990-1991 academic year, the island's college and university systems enrolled 462,492 students, more than 30% of whom studied engineering (Council for Economic Planning and Development, 1991). In 1990, about 44% of employed persons have completed a senior high school or earned a degree.

   b. Since 1981, the government has established 13 public vocational training institutes for students who are unable to go to college or vocational school, for the disabled, for workers who seek to change occupation, and for workers who are currently employed, but wish to obtain advanced skills training. In 1989, these institutes trained more than 20,000 workers (Council for Economic Planning and Development, 1990).

2. *Enterprise level*. Historically, private companies in Taiwan have viewed employee training and development as a cost to be tightly controlled rather than as an investment. According to Huang (1986), an average company in Taiwan spent less than 1% of its total labor costs on employee training and development. And more than two thirds of the companies spent less than one tenth of 1% of their total sales on training and development. This reluctance to invest in training and development may be due to three factors. First, the small size of the companies limits their resources to pay for training costs. Second, training is not viewed as an essential activity when companies are using cheap labor costs as their major competitive advantage. Third, training is considered risky because of high employee turnover rates, especially among skilled technical employees.

   As Taiwan's economy gradually moves from labor-intensive to skill- and capital-intensive industries, there appears to be an increasing awareness of the importance of training and development. This is especially true among large companies. According to a survey of large manufacturing firms (Wu, 1990), training was ranked third among various personnel functions, after staffing and compensation. In another survey of training practices focusing on large companies in Taiwan, 92% of the respondents indicated their company's willingness to increase the training budget over the present level in future years (Li, 1990).

Among the various training methods, job rotation is said to be most effective (69%), followed by in-house training (22%) and outside training (8%) (Li, 1990). There seems to be a greater interest among Taiwanese companies in managerial rather than technical training. It is widely perceived among employers that there exists a shortage for able, middle-level managers. The turnover rates among managers are generally lower than for technical personnel, a fact which makes such training investment less risky. In addition to job rotation and in-house training, companies also send their low- to middle-level managers to management development seminars offered by consulting firms and universities. In a recent survey, Kuo and Lin (1990) found that courses on interpersonal relations, communication skills, leadership, and motivation are particularly popular.

Gender and employment conditions. In most East Asian countries, women traditionally occupied a family-centered, domestic role in society. After World War II, as these countries became industrialized, women started to enter the work place in large numbers. Despite their increased presence, traditional values persist. For example, women in Japan were treated as a secondary labor force and practically isolated from management positions until the passage of Japan's equal employment law for male and female workers in 1985. Employment discrimination against female workers in Taiwan follows a similar pattern.

On the legal front, the government has not been actively involved in fighting gender-based discrimination. The ROC's all-encompassing Labor Standards Act does contain a simple provision concerning sex discrimination. Article 25 of the Act states: "An employer shall not show discrimination in the payment of wages based on gender; workers shall receive equal wages for equal work of equal efficiency." The law, however, is silent about other aspects of employment rights. As mentioned earlier, ROC labor laws have not been rigorously enforced. In practice, it is common for female workers to be subject to unequal treatment with regard to wage payments, promotions, and other employment conditions. Several common examples are in order: (a) employers use gender as part of the job qualifications and thus exclude women from certain high paying jobs; (b) among new hires, women often receive lower pay than their male counterparts for the same job, even when they have equal experience and educational attainments; and (c) before hiring, women are forced to sign a contract that requires them to quit their jobs when they are married or become pregnant.

In a recent survey conducted by the government (Council of Labor Affairs, 1990c), the average female worker's wage as a percentage of the male's stood at 65.13% in 1989. The same figure for 1979 was 66.32%. Thus, gender-based wage inequity has not improved in the last decade. The same survey also revealed a number of gender-based discriminatory practices.

1. About 50% of the employers surveyed indicated that they applied different selection criteria for male and female new hires. This percentage remained the same regardless of the applicant's education level. Restrictions typically applied to female employment include: (a) women are disallowed in jobs that require night shift work, frequent overtime, travel, outside contacts, high-level skill, physical effort, and judgment; (b) women were subject to stricter age limitation; (c) only single women were hired; and (d) women who were renters, etc., were not hired.

2. Except for basic training for new hires, for which men and women have equal access, women are frequently excluded from technical and managerial training. For example, 45% of the employers do not consider women for technical training that enables them to qualify for a more advanced job. Some 70% of the employers exclude women from training that prepares them to move into managerial jobs.

In such a discriminatory environment, it is not surprising that the survey reported sharply lower career aspirations and work motivation among women, compared to men. For example, fewer than 5% of female workers considered a managerial position their ultimate career goal, compared to 46.7% male workers. While more than one-third (37.5%) of the men reported a desire to work harder than their peers, only 17.3% of the women indicated so.

Today, working women in Taiwan are becoming more cognizant of their rights and of gender-based discrimination. Traditional values are deeply rooted, however, and it will take a long time for the society to change. At present, women's advocates are pushing for passage of comprehensive legislation that guarantees equal employment rights for male and female workers. Passage of the law appears likely in the newly elected, reform-minded Legislature Yuan. Even if the legislation passes and becomes law, however, it would still be years before it can be rigorously enforced and implemented.

The Role of Human Resource Managers in Organizations

Based on her recent survey of the top 500 manufacturing firms in Taiwan, Wu (1990) examined the role of human resource managers in these firms. Since her sample had a response rate of 47%, the survey results can be viewed as representative of current HR practices in large companies in Taiwan. It should be noted, however, that not all firms included in her sample are large by Western standards. About 12% of the sample had fewer than 200 employees, 57% had between 200 to 1,000 employees, and 31% had more than 1000 employees.

The major findings of her study are as follows:

1. About 88% of the firms had a formal personnel department.

2. About 80% of those firms that have a personnel department classify it as a mid- or low-level unit in the organizational hierarchy.
3. In 80% of the firms, the head of the personnel department bears the title of manager or lower. Only 20% have the title of vice president or assistant vice president. In comparison with the heads of other functional areas such as marketing, finance, and production, the head of the personnel department has a significantly lower (less prestigious) title.
4. Only about 25% of personnel managers participate frequently in overall business planning; 60% participate occasionally, and 14% do not participate at all.
5. The personnel department in most companies is generally small, with 47% of them employing fewer than 6 employees. Only 19% of the departments employ 20 or more people.
6. About 42% of the heads of personnel lack professional degrees or expertise in the personnel area. In contrast, only 11% of the heads of other functional areas lack a degree or experience in their respective areas.
7. In terms of overall performance, the personnel department was ranked lower than other functional areas.
8. Only 2% of the companies reported that their line managers were very satisfied with the performance of their personnel departments; 38% satisfied; 53% said it was okay; and 7% were dissatisfied.
9. More than 54% of the companies reported that their line managers always participate in personnel activities.
10. In terms of the order of importance of various HR activities, external staffing was ranked highest, followed by compensation and benefits (2), training and development (3), performance appraisal (4), communication (5), occupational safety and hygiene (6), labor relations (7), counseling and guidance (8), career management (9), and human resource planning (10).

Several conclusions can be drawn from these findings. First, personnel departments in general hold a lower rank than other functional areas in the managerial hierarchy of these manufacturing firms. Not only does the department head lack an impressive job title, but also the performance of his department is viewed less positively by line managers. From a strategic contingency perspective, a functional department is powerful only to the extent that it can help the firm cope with critical environmental uncertainty. The current macro environment in Taiwan does not seem to impose powerful constraints that can be addressed effectively only by the personnel function. As noted earlier, the ROC's labor laws have not been vigorously enforced. Its labor union movement, although revitalized after 1987, is still disorganized and too weak to assert itself. Although the current labor shortage accentuates the importance of external staffing activities as reflected in the ranking data, the shortage could be addressed in other ways that do not require heavy investment in human resources, such as raising worker wages, accelerating factory automation, foreign sourcing, or even employing foreign workers. More disturbing is the fact that 42% of the heads of personnel do not have a professional degree or expertise in the personnel area. This lack of professionalization makes it even more difficult to deliver superior performance and win respect from line managers.

Second, the ranking of the importance of various HRM activities indicates that personnel departments in these firms still assume a passive, reactive role in addressing HRM issues. Traditional activities such as recruiting and selection and compensation and benefits administration are the primary concerns of these departments. In contrast, forward-looking issues such as human resource planning and career management are taking a back seat among the various activities.

Finally, it is worth noting that the study's sample consists of some of the largest manufacturing firms in Taiwan. The personnel function in smaller firms is likely to be even less specialized and differentiated. Furthermore, there is little reason to believe that the personnel function will be accorded a higher status in service- oriented firms in Taiwan. The overall picture, therefore, is a state of underdevelopment of human resource management function in Taiwan.

The Future

Twenty years ago, Negandhi (1973) commented on the manpower practices of then local Taiwanese firms. He noted that manpower policies were not stated and documented; that the organization of the personnel department was not a separate unit; that job evaluation was rarely done; that selection and promotion criteria were not well-developed; that age and experience were emphasized for promotion; training programs were not well-developed; and that monetary rewards were the main promoting and motivational devices.

This review reveals that many of the HRM practices of Taiwanese firms have changed dramatically since 1973. As new industries emerge and the country's social/economic/political conditions evolve, so do its HRM practices. As the recent rise in popularity of Japanese HRM practices indicates, there is no single set of practices that work best for all countries (Hofstede, 1983). What are considered to be the best HRM practices in the West may not work well with companies in Taiwan.

With this caveat in mind, I believe that the HRM function in Taiwanese firms is likely to receive increasing attention in the future. My optimism is based on a number of fundamental social/economic factors that are currently converging in the country and that will underscore the pivotal role of human resources in the further development of the country's economy. These factors include:

1. *Continued shortage of labor.* Since the late 1980s, the country has experienced a severe shortage of labor. Lower birth rates in the 1970s and continued

economic expansion in the 1990s will further exacerbate this imbalance in the future.

2. *Industry in transition.* Because of high operating costs (especially labor costs), the country's labor-intensive industries are moving their operations overseas at an alarming rate (*The Economist*, 1992). The industries that are left behind in the 1990s will be increasingly capital-intensive, technology-intensive, and service-oriented. Human resource management plays a much more prominent role in the effective operation of companies in such industries.

3. *Changing work values.* Because of the steadily rising level of education and the increasing acceptance of Western democratic values, the new generation of Taiwanese workers is likely to have a much higher expectation for workplace participation and a stronger demand for fair, consistent treatment in personnel matters.

4. *Changing role of the government.* Over the last four decades, the ROC government, by and large, took a pro-business stand in dealing with labor-management relations. As democratization and liberalization continue in the 1990s, more protective labor legislation will be enacted in the Legislative Yuan. Under pressure from the union movements and with opposition from the DPP, which often sided with the country's blue collar working class, the government will be forced to tighten its labor laws and their enforcement, and take a more even-handed approach to labor issues in the future.

Above all, there is an increasing awareness among academics as well as practitioners in Taiwan that superior human resources practices are the ultimate competitive advantage if the country's industries are to continue their past success in future global competition.

Endnote

1. Before reviewing the current status of HRM practices in Taiwan, it should be noted that the ensuing discussion is not always based on solid empirical evidence for two reasons.

   The first is the paucity of research literature on this subject. The extant English literature almost always involves comparison of management practices between Taiwanese firms or employers and those of other countries. This literature relies on convenient samples and focuses on general management issues. These difficulties make this body of literature less useful. On the other hand, the Chinese literature on human resource management in Taiwan is often anecdotal and lack the rigor of scientific research. After all, HRM is a new field in Taiwan that began to attract research attention only in the last few years. Fortunately, there are a series of surveys conducted by the Council of Labor Affairs, the Executive Yuan, that examined selected HRM topics. These government-conducted studies often involve large samples and were an invaluable source for writing certain sections of this report. To fill in the gaps in the literature, I had to rely on my personal teaching, research, and consulting experiences in Taiwan.

The second difficulty in writing this report is how to present a broad and accurate view of Taiwan's HRM practices in light of the fact that there are wide differences in practices across different types of firms. The approach I took is first to classify Taiwanese firms into five major categories and then to describe the HRM practices of each in broad strokes. I then focused on the HRM practices in moderate- to large-sized local Taiwanese firms because of their importance in the economy and the availability of data.

References

Borthwick, M. (1992). *Pacific Century: The Emergence of Modern Pacific Asia*. Boulder, CO: Westview Press.

Carroll, S.J. (1987). "What Can HRM Do to Help U.S. Industrial Enterprises Cope with Current Change Pressures? Some Ideas from the Pacific Basin Nations." *Human Resource Planning*, 10(3), 115-124.

Chan, C.S. & J.L. Farh (1992). "An Investigation of the Quality of Work Life Concept in Taiwan." Working paper. Department of Industrial and Business Management, National Taiwan University, Taipei (in Chinese).

Cheng, B.S. (1991). "Familism and Leadership in Taiwan." In C.F. Yang & S.Y. Kao (eds.), *Chinese and Chinese Soul*. Taipei: Yeuan-Liou Publishing (in Chinese).

Cheng, B.S. (1992). "The Impact of Organizational Culture and Demographics on Company Performance." Working Paper. Department of Psychology, National Taiwan University, Taipei (in Chinese).

China (1990). *Republic of China Yearbook 1990-1991*. Taipei: Kwang Hwa Publishing Co.

Council for Economic Planning and Development (1990). *Manpower Indicators, 1990*. Taipei: Council for Economic Planning and Development, Executive Yuan.

Council for Economic Planning and Development (1991). *Taiwan Statistical Data Book, 1991*. Taipei: Council for Economic Planning and Development, Executive Yuan.

Council of Labor Affairs, Executive Yuan (1990a). *Labor Laws and Regulations of the Republic of China*. Taipei: Council of Labor Affairs, Executive Yuan.

Council of Labor Affairs, Executive Yuan (1990b). *A Survey of Year-end Bonus Distribution Practice in Taiwan Area of the Republic of China in 1988*. Taipei: Council of Labor Affairs, Executive Yuan (in Chinese).

Council of Labor Affairs, Executive Yuan (1990c). *A Survey of Current Employment Conditions for Male and Female Workers in Taiwan Area of the Republic of China*. Taipei: Council of Labor Affairs, Executive Yuan (in Chinese).

Council of Labor Affairs, Executive Yuan (1991). *A Survey of Current Benefits Conditions in Private Enterprises in Taiwan Area of the Republic of China*. Taipei: Council of Labor Affairs, Executive Yuan (in Chinese).

Deyo, F. (1989). *Beneath the Miracle: Labor Subordination in the New Asian Industrialism*. Berkeley: University of California Press.

Directorate-General of Budget, Accounting and Statistics (1988).*Yearbook of Labor Statistics, Taiwan Area, Republic of China, 1987*. Taipei: Council of Labor Affairs, Executive Yuan.

Directorate-General of Budget, Accounting and Statistics (1989).*Yearbook of Labor Statistics, Taiwan Area, Republic of China, 1988*. Taipei: Council of Labor Affairs, Executive Yuan.

Directorate-General of Budget, Accounting and Statistics (1990).*Yearbook of Labor Statistics, Taiwan Area, Republic of China, 1989*. Taipei: Council of Labor Affairs, Executive Yuan.

Directorate-General of Budget, Accounting and Statistics (1991).*Report on the Manpower Utilization Survey, Taiwan Area, Republic of China, 1990*. Taipei: Council of Labor Affairs, Executive Yuan (in Chinese).

Grosse, R. & D. Kujawa (1992). *International Business: Theory and Managerial Applications* (2nd ed.). Homewood, IL: Irwin.

Hofstede, G. (1983). "The Cultural Relativity of Organizational Practices and Theories." *Journal of International Business Studies*, Fall, 75-89.

Hofstede, G. & M.H. Bond (1988). "The Confucius Connection: From Cultural Roots to Economic Growth." *Organizational Dynamics*, 16(4), 4-21.

Huang, I.C. (1986). *Corporate Training*. Taipei: Chieh Yuan Publication (in Chinese).

Huang, I.C. (1990). "Contemporary Labor Relations in ROC: A Human Resource Management Perspective." *Proceedings of Conference on Human Resource Management, Labor Relations, and Business Development* pp. 63-78. Taipei: Council of Labor Affairs, Executive Yuan (in Chinese).

Huang, K.L. (1992). "The Past and the Future of Personnel Management in Taiwan." Working paper. Department of Industrial and Business Management, National Taiwan University, Taipei.

Kleingartner, A. & H.Y. Peng (1991). "Taiwan: an Exploration of Labor Relations in Transition." *British Journal of Industrial Relations*, 29(3), 427-445.

Kuo, S.W.Y. (1983). *The Taiwan Economy in Transition*. Boulder, CO: Westview Press.

Kuo, W.G. & C.D. Lin (1990). "A Survey and Evaluation of Management Training Practices in ROC's Private Sector." *Special Report*. Taipei: National Science Council (in Chinese).

Lawler, E.E. III. (1990). *Strategic Pay*. San Francisco, CA: Jossey-Bass.

Lee, J.S. (1988). "Labor Relations and the Stages of Economic Development: The Case of the Republic of China." *Conference on Labor and Economic Development*. Taipei: Chung-Hua Institution for Economic Research (in Chinese).

Li, K.T. (1991). *Experience and Belief*. Taipei: Commonwealth Publishing Co. (in Chinese).

Li, S. (1990). "Coping with a Shortage of Talents." *Common Wealth*, No. 4 (November), pp. 16-28. Taipei: Common Wealth (in Chinese).

Liu, B.T. (1992). "Small and Medium Businesses and Taiwan's Economic Development." *Taiwan's Economy*, 192, 19-45 (in Chinese).

Milkovich, G.T. & J.M. Newman (1993). *Compensation* (4th ed.). Homewood, IL: Irwin.

Moore, J. (1988). "Summer of Discontent." *Far Eastern Economic Review*, 146(36), 116-117.

Negandhi, A.R. (1973). *Management and Economic Development: The Case of Taiwan*. The Hague: Martinus Nijhoff.

Oh, T.K. (1991). "Understanding Managerial Values and Behavior Among the Gang of Four: South Korea, Taiwan, Singapore, and Hong Kong." *Journal of Management Development*, 10(2), 46-56.

Peng, H.C. (1989). "The Evolution of Owner Relationships in Taiwanese Enterprises: A Sociological Analysis." Unpublished Dissertation. Tung-Hai University, Taipei (in Chinese).

Porter, M.E. (1985). *Competitive Advantages: Creating and Sustaining Superior Performance*. New York: The Free Press.

Redding, S.G. (1990). *The Spirit of Chinese Capitalism*. Berlin, New York: de Gruyter.

Rozman, G. (1992). "The Confucian Faces of Capitalism." In M. Borthwick (ed.), *Pacific Century: The Emergence of Modern Pacific Asia*. Boulder, CO: Westview Press.

Stevenson, H.W. (1992). "Learning from Asian Schools."*Scientific American*, December, pp. 70-76.

The Economist (1992). Taiwan on the Move, pp. 3-18.

Wu, C.S. & N.T. Huang (1990). "On the Development and Utilization of Taiwan's Labor Force Reserve." *Proceedings of Conference on Human Resource Management, Labor Relations, and Business Development*, pp. 81-93. Taipei: Council of Labor Affairs, Executive Yuan (in Chinese).

Wu, S.H. (1990). "Human Resource Management and Organizational Effectiveness: An Analysis of Large Manufacturing Firms in Taiwan." *Proceedings of Conference on Human Resource Utilization and Labor Productivity*, pp. 235-264. Taipei: Council of Labor Affairs, Executive Yuan (in Chinese).

Yeh, R.S. (1991). "Management Practices of Taiwanese Firms: As Compared to Those of American and Japanese Subsidiaries in Taiwan." *Asia Pacific Journal of Management*, 8(1), 1-14.

Human Resource Management in Thailand

John J. Lawler and Vinita Atmiyanandana

Thailand, a central player in the ASEAN[1] group of nations, enjoys one of the highest rates of economic growth in the world. Yet the country's success on the economic development front has been, at times, only a mixed blessing. Economic growth has engendered severe environmental problems. Social and cultural changes have altered values and disrupted traditional patterns of interaction. Class boundaries are more readily crossed and kinship networks may no longer offer the security they once did. Foreign investment has changed power relationships and introduced new modes of behavior. The changes of this sort occurring in Thai society have profoundly impacted management practices in Thailand, including human resource management (HRM). This paper examines different HRM approaches in Thailand, focusing both on the evolution of employment practices over time and on similarities and differences between Thai-owned and foreign firms.

The paper is divided into three major sections. The first section examines important social, political, and economic forces as these affect HRM practices in Thailand. The second section constructs a typology of human resource strategies that distinguishes between Thai-owned firms and subsidiaries of multinational corporations. The final section of the paper reports the results of an empirical investigation of HRM practices in Thailand designed to assess the typology of HR strategies.

Thailand: National Characteristics

In order to understand HRM practices in Thailand, it is first necessary to consider the economic, social, political, and physical features of the country. HR management is clearly impacted by these external constraints, so we begin by examining some of the more significant aspects of contemporary Thailand.

Population and Geography

Thailand currently has a population of around fifty-six million, which is growing at an annual rate of approximately one and a half percent (Thailand Development Research Institute, 1992). Thailand has made tremendous strides in reducing its birth rate over the past several years, utilizing an aggressive and seemingly successful family planning and birth control program. Contemporary urban families, often with both parents employed, typically have only a few children in comparison to very large, traditional Thai families. Further development of the Thai economy is likely to accelerate this trend, which might, in the long term, generate labor shortages in some areas.

In terms of area, Thailand is roughly the size of Texas. It is bordered by Malaysia on the south, Burma on the west, Laos on the northeast, and Cambodia on the southeast. The country is traditionally divided into four major sections. Central Thailand is the area in and around Bangkok. Bangkok, with a population of approximately six million, is the economic, as well as political, center of the nation. Its rapid population growth has meant overcrowding, pollution, and a sorely taxed infrastructure. However, economic growth has generated a construction boom in Bangkok, though efforts to alleviate traffic congestion have so far had little effect.

Northern Thailand is quite mountainous. Its central city is Chaing Mai, in the heart of the famous "Golden Triangle". Although one of the largest cities in Thailand, Chaing Mai has a population of only around 200,000. Yet Chaing Mai, once primarily a tourist attraction, is also undergoing significant industrial growth. Southern Thailand consists primarily of the isthmus connected to Malaysia. This is a largely agrarian area, though the tourist industry is quite significant, particularly in coastal areas. Southern Thailand is the site of much of the country's mining, fishing, and forestry industries. The southern city of Had Yai, with a population of around 100,000, is another center of economic growth.

Northeastern Thailand, also known as Isarn, is the poorest region of the country. Mostly agricultural, it is the source of many of the migrants to Bangkok. There is considerable reliance here on small-scale subsistence farming, although the "Green Revolution" has impacted the area substantially. The Thai government has had numerous development projects underway in Isarn for many years, although some are quite controversial. Projects include dam construction and the "Green Isarn" initiative, intended to improve agricultural production through the introduction of modern farming methods. There is increasing industrial development in the region, especially in areas designated as enterprise zones by the Thai government (where new employers can obtain substantial tax breaks and other aid from the government). Development in the region is also likely to be promoted by the opening of Laos and Cambodia. In the long term, development of Vietnam would probably significantly affect this region as well.

Labor and Human Resources

The real rate of growth for the Thai economy was around eight to ten percent in the late 1980s (Thailand Development Research Institute, 1992), though it is now around seven percent. However, there is general optimism that, in the absence of further political turmoil, the economy will continue to grow rapidly in the foreseeable future. Per capita income is now somewhere around $1,800 per year. Thus, while Thailand is far behind the developed nations and also the newly industrialized countries of Asia (South Korea, Taiwan, Hong Kong, and Singapore), it has moved significantly beyond most of its other neighbors.

The labor force participation rate in Thailand, based on individuals twelve and older, is approximately seventy-one percent (Hongladarom, 1990b). Despite significant economic growth, Thailand remains a labor-surplus economy. Although the official unemployment rate is only two percent for the late 1980s (Thailand Development Research Institute, 1992), seasonal unemployment and underemployment can be quite high. Large numbers of Thais travel abroad, usually to other ASEAN countries, to Japan and Taiwan, or to the Middle East, in search of employment. However, growing labor shortages in certain sectors and increasing wages in Thailand are apt to reduce migration in coming years.

As with other developing countries, the labor markets in Thailand can be viewed as segmented. The majority of workers (about sixty-seven percent; Thailand Development Research Institute, 1992) remain in the agricultural sector, primarily working on family farms. With economic growth and industrialization, there has been substantial migration from agricultural areas into the cities, especially Bangkok. Migrants are most often in search of jobs in the modern, or industrialized, sector of the economy. Such jobs are characterized by relatively high pay, some fringe benefits, and some degree of protection from arbitrary employer treatment. Since modern sector jobs are limited (though increasing rapidly), most migrants spend at least some time awaiting such opportunities; mostly working in informal sector jobs as street vendors or domestic servants. Unfortunately, based on available statistics, it is difficult to differentiate between modern and informal sector employment. We know that approximately twelve percent of the labor force is employed in what are generally modern sector jobs in manufacturing, construction, mining and transportation. On the other hand, about twenty-one percent of the labor force is employed in trade and service sectors, which includes both modern and informal sector jobs (Thailand Development Research Institute, 1992).

The rural and relatively relaxed lifestyles of migrants creates certain problems for HR managers in socializing lower level employees to the discipline of industrial work. Absenteeism can be a significant problem. For example, during harvest season, workers may wish to return to their villages for an extended period to help out. This is particularly a problem in multinational firms, where expatriate managers might expect standards of work and organizational commitment that are alien to many Thai workers. Such cultural clashes have resulted in significant conflicts in some firms. Although the Thai labor movement is relatively weak, there are examples of very militant actions taken against some employers by company unions (Brown and Frenkel, 1993). Thus, cultural sensitivity on the part of employers is an important feature of human resource management in Thailand.

Literacy in Thailand is high by world standards. Education is compulsory through the equivalent of sixth grade and about eighty-seven percent of Thais have completed elementary school (Thailand Development Research Institute, 1992). This has clearly been a factor in making Thailand attractive to foreign investors. Unfortunately, the country's level of educational attainment at higher levels is lower than it should be to sustain development of greater value-added industries. Only about twenty-eight percent of the population has completed some secondary school and around sixteen percent has had some sort of post-secondary education (either college or vocational school). A plan is underway to increase mandatory school attendance, initially through the ninth grade. However, implementation will require significantly increasing the number of classrooms in the country.

The Thai higher education system is quite extensive and has been given considerable priority over the past several years. In the 1970s, Thailand could only accommodate about 30,000 students at the university level. However, a number of regional universities and teachers colleges have been constructed, several private colleges have been set up, and Thailand has created two large open universities. Consequently, there are now about 300,000 students enrolled at the university level. There is also an extensive system of vocational and technical schools. Graduate education has also been developed. Some universities now offer a Ph.D., there are several medical schools in the country, and numerous MBA programs are in operation. However, many Thai students still go abroad for higher education, particularly at the graduate level. Foreign degrees, primarily from European, North American, and Australian institutions, remain highly valued. In the past, foreign study generated something of a "brain drain", as students often remained abroad after completing their studies. However, economic growth in Thailand and more limited opportunities in the West appears to be luring some of these individuals back to Thailand.

Politics

The political environment in Thailand is complex and subject to change. However, there is generally greater political stability in Thailand than in many of its neighboring countries. Thailand was an absolute monarchy until 1932. At that time, the king was forced to relinquish most of his powers as the result of a coup led by both the military and senior officers in the civil service. The civilians participating in the revolution had something of a socialist bent, so Thailand proceeded to establish numerous state enterprises. The state enterprises often set the standard for personnel management practices, at least until the current period of economic growth. State enterprises are among the largest employers in Thailand and also have been a center of unionism.

Over the years, the military generally dominated Thai politics. During World War II, Thailand was technically allied with Japan. However, there was an extensive underground movement in the country that supported the Allies and a government in exile was established in the U.S. There have been numerous coups since 1932. Most were bloodless and typically resulted in one military faction displacing another. However, beginning in the early 1980s, under the leadership of Prime Minister Prem, Thailand began moving increasingly toward a more stable and democratic system of government. Thanks largely to the intervention of the current king (who exerts considerable power informally), at least two coups in the 1980s were quashed. However, a coup was successful in February, 1991, overturning a democratically elected – although apparently quite corrupt – government. A result of that coup was a proclamation outlawing unions in the state enterprises, but not in the private sector. However, since unionism in Thailand is largely concentrated in the state enterprise sector, this action effectively gutted the Thai labor movement.

A leader of the 1991 coup, General Suchinda Kraprayoon, became prime minister after national elections in early 1992. However, there was widespread opposition to the Suchinda government. Most significantly, a large and well-educated middle class, the product of years of economic expansion, became a center of opposition to the government. A major concern among this group was that political instability and military-dominated governments would undermine Thailand's reputation and discourage foreign investment and trade. Despite a bloody repression of opponents in May, 1992, the Suchinda government was forced from office. New elections were held later in the year, resulting the establishment of a centrist civilian government. The government is centrist in that it neither supports the nationalism of the military leaders nor the radical proposals of the left wing. In general, the government is strongly supportive of policies designed to promote economic development and streamline aspects of Thai government.

Society and Culture

In comparison to many other Southeast Asian nations, Thailand is much less ethnically diverse. Ethnic Thais (and their close relatives, the Lao) make up around eighty percent of the Thai population. The next largest group is the Chinese, constituting about twelve percent of the population. With the exception of certain enclaves in remote parts of northern Thailand, the Chinese population is highly assimilated, certainly in relation to most other Southeast Asian countries. Although the Chinese maintain aspects of an ethnic identity, they use Thai, rather than traditional Chinese, names. There has been considerable intermarriage among

Chinese and ethnic Thais, especially within the middle and upper classes. Yet Chinese families are clearly dominant in the business sector and most firms in Thailand are, or at least began, as Chinese-owned family enterprises.

Any real understanding of management practices in Thailand must be informed by a knowledge of Thai culture and values. A full treatment of this topic is beyond the scope of this chapter. However, we will discuss certain aspects of Thai culture. Of particular significance is the role of Buddhism. Almost ninety-five percent of Thailand's population is Buddhist and the religion impacts almost all aspects of Thai life.

The principal element of Buddhism is its emphasis on moderation, that is following the "middle path" in whatever one is doing. Buddha stressed the use of one's critical intellect, stating that an individual should follow his teachings only if they stood the test of one's own logic and personal experience. Buddhism is the religion of cause and effect, the logical system of "kharma". The Buddhist believes that one's actions bring upon oneself inevitable results, either in this life or in a reincarnation. The essence of Buddha's teachings is contained in the "Four Noble Truths": a) suffering (birth, death and decay, sorrow, pain, grief, despair, etc.), b) the cause of suffering (which is desire), c) the extinction of suffering (ridding one's self of desire), and d) the way to the cessation of suffering (the Noble Eightfold Path).[2]

Buddhism is neither pessimistic nor optimistic in outlook. It is viewed by believers as a truth that can only be understood through a combination of intuition and a pure state of mind. It is not wrong to say that the Thai version of Buddhism is the gentlest and most liberal form of the religion. The ultimate goal of the Buddhist is to achieve a state of "Nirvana".[3] But modern Thais, especially educated professionals such as those in management positions, are more apt to hope only for a better state of existence, or next chance, than for what is, in effect, complete extinction. Thai managers do not feel compelled to make every moment count. There seems always to be a next time, a next chance, or even a next life. Thais have a long range view of human existence that profoundly affects their behavior toward one another.

Although Thais may be dedicated to their work, career advancement is not often a dominant consideration. Rather, they prefer some moderate path that balances career and family life. Failure to achieve can also be understood in terms of Buddhist doctrine. Since all things are viewed as caused and predestined, a current failure must be the consequence of prior indiscretions, perhaps even in a past life. Thus, frustration and disappointment are explained; tolerance and patience have to be maintained.

Thai Buddhism, coupled with other elements of Thai culture, gives rise to a variety of attitudes and values typical of Thai workers. Work must be a source of "sanuk" (fun) and not overly demanding. The central focus of the Thai's life is family rather than work, so work that intrudes excessively into one's personal life and time with one's family is not acceptable. Thai workers seek to avoid confrontation, either with management or other workers. Confrontation sets the stage for someone to win and someone else to lose, resulting in a loss of face for the latter. Thais prefer to avoid either being so humiliated, or causing humiliation to others. As family life is central to a Thai's personal identity, there is considerable nepotism and this is facilitated by numerous relationships in one's extended family. Nepotism clearly extends into the work place and most Thais would tell you that personal connections involving one's relatives are critical to obtaining work and becoming successful within an organization. Thais also feel that overt expressions of emotion, particularly to those outside one's family, are inappropriate. In particular, anger is viewed as indicative of loss of control. Hence feelings are expressed indirectly. Thais find it preferable to act properly, rather than to be viewed as always correct.

HRM Implications

Thailand's rapid industrialization has had significant social and cultural, as well as economic, consequences, all of which have impacted human resource management practices in the country. Expansion has been driven by foreign investment and the subsidiaries of multinational companies (MNCs) have introduced a range of employment practices into Thailand. Initially, Thai firms had difficulty in competing with the MNCs in the labor market, as the foreign firms had greater resources and generally attracted the best talent. In fact, employment in a MNC tended to be socially prestigious, since it was recognized that foreign firms usually paid considerably higher salaries than Thai-owned firms and selected only the best applicants. Thai firms, mostly family-owned enterprises (see below), tended to utilize personnel management systems that lacked much sophistication. However, as the economy has grown rapidly in the past decade, management practices have changed in Thai-owned firms, particularly those heavily involved in foreign trade. In subsequent sections of this chapter, we trace the development of HRM practices within indigenous firms, noting the increasing use of sophisticated techniques, modeled to a considerable extent after the HRM systems typical of Western firms.

Growth has also meant that Thailand's labor supply is no longer so abundant relative to demand. Thailand underwent significant growth with little wage inflation because it was a surplus labor economy. This is less so today, as significant shortages have arisen in many of the more skilled and highly trained occupations. Firms must act more aggressively in the labor market to attract and maintain the best employees. There would appear to be greater emphasis on employee training and development, both in foreign and indigenous firms. Numerous HR consulting services, recruitment agencies, and training institutes now flourish in Bangkok and elsewhere in Thailand, indicative of the demand for such services.

Traditionally, Thai society has been highly stratified, with distinct class groupings and little mobility across class lines. The class system is, to some extent, supported by Buddhism. As Buddhists generally believe in reincarnation, one's current situation in life is seen to be a consequence of actions taken in one's last life. This tends to rationalize class distinctions. While those in lower classes may subordinate themselves to those in the upper classes, the more privileged nonetheless have an obligation to treat social inferiors in a kindly and fair manner. The class system is reflected in the organization and management of traditional family-owned enterprises in Thailand. In such organizations, there was little need for highly formalized personnel management systems, as the external social system largely defined patterns of interaction, rights, and obligations. Nepotism and social networking have been closely linked to the reliance on external class distinctions as a means of establishing and maintaining control within traditional Thai organizations. However, the pressures of modernization have inevitably weakened the class system. A relatively small, educated elite is increasingly being displaced by an educated and affluent middle class. Entrepreneurial opportunities abound, even for many in the lower classes. The mass opposition to the Suchinda government in 1992, essentially unprecedented in Thai history, is clearly indicative of this change. As the class system is undermined by economic advancement, traditional management systems must also be transformed. As we will discuss later, this clearly seems to be occurring in indigenous firms.

Human Resource Strategy in Thailand: A Typology

A central concept in the contemporary HRM literature is the notion of strategy and strategic choice (Butler, Ferris, and Napier, 1991). We shall use the strategy concept to distinguish the HRM practices of firms operating in Thailand. Our principal focus is on differences and similarities in HRM practices based on the firm's national origin, contrasting practices in Thai-owned firms and subsidiaries of multinational corporations (MNCs).

Strategies may be viewed as sets of choices that define the long-term relationship of the organization to its environment. Yet as Mintzberg (1989) notes, strategies need not be deliberate, emerging instead as unintentional consequences of prior, perhaps random, actions. Whatever the case, strategies ultimately shape the policies, procedures, and structural features of an organization. General organizational strategies shape the overall direction of the firm and give rise to more specific functional strategies, such as human resource (HR) strategy. HR strategy, in turn, specifies which employment practices will be utilized in the organization.

Strategies reflect the values of key organizational decision makers. To the extent that such value systems are influenced by external cultural forces, the national culture of a company may impact strategic choices. In a multinational firm, the parent firm's home country culture might be expected to affect employment practices at all levels of the organization, including foreign subsidiaries. Yet such linkages may be moderated by various factors, so the extent to which the parent firm's home country culture impacts employment practices in subsidiaries may vary.

In our prior research on HRM practices in Thailand (Lawler, Zaidi, and At-miyanandana, 1989), we have suggested stylized HR strategies that are related to a firm's country of origin. We distinguished among four modern-sector organizational forms prevalent in Thailand (subsidiaries of Western firms, subsidiaries of Japanese firms, Thai family enterprises, and publicly held Thai corporations). In each instance, we identified an underlying strategic theme, the structural characteristics of the HR subunit, and typical HRM practices. The HR strategies of Western and Japanese subsidiaries were as might have been expected; the significance of the study lies in contrasts drawn between the HR strategies of subsidiaries of foreign multinationals and those of domestically owned firms.

The typology we first proposed was based on a series of intensive case studies and was largely qualitative in character. Those observations will be assessed empirically below, based on results obtained from a larger data set. In this section, we summarize the salient characteristics of each component of the typology.

Western Subsidiaries

American firms are traditionally viewed as utilizing more systematic and structured personnel management systems than was generally the case in Europe though this now seems to be changing. In the case of multinational firms operating in Thailand, Lawler et al. (1989) found few differences between subsidiaries of American and European firms, consequently these were grouped together.

As expected, the dominant theme for HR strategy in Western subsidiaries was one of rational control and efficiency. Most of the managers in these firms were Thai nationals (versus expatriates) and these companies generally utilized professional HR managers who exerted considerable influence within the organization. However, the discretion of HR managers was often limited by rules and standardized procedures dictated by the firm's home office. In regard to HRM practices, these companies were seen as having highly structured internal labor markets, with an emphasis on performance-based compensation and job evaluation. Formal training appeared to be limited, as Western subsidiaries relied on high wages to attract workers who already possessed strong credentials. Employee involvement programs were limited and Western subsidiaries often endeavored to avoid unionization.

Japanese Subsidiaries

The dominant strategic theme for Japanese subsidiaries was found to be one of acculturation. Japanese firms placed considerable emphasis on the programs of indoctrination, stressing loyalty to the company. Japanese subsidiaries often lacked well-defined HRM roles and generally did not rely on HRM professionals. Expatriate Japanese typically occupied key management positions, which facilitated control of the subsidiary by the parent company, obviating the need for rules and standard procedures. Compensation systems stressed seniority rather than performance and internal labor markets were not highly structured. Japanese subsidiaries placed considerable emphasis on training, both on-the-job and formal programs; training often involved extended assignments at the parent company's facilities in Japan. Employee involvement programs, such as quality circles, were common. Although the Japanese subsidiaries did not formally guarantee "lifetime" employment, most did extend considerable job security to Thai employees.

Thai Family Enterprises

Family enterprises are common throughout much of Asia, as in the case of the Korean *chaebol* (Steers, Shin, and Ungson, 1989). We are, of course, referring to large-scale organizations owned and managed by the members of a single family or small group of families. There are numerous small enterprises – stores, workshops, restaurants – that are family owned and operated but are not of sufficient size to be of interest here.

Some of the largest and most powerful organizations in Thailand are family enterprises. As elsewhere in Southeast Asia, most of these firms are owned by entrepreneurial Chinese families. The "Chinese management system" relies heavily on family connections and interfamily networks, not only for internal coordination of the enterprise, but also for developing and maintaining external relationships. In the larger firms, world-wide family connections serve as a foundation for building international trading companies. The system is perhaps best characterized by the expression "management by entourage" (Isarangkun Na Ayuthaya and Taira, 1977).

Mintzberg's (1989) notion of "emergent" (as opposed to "deliberate") strategy is quite relevant to family enterprises, at least when it comes to HRM practices. Such practices are heavily rooted in traditional values and social practices rather than contemporary management theory. There is often little in the way of a formal HRM function within these firms, outside of a payroll office. Lawler et al. (1989) found professional HR managers to be a rarity in family enterprises; HR planning and the systematic analysis of employment issues were virtually absent in such organizations. Management control of employees is exerted largely through a hierarchical system that reflects the traditional class system in Thailand. Those in lower positions defer to higher level managers more out of a sense of duty than as a result of rules and regulations.

As most family enterprises in Thailand are owned by those of Chinese descent, it is also relevant to consider the role of Confucian values in shaping management practices in these organizations. Such an approach reflects a renewed interest among many Asian academics in understanding the relationship between Confucian tradition and contemporary Chinese life. The lessons of Confucianism are often applied in the political realm, suggesting something about the nature of Confucian leadership. Lee Kuan Yew, who virtually single-handedly forged modern Singapore, defines the ideal national leader as a "Confucian gentleman", a person who exudes moral authority, is an example to his subordinates, and thus commands their respect and obedience. The Confucian values that appeal to Lee include "hard work, thrift, filial piety, national pride" (*The Economist*, 1991).

Confucianism as management ideology (Chen, 1991) similarly demands the loyalty of those lower in the organizational hierarchy to those at the top. In return for their loyalty, subordinates can expect that organizational leaders will watch out for their welfare. What we have said is, of course, a rather simplified rendering of Confucian ideology, which is felt by adherents to promote social stability and prosperity. In addition, Confucian values are often moderated or supplanted by country-specific value systems. But almost all of these national value systems, which influence management practices, stress harmony, conformity, hierarchy, and the avoidance of direct conflict. This would certainly be so in the case of Buddhism in Thailand (Siengthai and Vadhanasindhu, 1991) and applies to other Southeast Asian nations as well (Widyahartono, 1991; Soriano, 1991).

Lawler et al. found employment practices in family enterprises to be ad hoc and limited. Recruitment and selection into these firms involved heavy reliance on social networks, personal contacts, and "mee sen" (literally, "to have strings" to pull). Compensation depended on seniority and social status. For example, Isarangkun Na Ayuthaya and Taira (1977) note the case of two janitors in a family enterprise who, while doing precisely the same work, received substantially different salaries. The lower paid worker came from "upcountry" (i.e., outside of Bangkok) and had fewer contacts and social credentials than the higher paid worker. Formal training programs were generally lacking and there was little use of such techniques as job analysis, job evaluation, or performance evaluation.

Publicly Held Thai Corporations

Thailand's rapid economic growth over the past decade has resulted in significant changes in traditional organizational forms. As family enterprises have increased in size and scope, it has often been difficult to staff all top level positions with family members. Moreover, capital requirements for expansion have necessitated issuing stock to the public. There are now in excess of two hundred firms listed on the Stock Exchange of Thailand (SET). While most are family enterprises that have "gone public", the country's many state enterprises are in the process of privatization and several are now listed on the SET.

The emerging corporate sector has increasingly turned to professional managers, many of whom are supplied by several MBA programs. A number of these programs are collaborative efforts involving American, Canadian, Australian and European universities. The most prestigious of these would be the MBA program operated by Northwestern's Kellogg School in conjunction with Chulalongkorn University. Northwestern faculty members teach courses in Bangkok and graduates are awarded a diploma from Northwestern. All of this suggests the development of a managerial elite increasingly attuned to Western methods.

Lawler et al. (1989) characterized publicly held Thai corporations as pursuing HR strategies that represent a hybrid of Western rationalism and the traditionalism of the family enterprise. They found that Thai corporations tend to be hierarchical, with authority patterns related to social class. There were distinct differences between HRM methods applied to professional and managerial employees and those applied to lower-level employees. In the former case, practices were similar to those encountered in Western firms. A variety of methods were used to recruit and retain professionals and managers, particularly given acute shortages in many fields. Structured internal labor markets and sophisticated training programs were also common for these employees. Conversely, employment practices utilized in the case of lower-level employees (production workers, clericals, etc.) were found to be much more like those in traditional family enterprises. Hence, there was little in the way of formal training, employees were often recruited through informal networks, and job evaluation and job analysis were generally not used.

Employment Practices in Thailand: Survey Methods

We have examined the types of private sector enterprises thought to be characteristic of Thailand's modern sector. These categories are based solely on a firm's national origin and, in the case of Thai firms, ownership patterns. There are certainly many other factors that might be expected to impact HR strategy, including a firm's industry, size, technology, and external market conditions. However, space does not allow a treatment of those factors. Moreover, empirical evidence suggests that cultural influences often dominate in determining HRM practices in the Thai context (Lawler, Atmiyanandana, and Zaidi, 1992).

Our original study (Lawler et al., 1989) was based on a series of in-depth case studies. However, the sample was relatively small (twenty-five cases) and data were collected in 1985, a time at which Thailand's economy was just beginning to undergo rapid growth. We collected additional data in 1988 and 1989. These data are used here to provide a more quantitative description of HRM practices in firms operating in Thailand. In addition, we provide at least a rudimentary test of the validity of the framework described above, as HRM practices are compared across the categories of the typology.

Data Collection

Personal interviews were conducted by the authors in a total of ninety-four firms. In each case, the individual interviewed was primarily responsible for personnel administration within the firm. These firms were randomly selected for the study from a listing of the largest 2000 companies operating in Thailand (sampled in International Business Co., 1985-1989). Approximately eighty percent of the companies contacted agreed to participate in the study. Unfortunately, the process of setting up interviews and commuting to various locations was extremely time consuming, so it was not possible to generate a larger sample within the time available to conduct the study.

The interviews typically took anywhere from sixty to ninety minutes to complete. Virtually all of the individuals interviewed were Thai nationals; while most respondents spoke English, one of the authors is Thai and translated when necessary. Roughly one-third of the interviews were conducted in each of three years (1985, 1988, and 1989). As the sampling procedure was identical across the three years in which the data were collected, there is no systematic relationship between time period and company characteristics.

Variables

The questions included in the survey instrument concerned the company's compensation, training, staffing, and employee relations practices. Semantic differentials were used to record responses to most questions on employment practices. These scales assessed the respondent's perception as to the relative importance of several different techniques within his or her company. Five categories were used in the scales, with the upper end indicating the firm extensively utilized a particular HRM technique and the lower end indicating little or no reliance on the method. The scale items were completed by the interviewer rather than the respondent, with answers based on probing questions. Certain other items were answered on a simple "yes" or "no" basis.

The level of HRM professionalism in a firm was measured by means of a five-point Likert scale. This scale reflects the perceptions of the interviewer (the same individual in all cases). Verbal anchors were attached to response categories as a point of reference. A value of five indicated one or more HR managers in the firm had graduate degrees in personnel or a related field, a value of four indicated that one or more HR managers had extensive prior work experience in personnel in a professionalized setting (though no HR manager had an advanced degree). Level four and five subunits also typically had multiple departments to deal with specialized HR functions (training, etc.). At the lower end of the scale, a level of one indicated that the firm had no manager with responsibilities exclusively in the

HR area (most common in the Japanese companies), while a level two company typically delegated the HRM function to a senior clerk or secretary.

To simplify the analysis, the items have been rescored to 0-1 dichotomous variables. This also allowed comparable treatment of those scored as dichotomous variables on the survey instrument. A score of 3, 4, or 5 on the semantic differential was taken to mean that the practice in question was used to a significant extent by the firm; this was scored as a 1 on the recoded scale, while other answers were coded as 0. HRM professionalism was similarly recoded to a dichotomous variable.[4]

The operational definitions of the variables analyzed in this study are presented in Table 1. The HRM practices examined fall into the following general categories: staffing and selection (recruiting methods, internal allocation of labor, compensation (pay setting methods and pay criteria), training (use of formal methods, for managers, professionals, and lower echelon workers), and employee evaluation methods (use of written performance evaluations and techniques such as MBO). We also examined use of quality control circles (in the miscellaneous category).

Employment Practices in Thailand: Survey Findings

Each of variables described in Table 1 have been broken into five categories: American firms, European firms, Japanese firms, Thai family enterprises, and publicly held Thai corporations. The results of these cross-tabulations appear in Table 2. The percentages indicate the proportion of cases in each category that received the higher score for that particular variable. For example, in the case of HRM professionalism, 95.5% of the American firms, but only 37.5% of the Japanese firms, scored "relatively high" on the professionalism scale (and thus 4.5% of the American, and 62.5% of the Japanese firms, scored "relatively low"). The average for all cases in the sample appears in the column labeled "total". Finally, the last column presents the significance level of the chi-square statistic associated with each cross-tabulation. In some instances (i.e., training, recruiting, and selection), we have differentiated between HRM practices as applied to blue and white collar workers. We discuss each of the major categories presented in Table 2 in turn.

HRM Professionalism

The results indicate a statistically significant relationship between HRM professionalism and a firm's national origin. As would be expected, Western firms are considerably more likely than Asian firms to professionalize the HRM function. In addition, American firms are more likely than European firms to go this route. Both the Japanese firms and Thai family enterprises were the least likely to utilize

Table 1:   Definitions of Variables

Variables	Coding Scheme
HRM Professionalism	1 = relatively high 0 = relatively low
Staffing Practices: General	
1) Written Job descriptions descriptions	1 = extensive use 0 = little or no use

2) Promotion from within	1 = most positions filled
	        by internal promotion
	0 = positions are often
	        filled externally

3) Succession planning	1 = used 0 = not used
Staffing Practices: Recruiting	
4) College recruiting	1 = extensive use 0 = little or no use
5) Employment services	1 = extensive use 0 = little or no use
6) Ads in English-language newspapers	1 = extensive use 0 = little or no use
7) Ads in Thai-language newspapers	1 = extensive use 0 = little or no use
8) Walk-in applications	1 = extensive use 0 = little or no use
Staffing Practices: Selection	
9) Interviews	1 = extensive use 0 = little or no use
10) Written tests	1 = extensive use 0 = little or no use
11) Internal references	1 = extensive use 0 = little or no use
12) External references	1 = extensive use 0 = little or no use
Staffing Practices: Selection	
13) Prior work experience	1 = extensive use 0 = little or no use
14) Level of education	1 = extensive use 0 = little or no use
Compensation Practices	
1) Job Evaluation	1 = extensive use 0 = little or no use
2) Role of seniority in compensation decisions	1 = very important 0 = unimportant
3) Profit sharing program	1 = used 0 = not used
Training proactices	
1) Formal training programs	1 = extensive use 0 = little or no use
Evaluation Practices	
1) Written performance evaluations	1 = used 0 = not used
2) Management by objectives (MBO)	1 = used 0 = not used

Table 2: Survey Results (percent)

Variables	American	European	Japanese	Thai (Family)	Thai (Public)	Total	Significance level
HRM Professionalism	95.5	73.7	37.5	41.2	60	63.8	.01
Staffing Practices: General							
1) Written Job descriptions	90.9	84.2	43.8	52.9	70.0	70.2	.01
2) Promotion from within	63.6	42.1	75.0	41.2	30.0	50.0	.05
3) Succession planning	31.8	47.4	25.0	23.5	20.0	29.8	ns
Staffing Practices: Recruiting (White Collar)							
1) recruiting	45.5	63.2	56.3	41.2	55.0	52.1	ns
2) Employment services	45.5	63.2	6.3	23.5	5.0	29.8	.01
3) Ads in English-language newspapers	77.3	89.5	68.8	70.6	60.0	73.4	ns
4) Ads in Thai-language newspapers	22.7	21.1	43.8	41.2	30.0	30.9	ns
5) Walk-in applications	18.2	31.6	12.5	29.4	35.0	25.5	ns
Staffing Practices: Recruiting (Blue Collar)							
1) Employment services	9.1	21.1	12.5	17.6	20.0	16.0	ns
2) Ads in English-language newspapers	13.6	10.5	31.3	11.8	15.0	16.0	ns
3) Ads in Thai-language newspapers	59.1	57.9	50.0	35.3	55.0	52.1	ns
4) Walk-in applications	36.4	47.4	18.8	47.1	65.0	43.6	.10
Staffing Practices: Selection (White Collar)							
1) Interviews	54.5	94.7	81.3	82.4	75.0	76.6	.05
2) Written tests	45.5	47.4	68.8	35.3	70.0	53.2	ns
3) Internal references	36.4	31.6	18.8	41.2	45.0	35.1	ns
4) External references	50.0	52.6	25.0	52.9	35	43.6	ns

Human Resource Management in Thailand 311

5) Prior work experience	36.4	68.4	37.5	58.8	55	51.1	ns
6) Level of education	63.6	84.2	56.3	82.2	80.0	73.4	ns
7) Foreign college degree	45.5	26.3	0.0	11.8	35.0	25.5	.01
Staffing Practices: Selection (Blue Collar)							
1) Interviews	50.0	94.7	68.8	82.4	65.0	71.3	.01
2) Written tests	45.5	57.9	62.5	58.8	65.0	57.4	ns
3) Internal references	54.5	57.9	56.3	64.7	45.0	55.3	ns
4) External references	27.3	57.9	31.3	52.9	35.0	40.4	ns
5) Prior work experience	9.1	21.1	12.5	11.8	25.5	16.0	ns
6) Level of education	40.9	63.2	43.8	52.9	25.0	44.7	ns
Compensation Practices							
1) Job Evaluation	90.9	52.6	12.5	17.6	45.0	46.8	.01
2) Role of seniority in compensation decisions	31.8	36.8	87.5	41.2	40.0	45.7	.01
3) Profit sharing programs	22.7	26.3	56.3	35.3	30.0	33.3	ns
Training Practices (White Collar)							
1) Formal training programs	86.4	100	75.0	76.5	85.0	85.1	ns
Training Practices (Blue Collar)							
1) Formal training programs	54.5	68.4	68.8	58.8	60.0	61.7	ns
Evaluation Practices							
1) Written performance evaluations	59.1	73.7	87.5	76.5	70.0	72.3	ns
2) Management by objectives (MBO)	36.4	47.4	18.8	11.8	25.0	28.7	.10

professional HR managers. In the case of Japanese firms, the HRM function was often fulfilled by the managing director or some other executive with operations responsibility. This, of course, is consistent with the tendency of Japanese firms in general to avoid highly specialized organizational roles. And in many of the cases in which Japanese firms did have a defined HRM function, managers from various fields were often rotated through HR management positions.

In the family enterprises, the HRM function seemed to have relatively low status; in the interviews, it often appeared that less talented family members were relegated to such positions. In contrast, the publicly held Thai firms are clearly striving to upgrade the HRM function. There are several reasons for this. Labor shortages in critical areas mean that these firms must devote greater resources to recruiting and attempting to retain the most competent employees. Second, as these firms strive to compete internationally, they have sought to model themselves after Western multinationals. Union avoidance considerations also have promoted a greater interest in the HRM function in Thailand.

Staffing/Selection Practices

Firms may employ a wide range of techniques to aid in hiring employees and staffing positions. We examined only a subset of these methods, choosing those that seemed conceptually most interesting. For example, informal networking and "string pulling" are often viewed as major features of organizations in Southeast Asia, so we asked the extent to which firms relied on internal and external references (really personal contacts) as a means of selecting new employees. Testing is seen as an especially important screening device in Japanese firms and managers in Thai-owned firms often stress its importance in informal conversations.

There is considerable variation across staffing practices with regard to statistically significant relationships. Again, as would be expected, Japanese firms rely heavily on internal promotion to fill vacancies and develop employees. American firms also are relatively high on this dimension. However, this would seem to be a more recent development, as American firms are no longer so readily able to fill vacancies from a large pool of job seekers. Also, as expected, Western firms are more prone to have clearly defined and written job descriptions. Notice again that this practice has also become rather common in the publicly held Thai firms.

What is most surprising, however, is that there were very few statistically significant differences across these categories for most of the other staffing practices. Formal succession planning is somewhat less common in Asian that Western firms, but still the differences are not especially pronounced. Only a few of the staffing and the recruiting practices examined were significantly related to the firm's national origin. Although there are no tests of significance, it appears that firm reliance on various selection methods did not differ much between white collar and blue collar workers. On the other hand, recruiting methods seem to have been much more intensively applied in the case of white collar workers. This result would be consistent with Thai labor market conditions. Labor shortages are more pronounced in the case of highly educated workers, resulting in "job hopping" and upward pressure on salaries.

Compensation Methods

As most companies were reluctant to provide actual wage data, it was not possible to compare firms in terms of wage levels or distributions. Based on the comments of the survey respondents, we are, however, able to offer some impressions regarding wages in general in Thailand.

There has been considerable upward pressure on wages in Thailand, especially in the Bangkok area. However, wage growth seems to be driven primarily by improvements in productivity, resulting from new investment, rather than by general inflation. In fact, consumer price movements have been quite modest, with the rate of inflation for the country as a whole running at around 6% per year (again, this rate is probably higher in Bangkok and other industrial centers). As noted, labor shortages are particularly acute in the case of skilled professionals. "Job hopping", a problem for employers in other rapidly developing Southeast Asian countries, is now a major concern for Thai employers. This has resulted in very significant salary increases for engineers, managers, computer experts, etc. One way of assessing the degree to which salaries have increased for such workers is to compare advertised starting salaries (in newspaper advertisements) to typical salaries for government officials. The latter have changed very little over the past several years. A college professor in Thailand, for example, might make only around $6,000 per year, yet starting salaries for graduating engineers may be $30,000 or more per year. Needless to say, this has resulted in a serious internal "brain drain", as government employees have left for private sector jobs in droves.

The wage picture for blue collar workers, and those who are not highly skilled, has not been so bright. In this sector, characterized by surplus labor, economic growth has resulted primarily in significant increases in employment. Factory workers in large-scale enterprises are normally paid the Thai minimum wage, which is now around five dollars per day. However, the minimum wage has increased over the last several years and was less than three dollars per day in the mid-1980s. However, the increase over this period is largely offset by inflation, so real wages for blue collar workers has changed very little in the past decade. There are, nonetheless, signs of a dwindling supply of labor in this sector that may soon generate upward pressure on wages. There seems to be increased reliance by employers in some areas on illegal immigrants from neighboring countries (especially Laos and Myanmar, formerly Burma). Domestic servants, once readily available in Bangkok, are increasingly difficult to find. This suggests that those once taking servant positions are finding more lucrative work. Such pressures may result in significant wage inflation in coming years.

Although we did not obtain hard wage and salary data from the companies in which interviews were conducted, we did ask questions about specific wage and salary practices. Job evaluation was extensively used in American firms and, to a somewhat lesser extent, in European firms. Job evaluation was virtually nonexistent in Japanese firms and little used in family enterprises. However, again, the publicly held firms seem to be adopting this method. Another important compensation issue is the extent to which seniority, versus job performance, serves as a basis for periodic adjustments in wages and salaries. Again, consistent with the stereotypical Japanese approach, most of Japanese subsidiaries placed primary importance on age or length of service. Nonetheless, managers in these firms indicated that the seniority factor was beginning to give way to performance indicators in these decisions. Although seniority is stressed much less in Western subsidiaries (relative to Japanese), there is not much difference between Thai and Western firms, a somewhat surprising finding. One suspects, that at least in the family enterprises, the performance dimension may be mostly related to what managers perceive as an employee's loyalty, rather than objective indicators of job performance. Finally, there is no significant difference with respect to profit sharing across firms, although the Japanese subsidiaries, with an emphasis on group incentives, are somewhat more likely than either Thai or Western firms to utilize profit sharing schemes.

Training Practices

In our original case studies (Lawler et al., 1989), respondents had suggested that training practices differed considerably across firms as a function of national origin. Japanese firms, with a strong emphasis on internal development of their work forces, were given high marks all around for their training efforts. Thai firms were, for the most part, seen to view extensive training as excessively costly. Finally, Western firms, especially American subsidiaries, seemed to rely on a high wage strategy to attract experienced and well-trained employees, thus obviating the need for anything more than rudimentary training programs. However, in our subsequent survey, we found that, at least with respect to formal training programs, there were no significant relationship between training efforts and national origin. This held for both white collar and blue collar workers. For white collar workers, reliance on training in Japanese companies was least of all, though these firms were somewhat above average for blue collar workers?

The apparent shift in training efforts among Thai and Western firms appears to be related to labor market conditions. As employers find it increasingly difficult to find quality workers, they necessarily turn to internal development and training. The prosperity now occurring in Thailand has meant that indigenous firms have the resources to conduct quality training programs. As an example, Siam Cement, one of Thailand's premier corporations, has utilized faculty from such prestigious American business programs as Berkeley, Northwestern's Kellogg School, and the Wharton School to conduct management development programs in Thailand. For the reasons discussed above, Western firms no longer find high wage strategies workable; consequently, they must now also devote resources to employee development.

Evaluation Practices

For the final set of HRM practices examined, we found no significant relationship between country of origin and use of written performance evaluations, though there was a weak but significant relationship in the case of management by objectives (MBO) programs. MBO programs, again as might be expected, were more common in Western subsidiaries.

Conclusion

We have examined a wide range of employment practices as utilized in both foreign and domestic firms operating in Thailand. As Thailand is a major emerging economy in the Pacific rim, the results of this study are relevant not only to Thailand itself, but to other countries in the region that are on similar growth paths (e.g., southern China, Malaysia, Indonesia, and, potentially, the Philippines) and those countries that may possibly begin rapid growth in the near future (e.g., Vietnam, Cambodia, and Laos). Of course, Thailand is, in many respects, socially and culturally distinct from its neighbors, so that the findings are not totally generalizable.

The empirical work in this study anticipated substantial differences in HRM practices among firms based on national origin, yet the results of our survey suggest more in the way of convergence than divergence. Why might this be so? We believe in most cases, market conditions, rather than cultural forces, are at work. Consider, for example, staffing policies. The identification and selection of new employees are particularly important in tight labor markets. There are, in many areas, severe shortages in Thailand of professional and managerial employees. Consequently, "job hopping" is a frequent problem for firms. As a result, firms may adopt the most efficient means of identifying quality employees regardless of cultural predispositions. In addition, labor shortages may compel firms to implement aggressive training programs. While Japanese firms have long stressed training, American MNCs have generally had a tradition in developing countries of paying high wages, thus attracting the most skilled workers and limiting the need for extensive training programs. And Thai firms have, in the past, tended to view formal training as too expensive. Perhaps this is no longer the case, resulting in a convergence of training and staffing practices. Anecdotal evidence derived from informal discussions with respondents supports such an interpretation of the findings.

How do we expect HRM practices to change in Thailand in coming years? Thailand is very open to external influences and we anticipate that reliance on Western HRM techniques is liable to increase. This is likely to result from the increasing presence of MNCs in Thailand, as well as the academic training typical of most younger Thai managers. Large-scale family enterprises will find it increasingly difficult to maintain their traditional structures and management systems. As they grow, there simply may not be enough trusted and competent family members to assume key positions. Also, the need to raise capital externally will continue to create the kind of accountability pressures mentioned earlier. So overall, it appears as though there will be greater professionalization of the HRM function in Thailand and greater reliance on relatively systematic and rationalized HRM methods.

One area that is likely to undergo considerable change, and this is already evident in our results, is employee training and development. To date, training and development activities focus primarily on professional and managerial employees. We anticipate that not only will training and development efforts will increase for that sector, but that such efforts will also increase substantially for lower-level employees. This will be the outcome of efforts to sustain Thailand's recent economic gains and to promote future growth. Employers in Thailand, except for Japanese companies, have often been reluctant to invest in training because of a concern that they would not be able to recover training costs (due to economic change, worker job hopping, etc.). To date, much of the country's growth has revolved around labor-intensive and low value-added industries. As wages increase in Thailand, the country will not be able to compete with lower-wage areas (e.g., Indonesia, China, Vietnam) without a substantial upgrading of the human resources. Some of this will be accomplished through the public education system, though it seems probable that private enterprise will need to take considerable initiative in this area as well.

Endnotes

1. Association of Southeast Asian Nations (Philippines, Indonesia, Brunei, Singapore, Malaysia, and Thailand).
2. The Eightfold Path consists of right understanding, right intention, right speech, right action, right livelihood, right effort, right mindfulness, and right concentration.
3. Nirvana can be defined as a state of perfect emptiness, the complete elimination of all mortal elements, and the final release from the cycle of reincarnations.

4. Though not reported here, some sensitivity analysis was performed by varying the break points used to generate the dichotomous variables; slight changes in the break points appeared to have no appreciable affect on the results of the analysis reported below.

References

Brown, A. and S. Frenkel (1993). "Union Unevenness and Insecurity in Thailand." In S. Frenkel (ed.), *Organized Labor in the Asia Pacific Region*. Ithaca, NY: ILR Press, pp. 82-106.

Butler, J.E., G.R. Ferris, and N.K. Napier (1991). *Strategy and Human Resources Management*. Cincinnati: South-Western.

Chen, C. (1991). "Confucian Style of Management in Taiwan." In J. Putti (ed.), *Management: Asian Context*. New York: McGraw-Hill, pp. 198-221.

The Economist (1991). "Where Tigers Breed: A Survey of Asia's Emerging Economies." *The Economist*, November 16, 4.

Hongladarom, Chira (1990a). "The Rise of Trade Unions and the Industrial Relations System in Thailand." In S. Prasith-rathsint (ed.), *Thailand On the Move: Stumbling Blocks and Breakthroughs*. Bangkok: Thai University Research Association, pp. 167-188.

Hongladarom, Chira (1990b). "Unemployment in Thailand." In S. Prasith-rathsint (ed.), *Thailand On the Move: Stumbling Blocks and Breakthroughs*. Bangkok: Thai University Research Association, pp. 133-166.

International Business Research Co. (1985-1989). *Million Baht Business Information*. Bangkok: IBR.

Isarangkun Na Ayuthaya, C., and K. Taira (1977). "The Organization and Behavior of the Factory Work Force in Thailand." *The Developing Economies*, 15, 16-37.

Lawler, J.J., V. Atmiyanandana, and M.A. Zaidi (1992). "Human Resource Management Practices in Multinational and Local Firms in Thailand." *Journal of Southeast Asia Business*, 8, 16-40.

Lawler, J.J., M.A. Zaidi, and V. Atmiyanandana (1989). "Human Resource Strategies in Southeast Asia: The Case of Thailand." In A. Nedd, G. Ferris, and K. Rowland (eds.), *Research in Personnel and Human Resources Management* (Supplement 1). Greenwich, CN: JAI Press, pp.201-222.

Mintzberg, H. (1989). *Mintzberg On Management: Inside Our Strange World of Organizations*. New York: Free Press.

Siengthai, S., and P. Vadhanasindhu (1991). "Management in a Buddhist Society – Thailand." In J. Putti (ed.), *Management: Asian Context*. New York: McGraw-Hill, pp. 222-238.

Soriano, E. (1991). "Management in *Pakikisama* Society – Philippines." In J. Putti (ed.), *Management: Asian Context*. New York: McGraw-Hill, pp. 61-77.

Steers, R.M., Y.K. Shin, and G.R. Ungson (1989). *The Cheabol: Korea's New Industrial Might*. New York: Harper and Row.

Thailand Development Research Institute (1992). *Thailand Economic Information Kit*. Bangkok: Thailand Development Research Institute.

Widyahartono, B. (1991). "The *Pancasila* Way of Managing in Indonesia." In J. Putti (ed.), *Management: Asian Context*. New York: McGraw-Hill, pp. 130-144

Human Resource Management in the United States

P. Devereaux Jennings and Larry F. Moore

Human resource management in the United States at the turn of this century appears to be in a state of transition, whether viewed by human resource specialists or industrial relations theorists:

the workplace of the 1990s promises to be very different from the 1980s... In today's highly competitive and changing economic environment, HR professionals are being asked to help lead their organizations into the future. Recruiting employees from a shrinking labor pool, coping with greater workforce diversity and helping employees balance work and family life are some of the more urgent matters that HR professionals need to address (Wagel and Levine, 1990, p. 18).

The cumulative effects of the decline of unions and the rise of alternative approaches to human resource management by the early 1980s had set the stage once again for an intense debate concerning the role of unions and collective bargaining in American society... We are currently moving through another one of those critical periods of transformation of American industrial relations (Kochan et al., 1986, pp. 4-6).

But not all observers agree that these changes are fundamental. Some argue that the employment relationship in the United States will continue to be governed primarily by the bureaucratic method of control (Baron et al., 1986; 1988; Edwards, 1979; Gordon et al., 1982; Jacoby, 1985; Villimez and Bridges, 1994). Jacoby (1985), who has traced the rise of this control regime, states:

unlike some recent observers, I do not see these structural adjustments as portents of a weakening employment relationship and a return to more casual labor markets. Instead, I believe that the basic practices which make up the internal labor market are likely to persist, not because they are carved in microeconomic stone, but because over the years they have become embedded in a structure of law, managerial principles,.and employee expectations (Jacoby, 1985, p. 285).

In this case, human resources will still be handled through a widespread use of rules, regulations, and procedures that govern all aspects of the employment relationship in the firm – from hiring to promotion to departure. Such practices will include in-house hiring quotas and screening tests; formal performance appraisal and other due process promotion procedures; seniority- and skill-based pay; and formal dismissal procedures, severance packages and retraining plans. While the external labor market's formalization is temporarily in flux, the internal labor market in most medium- and large-sized firms is just as elaborate and formal as in the past.

Analysts are able to argue about transformation because the *variation* in human resource practices and policy appears to be growing. In some sectors, there is still the more traditional overlay of technical and bureaucratic practices that are administered by HR functionaries with the help of management and within the constraints of union practices and the law (Noble, 1993; Norback and Russell, 1991). In other sectors, there are more experimental programs with HR practices, such as computerized linkages of employees to HR units allowing employees to select HR information and create their own benefit packages (Gavin, 1993; Radford and Kove, 1991, pp. 38-41). In fact, there is even some evidence of what Kochan et al. (1986) foresaw almost a decade ago: firms are becoming highly networked and subcontract most of their HRM work to smaller, specialized consulting units, which have firm-specific knowledge of advanced HRM practices and simply set up HRM programs for their larger counterparts (PNPMA/SHRMA, 1991).

Unfortunately, systematic, economy-wide, firm-level information on corporate HRM systems has not been readily available to address this debate on HRM's transformation. Most research on current HRM has relied on information of a much narrower scope, such as data on the HR managerial pay (Langer, 1991) or data on the practice of testing (Greenberg, 1990) or data on the development of HRM systems in one economic sector or state (Baron and Newman, 1990; Baron et al., 1991). Research within HRM has also conceptualized the development of U.S. HRM in narrow, nation-centered terms, rather than in the broad context of the HRM systems that have evolved in other countries (Fombrun et al., 1984; Schuler and Jackson, 1986; but see Brandt, 1991, p. 38; Schuler et al., 1993).

However, some researchers are trying to provide more comprehensive pictures of the employment relationship within the United States. Many of these researchers are doing work within sociology, which has an intellectual commitment to examining the role of larger, societal or market structures in the development of social subsystems, such as the internal labor markets within the firm. Kalleberg and Berg (1987) have summarized the different efforts to understand the work in organizations from macro sociological perspectives. They argue that work must be understood within the context of the specific industry and market in which it is placed, and then organization-specific variables must be added into the picture as additional mediating effects. Villimez and Bridges (1994) are currently assessing the role of bureaucratic practices in modern industry by building on the work of Baron et al. (1986; 1988) and Jacoby (1985) that examined the evolution of the bureaucratic labor regime in personnel during the first half of the century. Baron and Kreps (forthcoming) and Pfeffer (1994) are in the process of translating classical approaches to personnel management into new, sociological approaches to macro HRM, in part by framing all personnel activities within the larger context of the employment relationship.

In this chapter we work along similar lines. We assess HRM in the U.S. by analyzing HRM within the context of the employment relationship and using a macro organizational framework – in particular, Neoinstitutional Theory (Meyer and Scott, 1983; Powell and DiMaggio, 1991; Scott, 1987; Zucker, 1987). We move across different levels of analysis, from the macro level of the employment relationship to the micro level of HR managerial attitudes, and we put each of these levels into historical context with preliminary discussion of HRM's development. In keeping with the work of Baron et al. (1986; 1988); Baron and Newman (1990); Pfeffer and Cohen (1984), and others we try to provide a comprehensive picture of corporate HRM systems by relying on survey and demographic data on HR departments and managers taken from the national association of HR Practitioners, the Strategic Human Resources Management Association (SHRMA), and by using our own in-depth survey of HR practices and HR managerial views in one of SHRMA's regional associations, the Pacific Northwest Personnel Management Association (PNPMA/SHRMA). Finally, like Villimez and Bridges (1994) we consider whether or not bureaucratic control is still relied upon in many of the medium- and large-sized firms found in our sample of firms in the Pacific Northwest.

Our approach seems well suited for a study of current HRM in the United States because of the large, structural changes occurring in corporate HRM systems that have been acknowledged by so many researchers (Kochan et al., 1986; Springer and Springer, 1990). These changes are noticeable both within the firm and in the types of contracts that are being struck in the external labor market. Starting with a macro level of analysis allows us to discuss both the external and internal labor markets as well as two traditional units of analysis in HR studies in the wider context of the employment relationship: HR departments and HR managers. The unravelling of the bureaucratic regime – at least at the edges – can be seen by the differences that are beginning to appear among HR departments in their use and types of interpretation of what were once considered standard bureaucratic practices, such as job analysis and job classification. The ability of HR managers to affect the employment relationship and to advance the cause of HRM as a field can be seen by examining the perceptions of managers about their role in the firm and about the degree of professionalism they believe exists in HRM today.

Our ultimate objective in the chapter is to present some overall, coherent pattern of HRM in the U.S. This pattern will help us answer the three fundamental questions: Is a new control regime beginning to arise in the employment relationship? Have HR managers changed their training and interpretation of HR practice? And are some of these patterns recognizable in other Pacific Rim countries?

The Employment Relationship in the U.S.

All HR practice takes place within the context of the employment relationship, the set of all relations and supporting institutions between employees and employers (Flanagan et al., 1989; Pfeffer, 1994). The employment relationship from the point of view of macro organization theory involves not simply the neoclassical market factors associated with work, but the structures (organizations, regions, nations) in which markets exist (Kalleberg and Berg, 1987). This "multivariate" or structuralist view of the employment relations implies that in order to understand HR practices it is necessary to understand the historical and social context in which work practices evolve. In the case of HRM, the following section will sketch the evolution of different regimes that have dictated the nature of employment practices over time.

The Historical Changes

The modern employment relationship in the U.S. began in the mid-1800s with the advent of the mechanized factory, which required the availability of more unskilled and skilled labor on a longer term, reliable basis (Chandler, 1962; Dobbin, 1992; Jacoby, 1985). Along side the development of industry on this more massive, rationalized scale was the development of labor's ability to take collective action to manage the terms of the employment relationship (Bernstein, 1960; 1970; Jacoby, 1985). The first HRM or "personnel" departments developed at the point of contact between the growing firm and organizing labor.

National Cash Register (NCR) is widely credited with one of the first HR departments in the U.S. (Springer and Springer, 1990). At NCR, the focus was on programs to train large numbers of workers to make cash register parts. Other innovators in personnel, like Goodyear Tire and Rubber and Plimpton Press, also experimented with the basics of human resource administration, such as screening applicants with tests and using systematic wage data (Eibert, 1959). Methods for administering large groups of workers according to the discipline set by the factory system were also developed by engineers and business analysts at MIT, a group later credited with the creation of Scientific Management Theory (Jacoby, 1985, pp. 47-48; Springer and Springer, 1990; Taylor, 1911). In such a system, technology determined the basic characteristics of the tasks and skills required of workers. The time and motion principles of the assembly line were used to design the tasks and jobs of laborers working on the line. But because many jobs off the assembly line were difficult to adapt to time and motion principles, departments relied on these practices in only a small number of jobs (Jacoby, 1986; but see Edwards, 1979).

Size appeared to be as important a factor as technology for the rationalization of the employment relationship (Baron et al., 1986; Doeringer and Piore, 1971;

Jacoby, 1985). Average firm size increased dramatically from 1850 to 1950, even after anti-trust legislation broke up many of the largest firms in the petroleum, chemical, steel, and rail industries (Chandler, 1962). The increased size meant more workers were being included on a permanent basis in the firm. Adminis-trating this longer term contract was easier from a single corporate unit, such as the personnel department. Such units could also be used to screen and to develop applicants. In fact, Scientific Management theorists such as Taylor advocated us-ing personnel departments to handle the administrative problems created by scale (Taylor, 1911). Not surprisingly, data from the National Industrial Conference Board (1927; 1936; 1940; 1946) indicated a strong relationship between firm size and the percentage of firms with personnel departments during very distinctive decades – the 1920s, the 1930s, and the 1940s.

Personnel departments were also developed to help forestall unionization within firms (Edwards, 1979; Stone, 1974). While personnel departments were not im-portant in this regards during the first great round of unionizing, which began in the late 1870s and ended in the 1890s (Voss, 1994), they were important in the second round of unionizing, just after World War I, and in the third round, just after the creation of the Wagner Act in 1935 (Jacoby, 1985). In the later two time periods, personnel departments used so-called "welfare practices" to promote long-term commitment and undermine unionizing efforts, practices such as pension plans and health care provisions. In some cases, companies formed their own in-house unions to give employees an alternative method of expressing their grievances (Bernstein, 1960; 1970; Slichter, 1919). Many of these welfare practices and company unions were dropped by firms in the 1930s, after their failure to arrest unionization. The few that were kept, such as pension plans and the use of health insurance, were still used not because of their success at combat-ing unionization, but because of government mandates about pension and health insurance during that time period (Baron et al., 1986; Dobbin, 1992; Stevens, 1986).

During each World War the State played a large role in controlling the conflict between labor and management (Baron et al, 1986; 1988; Jacoby, 1985; but see Edwards, 1979). The government centralized resource allocation in the economy through various standing committees like the War Labor Board (WPB, 1942). These resource planning boards monitored the number and types of workers attached to different firms in different industries in order to regulate manpower flows. Monitoring required that units like personnel departments classify and evaluate jobs and carefully track workers. The government also tried to regulate how much workers were compensated in order to keep employees or employers from exploiting one another during these critical periods (Gray, 1943).

But the government did not choose to focus on all industries and all aspects of work to an equal degree: War materials industries were essential, and their large, short-run profits (windfalls) were highly visible and potentially embarrass-ing politically in times of hardship, which required much more careful regulation of these industries than of others. Firms outside of war materials industries were allowed to chose whether or not to follow suit with other wartime industries. Nevertheless, Baron et al., (1986) found a high level of mimicry in non-essential industries, such as the wholesale adoption of job classification and job evaluation procedures in non-manufacturing sectors. In some cases, fear of future legislation and the need for efficient interaction with war-related industries may have been the reasons for mimicry. But imitation also seemed to occur for less direct reasons. Dobbin (1992) found that pension plans in industries varied more dramatically than labor allocation and assessment. This seems to have been because the government chose not to regulate these plans directly, but simply to offer workers a small pension through social security, which firms could then supplement in any way firms saw fit. Consequently, these firms developed practices that would complement the actions of the State and, at the same time, fit the unique circumstances facing the firm.

By the end of World War II, the joint effects of organization, technology, size, unionization, and government regulation helped create what is known as the "bureaucratic control regime" or the bureaucratic method of handling the employment relationship in most industries (Baron et al., 1986; Edwards, 1979; Jacoby, 1985). The bureaucratic regime has been characterized by a strong reliance on complex, formal practices for due process in hiring, training, rewarding, moving and releasing workers. These practices have normally been under the control of the HR department, or at least have had its active involvement. Bureaucratic control differs from control regimes associated with earlier systems, such as "simple control" used in the small organizations and "technical control" used in the first mass production factories. Simple control relied on the personal decision making of the foreman in all human resource areas, and technical control relied on the needs of the factory's technology – the pace of its assembly line, the number of parts made, the rate of mishaps – to determine how labor should be hired, trained, moved and released (Edwards, 1979).

The elaboration and diffusion of the bureaucratic regime has continued up to the present time. A look at HRM practices in the 1950s shows that job design, classification, and evaluation; compensation and benefits; company information and HR planning; and many other practices were still widespread and in firms with personnel departments (NICB, 1954). In the 1960s and 1970s HR departments became even more involved in the establishment and administration of due process procedures for workers. The 1964 Civil Rights Act changed advertising, recruiting, selection, promotion and dismissal procedures; and more recent legislation like EEO and ADA intensified this need for due process in corporate HRM systems (Edelman, 1992; Sutton et al., 1993). According to Villimez and Bridges (1994), the bureaucratic regime in the 1990s is still widespread in U.S. industry and still associated with the use of personnel departments, due process, and firm size. More importantly, the State continues to be a strong contextual and direct factor in the use of bureaucratic control within firms – even when unionization,

competition, size and industry are considered. The State regulates the employment relationship through laws and rules affecting both the external labor market
and internal labor market of private firms. It is also the largest single employer in
the country, which means many workers are covered directly by its human rights
policies and statutes.

However, major changes have occurred in the roles played by two other actors
involved in the original development of the bureaucratic regime – labor and
management. Labor can no longer focus its will as clearly by drawing on the
clout of a few dominant unions. Since the 1970s there has been a decrease in the
percentage of workers unionized in most industries and a lack of new unionization
in non-traditional sectors, like whitecollar work in service industries. The absolute
number of unionists has also fallen, with no apparent end to this trend in sight
(BLS, 1994; Kochan et al., 1986, p. 50). As might be expected, labor's impact
on local and federal politics has also been on the downswing. In the Reagan Era
of the 1980s, fundamental labor causes, such as plant closing legislation, limits
on immigration, and protection for labor-intensive industry either failed or led to
minimal results (Bluestone and Harrison, 1982; Sabel and Piore, 1984). Today,
unions are primarily a force in only three sectors – transportation, education,
and government work. Not surprisingly, Villimez and Bridges (1994) reported no
consistent, current association of unionization with bureaucratic control in their
studies.

Management has regained some of the initiative to enact human resource policies that it lost to labor, although the government is more watchful than ever. In
non-unionized sectors, managers have allowed HRM practitioners to experiment
with more customized methods of handling groups of workers, such as using
cafeteria-style benefit plans (Rothwell and Kazanas, 1988; Springer and Springer,
1990). In unionized sectors, managers have circumvented both union and government initiatives by threatening or actually closing plants and declaring bankruptcy
in order to gain concessions (Kochan et al., 1986; McKenzie, 1982; Norback and
Russell, 1991). Ironically, it is still HR managers who are involved in handling
union problems that earn the highest salaries (Langer, 1991, p. 25), even though
their goal is to make sure unions are no longer the source of difficulties for firms.

Two unforeseen changes have also taken place with regards to the standing
of HRM in organizations. On the one hand, the professionalization process of
HR management has not yet succeeded in transforming the HR occupation into
an independent, professional discipline. Professionalization began at the turn of
the century with the use of Scientific Management Theory as an ideology for
handling human capital, and it gained speed in the 1940s and 1950s with detailed
job classification, analysis and evaluation (Nkomo, 1980; Ritzer and Trice, 1969).
Currently, HR management has subspecialties that require highly skilled work,
but the field does not have the classic characteristics of a profession (Jacoby,
1983; Jennings, 1992). On the other hand, there has actually been an increase in
HR managerial power within firms because of HRM's involvement in business

planning and corporate strategy (Fombrun et al., 1984; Schuler, 1987). The call for a more strategic approach to HRM was first sounded in the early 1980s and can still be heard in the field from a number of top ranking representatives:

More than ever, it is necessary that the highest levels of HR be tied into the overall corporate strategic-planning cycles. The need to model and simulate current and future workforce requirements will call increased attention to the lack of HR planning systems able to support those concerns (Wagel, 1990, p. 14).

Strategic management requires that a reactive, bureaucratic approach to the employment relationship should give way to a proactive, managerial approach in which the HR department helps tailor the employment contract to the firm's strategic needs (Anthony and Norton, 1991, pp. 75-86).

As discussed at the outset, these changes in the balance among government, labor and management, as well as specific changes within firms have created a fundamental shift in the character of the employment relationship. In simplistic terms, it has become more of a buyer's market, yet the costs of screening and training and conforming to the law mean that making a good buy is not easy. The system is attempting to adapt: It is out-sourcing many of these costly components of HR; it is trying to make its own human capital more flexible through additional education and development; and it is moving many facilities off-shore to countries with completely different labor pools. The State as a dual advocate for business and labor concerns has become a major determinant as to which options firms are most likely to take in the 1990s.

The Present Employment Relationship

Our discussion of the employment relationship from a macro, neoinstitutional perspective requires a consideration of the external and internal labor markets and then the role played by the HR department and HR manager in them. The external labor market forms the environment for the firm's HR system, and the internal labor market contains all of the elements of the employment relationship in the firm, which the HR unit sees as its job to administer.

The External Labor Market

The labor market is composed of all buyers and sellers of labor (Baron and Kreps, 1994; Flanagan et al., 1989, p. 16). The market matches buyers and sellers – in particular, firms and laborers in jobs. In the U.S. the characteristics of the laborers are described in Table 1. There has been an increasing occupational bulge in white-collar work in the so-called service sector. By 1993, almost 60% of all workers were clerical or white collar of some sort, and almost 70% of all

Table 1:   Changing Profile of Industrial Employment

Industry	1970	1980	1990				1993
			Total	Female	Black	Hispanic[1]	
Total employed	78,678	99,303	117,598	45.7	10.1	7.6	188,451
Agriculture	3,463	3,364	3,210	21.0	4.8	14.5	2,681
Mining	516	979	664	16.0	3.6	7.0	631
Construction	4,818	6,215	7,013	8.9	6.3	8.3	6,856
Manufacturing	20,746	21,942	19,972	32.9	10.4	8.7	19,278
Transportation, communica tion and other public utilities	5,320	6,525	8,245	28.3	13.4	6.7	8,224
Wholesale and retail trade	15,008	20,191	24,354	46.7	8.1	8.4	24,354
Finance, insurance, real estate	3,945	5,993	7,764	59.0	8.8	5.9	7,649
Services[2]	20,385	28,752	40,758	61.7	11.4	6.8	41,667
– Business services and repairs[2]	1,403	2,361	6,533	35.3	10.7	9.4	6,571
– Personal services[2]	4,276	3,839	4,400	69.3	14.9	13.6	4,400
– Entertainment and recreation	717	1,047	1,957	40.3	8.3	7.4	1,511
– Professional and related services[2]	12,904	19,853	27,677	68.5	11.3	5.2	28,604
Public administration[3]	4,476	5,342	5,620	42.7	14.4	5.6	5,665

NA Not available.

[1] Persons of Hispanic origin may be of any race.
[2] Includes industries not shown separately.
[3] Includes workers involved in uniquely governmental activities, e.g., judicial and legislative.

Source: U.S. Bureau of Labor Statistics, *Employment and Earnings*, January issues.

employment was in service (from transportation and public administration) (BLS, 1994; U.S. Government, 1994). By the year 2000, some have estimated that 90% of all labor is expected to be in white collar and service sector jobs (ILO, 1988, p. 53).

However, it is also noteworthy that this service sector is becoming less stable with time, meaning more white-collar workers will be shifting among jobs than ever before. For instance, the growth rate in business service far exceeded that in other services between 1970 and 1990. Yet in this current time of recession, service sector jobs appear more vulnerable than those in manufacturing, where a restructuring has been occurring for years. Moreover, white-collar work is more vulnerable than clerical work, if current business literature is any guide (e.g., Peters, 1987).

A change in the stability of white collar occupations is also accompanied by a change in the composition of the employed labor force, both across occupations and industries. The rate of female worker participation has increased from 22.9% of women in 1920 to 55.2% of women in 1988 (BLS, 1989). In 1992 women were 45.7% of the total labor force (BLS, 1994). By the year 2000, women will constitute 65% of all labor force entrants and 47% of all U.S. workers (BLS, 1992; Kovach and Pearce, 1990, p. 52). Professional occupations, such as medicine and law will have one-third female membership, which will be reflective of the predominately female composition of those industries.

Different racial and ethnic groups are also now very much a part of the permanent labor force, as shown by the statistics in Table 1 on the employment of blacks and Hispanics by major industry category (BLS, 1994). Blacks are 10.1% of the workforce and Hispanics, 7.6%. As the percentage of blacks, Hispanics, and Asians in the labor force increases, the overall composition will become much more diverse. The high level of diversity will mean that the assimilation of workers into the dominant culture of the firm cannot be expected to occur. Furthermore, HR departments cannot expect workers to be relatively passive once their separate group identities have been recognized and enclaves of these workers created in the firms. Instead, each group of workers is likely to demand its own set of rights as employees and to have these rights reflected in items as basic as the firm's mission statement (Gordon, 1992, p. 23; Jemison and O'Mara, 1991).

Traditional methods of organizing the labor force to direct their collective actions are not likely to be of the same use in the next decade. It is well known that traditional industrial unions, such as the AFL-CIO have declined (Kochan et al., 1986, p. 50). Only 20% of the U.S. labor force is presently represented in some form by unions. Furthermore, service unions have not grown at the rate that was anticipated. At this point, the most organized sector appears to be in municipal, state and federal government services. The breakdown on unionization statistics appears in Table 2.

The composition of "buyers" (of the firms that employ these workers) has changed along with the industries in which they produce. As was illustrated in Table 1 above, the number of firms in manufacturing has remained relatively constant, while most growth has occurred in service sectors, such as in high technology. While the movement of employees into services and the maturation of manufacturing have led to more capital- and skill-intensive, production firms, even service firms are using more skilled labor than ever before. Firms are complaining that the labor force is no longer adequately skilled to meet market demand in the coming decade. In a recent survey of AMA members, between 15% and 30% of workers who applied to firms were considered deficient in skills, and most firms reported at least 10% of their current workers as having deficient skills, except in

Table 2:   Profile of Union Membership, 1983, 1992

Industry	Employed Wage and Salary Workers			
	Number represented by unions[1] (1000)		Percent represented by unions	
	1983	1992	1983	1992
Full-time workers	18,745	16,886	26.4	20.1
Part-time workers	1,787	1,654	10.3	8.5
Managerial	4,307	4,687	21.9	17.8
Technical sales, and administration support	4,199	4,052	15.0	12.1
Service occupations	2,306	2,322	17.9	15.6
Precision, production, craft and repair	3,760	2,958	35.7	26.8
Operators, fabricators, and laborers	5,839	4,418	37.5	27.3
Farming, forestry and fishing	122	104	6.9	5.7
Agricultural wage and salary workers	55	42	3.8	3.8
Private nonagricultural wage and salary workers	13,369	10,660	18.8	12.7
Mining	201	100	23.1	16.1
Construction	1,207	955	29.4	21.4
Manufacturing	5,812	4,005	30.5	21.0
Transportation and public utilities	2,376	2,052	46.7	32.9
Wholesale and retail trade, total	1,775	1,542	9.8	7.2
Finance, insurance and real estate	228	196	4.1	2.9
Services	1,770	1,810	9.6	7.1
Government	7,109	7,838	45.5	43.2

[1] Members of a union or an employee association similar to a union as well as workers who report no union affilliation but whose jobs are covered by a union or an employee association contract.

Source: U.S. Bureau of Labor Statistics, *Employment and Earnings*, January issues; Statistical Abstracts of the United States, 1993

health care and education where the percentage of current workers with deficiency was near zero (Greenberg, 1990, p. 51).

A second change in the composition of buyers is that large firms may no longer employ as many workers as small firms or be as big a source of new jobs (Birch, 1979; Brock and Evans, 1986; but see Brown et al., 1990). Analysts now maintain that agglomerations of small firms in growing industries, like software manufacturing, create local economic synergies, leading to increased community growth. Of course, this exacerbates regional differences in the labor market, with these local "growth pole" areas (e.g., the Silicon Valley, Phoenix's outer rim, or Seattle-Bellevue) experiencing much more prosperity than other areas.

Small firms are often started by a few owners who both invest capital and work in the firm, and who are interested in retaining control – especially by resisting the power of organized labor. However, ownership of larger firms has begun to shift away from as much founder or family control (Herman, 1982; Fligstein, 1990; Fligstein and Brantley, 1992). The implication of this shift is that the impact of owning-family interests may not be felt as directly as it was earlier in the century. A second group of owners, financial institutions, have become even more important sources of capital for firms, and, like family owners, the interests of these institutions may also have changed. Today they appear less concerned with controlling the firm's operating decisions than with strategic decisions in times of crisis in order to guarantee a return on their investments (Mintz and Schwartz, 1985). Such control activity in financial arenas only has an indirect effect on labor policies (Kochan et al., 1986, p. 66). In fact, traditional financial institutions such as commercial banks are themselves threatened by competition from smaller institutions that now compete across multiple financial markets and by the cost of the Savings and Loan Bail Out. So both family and financial control over corporate policy regarding labor appears more circumscribed than ever before.

The most identifiable interest group that currently has an impact on labor is the coalition between top shareholders and the professional managers who run the firm. They express their interests primarily through their choice of production and market strategies. In the last two decades, firms with very different ownership structures have all closed plants, dodged labor demands, and intensified their capital investments (Kochan et al., 1986, p. 66; McKenzie, 1982). Within the firm's internal labor market, the net result of these production and marketing strategies has been the erosion of the union's role in contract formation and administration. In the external labor market, the net result has been that the strengthening of the buyer over the seller of labor.

How might these changes have influenced the overall performance of the labor market system? The real wages of workers are beginning to drop, according to some (Flanagan et al., 1989, p. 24), and unemployment has reached higher percentages than in earlier periods, except for the Great Depression (BLS, 1992). Productivity accelerated in the late 1970s and early 1980s, but has had a relatively level rather than exponential rate of increase in more recent years, with the lowest gains being shown in manufacturing (Table 3).

Not surprisingly, the experience of the worker within the firm in the U.S. has become one of insecurity, especially when compared to that of workers in many other industrialized countries. The turnover rate for the American worker is higher than for workers in Britain, Germany, France, and Japan (ILO, 1988). Nevertheless, attitudinal measures show that many American workers are somewhat "satisfied" relative to workers in comparable settings in other countries. For instance, Lincoln and Kalleberg (1985; 1991) report that Japanese auto workers are more dissatis-

Table 3:   Productivity of Labor from 1960-1992, Selected Years.

Item	1960	1970	1975	1980	1985	1987	1989	1992
Unit labor costs business sector[1]	32.2	42.3	57.6	85.8	105.4	111.2	118.0	134.3
Nonfarm business	31.8	41.8	57.1	85.2	105.6	111.6	118.1	133.8
Manufacturing	39.5	47.7	61.6	87.8	95.9	95.5	97.4	104.3

[1] Hourly compensation divided by output per hour.

fied than American auto workers in similar jobs, even though American workers are also more prone to confrontation with management. This difference in attitude may be a residual disposition reflecting the role of national culture, since it did not seem directly attributable to specific differences in work or management practices within the firms.

The Internal Labor Market

Most medium- and large-sized firms still rely on some form of internal labor markets, which affects workers quite differently than the external labor market (Edwards, 1979; Kalleberg and Berg, 1987; Pinfield, 1994). Internal labor markets provide a system of selection, training, reward, and movement for workers that is based on the relationship among the firm's jobs rather than just on the market itself; it is a form of localized labor market in a non-geographic, firm-specific sense. These internal labor markets are typically administered with the help of HR units or HR personnel (Althauser, 1989; Baron and Bielby, 1980; Doeringer and Piore, 1971; Jacoby, 1985).

The HR Department

According to data from the Strategic Human Resource Management Association (SHRMA), the national society for HR administrators, the average size of member HR departments in 1992 was small, with 67% of all departments averaging less than 10 members and only 7% averaging more than 50 members. Yet the average firm size of these HR units was moderate to large, with only 12% of firms having under 100 employees, and 44% having more than 1,000 employees (PNPMA/SHRMA, 1991). These data indicate that firms are not employing large numbers of permanent, full-time HR staff (also see Jennings, 1992).

The types of practices that are being administered by these HR departments is difficult to determine. At a national level, most surveys are of clusters of related practices, such as training (e.g., Greenberg, 1990) or compensation methods (e.g., Langer, 1991). The author conducted a survey of regional members of SHRMA – members of the Pacific Northwest Management Association that is affiliated with U.S. SHRMA (PNPMA/SHRMA). In the survey, which contained slightly smaller firms but slightly larger HR departments than the national chapter, the author found that firms had many practices considered standard in the literature on human resource management (Maidment, 1991; Norback and Russell, 1991; Rothwell and Kazanas, 1988; Springer and Springer, 1990). These practices included recruiting, selection, hiring, promotion, performance appraisal, compensation, job evaluation, job design, job safety, and affirmative action (see Table 4). Surprisingly, very advanced practices like incentive/merit systems, job enrichment, EAPs and HR planning were also used by most firms. However, the HR department did always have strong control over the administration of the firm's HR practices. Promotion, additional benefits, training, job enlargement or enrichment, and teams or quality circles were controlled to a larger extent by units outside of HR – most likely the specific units in which the work was being done. The employment relationship was not completely managed by the HR unit.

The Continued Existence of a Bureaucratic Regime?

The information on practices is useful for assessing arguments about the type of control that exists within firms over the employment relationship. As mentioned previously, the Neoinstitutional Approach argues that the bureaucratic regime still dominates the employment relationship (Baron et al., 1986; Dobbin et al., 1991; 1993; Jennings, 1992). Firms use elaborate, highly formalized, internally controlled employment procedures to govern their internal labor markets. In particular, Edwards (1979, p. 145) has claimed that the "elaboration of job titles, rules, procedures, rights and responsibilities" are the means of guiding workers in the system. This includes the use of testing and the use of long-term provisions for seniority. In principal component factor analyses, Baron et al., (1988, p. 507) found that by 1946 well-developed compensation systems, company information policies, employment tests, and job evaluation all loaded heavily on a first principal component that could be characterized as "bureaucratic control". Both manufacturing and non-manufacturing industries scored highly on this component, indicating a widespread use of bureaucratic control in each sector.

In the 1991 data on firms collected in our survey, there is even greater usage of bureaucratic procedures than in the 1946 data (Baron et al., 1986). Over 90% of firms have entry, transfer, and exit procedures in the detailed sample of the Pacific Northwest, and over 80% of HR departments had at least moderate control over these practices. Firms are also using large numbers of compensation and benefits procedures, again under the control of HR departments. However, job evaluation, job description, job enlargement, and job enrichment appeared to be less under the control of the HR department than under the control of other units (see Table 4).

Table 4:   Percentage of HR Units Reporting Existence of and Control over Different
           Types of HR Practices

Practice	Ext.[1]	Cnt.[2]	Practice	Ext.[1]	Cnt.[2]
Recruiting	99	95	Job Analysis	92	75
Selection	100	88	Job Description	98	88
Hiring	100	88	Job Evaluation	94	81
Promotion	100	70	Job Enlargement	82	53
Transfer	98	65	Job Enrichment	80	52
Voluntary Sep.	99	65	Quality Circles	48	26
Involuntary Sep.	100	93	Suggestion Systems	74	51
Exit Interview	94	83	Work Groups/Teams	73	39
Performance App.	99	78	Employee Recog.	95	80
Job Training	98	39	Job Design Changes	91	60
Management Training	97	74	EAP (fit./abuse)	82	72
Cosponsored Ed.	89	65	Career Counselling	86	61
Employer Ins.	100	90	Child Care Program	39	23
Pension	94	73	Contract Neg.	57	44
Other Benefits	100	89	Grievance Proc.	89	83
Comp. Design	99	85	Safety Programs	95	70
Comp. App.	99	91	Org. Reviews	86	60
Bonus Plans	83	59	HR Research	84	67
Incentive/Merit	88	73	Affirm Act/EEO	96	90
Control/Discip.	100	90	HR Planning	97	89
Time & Motion	44	13	Subcontract Out	75	66

Number of respondents is 345 firms on average for each practice; but only 243 firms
responded completely.

[1] The existance of a practice is indicated by "Ext."
[2] Having at least moderate control over the practice is indicated by "Cnt."

Enlargement and enrichment, while present in over three-quarters of the firms,
were only under at least moderate HR department control in about half the firms.

Nevertheless, unconstrained principal component factor analyses of practices
(excluding those practices on which no variance existed) showed that there were
at least five components with eigenvalues greater than one; and no one component
explained more than 15% of the variance before or after rotation. This lack of a
single, "bureaucratic" factor could indicate that there is such a diffusion of basic
bureaucratic practices, like recruiting, separation, training and appraisal practices,
that no real contrasts across firms or industries can be determined. A closer look at
the analyses reveals that two components did appear consistently in three, five and

N factor solutions, before and after rotation, and counting either all practices that existed in the firm or just practices under the HR department's control. The first factor was composed of job evaluation, description, enlargement and enrichment; the second factor, of compensation, benefits, and appraisal (and defined as *not* being composed of suggestion systems and safety programs). Current corporate HRM then can be distinguished by at least the two characteristics: first, by having a developed versus undeveloped job analysis system, and, second, by having a developed versus undeveloped compensation system. This leads us to believe that there is still some quantitative difference in how much rationalization the employment relationship has undergone within firms – if not in some qualitative difference in the underlying control regimes used in most firms. While the raw percentages indicate the use of bureaucratic control in many medium- and large-sized firms, the amount of control and number of bureaucratic practices used in the regime still varies across firms. At this point, some of this variation may even be due to debureaucratization of the employment relationship in some firms and some industries, a theme we will consider in our final section.

The Existence of Strategic HRM?

In the 1980s, HRM theorists and practitioners argued that human resource management should become more strategic in nature if it wished to survive the rapid changes facing the firm (Dyer, 1983; Fombrun et al., 1984; Schuler, 1987). From Table 3 we know that HR units vary in the degree of control that they have over practices; also, some HR units have more advanced practices, such as job enrichment or HR research, while many others do not. This indicates that a sizeable group of HR departments are either not involved in such fundamental decisions as work redesign or they do not have control over the process of implementation. It is hard to imagine those departments are being strategic in nature, but what about those departments with a wide array of advanced practices over which they have control?

In our survey of PNPMA members, we asked HR managers about their involvement in strategic decision making in order to assess the HR unit's role more directly. The results in Table 5 show that the majority have at least moderate involvement in even high-level planning and implementation of business plans.

Further analysis reveals that having a wide array of advanced practices over which the HR unit has control is strongly correlated with involvement in strategic decision making (r=.50, p<.01). As Fombrun et al. (1984) have said, having a well-developed set of HR practices provides the cornerstone for becoming more strategic. In addition, involvement in strategic decision making by HR mangers also has an impact on some *intra*departmental outcomes. It is associated strongly with the amount of skill that an HR manager has and with his or her job responsibility. Through its association with having strategic HR practices

Table 5:   HR Involvement in Strategic Decision Making

Question Asked	Mean[1]
Participate in developing HR strategies	3.98
Initiate more human resource programs	4.09
Implement human resource programs	4.22
Participate in overall business planning	3.25
Participate in implementing business plans	3.15

[1] Mean on a 5 point Likert Scale, with 5 = "To A Very Large Extent" and 1 = "A Very
Small Extent"

and through its impact on job responsibility and skill level, an HR department's
involvement in strategic decision making also influences rewards for HR managers
(Jennings, 1992).

Other research indicates that strategic HRM may also have an effect on *in-
ter*departmental and organizational outcomes. Fombrun et al. (1984) have assem-
bled several articles that illustrate the impact of strategic HRM on the quality
of its human resources – in particular, on the level of training and commitment
of employees. Schuler and Jackson (1986) have reported that firms engaging in
strategic HR tend to perform better. Adler (1991) has made a convincing case that
firms with subunits in different cultures require the involvement of HR practitioners in overall human resource planning to succeed. Finally, many CEOs and other
top corporate executives have recognized the contribution HR departments can
make to corporate strategy if the HR department estimates its own internal costs
and benefits accurately and learns to speak the language of general management
(Maidment, 1991; Norback and Russell, 1991; Wagel and Levine, 1990).

The HR Manager

Macro organizational and neoinstitutional approaches to HRM do not accentuate
the role of the HR manager in the development of the field (Jennings, 1994). However, HR managers are assumed to be a political interest group that has benefited
from conflicts between management and labor insofar as they are able to focus
the firm's employment policies and bring them under HRM's control (Baron et
al., 1986; Edwards, 1979; Jacoby, 1985). HR managers have also influenced the
bureaucratization of the employment relationship by rationalizing work through
the use of rules and formal HR practices. Finally, HR managers have maintained
their power and increased the rationalization of the employment by professionalizing (Baron et al., 1986; Jennings, 1992; but see Jacoby, 1985). Therefore, even
from a macro perspective it is important to consider the characteristics of the HR
manager.

In 1992, U.S. SHRM reported the following demographic data about its members: 50% were over forty, 90% were white, and just over 50% were male. Our more detailed study of HRM in the Pacific Northwest in 1992 confirms this picture: the average age was 41 years, most members were white, and males outnumbered females slightly.

Association members tended to be highly placed in the firm, well trained, and fairly well educated. In both the U.S. and the Pacific Northwest samples, a member was usually an HR manager or HR director, rather than a line worker or supervisor. Fifty-five percent of the SHRM members were generalists; yet 17% specialized in employment, and 14% specialized in compensation or benefits. Fifty percent of SHRM members worked at corporate headquarters rather than in branch locations. And, on average, managers in the Northeast had 11 years in the HR field and a university degree. Similarly, 88% of national SHRM members had at least a bachelor's degree, and 32% had advanced degrees.

As might be expected, HR managers are compensated in a way that is commensurate with their training and experience. In a nation-wide survey of compensation in 830 companies, Langer (1991) found that the average HR director earned $57,595 annually, and some of the nation's top directors earn as much as $150,000. While structural or organizational factors like the company's growth and the number of individuals supervised by the manager made a great deal of difference in salary, having a lot of experience increased income as much as 69%. Education also had some impact on income, although a less substantial one. Median income increased 14% with a bachelor's degree and 26% with a master's degree. Our detailed study of PNPMA members showed a similar pattern of results, with five years of experience increasing income as much as moving up one quantitative step in education level, such as from high school to college.

Apart from these more objective indicators of HR managerial standing, it is important to understand how HR managers perceive themselves – both in terms of their jobs and their roles in the firm. Ritzer and Trice (1969), Moore and Longbottom (1971) and others have noted that HR managers have problematic jobs: their work is not easily evaluated because of its ambiguous nature; and HR managers sit between labor and management, which means their role sets contain parties with conflicting interests and expectations. Consequently, HR managers experience a fair amount of stress.

Our study of PNPMA/SHRMA members examined HR managerial satisfaction. While the perception of others and of HR managers of satisfaction provides only indirect evidence about roles and stress, the results actually showed an unexpected pattern: When asked about what the impressions that others in the firm had of HRM, as opposed to what they themselves had, HR managers reported quite positive opinions in both cases (see Table 6). The vast majority of respondents believed that the personnel office was thought by others in the firm to be an aid, not a nuisance, and that the language of personnel specialists was understood by others in the firm. The only indication of conflicting expectations is in the third question

Table 6:   Perceptions of HR Practitioners about HRM

Questions about HR practitioners	Agree?	In-firm	Out-of-firm
The personnel office is a nuisance, not an aid	Disagree	74.3%	61.0
	Agree	23.0	23.0
Personnel people tend to speak their own special	Disagree	71.4%	46.8
language that is hard for others to understand	Agree	22.9	33.9
The primary responsibility of the personnel office	Disagre	54.4%	31.1
is to management rather than to employees	Agree	42.9	45.2

HR managers were asked what views they thought others in and out of the firm had of the following questions. Strongly disagree and disagree categories have been combined, as have strongly agree and agree; neither agree nor disgree is the ommitted category.

concerning the responsibility of HR managers: HR managers appeared uncertain whether or not they were allied with other managers versus with employees – a finding consistent with studies done two decades ago (Ritzer and Trice, 1969). In keeping with this relatively positive view of their standing, HR managers reported moderate to high job satisfaction on the JDS (score = 11.85 of 17.00), and at least moderate levels of satisfaction on a 5-point, Likert scale item for overall professional satisfaction (mean = 3.25 out of 5.00).

Table 7:   Perceptions of Professionalization of HRM (percentages)

How well do the following characteristics of a profession describe the HRM field?	Not descriptive	Some-what descriptive	Very descriptive
A body of specialized knowledge with standardized terminology	11.0	76.8	12.2
Widely recognized certification based on standardized training	51.9	46.3	1.8
Code of ethics	25.7	56.6	17.7
Members oriented towards a service objective	9.9	65.6	24.6
Recognized by the general public as a distinct profession	26.5	59.5	14.0
Limited acces to the field, based on acquisition of standard skills/know	38.6	53.9	7.5
A professional society or association, which, among other things gives voice to the entire field	21.6	66.3	12.2
Practitioners are licensed	85.2	14.2	.5
Close collegiality among practitioners	27.0	64.3	8.7

Table 8:   Major Issues Facing HRM in the Next Five Years

Major issue	# Citing issue
Legislative changes	89
Changing workforce	78
American disabilities act	71
Benefit vs. cost of HRM	59
Unskilled workers	49
Change in worker values	13
Workforce 2000	13
Productivity	12
Compensation	12
Organizational change	12

Consistent with the strong assessment of their role in the firm, HR managers also believed the HRM discipline to be somewhat professional. When asked their opinions about which characteristics of a profession the HRM field presently possessed, HR managers thought it was at least "somewhat descriptive" to say that HRM has a body of specialized knowledge, a code of ethics, a service objective, recognition from the public as a profession, barriers to entry, an effective professional society, and collegiality among practitioners. However, they tended to think it was "not descriptive" to say that HRM has licensing or widely recognized certification based on standardized training (see Table 7).

The Future of HRM in the U.S.

The Employment Relationship

Studies of the U.S. economy have pointed to several issues that should have a direct impact on the employment relationship, in particular, to the characteristics of labor, the increased power of management over workers, and the role of the government (Althauser, 1989; Baron and Kreps, 1994; Norback and Russell, 1991; Jemison and O'Mara, 1991; Pfeffer, 1994; Springer and Springer, 1990). The likelihood of an impact of these issues on HRM has also been corroborated by our survey of HR practitioners, who were asked to identify the most important issues facing HRM in the next five years.

The most critical changes revolve around the role of the government actions in the workplace. In the first half of the 1990s the American Disabilities Act (ADA) has caused great concern on the part of HR managers, who must determine how hiring, promotion, and compensation standards must be adjusted for physically and mentally challenged workers, not to mention how to change the design of workplaces to accommodate these workers or physically challenged customers (Hirsch, 1993; Norback and Russell, 1991). Other influential legislative changes that are on the horizon revolve around company pension and health plans, as pressure grows to create a more comprehensive national health care system in which the older, firm-based system can fit (Dobbin, 1992; Stevens, 1986).

The second set of changes cited by PNPMA managers revolves around the characteristics of the worker. Demographic studies have shown that by the year 2000 more workers will be over forty years old than under (BLS, 1992; Springer and Springer, 1990). More women will be in the workforce, as well as minorities, causing adjustment in the traditional expectations that firms have had for white males with spouses who worked part-time and reared children part-time. In addition to these demographic changes in the profile of workers is the lack of workers with requisite skills and productivity, compared to workers in other industrialized countries. This is attributed in part to the U.S.'s educational system, and, in part, to the values of U.S. workers (see Jemison and O'Mara, 1991).

The role of management in HR practice was not considered by PNPMA managers to be as large an issue as either the role of government or the nature of the workforce. The two issues concerning corporate management that appear in Table 8 are the cost of HR management to corporate actors and adapting to organizational change; but neither is highly ranked. Given that it is now more of a buyer's market than ever before, we find this lack of concern over management interests and corporate strategies surprising. Perhaps the changing composition of buyers and sellers implies that corporate America may no longer be centralized and stable enough to make policy about employment as it did in the past. The result may be an increasing divergence of HR practices across firms, as has already been witnessed in the case of pension and benefit plans. Many small firms cannot afford either type of plan, and some of the largest firms have decided to leverage their pension plans to borrow capital for growth. These dramatic "policies" have a strong impact on the rewards that are available to labor within different industries.

As noted at the outset of this chapter, the changing balance among the major actors in the industrial relations system – the government, labor and management – has suggested to some theorists that the employment relationship itself will be fundamentally transformed. Labor relations theorists such as Kochan et al. (1986) believe that transformation is fundamental – in particular, because firms have more strategic choice, forcing labor unions to be reactive. Other theorists do not think that change is as fundamental as Kochan et al. (1986); Jacoby (1985) sees change primarily as "structural adjustment".

Our investigation indicates that labor may have lost power to management, but the role of the State has become much more important than either. This suggests that more than just structural adjustment of the labor markets is at work, since power of the actors that created these structures has changed. Our argument is in keeping with the research of Baron and Newman (1990); Baron et al. (1991); Bridges and Villimez (1991); Dobbin (1992); Dobbin and Boychuck

(1993); Sutton et al. (1993); and Villimez and Bridges (1994) who maintain change is fundamental, but the control regime still has a bureaucratic foundation. In the new system, the complex web of laws, rules and norms promulgated by government activities has modified the role of labor in the firm. Workers have rights and obligations to corporations that are becoming similar to their rights and obligations to the nation-State; that is, workers are becoming organizational citizens (Sutton et al., 1993). The legalistic aspect of bureaucratic control has become so predominant in the employment relationship that only through the use of due process and longer term consideration of the worker, can labor be motivated to produce and to attach themselves to a given firm's destiny. At some point a clan-type culture emphasizing long-term work commitments, continuous learning, and international competitiveness may be necessary to cement this system into place (Kunda, 1992; Lincoln and Kalleberg, 1991).

HR Departments and Managers

Given the changes in the employment relationship, what are the implications for HR departments and HR managers? There are at least three competing possibilities: first, HR departments will continue to become more strategic as human resources are recognized as the key to succeeding in international competition; second, HR departments will become less important, as knowledge of HRM diffuses, just as management information systems departments have become less important as knowledge of computing has become widespread; and third, HRM will remain important but become located in different organizational forms than in the past – in out-of-house consulting units and government agencies rather than in large, private firms.

Currently, there is evidence to support each possibility: no one outcome seems most likely. We have seen that some departments have become more strategic in nature, with consequences for interdepartmental outcomes like managerial pay; yet at least half of our departments were not involved in strategy formulation or implementation (Anthony and Norton, 1991; Jennings, 1992; Wagel, 1990, p. 14). We have also seen that HR managerial practices are present in firms of different sizes and in widely different industries, corroborating the picture of diffusion put forward by others (Baron et al., 1986; Dobbin et al., 1993; Jacoby, 1985); yet HR management is still viewed as a managerial specialty, and information from business schools leads us to believe that HR concepts and skills have not been transmitted to the majority of managers (UBC, 1994). Finally, we have witnessed the creation of more and more HR consulting businesses and the downsizing of HR units in firms. In our sample of association members in the Pacific Northwest, almost 20% were not associated with a large firm or HR department; they appeared to be at least part-time HR consultants. This could indicate some debureaucratization of HRM (Oliver, 1992). Yet interviews with HR practitioners suggest that top players in HRM typically start out with HR departments in large firms and that large firms still have the resources to experiment with new HRM programs (Harrison, 1994).

Of course, these three possibilities for HRM are not mutually exclusive outcomes. If the development of the accounting profession is any guide, HRM as a field could continue to develop along all three lines simultaneously. Accounting has become more strategic within firms; more general managers have absorbed accounting knowledge; and many more external consulting units have developed, making accounting one of the major specialty areas in advanced business services (Hinings et al., 1990; U.S. Government, 1991). It is only if growth does not occur in the HR occupation that a conflict among these lines of development is likely to occur.

During the 1970s and 1980s the number of registered HR workers increased (BLS, 1991), as did HR association memberships (PNPMA/SHRMA, 1991). However, recent rates, from 1988 to 1992, are ominous: growth has dipped due to the continued recession; and it has dipped more than in other managerial occupations. Membership in HRM associations has also declined slightly (SHRMA, 1992). We believe that, in the future, national level organizations of HRM must promote themselves more systematically to the largest player, the government – even at the expense of the promoting themselves to large corporations. Managers in key HR consulting firms and HR specialists in government agencies must also be mobilized if the visibility and power of HRM is to be retained and the field of HRM given a chance to advance.

Appendix 1: The industries represented by the Pacific Northwest Sample are as follows:

Industry	#	%	Industry	#	%
Agriculture	5	1.3	Health Care	42	10.9
Primary Manufacturing	30	7.8	Education	17	4.4
Manufacturing	104	27	Wholesale Trade	17	4.4
Construction	1	0.3	Financial	54	14
Service	57	14.8	Public Utilities	15	3.9
Transportation	8	2.1	Other Industry	27	7
Communication	8	2.1	Total	385	100

References

Adler, N.J. (1991). *International Dimensions of Organizational Behavior*. Boston, MA: P.W.S. Kent.

Althauser, R. (1989). "Internal Labor Markets." *Annual Review of Sociology*, 15, 143-161.

Anthony, P. and L.A. Norton (1991). "Link HR to Corporate Strategy." *Personnel Journal*, 70(4), 75-86.

Baron, J.N. and W.T. Bielby (1980). "Bringing the Firm Back IN: Stratification, Segmentation, and the Organization of Work." *American Sociological Review*, 45, 736-765.

Baron, J.N., F.R. Dobbin and P.D. Jennings (1986). "War and Peace: The Evolution of Modern Personnel Administration in U.S. Industry." *American Journal of Sociology*, 92(2), 350-383.

Baron, J., P.D. Jennings and F.R. Dobbin (1988). "Mission Control? The Development of Personnel Systems in U.S. Industry." *American Sociological Review*, 53, 497-514.

Baron, J.N. and D. Kreps (forthcoming). *Human Resources: A Framework for General Managers*. New York: John Wiley & Sons.

Baron, J.N., B.S. Mittman and A.E. Newman (1991). "Targets of Opportunity: Organizational and Environmental Determinants of Gender Integration Within the California Civil Service." *American Journal of Sociology*, 96(6), 1362-1401.

Baron, J.N. and A.E. Newman (1990). "Organizations, Occupations, and the Value of Work Done by Women and Nonwhites." *American Sociological Review*, 55, 155-175.

Bernstein, I. (1960). *The Lean Years: A History of the American Worker, 1920-1933*. Boston: Houghton Mifflin.

Bernstein, I. (1970). *The Turbulent Years: A History of the American Worker, 1933-1941*. Boston: Houghton Mifflin.

Birch, D.L. (1979). *The Job Generation Process*. Cambridge, MA: MIT Program on Neighborhood and Regional Change.

Bluestone, B. and B. Harrison (1982). *The Deindustrialization of America*. New York: Basic Books.

Brandt, E. (1991). "Global HR." *Personnel Journal*, 70(3), 38-44.

Bridges, W.P. and W.J. Villimez (1991). "Employment Relations and the Labor Market." *American Sociological Review*, 56(6), 748-764.

Brock, W.A. and D.S. Evans (1986). *The Economics of Small Businesses: Their Role and Regulation in the U.S. Economy*. New York: Homes and Meier.

Brown, C., J. Hamilton and J. Medoff (1990). *Employers Large and Small*. Cambridge: Harvard University Press.

BLS (Bureau of Labor Statistics) (1989). *Employment and Earnings*. Washington, DC: U.S. Government Printing Office.

BLS (Bureau of Labor Statistics) (1990). *Handbook of Labor Statistics*. Washington, DC: U.S. Government Printing Office.

BLS (Bureau of Labor Statistics) (1991). *Employment and Earnings*. Washington, DC: U.S. Government Printing Office.

BLS (Bureau of Labor Statistics) (1992). *Outlook 1990-2005*. Washington, DC: U.S. Government Printing Office.

BLS (Bureau of Labor Statistics) (1994). *Employment and Earnings*. Washington, DC: U.S. Government Printing Office.

Carlson, D. (1945). "Annual Report of the President." *Personnel Administration*, 7(10), 18-19.

Chandler, A. Jr. (1962). *Stategy and Structure*. Cambridge, MA: The MIT Press.

Corporate Data Exchange (1981). *CDE Stock Ownership Directory: Fortune 500*. New York: Corporate Data Exchange, Inc.

DiMaggio, P. (1985). "Interest and Agency in Institutional Theory." Paper presented at UCLA/NSF Conference on Institutional Theory, Los Angeles. (Published in L.G. Zucker (ed.) (1988), *Institutional Patterns and Organisations: Cultures and Environment.* Cambridge, MA: Ballinger.)

DiMaggio, P. and W.W. Powell (1983). "The Iron Cage Revisited: Institutional Isomorphism and Collective Rationality in Organizational Fields." *American Sociological Review*, 48, 147-160.

DiMaggio, P.J. and W.W. Powell (1991). "Introduction." In W.W. Powell and P.J. DiMaggio (eds.), *The New Institutionalism in Organizational Analysis.* Chicago, IL: University of Chicago Press, 1-38.

Dobbin, F.R. (1992). "The Origins of Private Insurance, 1920-1950." *American Journal of Sociology*, 97(5), 1416-1450.

Dobbin, F.R. and T. Boychuk (1993). "Job Autonomy and National Context: Evidence from Nine Nations." Paper presented at the American Sociological Annual Meeting, Washington, DC, 1991.

Dobbin, F.R., L. Edelman, J.W. Meyer, W.R. Scott and A. Swidler (1988). "The Expansion of Due Process in Organizations." In L. Zucker (ed.), *Institutional Patterns and Organizations.* Cambridge, MA: Ballinger, pp. 70-98.

Dobbin, F.R., W.R. Sutton, J.W. Meyer and W.R. Scott (1991). "The Renaissance of Internal Labor Markets: The Effects of Affirmative Action." Paper presented at SCOR Conference, Asilomar, CA.

Dobbin, F.R., W.R. Sutton, J.W. Meyer and W.R. Scott (1994). "Equal Opportunity Law and the Construction of Internal Labor Markets." *American Journal of Sociology*, 99 (4), 396-427.

Doeringer, P.B. and M.J. Piore (1971). *Internal Labor Markets and Manpower Analysis.* Lexington, MA: Lexington Books.

Dunlop, J.T. (1950). *Wage Determination Under Trade Unions.* New York: August M. Kelley.

Dunlop, J.T. and W. Galenson (1978). *Labor in the Twentieth Century.* New York: Academic Press.

Dyer, L. (1983). "Bringing Human Resources into the Strategy Formulation Process." *Human Resources Management*, 22(3), 257-271.

Edelman, L.B. (1992). "Legal Ambiguity and Symbolic Structures: Organizational Mediation of Civil Rights Laws." *American Journal of Sociology*, 97(6), 1531-1576.

Edwards, R. (1979). *Contested Terrain: The Transformation of the Workplace in the Twentieth Century.* New York: Basic Books.

Eibert, H. (1959). "The Development of Personnel Management in the United States." *Business History Review*, 33(3), 346-360.

Flanagan, R.J., L.M. Kahn, R.S. Smith and R.G. Ehrenberg (1989). *Economics of the Employment Relationship.* Glenview, IL: Scott, Foresman and Company.

Fligstein, N. (1990). *The Transformation of Corporate Control.* Cambridge, MA: Harvard University Press.

Fligstein, N. and P. Brantley (1992). "Who Controls the Large Modern Corporation?" *Amercian Journal of Sociology*, 98(2), 280-307.

Fombrun, C., N.M. Tichy and M.A. Devanna (1984). *Strategic Human Resource Management.* New York: John Wiley and Sons.

Freidson, E. (1986). *Professional Powers: A Study of the Institutionalization of Formal Knowledge*. Chicago: Chicago University Press.

Gavin, D.A. (1993). "Building a Learning Organization." *Harvard Business Review*, July-August, 78-92.

Gordon, D.M., R. Edwards and M. Reich (1982). *Segmented Work, Divided Workers*. London: Cambridge University Press.

Gordon, J. (1992). "Rethinking Diversity." *Human Resource Training*, 29(1), 23-30.

Gray, R.D. (1943). *Systematic Wage Administration in the Southern California Aircraft Industry*. Industrial Relations Monograph No. 7. New York: Industrial Relations Counselors.

Greenberg, E.R. (1990). "Workplace Testing: The 1990 AMA Survey, Part I." *Personnel*, 67(6), 43-51.

Harrison, J. (1994). "Manage The People Issues, The Dollars Will Flow." Vancouver, B.C.: KPGM Management Consulting.

Herman, E.S. (1982). *Corporate Control, Corporate Power*. Cambridge, UK: Cambridge University Press.

Hinings, C.R., R. Greenwood, and J. Brown. (1990). "The P^2-Form of Stategic Management: Corporate Practices in the Professional Partnership." *Academy of Management Journal*, 33, 725-755.

Hirsch, J. (1993). "The Americans with Disabilities Act: An Analysis of the Impact on Increased Awareness of the Rights and Abilities of Persons with Disabilities." Unpublished Master's graduating essay. University of British Columbia, Vancouver.

Hudson Institute (1987). *Workforce 2000*. Indiannapolis: U.S. Department of Labor Report.

ILO (International Labour Organization) (1988). *World Employment Review*. Geneva: ILO Press.

Jacoby, S.M. (1983). "The Early Years of Personnel Management in the United States: 1900-1930: The Rise and Fall of Professionalism." Unpublished manuscript.

Jacoby, S.M. (1985). *Employing Bureaucracy: Managers, Unions and the Transformation of Work in American Industry, 1900-1945*. New York: Columbia University Press.

Jemison, D. and P. O'Mara (1991). *Managing Workforce 2000: Gaining the Diversity Edge*. San Francisco, CA: Jossey-Bass Publishing.

Jennings, P.D. (1992). "SHRM Makes a Difference: The Impact on HR Managerial Training, Job Experience and Salary." Unpublished paper.

Jennings, P.D. (1994). "Viewing Macro HRM from Without." *Research in Personnel and Human Resources Management*, Vol. 12, Greenwich, CT: JAI Press.

Kalleberg, A.L. and I. Berg (1987). *Work and Industry: Structure, Markets and Processes*. New York: Plenum Press.

Kochan, T.A., H.C. Katz and R.B. McKersie (1986). *The Transformation of American Industrial Relations*. New York: Basic Books.

Kovach, K.A. and J.A. Pearce (1990). "HR Strategic Mandates for the 1990s." *Personnel*, 67(4), 50-55.

Kunda, G. (1992). *Engineering Culture: Control and Commitment in a High Tech Corporation*. Philadelphia, PA: Temple University Press.

Langer, S. (1991). "What You Earn – and Why." *Personnel Journal*, 70(2), 25-27.

Licht, W. (1988). "How The Workforce Has Changed in 75 Years." Monthly Labor Review, February, 19-25.

Lincoln, J.R. and A.L. Kalleberg (1985). "Work Organization and Workforce Commitment: A Study of Plants and Employees in the U.S. and Japan." *American Sociological Review*, 50, 738-760.

Lincoln, J.R. and A.L. Kalleberg (1991). *Culture, Control and Commitment: A Study of Work Organization and Work Attitudes in the United States and Japan.* Cambridge: Cambridge University Press.

Little, B. (1992). "Guru Has a Passion for Slashing Managers." *Toronto Globe and Mail.* June 2, B1 and B8.

Maidment, F. (1991). *Human Resources Annual: 1990/91.* Guilford, CT: Dushkin Publishing Group.

McKenzie, R.B. (1982). *Plant Closings: Public or Private Choices?* Washington, DC: The Cato Institute.

Meyer, J.W. and W.R. Scott (1983). *Organizational Environments: Ritual and Rationality.* Beverly Hills, CA: Sage Publications.

Mintz, B. and M. Schwartz (1985). *The Power Structure of American Business.* Chicago: University of Chicago Press.

Moore, L.F. and P.D. Jennings (1993). "Human Resources Management at the Crossroads." *Asia Pacific Journal of Human Resources*, 31(2), 12-25.

Moore, L.F. and R. Longbottom (1971). "B.C. Study of Personnel Managers: Preliminary Items of Interest." *Canadian Personnel and Industrial Relations Journal*, 18, 45-49.

NICB (National Industrial Conference Board) (1927). *Industrial Relations in Small Plants.* New York: NICB.

NICB (National Industrial Conference Board) (1936). *What Employers Are Doing for Employees.* New York: NICB.

NICB (National Industrial Conference Board) (1940). "Personnel Activities in American Business." *Studies in Personnel Policy*, no. 20. New York: NICB.

NICB (National Industrial Conference Board) (1946). "Organization of Personnel Administration." *Studies in Personnel Policy*, no. 73, New York: NICB.

NICB (National Industrial Conference Board) (1954). "Personnel Practices in Factory and Office." *Studies in Personnel Policy*, no. 145. New York: NICB.

Nkomo, S.M. (1980). "Stage Three in Personnel Administration: Strategic Human Resources Management." *Personnel*, 57, 69-77.

Noble, B.P. (1993). "Reinventing Labor: An Interview with Union President Lynn Williams." *Harvard Business Review*, July-August, 115-1175.

Norback, C.T. and N.R. Russell (eds.) (1991). *The Human Resource Yearbook, 1990.* Englewood Cliffs, NJ: Prentice-Hall.

Oliver, P. (1992). "The Antecedents of Deinstitutionalization." *Organization Studies*, 13, 563-588.

Parks, D.S. (1936). "1936 Personnel Trends." *Factory Management and Maintenance*, 12, 39.

Peters, T. (1987). *Thriving on Chaos: Handbook for a Management Revolution.* New York: Alfred Knopf.

Pfeffer, J. (1994). *Competitive Advantage Through People.* Cambridge, MA: Harvard Business School Press.

Pfeffer, J. and Y. Cohen (1984). "Determinants of Internal Labor Markets in Organizations." *Adminstrative Science Quarterly*, 29, 550-73.

Pieper, R. (1990). *Human Resource Management: An International Comparison*. Berlin: Walter de Gruyter.

Pinfield, L.T. (1994). *The Operation of Internal Labor Markets: Staffing Practices and Vacancy Chains*. San Francisco, CA: Jossey Bass.

Pinfield, L.T. and M.F. Bernier (1994). "Internal Labor Markets: Towards a Coherent Conceptualization." In G.R. Ferris (ed.), *Research in Personnel and Human Resources Management*, Vol. 12, Greenwich, CT: JAI Press, pp. 1-40.

PNPMA/SHRMA. (1991). "Report to the Board of Directors, PNPMA/SHRMA." Unpublished Report. Portland, Oregon.

Porter, M. (1990). *Competitive Strategy: Techniques for Analyzing Industries and Competitors*. New York: Free Press.

Porter, M. (1991). *Canada at the Crossroads: The Reality of a New Competitive Environment*. Ottawa: Business Council on National Issues and the Government of Canada.

Powell, W.W. and P.J. DiMaggio (1991). *The New Institutionalism in Organizational Analysis*. Chicago: University of Chicago Press.

Radford, J. and S. Kove (1991). "Lessons from the Silicon Valley." *Personnel Journal*, 70(2), 38-44.

Reskin, B.F. and R.F. Putnam (1990). *Job Queues, Gender Queues*. New Brunswick, NJ: University of Rutgers Press.

Rhodeback, M.J. (1991). "Embrace the Bottom Line." *Personnel Journal*, 70(5), 53-59.

Ritzer, G. and H. Trice (1969). *An Occupation in Conflict: A Study of the Personnel Manager*. Ithaca, NY: New York State School of Industrial Relations.

Rothwell, W.J. and H.C. Kazanas (1988). *Strategic Human Resources Planning and Management*. Englewood Cliffs, NJ: Prentice-Hall.

Sabel, J. and M. Piore (1984). *The Second Industrial Divide: Possibilities for Prosperity*. New York: Basic Books.

Saha, S.K. (1989). "Variations in the Practice of Human Resource Management: A Review." *Canadian Journal of Admistrative Sciences*, 34, 37-45.

Schuler, R.S. (1987). *Personnel and Human Resource Management*. (3rd ed.) St. Paul, MN: West Publishing.

Schuler, R.S., P.J. Dowling and H. De Cieri (1993). "An Integrative Framework of Strategic International Human Resources Management." *Journal of Management*, 19(2), 419-459.

Schuler, R.S. and Jackson, S.E. (1986). "Managing Stress through PHRM Practice." *Research in Personnel and Human Resources Management*, 4, 183-224.

Scott, J. (1986). *Capitalist Property and Financial Power*. Brighton, UK: Wheatsheaf Books.

Scott, W.R. (1987). "The Adolescence of Institutional Theory." *Administrative Science Quarterly*, 32, 493-511.

Shetty, Y.K. and P.F. Butler (1990). "Regaining Competitiveness Requires HR Solutions." *Personnel*, 67(6), 8-12.

SHRMA (1992). [Interview with PNIMA/SHRMA executive assistant.] August.

Slichter, S. (1919). *The Turnover of Factory Labor*. New York: Appleton.

Springer, B. and S. Springer (1990). "Human Resources Management in the U.S. – Celebration of its Centenary." In R. Pieper (ed.), *Human Resource Management: An International Comparison*. Berlin: Walter de Gruyter, 41-57.

Human Resource Management in the United States 347

Stevens, B. (1986). "Complementing the Welfare State: The Development of Private Pension, Health Insurance and Other Employee Benefits in the United States." *Labor Management Relations Series*, no. 65. Geneva: ILO.

Stone, K. (1974). "The Orgins of Job Structures in the Steel Industry." *Review of Radical Politics and Economics*, 6, 113-73.

Sutton, J.R., F. Dobbin, J.W. Meyer and W.R. Scott (1994). "The Legalization of the Workplace." *American Journal of Sociology*, 100, 944-971.

Swiercz, P.M. and B.A. Spencer (1992). "HRM and Sustainable Competitive Advantage: Lessons from Delta Airlines." *Human Resources Planning*, 15(2), 35-46.

Tolbert, P.S. and L.G. Zucker (1983). "Institutional Sources of Change in the Formal Structure of Organizations: The Diffusion of Civil Service Reforms, 1980-1935." *Administrative Science Quarterly*, 23, 22-39.

Taylor, F.W. (1911). *Shop Management*. New York: Basic Books.

UBC (University of British Columbia) (1994). "Report of the MBA 2001 Design Committee." Unpublished Committee Report on Teaching.

U.S. Government (1992). *Statistical Abstracts of the United States, 1991*. Washington, DC: U.S. Government Printing Office.

U.S. Government (1994). *Statistical Abstracts of the United States, 1993*. Washington, DC: U.S. Government Printing Office.

Villimez, W.J. and W.P. Bridges (1994). *The Employment Relationship: State, Industrial, Organizational and Job Effects on Bureaucratic Control and Due Process*. New York: Plenum Press.

Voss, K. (1994). *The Making of an American Exceptionalism: The Knights of Labor and Class Formation in the Nineteenth Century*. Ithaca, NY: Cornell University Press.

Wagel, W.H. (1990). "On the Horizon: HR in the 1990s." *Personnel*, 67(1), 11-16.

Wagel, W.H. and H.Z. Levine (1990). "HR '90: Challenges and Opportunities." *Personnel*, 67(6), 18-42.

Wolf, W.B. (1980). *Top Management of the Personnel Function: Current Issues and Practices*. Ithaca, NY: ILR School, Cornell University.

WPB (War Production Board) (1942). *Job Instruction: A Manaul for Shop Supervisors and Instructors*. Washington, DC: War Production Board.

Zucker, L.G. (1987). "Institutional Theories of Organizations." *Annual Review of Sociology*, 13, 433-464.

Conclusion

Human Resource Management on the Pacific Rim: An Integration

P. Devereaux Jennings, Dianne Cyr and Larry F. Moore

> The world's trends point overwhelmingly toward political independence and self-rule on the one hand, and the formation of economic alliances on the other (John Naisbitt, 1994, p. 49).

In this book we have pursued two opposing research strategies simultaneously: specialists on each of the selected Pacific Rim countries and city-states have provided "stand-alone" treatises on human resource management in their area of expertise; at the same time, they have drawn on common framework to guide comparisons across chapters. While we may have been learned much about the eleven places on the Pacific Rim by concentrating on the realities of HRM in each, we have also sought to uncover a deeper reality that exists across the various HRM systems. We are among the growing number of HRM scholars who believe that there are patterns and linkages among international HR management practices (Begin, 1993; Evans et al., 1990; Schuler et al., 1993).

The investigation of patterns across HRM systems found in different countries is still in its infancy. In his review of the international HRM literature, Begin (1993) found little research that attempted to identify consistent patterns of HRM systems across countries. Furthermore, much of the research thus far has focused on specific aspects of HRM first and has investigated the environment second. For instance, Baglioni and Crouch (1990) and Bamber and Lansbury (1987) examined the collective bargaining functions in different firms in Australia before extending their analysis comparatively. Similarly, Begin (1993) argued for the utility of Mintzberg's (1983) lifecycle framework for assessing the relationship between different types of HRM systems within firms and only then moved on to discuss how such HRM systems may match with different industrial structures and national contexts.

In contrast, the Neoinstitutional Approach begins with an assessment of the environmental context and then incorporates the eco-political and socio-cultural configurations into investigations of the employment relationship in the firm. The elements of these two constellations are considered in terms of their constraints and limits on the firm's internal labor market and type of HRM system used.[1] Neoinstitutionalists view institutionalization as occurring at the sectoral or societal levels; hence, the approach argues for an essentially interorganizational locus of action. Neoinstitutionalists also see organizations as loosely coupled arrays of standardized elements that create networks of varying homogeneity (Powell and DiMaggio, 1991, p. 14). Internal networks interact highly with the actors in the interorganizational field to help create diffusion. Therefore, environmental fit or matching is viewed descriptively as a process starting with innovation and moving on to diffusion.

In this final chapter we operationalize the Neoinstitutional Approach by first examining the cogent elements of the political/structural and the cultural/social configurations in each Pacific Rim country that give rise to different character-istics of firm internal labor markets and HRM systems. We then examine the implications of the Neoinstitutional Approach for international strategic human resources management (ISHRM). Ultimately, we strive for insights not only into what HRM is like, but also into what the future may hold for HRM.

Characteristics of HRM Systems

The supply of and demand for labor and the dynamism of the external labor market, the direct and indirect effects of the State, the organization of labor, and the diversity of the local country culture are each associated with the complexity, formalization, and centralization of the firm internal labor markets found within medium- and large-sized organizations in a country or city-State. The relationship between the two types of labor markets (i.e., external and internal) is, in turn, associated with the features of the firm's HRM system; that is, with its degree of bureaucratization and the professionalization of the HR staff (Althauser, 1989; Baron et al., 1986; 1988; Baron and Kreps, forthcoming; Pfeffer and Cohen, 1984; Kalleberg and Berg, 1987; Pfeffer, 1994). In the preceding chapters we have noticed the pattern of institutional features across the selected Pacific Rim countries and cities that are summarized in Table 1.

Bureaucratization

The most bureaucratic corporate HRM systems within firms are found in Australia, Canada, New Zealand, and the United States; the least bureaucratic, in Hong Kong and the PRC. Yet there is an increasing amount of bureaucratization in the corporate HRM systems in Hong Kong, the PRC, South Korea, Taiwan, and Thailand; while there is a decreasing amount of bureaucratization in the corporate HRM systems in Canada and the United States. In the bureaucratized systems, large numbers and varieties of HR practices are found, ranging from basic compensation and benefits programs to advanced HR research, EEO policies and contract negotiation. The HRM practices are well documented through policy manuals, procedures, and rules. And, in the case of most practices, control or administration is moderately centralized around the HR function; that is, there is direct involvement of HRM staff in the decisions within these practice areas. In bureaucratizing systems, a number of new practices are added, then some formalization and centralization occurs; while in a de-bureaucratizing system,

Table 1: Institutional Features of Pacific Rim HRM Systems

Country/City-State	AUS	CAN	HK	JAP	NZ	PRC	SIN	SK	TAI	THA	US
External labor market											
Surplus unskilled labor	H	H	L	M	H	H	L	L	M	M	H
Surplus skilled labor	M	M	L	L	M	L	L	L	L	L	M
Volatile market	M	M	H	H	M	M	H	H	H	M	M
Direct state involvement	H	M	L	L	H	H	H	H	H	M	H
Indirect state involvement	M	H	M	M	H	M	M	M	M	L	M
Labor organization	H	H	L	M	H	L	M	H	M	M	M
Cultural diversity	H	H	M	L	M	L	M	L	L	L	H
Large firm presence	H	H	M	H	M	H	M	H	H	M	M
Firm internal labor market											
Complexity	H	H	M	H	H	M	M	H	M	M	H
Formalization	H	M	L	L	H	L	M	M	M	M	H
Centralization	H	M	L	M	M	L	M	L	M	L	M
Firm's HRM system											
Bureaucratized	H	Hd	Li	M	H	Li	Mi	Mi	Mi	M	Hd
Professionalized	Mi	Li	Mi	L	Li	L	Mi	L	Mi	L	H

"H"= high; "M"=medium; "L"=low; "i"=increasing; "d"=decreasing

control and formalization are rolled back before practices actually seem to be lost.

There is no one factor that seems to covary neatly with the degree of an HRM system's bureaucratization. Contrary to the belief of some institutional labor economists (e.g., Doeringer and Piore, 1971), having a volatile labor market, a high demand for labor – particularly for skilled workers – and large firms in control of the economy do not by themselves seem to be uniquely associated with bureaucratization. The PRC has an increasingly volatile market, a lack of skilled workers, and the presence of many large firms, but less bureaucratization of the FILM than many other countries have. Instead, the Chinese State has several bureaus and agencies that are involved in labor allocation, training, and remuneration – such as the Chinese State Economic Commission (Wang, 1991). A strong external framework is provided for handling the demand and scale problems within the vast labor market of China.

However, the case of the PRC shows that having strong, direct State involvement in labor is not uniquely associated with bureaucratization of the HRM system of firms within a country. Not only does the PRC have strong direct involvement, but so do Singapore, South Korea, Taiwan, and Thailand – none of which have extremely bureaucratized corporate HRM systems. As in the PRC, direct State involvement in Singapore comes in the form of agencies for labor allocation, laws governing the movement of skilled workers, training and remuneration programs, and State-run firms controlling critical sectors like transportation and utilities. Indirect State involvement also occurs through employment relations policies that establish some formal industrial systems among government, workers and managers (e.g., the "Enterprise Laws" in the PRC and the NWC in Singapore) and through the development of models in the State-run sectors that are then used in the private sector (e.g., by firms involved in the "private contract" sector in China). Indirect State involvement is strongest in the PRC and is also relatively strong in Canada and New Zealand. It is at least moderate in most nations. When the corporate HRM system is bureaucratized, it is rare to find a lack of indirect State involvement.

Neither the organization of labor nor cultural diversity provides a unique rationale for bureaucratization of the HRM systems. Not only do Australia, Canada and New Zealand have strong unions in several sectors, but so does South Korea. Even in Japan, company unions are essential for establishing labor peace, which is the key to competitiveness. Cultural diversity is high in Australia, Canada, and the United States – all of which tend to have more bureaucratic corporate HRM systems – yet there is a moderate amount of diversity in Hong Kong and Singapore, places without very bureaucratic HRM systems. Furthermore, there is a great deal of cultural homogeneity in Japan, yet a moderate amount of bureaucratization in the corporate HRM systems. Nevertheless, it does seem that diversity may force the development of more formal rules to ensure workplace values are followed; while homogeneity may allow for such rules to be unstated norms. The actual effect of homogeneity will ultimately depend on the characteristics of the core culture of the homogeneous group. The core culture may emphasize formalization, and thus create more bureaucratization than a diverse set of cultural groups would (Pieper, 1991).

While no one factor seems to provide a unique rationale for bureaucratization in corporate HRM systems, several factors seem *necessary* for its development. These factors include some direct State involvement, the organization of labor, and the importance of large firms in the economy. This is consistent with the argument that employment practices are embedded in a complex, larger system formed by the characteristics of the external and internal labor market; it is also consistent with research that has shown the simultaneous impact of scale, technology, unionization, and State action on the bureaucratization of personnel systems (Baron et al., 1986; 1988; Kalleberg and Berg, 1987; Lincoln et al., 1985; Moore and Jennings, 1993). Conversely, bureaucratization is not evident when there is a tight labor market, a minimal amount of labor organization, and low cultural diversity; and when indirect State involvement is more important than direct State involvement and large firm size is less important, often due to the existence of numerous small, family-run businesses.

In Australia, Canada, New Zealand, and the United States there has been a great deal of labor unrest and unionization, which has stimulated the development of labor relations boards, contracting systems, and methods of contract monitoring within firms. Grievance systems and even some adjudication is handled jointly with the HR department in many firms in these countries. Furthermore, HRM systems react to labor demands, re-designing jobs, safety standards, and compensation and benefit packages. The HR unit is normally in change of detailing such responses, if not initiating them. In the United States and Canada, the State was instrumental in establishing the first labor relations boards through legislation such as the U.S.'s Wagner Act (1935) and Canada's PC1003 (1944). Australia, Canada and New Zealand were also governed by Commonwealth legislation such as Canada's British North America Act (1867) and the IDI (1907). In all four nations between 1964 and 1990, the central State has created judicial frameworks for the protection of individual rights, such as equal opportunity and employment equity. The HRM systems in firms have responded by becoming more legally oriented. In particular, there is increasing formalization of hiring and firing practices and greater involvement of the HR department as overseers of due process.

The importance of large firms – that is, of "scale" – as a contributing factor for bureaucratization of corporate HRM systems is also evident (as several country authors have noted). The degree of bureaucratization depends not only on having important, large firms in a country that are willing to develop complex HRM systems but also on how important large-sized firms are in the country's economy compared to smaller firms. In Australia, New Zealand and Canada, large crown corporations or their equivalent have always been in control of most of the transportation and utilities sector, and in mining, forestry, oil and gas, and other natural resource industries, many of the original colonial firms set up to develop these markets are still in control of large market shares. These firms have the reputation for being more progressive than their average, smaller competitor, although not on the leading edge of HR development. They typically have standard compensation and benefit policies; most face unionized work environments and thus they are involved in labor relations through their HR department; and, given their size and affiliation, they are scrutinized by the government for conformity to employee rights policies. In Japan, the PRC, South Korea, and Taiwan where large firms have a real presence in most economic sectors, the firm internal labor markets are complex, and there is pressure to formalize practices in order to efficiently handle the pressures generated by managing a large workforce. For example, compensation systems in Japan are quite refined and formal, compared to promotion and feedback systems. In South Korea, procedures for screening new hires from college and training them in the firm are elaborate. In the PRC, procedures to document worker movement have been formalized to meet the needs of the external State bureaucracy. And in Taiwan the size and complexity of some of the largest holding companies, plus the international movement of capital and personnel, are pressuring firms to begin formalizing and centralizing their HR policies.

However, the PRC poses a particularly challenging and complex picture for our generalizations about the multiple factors associated with bureaucracy. Like the former USSR and other Eastern socialist bloc countries (Pieper, 1991), it has a centralized, State-run system controlling essential labor allocation practices and remuneration for 80% of the workforce. In a sense, then, the system is highly bureaucratized – but outside the firm. Within many firms there is still a reliance on general managers and foremen to hire, train, and dismiss workers. Standard compensation is modified considerably by the bonus system and by company perquisites, which are given for what, to some Western observers, appear to be personalistic reasons. However, managers or "cadres" are now receiving HRM training in Western firms and universities, which further blurs the picture. In addition, there are many foreign joint-ventures in the major cities of China, and the practices of the foreign national firms have seeped down to the shop-floor level, creating a situation similar to that in Thailand, where HRM systems can be distinguished based on their MNC affiliation.

Professionalization

Like bureaucratization of the corporate HRM system, the level of professionalization of those involved in HRM activities varies considerably among the Pacific Rim countries and city-states surveyed. There tends to be significant acknowledgement of HRM as a profession by HR managers and practitioners in Australia, Canada and the United States. In all three places, the strategic involvement of HR managers has increased due to greater perceived professionalism and a renewed emphasis on the role of human resources in international competitiveness. The enhanced status of HR managers is evident by their greater participation on senior management boards and committees, more direct reporting relationships with senior line managers, and higher levels of remuneration. The establishment of formal associations has also raised the level of professionalism attained by HR managers by heightening their images and by providing opportunities for furthering member knowledge and skill. In Hong Kong the founding of the Hong Kong Institute of Personnel Management (HKIPM) in 1977 has had an important impact on the professionalization of HRM in that jurisdiction, especially considering how non-bureaucratic corporate HRM systems tend to be in that city-state. The HKIPM is not only an institute with which HR practitioners can identity, but it also offers information and seminars to members.

Yet even when formal associations for HR managers exist, it would appear that their enhancement of professionalization takes time. Hong Kong still only reports a low, if increasing, amount of professionalization. In New Zealand, HRM has only recently been recognized as a distinct body of professional knowledge and practice, and only a moderate level of professionalism is reported there. Similarly in Taiwan the HRM professional associations (e.g., Human Resources

Management and Development Committee; Human Resources Development Association) have had a relatively short history, and a 1990 survey there indicated only a moderate level of perceived professionalism in HRM.

In Japan and Korea the professionalization of HRM is in the early stages. Japanese management tends to rely on a generalist approach to management skills, which makes HRM one of only many areas of individual managerial competence. South Korean management tends to be characterized by family management practices, and Korean HR managers do not consider themselves as belonging to a distinct profession. In Singapore HR staff lack specialized training and qualifications, and in Thailand professional HR managers are also rare (Von Glinow and Chung, 1989).

Glancing at Table 1 and considering some of the data from the preceding chapters helps us summarize the multiple factors associated with high levels of professionalization in the HRM on the Pacific Rim.

1. Longer-Run Existence of Professional Associations – In Canada, the U.S., Australia, and Hong Kong, the historical presence of HRM as a formal function and the development of professional HRM associations have both legitimated the HR function and provided a body of professional knowledge to which HR staff have access.

2. Existence of A Highly Bureaucratic HRM System – Australia, Canada, and the United States all have bureaucratic HRM systems and moderate or high levels of professionalization. And New Zealand, which also has a bureaucratic HRM system, has an increasing amount of professionalization in its HRM system.

3. Importance and Type of Large MNC – The level of perceived professionalism is higher in countries with many large multinational companies (MNCs) than in countries with bureaucratic and professionalized HRM systems. As Lawler and Atmiyanandana suggested in their chapter on Thailand (in this volume), "Western firms are considerably more likely than Asian firms to professionalize the HRM function." In American MNCs professionalism is reported to be 95.5 percent; in Japanese MNCs the figure is 37.5 percent, and both Japanese firms and Thai family enterprises were the least likely to utilize professional HR managers. In Japanese firms, HRM responsibilities were often fulfilled by the managing director or an executive with operations responsibility – reflective of a Japanese tradition to avoid specialized roles. In family enterprises in Thailand, the status of the HR department was lower than in publicly held Thai firms.

4. National Culture – Professionalism is found more in places that have cultures relying on specialization (Gannon and Associates, 1994; Von Glinow and Chung, 1989). There is a tendency for Western countries to specialize functions and, alternately, for Asian countries to generalize them. For example, in Canada or the United States HR specialists are usually trained and qualified in

HRM policy and practices; while in Japan, Korea or Singapore, broad training and skill development and a generalist perspective is more valued.

5. Organization of Labor – Countries where organized labor has been able to influence labor market decisions consistently tend to rely on more professionalized HR managers, although in countries like the United States that influence may be waning. In the U.S., HR managers began to professionalize as a means of handling worker demands and forestalling unionization. Once unionization had developed, HR professionals became well versed in union contract negotiation and employment law (Baron et al., 1986; Edwards, 1979; Jacoby, 1985).

6. State Involvement – The legitimation of the HR function and the professional associations themselves by the State is critical to the level of professionalism. In Australia and the United States, HR professionals have been involved closely with the government in the development of labor legislation. The State has given different types of certification to HR specialists involved in personnel counselling, EAPs, compensation and even in contract negotiation.

7. Surplus of Skilled Workers – A surplus of large groups of skilled workers is a signal that an economy has large groups of educated, specialized workers. Educated and specialized workers set the foundation for professionalization of work (Abbott, 1988; Cullen, 1985; Freidson, 1986).

The professionalization of HRM on the Pacific Rim is aided by these within-country factors, but it is also aided by between-country elements. Multinationals from countries with well-developed, bureaucratic HRM systems tend to import HRM expertise and HR managers to help set up new business units (Adler, 1991; Lawler and Atmiyanandana, in this volume). The core HRM practices in these units are transmitted from the home office and home country by the HR professionals, and the use of HRM expertise in employment matters are legitimated in the new workplace. Equally important are the development of networks and associations of HRM professionals that span several Pacific Rim countries. ASEAN and APEC have subgroups specifically examining HR problems (PECC, 1993), and PACIBER (1993) has connected various academic and business specialists for the past fifteen years. Every year there is also a meeting of the International Personnel Management Association, and there are now several outlets for the work of HR academics and practitioners – especially the *Asia Pacific Journal of Human Resources*.

The new organizations created by HR academics and practitioners serve as alternative sites for HR knowledge and policy; ones quite apart from the HR department within a large firm's internal labor market. Many would say that the traditional HR department is gradually fading away, being replaced by smaller, flexible external HR units staffed by a few highly trained and experienced HR specialists. These professionals are brought in as management consultants, change agents, systems experts, or temporary staffers to address difficult corporate HRM problems – problems that go beyond simple staffing and compensation issues that are being handled by a few lower level, clerical employees (Harrison, 1993; Jennings and Moore, 1992; Moore and Jennings, 1993).

Meaning and Value in Different HRM Systems

Neoinstitutionalists argue that once a method of doing work becomes a recognizable practice and has been objectified in language and consciousness, it becomes meaningful (Berger and Luckmann, 1967). Furthermore, once this practice becomes accepted (legitimated) within the firm as a means of doing business, it gains a longer-range value (Berger and Luckmann, 1967; Meyer and Scott, 1983; Scott, 1989). The meaningfulness and longer-range value of a practice for the HRM system is reflected, in part then, by how widespread a practice is and, in part, by the degree of involvement of HR managers in it. For instance, in the United States HR managers have gained a central, legitimate position in the administration of Affirmative Action (hereafter, also AA) programs. The initial need for this practice grew out of legislation (i.e., the Civil Rights Act of 1964). Between 1964 and 1979 the interpretation of these rights in the courts and the development of complex hiring schemes (e.g., modified quotas) directly involved the legal and personnel groups of large firms. The components of AA practices have ranged from hiring to review to promotion of minorities, and each currently involves HR departments. Research has shown that interpreting and administering AA practices is now a key source of power and legitimacy for HR departments in large firms (Edelman, 1992; Sutton et al., 1993).

However, in North America, "contract negotiation" never gained the same meaning and value as a practice. It did become a recognized practice for an HR manager from the time of early unionization in the 1930s to the height of the industrial relations system in the late 1950s. In several large firms in key sectors, personnel managers became involved between labor and general management as arbiters of the details of employment (NICB, 1940). This involvement was part of the longer range process of setting up labor-management relations and managerial efforts to bring some negotiation in-house using the HR department. Yet HR managers have never gained complete acceptance in the country as contract negotiators (Jacoby, 1983; Ritzer and Trice, 1969; Wolf, 1980). There has been distrust of HR staff members by union members, and management was reluctant to let the HR department have a direct hand in such important, strategic outcomes.

Looking at Table 2, we can see that the most pervasive practices involving HR functionaries seem to be around hiring and firing – "selection" and "involuntary dismissal". Also rating quite high in most countries are performance appraisal, basic compensation, and training. For instance, in the United States 98% of the managers in the Pacific Northwest were involved in hiring; 78% in performance appraisal; and 93% in compensation application. In the PRC performance appraisal and wage application ranked as the highest HR activities for cadre with HR training.

But the meaning of "recruiting and selection" practices varies considerably across the countries. In Canada, recruiting and selection refer to the placement of job notices in local papers, company listing sources, and informal networks. In most medium- to large-sized companies the HR department or HR manager is typically in charge of sorting through applications and candidates. Selection at this stage becomes separate from recruiting as efforts are made to determine with which of the final candidates a contract will be struck. In Hong Kong recruiting takes place through both similar and dissimilar means, from advertising in Chinese language newspapers (87.5%) to personal recommendations (75.8%) to notices outside of company's premises (36.2%); yet the tight labor market and dynamic economy has increased the velocity of the process and also created new recruitment methods (Kirkbride and Tang, 1989). The increased velocity and dynamism can be seen by the turnover in number of advertisements on company walls each week and in the willingness to hire interested parties on the spot, rather than to screen them. The line between recruitment and selection becomes blurred. Furthermore, the use of selection tests is quite low; the use of inside contacts and prior knowledge of the person, quite high. As a contrast to Hong Kong and even to the U.S. and Canada, in South Korea the recruiting and selection system for medium and large companies is much more formalized: first, recruiting through universities and newspapers is used; second, selection and placement tests are employed to judge the qualifications of candidates; third, personal contact or knowledge of the candidate is drawn upon to further screen individuals; and fourth, work groups are even involved in the decision of the acceptability of the candidate. The candidates are reviewed as if they were becoming members of a large corporate family (Koch et al., in this volume; Steers et al., 1990).

Performance appraisal is also used heavily in several countries – in Australia, Hong Kong, Japan, and the PRC. Performance appraisal in Australia takes the form of inventory-type assessments of the candidates at different periods during the year, usually by the supervisor, with review and feedback from the HR/personnel department. Similarly, large, public firms in Hong Kong use inventory check lists of work behaviors on an annual or semi-annual basis, although there is a tendency to rely on personnel department managers to gather data as well as to feed it back to the appraisee (Kirkbride and Tang, 1989; Poon, in this volume). In Japan, performance appraisal is less formal, relying on personal communication between a worker and both his/her managers and fellow workers. There is some periodic, formal write-up of such reviews to maintain the files in the central records area, but the administrative arm of the HR department is not as directly responsible for the actual act of appraising. In the PRC, performance appraisal occurs in new enterprises that are under the enterprise (market) scheme as part of the job design and evaluation programs for performance pay, and it also occurs in medium-and large-sized firms that are staffed with direct influence

Table 2:   HRM Practices in Selected Pac Rim Countries

Pacific Rim country/ City-State	Most Pervasive & Highest HRM Involvement Practices (% or Rank)	Least Pervasive & Lowest HRM Involvement Practices (% or Rank)
Australia	Performance Appraisal (83%); Job Analysis	Skills Audit (7%); JIT (7%)
Canada	Recruiting (79%); Involuntary Separation (78%)	Incentive Pay (34%); Job Design (35%)
Hong Kong	Recruiting & Selection (68%); Training and Development (72%); Performance Appraisal (72%)	Contract Negotiation (13%); Management Development (37%)
Japan	Performance Appraisal (1); Administration of Rewards (2); Strategic Hiring (3)	Counselling
New Zealand	Employment – Hiring, Firing, Promotion (87%); Salary Administration (90%); Planning and Research (88%)	Incentive Programs (34%); Production and Participation (48%)
PRC	Performance Appraisal (1); Training (2); Wage Administration (3)	Labor Disputes; Retirement
Singapore	Record Keeping (1); Recruitment (2); Selection (3); Wage and Salary (4)	Selection and Testing; Counselling; Public Relations
South Korea	Recruitment & Selection (87%); HR Research (81%); HR planning (79%); benefits (74%); Contract Negotiation (79%)	Safety (26%); Incentive Pay (37%); Job Design (35%)
Taiwan	Staffing (1); Compensation (2); Training (3)	HR Planning (10); Career Planning (9); Counselling (8)
Thailand	White Collar Training (80%); Performance Appraisal (70%)	Profit Sharing (30%); Compensation (40%)
United States	Recruiting (95%); Involuntary Separation (93%); Compensation Application (91%); Employer Insurance (90%); Control & Discipline (90%)	Work Groups/Teams (39%); Child Care (23%); Time & Motion (13%)

from government administrators. These administrators evaluate the "suitability" of cadre members and workers on various work behavior and attitude dimensions, some of which would appear to the Western eye to be political in nature (Chow and Shenkar, 1989; Wang, 1991). In Thailand, performance appraisal is beginning to take hold and is certainly one of the most pervasive of all HR practices in medium- and large-sized firms. Written inventory instruments are used by supervisors or HR managers to evaluate workers on a periodic basis. There is a tendency for such forms to be generic rating scales about attitude, rather than customized scales concerning behavior appropriate to the job. Many of these forms are used primarily in subunits of foreign national firms – U.S., British, or Japanese (Lawler and Atmiyanandana, in this volume). In other words, performance appraisal seems to have been adopted as an easily recognizable and reproducible practice, one which on the surface appears to fit well with other home units of these firms. Similarly, Poon (in this volume) citing Kirkbride and Tang (1989) notes that performance appraisal has been adopted in large measure because of the "Western influence" of British firms in Hong Kong. The PRC is currently beginning to adopt Western-style personnel instruments because its managers are being educated by Western HR practitioners or academics.

Many of these performance appraisal practices are diffused from other systems where performance appraisal is currently valued and pervasive (e.g., Australia, Britain, Canada, the United States). This means that not only do the practices look similar in form but have quite a different meaning; in fact, they may not have any meaning at all within the HRM system of the adopting countries. Lawler and Atmiyanandana suggest that there is a strong segregation between core home culture and that brought in by foreign nationals. The role of the family, the emphasis on Buddhism, and the tendency to view such evaluation in a longer run relationship as unnecessarily formal (Bolman and Deal, 1991; Lawler and Atmiyanandana, in this volume) all make formal appraisal difficult to adopt in a meaningful fashion within Thai-run firms. In a sense, methods like performance appraisal symbolize the "new", "outside" culture. Similarly, in Hong Kong, formal appraisal within large firms by HR managers runs counter to local traditions stressing paternalistic treatment of workers whom one has known well for a long period of time, and it tends to be associated with a bureaucratic arm of companies, which is viewed as a necessary but inefficient evil. One of the chapter authors when working in Hong Kong on a change in HRM policies in a large hotel heard the general manager report that formal, periodic performance evaluation actually riled workers, only further increasing the probability of their departure. In the PRC, Western-style performance appraisal has not been quite so difficult to adopt in principle, since there is a tradition of testing and of evaluating individuals for political correctness; however, getting managers to accept it as a critical component of the evaluation and promotion process has been more difficult. In fact, managers who have received M.B.A. training in the West are reported to have a hard time finding work in an economy starved for middle managers

(Lam, 1989). In other words, human resource management methods are seen as meaningful, but they have not been legitimated to the point that they are valued in the workplace. Finally, in Japan performance appraisal has existed in various forms for more than twenty years, having been adopted along with other Western management practices during the fifties and sixties; yet it is viewed as part of a larger, integrated effort to refine performance under the *Kaizen* system and in "on-the-job, off-the-job" training, rather than as a separate, evaluation of a specific individual's behavior within a given job for a given time period. Appraisal comes in many forms, rather than having forms define appraisal: the final write-up is a cumulative summary of minute evaluation of a longer range set of behaviors and of employee development (Morishima, in this volume; Takahashi, 1991).

Compensation as a practice is prevalent in most countries' corporate HRM systems to an even greater degree than is indicated in Table 2. Assigning and keeping track of basic salary and standard hourly wages tend to be administratively-intensive duties, especially in firms without computer systems (computers are still uncommon in many Pacific Rim firms). HR departments and accounting activities are lumped together for the purposes of compensation. Sometimes the HR group is in charge; at other times, the accounting group. However, in most firms and countries on the Pacific Rim the HR group is rarely in charge of assigning original salary or in dealing with major salary increases. Furthermore, the nature of pay increases within the compensation system varies tremendously by country. In Australia, Canada, New Zealand and the United States there is a tendency to rely on base salary or hourly wages for a large part of remuneration and to use more formal means of increasing the increments of pay. In the PRC, Taiwan, Hong Kong, and Singapore, base pay is not nearly as large a proportion of final pay compared to other countries, meaning that bonuses, merit pay or pay-for-performance are used to make up large differences. In such situations, the HR department has little say over compensation; decisions tend to be made by the managerial staff at least two levels above the individual being reviewed, with the input of the direct supervisor as a critical factor. While there is also a tendency for merit or bonuses to be discretionary in countries that are "westernized", there is a greater precedence for substantial pay increases to be set by contract or by a formalized pay system (e.g., the Hay method) and administered directly by the HR department. Furthermore, there tends to be direct involvement of HR managers in forms of acute assistance to employees. In Australia, Canada, New Zealand and the U.S., HR managers usually set up and administer employee assistance programs and other holdover, "welfare type" practices. The notion that the firm is an integral part of the Welfare State seems stronger in these countries (Stevens, 1986).

Training is one other area of HRM in Pacific Rim countries where managers appear to have increasing involvement, although not to the same degree as in recruiting, performance appraisal and compensation. HR managers seem to be charged with setting up retraining programs, searching the market for specific retraining programs or information for the firm to apply, and with delivering the message to the organization's workforce that continuous learning and improvement are critical in a competitive world. But training does not mean the same thing to a worker in China as in Japan or in Hong Kong or in Taiwan. Training in China means an avenue to a new job and employment as well as a status reward. Since salaries are low and mobility is controlled, skill-based pay and promotion are *de facto* methods of moving forward in the employment system. Training in Japan is part of the larger *Kaisen*, *Ringi* and job rotation systems, which means the HR department has a large involvement, just like any other department has a large involvement in training. Training is along generalist lines and involves a long-range investment of time and effort in many jobs. In Taiwan, training is more specialized, and like the PRC, it is offered as an additional perquisite to a job, beyond pay and benefits, because it is difficult to keep skilled employees in the volatile economy with a tight labor market. Canada and the United States do not have HR departments that are as strongly involved in training as some other Pacific Rim counterparts. In fact, HR departments in these countries tend not to be as involved in performance-related and job design activities, as can be seen in the third column of Table 2. The training and job design and performance pay occurs in conjunction with the production department and work group.

A similar point about practices which appear similar on the surface are quite different underneath has been made by Von Glinow and Chung (1989). Comparing recruiting/training, rewards, and promotion in the U.S., South Korea, Japan and the PRC, they note that in the United States selection tends to be based on standardized techniques, and the use of educational institutions and search firms is quite popular; in Korea selection is based on employment tests and family/personal contacts; in Japan, on university placement; and in the PRC, on "closed" selection systems for cadres within the Communist Party (Von Glinow and Chung, 1989, pp. 156-157). However, Von Glinow and Chung did not analyze the source of these variations – why "recruiting" means such different things to employees in each place. Our work suggests that the State and organized labor play a critical role in negotiating the interface between the external and internal labor market. Volatile external labor markets with a high demand for unskilled or skilled labor compel FILMs to adapt or be minimalized. The government or organized labor steps in to force change. For instance, the State may influence recruiting through the development of immigration polices, as in Hong Kong, the PRC and the United States. When there is slack in the system, company-specific HR systems have time to be developed; that is, practices can become embedded within an HR system, increasing their meaning and value. Yet, ironically, these meaningful and valued practices developed by HR groups in conjunction with workers can act as an inertial force when it comes time for the HR system, as a whole, to respond to a new, competitive, environment. The attachment to refined job classifications and particular work weeks and wage schedules of workers in Canada have been cited as major drawbacks to productivity (Porter, 1991).

Imitable and Inimitable Competitive Advantage

We have seen that at least three core sets of practice – recruiting and selection, performance appraisal, and basic compensation – are prevalent in most of our selected Pacific Rim countries, and that the HR departments or managers in those countries have a large involvement in these practices. We have also seen that the meaning of these practices, which appear similar on the surface in terms of their form – even down to the instruments used – are different underneath. They are interpreted differently and the background factors that give rise to the practices differ. The real paradox is that many of these practices have been adopted from other HRM systems where they had first become highly institutionalized – recognized, defined, and accepted as legitimate. But once adopted in the new place, industry or firm, the real meaning and use of the practice could not be the same. It might even be argued that once the practice had become fully institutionalized, it was already in danger of losing all its original meaning. Meaning might have been at a maximum just at the first stage of legitimation; for only if a practice remains deeply embedded in the set of original relations that created the practices or give it its unique form, does it retain its significance.

This discussion of the diffusion of the real value of a practice raises the question of which elements of an HRM system are truly imitable and which are not. Our observations suggest that only those practices that emerged simultaneously in a large number of firms and industries in a given country or that were diffused on the basis of some technical rationality among a small, progressive group of firms will retain their embedded quality. These cohort and emergence effects imply that only pervasive practices that were adopted and used by HR functionaries at almost the same time and practices that have diffused (or are diffusing) among a small group of homogeneous actors will be those imbued with the most meaning and direct use. It is these practices that should be least imitable. In contrast, practices that are pervasive because of gradual diffusion or practices that are not adopted by quite similar actors within a reasonable time period will be less imbued with special use and significance, and probably easier to copy.

This logic runs somewhat counter to current ideas about strategy found in both the strategic management and SHRM literature. Cohort effects and emergence effects are deemed to be precisely the source of new strategies, which players then attempt to imitate in the market. The context around those practices – e.g., the culture of the country – are spoken of as mediating elements that make them difficult to adopt, beyond mimicking certain structural features. Neoinstitutional Theory suggests that it is precisely those practices that one wants to imitate that will always be the most difficult to imitate and those that are easiest to adopt will have the least value. So the notion of successful adoption of core practices from other countries seems unlikely in most circumstances.

In keeping with the other neoinstitutional work on diffusion (Baron et al., 1986; DiMaggio and Powell, 1984; Powell and Dimaggio, 1991; Sutton et al.,

1993), only those practices in the first column of Table 2 that were created as part of a cohort effect and those practices that lie somewhere between the first and second column in terms of pervasiveness and HR involvement are likely to be inimitable. For instance, in the first column of Table 2, the true cohort practices in the various countries seem to be: performance appraisal and strategic hiring in Japan; contract negotiation in Korea; wage administration in the PRC; methods of record keeping in Singapore; training in Taiwan; and involuntary separation/discipline and employer insurance in the U.S. The emergent practices, based on the discussion in the preceding chapters seem to be: incentive schemes in Canada and New Zealand; management development in Hong Kong, job design in South Korea, wage administration in the PRC, Singapore and Thailand; and EAP components like counselling and child care in the United States.

But are inimitable practices a source of "competitive" advantage? Neoinstitutionalists and strategists beg the question to some degree. Neoinstitutional theorists maintain that practices become institutionalized because they solve important crises – especially around meaning (e.g., goals, technologies, etc.). Parties then recognize the practices as solutions and accept (legitimate) them to varying degrees (Berger and Luckmann, 1967; Meyer and Scott, 1983; Scott, 1989). In this sense, such practices must provide some source of advantage. For instance, in Japan, performance appraisal and hiring were used to overcome several problems: arranging transitions between educational institutions and work institutions; guiding worker training after the war within a highly hierarchical system; and applying methods learned in Western universities and businesses by Japanese managers. Similarly, in Hong Kong, recruiting methods have been developed to handle the chronic problems of labor shortage and high turnover: the methods are relatively low cost, high in information richness, and directly tap the external labor market (without mediation).

Strategic HRM theorists and those taking a resource-based approach to strategy also assume that core practices in HRM systems must have some competitive advantage. The former group tends to define different HRM systems precisely by core practice that developed at key points in a firm, industry or country's history. For example, Begin (1993) says HRM systems are part of the corporate lifecycle, in which firms progress from simple bureaucracies to adhocracies in accordance with the external environment. HRM systems simply follow suit. Schuler et al. (1993) argue that practices involving exogenous features like a country's culture, and endogenous factors like the composition of the firm's labor force, determine core practices and, ultimately, effectiveness. Similarly, strategists using a resource-dependence approach say that the least tangible practices directly involving the deeper values of a culture as well as the core business activities of a firm are most likely to be a source of competitive advantage (Barney, 1991; 1992). It is precisely those practices that became pervasive at one point in time as solutions to critical problems facing firms in an industry that would become core practices and that would also be likely to help the group survive in their environments. Furthermore,

Table 3: HR Activities Perceived Critical in Near Future

Pacific Rim Country/City-State	Practice Areas Perceived to Be Critical
Australia	Continuous Improvement; Change of Workplace Rules; Multiskilling; Communication
Canada	EEO Legislation; Labor Competitiveness; Training and Flexibility; Union-Management Cooperation
Hong Kong	Training and Development; Professionalization of HR Managers
Japan	Protection and Representation of Employees; Extending HRM to White Collar Workers; Motivating Aging Workforce; Decentralizing HRM
New Zealand	Professionalizing HRM; Decentralizing HRM
PRC	Training of HR Managers; Job Evaluation; Compensation
Singapore	Training and Development; Management Planning; Employee Compensation
South Korea	Collective Bargaining; Wages; Training
Taiwan	Labor Recruitment; Retraining; Participation; Union Protection
Thailand	Selection; Training and Development
United States	Interpreting Legislative Initiatives (e.g., ADA); Retraining

it is those practices that are emergent, based on their contact with the needs of production technology, that would be most related to some competitive edge in the marketplace.

The actual performance data on the different sets of institutionalized and emergent practices that are tied to the specific countries are more difficult to unearth. Measuring the contribution of HRM to the bottom line is difficult under even controlled conditions. Nevertheless, comparing current pervasive practices with managerial responses to questions such as "what practices may be of some use to the firm in the coming five years" may be of some use in determining whether current pervasive or emergent core practices are likely to be a longer run, intangible source of value-added for the firm. The managerial attitudes about future practices actually form the preference functions that will be used to maintain or adopt the practices – particularly given the absence of any objective utility data on their worth. In our and other surveys of managerial attitudes about HRM in the different countries, we have found the practices featured in Table 3 to be perceived as having particular importance over the next five years:

Among the practices in Table 3, training and development stand out as the most consistently mentioned. However, training is currently only a pervasive practice in the corporate HR systems in Hong Kong, the PRC, Taiwan, and Thailand. It is also worth noting that those places where more bread and butter practices have taken a back seat to training have had the strongest economic growth rates for the last five years. This suggests that many corporate HR systems are lagging behind immediate needs of their firms. However, just adopting training practices from other countries is not likely to help a firm regain its edge. First of all, "training" refers to different things in different countries, if Table 3 is any guide. It ranges from "continuous improvement and multiskilling" in Australia; "training and flexibility" in Canada; "training of managers" in the PRC; to "retraining" in Taiwan. Therefore, if our past observations are any guide, training will have to emerge from particular application and experimentation by firms within those places if it is to gain a unique value and be a source of advantage. Yet having training rank so highly as a future practice is ultimately a great irony for long-range effectiveness and competitive advantage: It implies that no current method of doing work will be sufficient in the near future, which means that the practice of training itself is likely to change continuously, eroding any competitive advantage. Perhaps this is why strategists now emphasize the role of "learning to learn" or "double-loop learning" or "innately recursive systems" as the ultimate source of competitive advantage. Unfortunately, at this point there appears to be no emerging cohort of corporate HR system that truly has this type of practice as its cornerstone.[2]

Professionalizing and decentralizing HRM also appear to be important in several countries as future HRM activities, yet they are certainly not the most pervasive elements of current corporate HR systems (see Table 2). As mentioned, the professionalization of HRM that is taking place occurs outside most medium- and large-size firms. The associations of HR practitioners and the small consulting firms that they are forming around the world seem to be a more important source of new expertise and professional standards today (Harrison, 1993; Moore and Jennings, 1993). As expertise moves out of the firms, there is some decentralization of the HR function down to the line personnel staff; some might even call it the "dismantling" or "cannibalizing" of the HR function. Of course, those who stay in HR units cannot be expected to take part in their own demise. The institutionalized bureaucratic structure is more likely to be changed by environmental shifts and internal changes in resource flows (Meyer and Scott, 1983; Oliver, 1992).

International Strategic HRM (ISHRM)

In organizations competing in the international arena, HRM units may indeed exercise strategic influence. To do so, they must align and reinforce those HR activities that are consistent with the business objectives of the firm (Evans, 1986; Kossek, 1987; Tichy, 1988). Specifically, HR managers can help to determine the strategic capability of an organization through the methods they use for staffing, appriasal, reward and development (Evans, 1984; Tichy, 1988).

On the Pacific Rim, there are variations in the degree to which HRM systems are able to function strategically. Based on the preceding chapters, the following summary observations seem warranted. International strategic HRM is more likely to occur:

1. in countries where HRM has a more established history and HRM system (e.g., the United States, Canada, Australia), managers are seeking to make HRM operations strategic as a vehicle to enhanced competitiveness,
2. where legislative and government statutes provide guidelines for HRM policy; however, such legislation may limit managerial autonomy at the organizational level related to the implementation of strategic HRM,
3. where, in a heavily unionized environment, line managers typically have restricted freedom to create innovative HRM policy and practice that supports strategic business objectives,
4. when HRM programs are highly valued in the workplace, and
5. where HR responsibility is shifting from the unilateral jurisdiction of the HR department, and is instead shared with line managers.

To elaborate, in Australia, an emphasis on strategic HRM is viewed as imperative to international competitiveness. In an effort to significantly revise industrial relations systems and the structure and management of work practices, "HRM has been identified as an important strategic tool in changing the Australian workplace culture from one of complacency to one of competitiveness" (Dunphy, 1989; Stace, 1987; Collins, 1987). To realize strategic goals, a highly regulated and centralized system is undergoing change to become more flexible and decentralized. In both Canada and the United States, HRM is slowly but consistently becoming more strategic. For example, in the United States, HRM departments remain small, but HR managers are involved in the implementation of standard HR practices along with the creation of strategic incentive/investment systems, job enrichment programs, and HR planning systems. As organizations become less bureaucratic, HR professionals have greater autonomy to interpret "standard" HR practices (e.g. job analysis or job classifications) to better match company-specific and competitive needs. In Canada, two-thirds to three-quarters of survey respondents indicated their HRM departments participated in the development and implementation of HR strategies. Although less than 45% of respondents saw the HR group as having strong participation in overall corporate planning, this was perceived as a significant increase in involvement from five years previously.

In contrast, many of the countries on the South Asian portion of the Pacific Rim have a shorter HRM history – and place less emphasis on policies that link HRM and the strategic business objectives of the firm. For example, in Singapore, HRM activities focus on personnel administration, recruitment, welfare, discipline and grievance handling. In Taiwan, only twenty-five percent of survey respondents indicated they participated in overall business planning (although bonuses related to business performance were used in privately owned enterprises). HR planning and systematic analysis of employment issues also tend to be absent in Thailand.

Further, the unionization of companies has traditionally restricted strategic capabilities. Sack and Lee (1989) suggested public sector unions in Canada have resulted in legal regulations that shape HR policies and constrain HRM practices. Unions perpetuate static reward systems and narrow job descriptions that often interfere with the creation of innovative incentive systems or "broad jobs" identified as important in highly competitive companies (Blackburn and Rosen, 1993). A diffusion of HRM responsibility away from unions as well as from HRM managers may result in new systems of HRM that are developed and implemented by a wide range of company employees. For instance, in Hong Kong, HRM is becoming more strategic as manpower planning is done in conjunction with line managers. In North American corporations, an increased emphasis on self-managed work teams suggests that in many instances HRM will operate in the jurisdiction of peer teams at the shop floor level.

How, then, might strategic HRM be characterized within an historical or neoinstitutional framework? One might speculate that in the early stages of HRM development, comprehensive legislation and unionization are required to ensure basic individual rights of workers. This was the case in the 1950s in North America; and in the evolving economies of South East Asia a similar pattern is more recently occurring. In the chapter on Taiwan, Fahr indicated that as "democratization and liberalization further blossom" the government will be forced to tighten labor laws and their enforcement. Under the pressure of union movements and heightened worker expectations for workplace participation, institutionalized forms of worker protection will be created. HR policy will initially focus on basic worker rights (e.g., policies to ensure a fair standard of living and good working conditions). Over time, HR-related policies and practices will be legitimized, and if serving a perceived useful purpose, will be valued by members of the organization. At this stage of HR development, greater emphasis is placed on the establishment of separate policy areas than on the integration of HR policy to match strategic demands. As HRM systems continue to evolve and to become more closely related to competitive demands, one might expect to see both flexibility and integration in HR-related policy. For example, in organizations practising a TQM philosophy, rewards, training and staff selection may be used to reinforce quality objectives. These HR practices support strategic objectives, but are also flexible in their capability to alter to meet new or changing environmental conditions.

International Human Resource Management in the Future

The rapid social and economic changes that have already occurred in all countries surveyed in this book will likely appear moderate in contrast to anticipated Pacific

Rim growth as predicted for the future. Trade and foreign ministers who attended the Asia Pacific Economic Cooperation (APEC) summit at Seattle in November, 1993, advocated a "broad vision" for commerce on the Pacific Rim. The vision is intended to promote trade, investment and regional economic ties between countries which would form the largest international trading block in the world. Such change will inevitably signal greater competitiveness among corporations, internationalization as foreign MNCs or joint ventures cross national borders, and social-economic-political changes in response to changing market or other demands. On the Pacific Rim what might be the role of HRM departments of personnel in the change process?

Related to the expansion of trade both in North America (NAFTA) and more broadly on the Pacific Rim, the focus and form of many industries is likely to be altered. In some cases, labor intensive industries will shift locations to reduce costs. In Southeast Asia, for example, Taiwan, Singapore, South Korea, and Hong Kong had traditionally been preferred low-cost manufacturing sites. As wages and other cost-related factors began to escalate in these countries, many MNCs began to look toward the PRC, Thailand, Malaysia, and Indonesia for their operations (Teagarden et al., 1992). Some industries will become more capital intensive, technology intensive, or service oriented. The role of HRM will change to accommodate shifts in industry requirements, and will be related to needs for enhanced competitiveness. For example, to increase worker productivity in high technology industries, new forms of training, rewards, or performance review may be required in order to enhance learning at the organizational level. In addition, and related to industrial and political shifts, government legislation will undergo some modification. In this context, a new role for HRM will be to balance labor and management priorities, and to forge cooperative frameworks for the application of HRM initiatives.

As corporations internationalize and create subsidiary operations or joint ventures in foreign locations, the form and function of HRM policy and practice is expected to undergo revision (Cascio and Serapio, 1991; Teagarden and Von Glinow, 1989). The existence of MNCs is already prevalent in countries like South Korea, Taiwan, or Singapore. To keep pace with international demands, in many cases knowledge and technology are imported by professional managers trained in Western-oriented MBA programs. Do HR managers intend to simply implant Western-style management practices into Eastern cultures? Or alternately, will HR managers with international skills be able to create new and culturally sensitive HR policy? To what degree then, is a balance forged between local customs and values and more "modern" management practices which reinforce the attainment of strategic business objectives? As described in the chapter on Thailand, in publicly held companies, HRM strategies were created which represented a hybrid of "Western rationalism and the traditionalism of the family enterprise". In this sense, new forms of HRM policy can be devised that match corporate goals as well as the cultural expectations of local employees. In the development of culturally relevant HRM practices, HR managers find a new role as integrators, facilitators and trainers of new forms of HRM.

To elaborate further, Cyr (forthcoming) found that in international joint ventures "hybrid" forms of HR policy could be developed to accommodate cultural preferences of diverse groups of managers and other employees. More specifically, in one Japanese-American joint venture, the implementation of a performance review process was problematic due to hesitancy on the part of Japanese managers to participate. Subsequently, HR managers created a simplified review format based on the suggestions from Japanese managers, "sold" policy when necessary, and provided training in order to implement the new system.

To be most effective as change agents, a broad skill set is suggested for HR managers which includes technical, personal and political skills. For example, Cyr (forthcoming) found that in a sample of progressive joint ventures HR managers functioned as "process experts" in addition to possessing traditional HR abilities in the areas of staffing, training, reward or performance review. In an expanded role, HR staff ideally were aware of business values and priorities, understood the goals and values of various stakeholders in the organization, and were excellent communicators. HR professionals gained credibility in the eyes of other members of the organization if they were able to consistently define a set or HR values and priorities, and to translate these priorities into timely and innovative HR policy and practice. Alternately, in less successful joint ventures, problems often arise due to blurred organizational culture, blocked communication and incomplete information, or inequality in the compensation systems offered to employees (Shenkar and Zeira, 1990), or the imposition of Western values or management practices (Csath, 1992).

Based on information presented in earlier chapters, in an effort to infuse organizations with decentralized HRM strategic operations, HR responsibility was shared between HR managers and other line managers in the company. In countries such as Canada, the United States, New Zealand, or Hong Kong, for example, HRM activities such as promotion, training, job enlargement and enrichment, and the development of teams or quality circles is controlled by units outside the HR department. In Japan, the HR group has an "ancillary role" in determining strategic policies and as such, acts as a coordinating body for corporate-wide personnel policies and practices. Central HRM-related activities are handled by line managers in Japanese corporations, located in Japan or elsewhere.

By the year 2000, we expect to see continued decentralization and debureaucratization of corporate HRM systems in Australia, Canada, and the United States. HRM professionals will operate more as strategic generalists or "process experts" than as technical HRM specialists. In this new role, HR managers will help to craft a direction for the organization that is both strategic and culturally appropriate. An increased emphasis will exist on organizational learning as environmental, social, or market situations change. In Hong Kong, Japan, the PRC, South Korea, Taiwan and Thailand, we expect to see a period of HRM formalization and bureaucratization, followed by greater flexibility and stategic emphasis in HRM operations. For example, increased complexity in the firm internal labor market will likely necessitate a formalization of practices (e.g., compensation) in order to handle a large workforce. Initial formalization, once legitimized might then be opened to less static, more creative forms of reward for workers that supports the strategic direction set for the firm.

Eventually, at the legislative level the creation of more flexible policy initiatives might permit employers to have both control and flexibility to meet demands of international or national competitiveness. At the organizational level, strategic HRM can further be enhanced by collaborative union-management relations is which joint steering committees consider what is best for both employees and for the organization. Also at the organizational level, HR managers may be able to set a careful and strategic vision for HRM policy which is shared with other managers and employees – and realized in practice by various units or departments.

In addition to within-firm HRM, increased globalization has given rise to various forms of organizations such as joint ventures and strategic alliances that require interunit linkages. Some key issues involved in the creation and operation of such linkages include balancing the needs for diversity, coordination and control to enhance competitiveness, flexibility and organizational learning (Bartlett and Ghoshal, 1991). The overall challenge to HRM managers and others responsible for HRM is one of identifying and understanding diverse needs and perspectives, not only in a single unit, but across organizational units as well. Flexibility is important, but may operate simultaneously with requirements for control. As Evans (1986) described, complex organizations are likely to exhibit paradoxical qualities such as formalization and informality, or individuality and teamwork. "Dynamic balances" may be created in turbulent, complex organizations when, for example, teamwork is created among strong individuals or rewards are offered for both individual and group participation.

In many ways this book has been about context. The various contributors have outlined HRM systems and how they operate relative to their respective countries, societies, legislative prescriptions, firm internal labor markets, competitive requirements, company strategic objectives, and employee needs and expectations. Of particular interest, and consistent with a Neoinstitutional Approach, the role of the State has received attention related to the development and diffusion of HRM systems. HRM is interpreted and reinterpreted resulting in new practices. Over time, convergence of practices is likely to occur across countries through networks that disperse policy and practices. For instance, integration occurs as one facet of industrial globalization when multinational corporations share practices among their various subunits. Ultimately, the effective institutionalization of practices will depend on adaptiveness to local conditions and cultures. Over time, new versions of ISHRM likely will emerge that exhibit system characteristics of flexibility, moderate bureaucracy, and professionalization. Under such conditions, the strategic capability of HRM will likely escalate in countries around the Pacific Basin – and elsewhere.

Endnotes

1. In a sense, this is saying that the HRM system cannot be treated as a separate, "dependent variable" apart from the external and internal labor markets in which it is embedded. Instead, factors such as those in Table 1 are tightly associational. Only when elements of an HR system have become highly institutionalized locally can they be partly transferred.
2. General Electric and Lincoln Electric and GM's Saturn plant have been discussed as having learning as central practices, but the role of HR in their development and administration is not as central as the role of production and R&D; and these practices have not yet been picked up by similar firms competing in their niches.

References

Abbott, A. (1988). *The System of Professions: An Essay on the Division of Expert Labor.* Chicago, IL: University of Chicago Press.

Adler, N. (1991). *International Dimensions of Organizational Behavior.* (2nd Edition.) Boston, MA: PWS-Kent.

Althauser, R. (1989). "Internal Labor Markets." *Annual Review of Sociology*, 15, 143-161.

APEC (1993). "APEC Ministerial Meeting, Seattle." *APEC-HRD-NEDM Newsletter*, 1(2), 1-12.

APRRC (1992). "ASEAN Celebrates 25 Years." *APRRC Newsletter*, 2(3), 1-12.

Baglioni, G., and C. Crouch (eds.) (1990). *European Industrial Relations: The Challenge of Flexibility.* London: Sage Publications.

Bamber, G.J. and R.D. Lansbury (eds.) (1987). *International and Comparative Industrial Relations.* London: Allen & Unwin.

Barney, J. (1991). "Firm Resources and Sustained Competitive Advantage." *Journal of Management*, 17(10), 99-120.

Barney, J. (1992). "Integrating Organizational Behavior and Strategy Formulation Research: A Resource Based Analysis." In P. Shrivastava, A. Huff and J. Dutton (eds.), *Advances in Strategic Management: A Research Annual, Vol. 8.* Greenwich, CT: JAI Press.

Baron, J., F. Dobbin and P.D. Jennings. (1986). "War and Peace: The Evolution of Modern Personnel Administration in U.S. Industry." *American Journal of Sociology*, 92(2), 350-383.

Baron, J., P.D. Jennings and F. Dobbin. (1988). "Mission Control? The Development of Personnel Systems in U.S. Industry." *American Sociological Review*, 53, 497-514.

Baron, J. and D. Kreps (Forthcoming). *Human Resources: A Framework for General Managers.* New York: Wiley.

Bartlett, C. and S. Ghoshal. (1991). *Managing Across Borders: The Transnational Solution.* Cambridge, MA: Harvard Business School Press.

Begin, J.P. (1993). "Identifying Patterns in HRM Systems: Lessons from Organizational Theory." In G.R. Ferris (ed.), *Research in Personnel and Human Resources Management*, Supplement 3. Greenwich, CT: JAI Press, 3-20.

Berger, P.L. and T. Luckmann. (1967). *The Social Construction of Reality*. New York: Doubleday.

Blackburn, R. and B. Rosen (1993). "Total Quality and Human Resources Management: Lessons Learned from Baldridge Award-winning Companies." *Academy of Management Executive*, 7(3), 49-66.

Bolman, L.G. and T.E. Deal (1991). *Reframing Organizations*. Beverly Hills, CA: Sage.

Cascio, W.F. (1992). "International Human Resource Management Issues for the 1990s." *Asia Pacific Journal of Human Resources*, 30(4), 1-18.

Cascio, W.F. and M.G. Serapio (1991). "Human Resources Systems in an International Alliance: The Undoing of a Done Deal?" *Organizational Dynamics*, Winter, 63-74.

Chow, I.H.S. and O. Shenkar (1989). In J.B. Shaw, J.E. Beck, K.M. Rowland and P.S. Kirkbride (eds.), *International Human Resources Management: Issues and Research for the 1990's. Proceedings of the Second International Conference on Personnel/Human Resources Management*. Hong Kong: International Personnel and Human Resource Management Association.

Collins, R. (1987). "The Strategic Contributions of the Personnel Function." *Human Resource Management Australia*, 25, 3.

Csath, M. (1992). "Strategic Alliances: Joint Venturing in Central and Eastern Europe (Problems and Opportunities). The Case of Hungary." *International Review of Strategic Management*, 2(2), 73-107.

Cullen, J.B. (1985). "Professional Differentiation and Occupational Earnings." *Work and Occupations*, 12(3), 351-372.

Cyr, D.J. (forthcoming). *International Joint Ventures: The Strategic Human Resource Management Challenge*. New York: Quorum Books.

Cyr, D.J. and P.J. Frost (1992). "Human Resource Management Practice in China: A Future Perspective." *Human Resource Management*, 30(2), 199-215.

Deal, T. and L. Bolman (1992). *Reframing Organization Theory*. San Fransisco, CA: Jossey-Bass.

DiMaggio, P. (1985). "Interest and Agency in Institutional Theory." Paper presented at UCLA/NSF Conference on Institutional Theory, Los Angeles. (Published in L.G. Zucker (ed.) (1988), *Institutional Patterns and Organizations: Culture and Environment*. Cambridge, MA: Ballinger.)

DiMaggio, P. and W.W. Powell. (1984). "The Iron Cage Revisisted: Institutional Isomorphism and Collective Rationality in Organizational Fields." *American Sociological Review*, 48, 147-160.

DiMaggio, P.J. and W.W. Powell (1991). "Introduction." In W.W. Powell and P.J. DiMaggio (eds.), *The New Institutionalism in Organizational Analysis*. Chicago, IL: University of Chicago Press, pp. 1-38.

Dobbin, F.R. (1992). "The Origins of Private Insurance, 1920-1950." *American Journal of Sociology*, 97(5), 1416-1450.

Dobbin, F.R. and T. Boychuk (1993). "Job Autonomy and National Context: Evidence from Nine Nations." Paper presented at the American Sociological Annual Meeting, Washington, DC, 1991.

Dobbin, F.R., L. Edelman, J.W. Meyer, W.R. Scott and A. Swidler (1988). "The Expansion of Due Process in Organizations." In L. Zucker (ed.), *Institutional Patterns and Organizations*, pp. 70-98. Cambridge, MA: Ballinger.

Dobbin F.R., W.R. Sutton, J.W. Meyer and W.R. Scott (1991). "The Renaissance of Internal Labor Markets: The Effects of Affirmative Action." Paper presented at SCOR Conference, Asilomar, CA.

Dobbin F.R., J.R. Sutton, J.W. Meyer and W.R. Scott. (1993). "Equal Opportunity and the Institutional Construction of Internal Labor Markets." *American Journal of Sociology*, 99, 396-427.

Doeringer, P.B. and M.J. Piore (1971). *Internal Labor Markets and Manpower Analysis*. Lexington, MA: Lexington Books.

Dunlop, J.T. (1950). *Wage Determination Under Trade Unions*. New York: August M. Kelley.

Dunphy, D. (1989). "The Historical Development of Human Resource Management in Australia." *Human Resource Management in Australia*, 25(2), 40-47.

Edelman, L.B. (1992). "Legal Ambiguity and Symbolic Structures: Organizational Mediation of Civil Rights Laws." *American Journal of Sociology*, 97(6), 1531-1576.

Edwards, R. (1979). *Contested Terrain: The Transformation of the Workplace in the Twentieth Century*. New York: Basic Books.

Evans, P.A. (1984). "On the Importance of a Generalist Conception of Human Resource Management: A Cross-National Look." *Human Resource Management*, 23(4), 347-363.

Evans, P.A., Y. Doz, and A. Laurent (eds.) (1990). "The Dualistic Organization." In P. Evans, Y. Doz and A. Laurent (eds.), *Human Resource Management in International Firms: Change, Globalization, Innovation*. New York: St. Martins Press.

Freidson, E. (1986) *Professional Powers: A Study of the Institutionalization of Formal Knowledge*. Chicago: Chicago University Press.

Frost, P.J. and D. Cyr (1990). "Selective Frames, Findings, and Futures: A Review of the Second Conference on International Personnel and Human Resources Management." In B.B. Shaw and J.E. Beck (eds.), *Research in Personnel and Human Resources Management*, Supplement 2. Greenwich, CT: JAI Press.

Gannon, M.J. and Associates (1994). *Understanding Global Cultures: Metaphorical Journeys Through 17 Countries*. Beverly Hills, CA: Sage Publications.

Gordon, D.M., R. Edwards and M. Reich (1982). *Segmented Work, Divided Workers*. London: Cambridge University Press.

Harrison, J. (1993). "Manage the People Issues, the Dollars Will Flow." Vancouver: KPGM Management Consulting.

Jacoby, S.M. (1983). "The Early Years of Personnel Management in the United States: 1900-1930: The Rise and Fall of Professionalism." Unpublished manuscript.

Jacoby, S.M. (1985). *Employing Bureaucracy: Managers, Unions, and the Transformation of Work in American Industry, 1900-1945*. New York: Columbia University Press.

Jennings, P.D. and L.F. Moore (1992). "A Comparison of the Functional, Political and Institutional Perspectives on Professinal Rewards: The Case of Human Resource Specialists." Vancouver: University of British Columbia Faculty of Commerce and Business Administration, Working Paper.

Kalleberg, A.I. and I. Berg (1987). *Work and Industry: Structure, Market and Processes*. New York: Plenum Press.

Kirkbride, P.S. and S.F.Y. Tang (1989). "Personnel Management in Hong Kong: A Review of Current Issues." *Asia Pacific Human Resource Management*, 27(2), 43-57.

Kossek, E.E. (1987). "Human Resource Management Innovation." *Human Resource Management*, 26(1), 70-92.

Lam, K.H. (1989). "Motivating the Chinese Workforce." *Asia Pacific Human Resource Management*, 27(3), 65-73.

Latham, G.A. and N.K. Napier (1989). "Chinese Human Resource Management Practices in Hong Kong and Singapore." In G.R. Ferris and K.M. Rowland (eds.), *Research in Personnel and Human Resources Management*, Supplement 1. Greenwich, CT: JAI Press, 173-199.

Lincoln, J.R. and A.L. Kalleberg (1985). "Work Organization and Workforce Commitment: A Study of Plants and Employees in the U.S. and Japan." *American Sociological Review*, 50, 738-760.

Lincoln, J.R. and A.L. Kalleberg (1993). *Cultural Control and Commitment: A Study of Workplace Organization and Work Attitude in the United States and Japan*. Cambridge, MA: Cambridge University Press.

Meyer, J.W. and W.R. Scott (1983). *Organizational Environments: Ritual and Rationality*. Beverly Hills, CA: Sage.

Mintzberg, H. (1983). *Structure in Fives: Designing Effective Organizations*. Englewood Cliffs, NJ: Prentice-Hall.

Moore, L.F. and P.D. Jennings (1993). "Human Resources Management at the Crossroads." *Asia Pacific Journal of Human Resources*, 31(2), 12-25.

Naisbitt, J. (1994). *Global Paradox*. New York: William Morrow & Co.

NICB (National Industrial Conference Board) (1940). *Personnel Activities in American Business. Studies in Personnel Policy*, No. 20. New York: NICB.

Oliver, P. (1992). "The Antecedents of Deinstitutionalization." *Organization Studies*, 13, 563-588.

Paciber (1993). "Paciber Membership Directory." *Paciber Bulletin*, 6(2), 7-8.

PECC (1993). "Pacific Economic Cooperation Council." CANCPEC Secretariat: Jan., 1994, 1-3.

Pfeffer, J. (1994). *Competitive Advantage Through People*. Boston: Harvard Business School Press.

Pfeffer, J. and Y. Cohen. (1984). "Determinants of Internal Labor Markets in Organizations." *Adminstrative Science Quarterly*, 29, 550-73.

Pieper, R. (1991). *Human Resource Management: An International Comparison*. Berlin: Walter de Gruyter.

Pinfield, L.T. and M.F. Bernier. (1994). "Internal Labor Markets: Towards a Coherent Conceptualization." In G.R. Ferris (ed.), *Research in Personnel and Human Resources Management*, Vol. 12. Greenwich, CT: JAI Press, pp. 1-40.

Porter, M. (1991). *Canada at the Crossroads: The Reality of a New Competitive Environment*. Ottawa: Business Council on National Issues and the Government of Canada.

Powell, W.W. and P.J. DiMaggio (eds.) (1991). *The New Institutionalism in Organizational Analysis*. Chicago: University of Chicago Press.

Ritzer, G. and H.M. Trice. (1969). *An Occupation in Conflict: A Study of the Personnel Manager*. Ithaca, N.Y.: New York School of Industrial and Labor Relations.

Sack, J. and Lee, T. (1989). "The Role of the State in Canadian Labour Relations." *Relations Industrielles*, 44, 195-221.

Schuler, R.S. (1987). *Personnel and Human Resource Management*. (3rd Edition.) St. Paul, MN: West Publishing.

Schuler, R.S., P.J. Dowling and H. De Cieri (1993). "An Integrative Framework of Strategic International Human Resources Management." *Journal of Management*, 19(2), 419-459.

Scott, W.R. (1989). "The Adolescence of Institutional Theory." *Administrative Science Quarterly*, 32, 493-511.

Shenkar, O. and Y. Zeira (1990). "International Joint Ventures: A Tough Test for HR." *Personnel*, 67, 26-31.

Stace, D. (1987). "The Value-added Organisation: Trends in Human Resource Management." *Human Resource Management Australia*, 22, 52-62.

Steers, R.M., Y.K. Shin, G.R. Ungson and S. Nam (1990). "Korean Corporate Culture: A Comparative Analysis." In B.B. Shaw and J.E. Beck (eds.), *Research in Personnel and Human Resources Management*, Supplement 2. Greenwich, CT: JAI Press, 247-262.

Stevens, B. (1986). "Complementing the Welfare State: The Development of Private Pension, Health Insurance and Other Employee Benefits in the United States." *Labor Management Relations Series*, no. 65. Geneva: ILO.

Sutton, J.R., F. Dobbin, J.W. Meyer and W.R. Scott (1994). "The Legalization of the Workplace." *American Journal of Sociology*, 100, 944-971.

Takahashi, Y. (1991). "Human Resources Management in Japan." In R. Pieper (ed.), *Human Resources Management: An International Comparison*. Berlin: Walter de Gruyter.

Tang, S.F.Y. and P.S. Kirkbride (1989). "Training and Development in Hong Kong." In J.B. Shaw, J.E. Beck, K.M. Rowland and P.S. Kirkbride (eds.), *International Human Resources Management: Issues and Research for the 1990s. Proceedings of the Second International Conference on Personnel/Human Resources Management*. Hong Kong: International Personnel and Human Resource Management Association.

Teagarden, M.B., M.C. Butler and M.A. Von Glinow (1992). "Mexico's Maquiladora Industry: Where Strategic Human Resource Management Makes a Difference." *Organizational Dynamics*, Winter, 34-47.

Teagarden, M.B. and M.A. Von Glinow (1989). "Human Resource Management Factors in International Joint Venture Effectiveness: The Case of the PRC," unpublished paper.

Tichy, N.M. (1988). "Setting the Global Human Resource Management Agenda for the 1990s." *Human Resource Management*, 27(1), 1-18.

Tsui, A. (1987). "Defining the Activities and Effectiveness of the Human Resource Department: A Multiple Constituency Approach." *Human Resources Management*, 26(1), 35-69.

Tung, R. (1989). "Strategic Management of Resources in the Multinational Enterprise." *Human Resources Management*, 23(2), 129-144.

Tung, R. (1990). "International Human Resource Management Policies and Practices: A Comparative Analysis." In B.B. Shaw and J.E. Beck (eds.), *Research in Personnel and Human Resources Management*. Supplement 2. Greenwich, CT: JAI Press.

Von Glinow, M. and B.J. Chung (1989). "Comparative Human Resource Management Practices in the United States, Japan, Korea, and the People's Republic of China." In A. Nedd (ed.), *Research in Personnel and Human Resources Management*. Supplement 1. Greenwich, CT: JAI Press.

Wang, Z. (1991). "Human Resources Management in China: Recent Trends." In R. Pieper (ed.), *Human Resources Management: An International Perspective*. Berlin: Walter de Gruyter.

Wolf, W.B. (ed.) (1980). *Top Management of the Personnel Function: Current Issues and Practices* Ithaca, NY: ILR School, Cornell University.

About the Contributors

Vinita Atmiyanandana earned her doctorate in mass communication from Florida State University. She has been on the faculties of both Chulalongkorn University and Thammasat University in Bangkok and is currently affiliated with the Urbana, Illinois public school system. Her research interests include cross-cultural psychology and human resource management practices in Southeast Asia.

Dianne Cyr is President of Global Alliance Management Inc. She completed her Ph.D. at the University of British Columbia. Her dissertation research was focused on how strategic HRM policy and practices operate in international joint ventures. Her current research interests continue in this area; particularly with respect to Central/Eastern Europe and the Pacific Rim. In 1992, she was a visiting post doctoral fellow at INSEAD in France. She is the author of a forthcoming book, *International Joint Ventures: The Human Resource Management Challenge*, which offers new perspectives for HRM related to corporate success.

Alan J. Geare is Professor and Head of the Department of Management, University of Otago, in Dunedin, New Zealand. He originally trained as an economist, and his Ph.D. was on industrial relations ideologies of managers. He is author of a number of books in industrial relations and human resource management and articles in such journals as *Academy of Management Review*, *Labor Law Journal* and *International Academy of Management Review*. He is currently editor of the *New Zealand Journal of Industrial Relations*, and is a partner in Management Development Associates and a director of a private consulting company.

Jiing-Lih (Larry) Farh is an Associate Professor of Management at the Hong Kong University of Science and Technology. He received his Ph.D. degree in organizational behavior and personnel from Indiana University at Bloomington in 1983. His current research interests include performance appraisal, organization rewrd system, motivation theories, and cross-cultural management.

Peter J. Frost is Associate Dean, Faculty of Commerce and Business Administration, University of British Columbia. Additionally, he holds the Edgar F. Kaiser, Jr., Chair in Organizational Behavior. A prolific author with many academic and professional publications, he has recently published several books in collaboration with other scholars, including *Doing Exemplary Research* (Sage, 1992), *Reframing Organizational Culture* (Sage, 1991), *Management Live: the Video Book* (Prentice-Hall, 1991). Dr. Frost is an editor of *Organizational Science* and has been the Executive Director of the Organizational Behavior Teaching Society. In 1993, he received the David Bradford Award from the OBTS to recognize his outstanding contributions to the advancement of management education.

P. Devereaux Jennings is an Associate Professor of Organizational Behavior in the Faculty of Commerce and Business Administration at the University of British Columbia. He has studied the evolution of U.S. personnel administration (with Baron, and Dobbin, 1986, 1988) and is presently examining development of HRM in different Pacific Rim countries (with Moore, e.g., this volume). Dev has also studied the diffusion of the multidivisional form from a political and institutional perspective (with Palmer, Friedland, and Powers, 1986; with Palmer and Zhou, 1993) and is presently investigating the impact of embeddedness on the changes over time in manufacturing location (with Palmer and Friedland, 1993; with Palmer, Friedland and Shin, 1993). Dev received his Ph.D. and M.A. in sociology from Stanford University.

Marianne J. Koch is an Assistant Professor of Management in the Graduate School of Management, University of Oregon. She completed her Ph.D. at Columbia University in the fields of human resource management and industrial relations. Her current research concerns hiring practices in organizations and how they are affected by the increasingly diverse workforce.

John J. Lawler is currently an Associate Professor of Labor and Industrial Relations at the University of Illinois at Urbana-Champaign. He earned his doctorate at the University of California (Berkeley). Prior to joining the faculty at Illinois, he was on the faculty of the Industrial Relations Center at the University of Illinois. His research interests include industrial relations and human resource management practices in Southeast Asia and information systems applications in industrial relations and human resource management.

Larry F. Moore is an Associate Professor in the Faculty of Commerce and Business Administration, University of British Columbia. He obtained an M.B.A. and a D.B.A. from the University of Colorado, Boulder, and is past president of the Administrative Sciences Association of Canada. He is co-editor of *Reframing Organizational Culture* (Sage, 1991) in addition to authoring numerous other academic and professional books and journal articles. He serves on the editorial board of the *Asia Pacific Journal of Human Resources*. Larry's research interests include the cultural aspects of organizations, multiculture workforces, and human resource management in the Pacific Rim.

Motohiro Morishima was stunned when he returned to Japan four years ago and learned how little serious research is being conducted on Japanese HRM. Since then, he has been actively studying Japanese HR and Industrial Relations, putting his training at the University of Illinois (Ph.D., 1986) to good use. To earn a living, he teaches in the Faculty of Policy Management, at Keio University in Fugisawa, Japan, where he is an Associate Professor. His publications have appeared in such journals as *Industrial Relations* and *Industrial and Labor Relations Review*. He also conducts research with a number of organizations including the Japanese Ministry of Labor and the Japan Productivity Center.

Sang H. Nam is an Assistant Professor of Management in the School of Business, University of Victoria, Canada. He holds a Ph.D. from the University of Oregon in the field of organizational studies. His current research interests include international HRM and attribution theories of employee behavior.

Mee-Kau Nyaw is Professor of Management and Director of M.B.A. Programmes, Faculty of Business Administration, The Chinese University of Hong Kong (CHUK). He obtained his B.S.Sc. *magna cum laude* from CHUK, an M.A. from Vanderbilt University in the U.S.A., an M.B.A. from the University of British Columbia, and a Ph.D. from Simon Fraser University, Canada. He has been teaching at CHUK since 1977. He spent a year as a post-doctoral fellow at the University of Edinburgh during 1983-84. Professor Nyaw specializes in HRM and strategic management. His current research interests focus on the enterprise management system with special reference to joint ventures in the People's Republic of China.

Wai K. Poon is a Senior Lecturer of the Department of Management at the Chinese University of Hong Kong. Dr. Poon received training both in Canada and the U.K. He earned a Ph.D. from the University of Toronto, and holds several professional designations: FIMgt, FITD, FIPM (HK). He has been active in the area of Management Development for more than 15 years. Dr. Poon launched the first Diploma in Training Management in Hong Kong in 1982 and was its program director for nearly 10 years. He was the Director of Management Development for the Asia-Pacific Institute of Business from 1990-92. In addition to his teaching duties, he has also been appointed Director of Diploma in Management Studies for Hong Kong government officers as well as Chairman of the Committee on the Behavioral Laboratory of the Faculty of Business Administration.

Diane Shelton is currently a Senior Lecturer at the Melbourne Business School at the University of Melbourne. She is primarily interested in the study of organizational culture and its relationship to human resource management processes. Diane's current work focuses on the linkages between overall corporate strategics and human resource management practices in organizations. She is specifically concerned with the way that human resource management practices reflect and are influenced by underlying organizational cultural values and assumptions.

Ralph E. Stablein is a Senior Lecturer of Organization Theory in the Department of Management of the University of Otago, Dunedin, New Zealand. He received his B.A. (1974) in economics and psychology from Illinois Benedictine College, an M.A. (1979) in economics from Western Illinois University, and a Ph.D. (1985) in organization behavior from Northwestern University's Kellogg Graduate School of Management. In addition to the development of personnel practices, he is interested in the theory and practice of organizational research. He is on the Editorial Board of the *Asia Pacific Journal of Human Resources* and is co-editor (with Peter Frost) of *Doing Exemplary Research* (Sage, 1992).

Richard M. Steers is the Kazumitsu Shiomi Professor of Management and International Studies in the Graduate School of Management, University of Oregon. He holds a Ph.D. from the University of California, Irvine. He is the author of several books, including *The Chaebol: Korea's New Industrial Might* (Harper & Row, 1989), and his current research interests focus on cross-cultural management and organizational change.

Keng-Choo Yeo is currently a Director/Principal Consultant with a management consultancy based in Singapore. She obtained her M.B.A. from the National University of Singapore (NUS). Ms. Yeo has worked for many years in industry, primarily in the human resource management (HRM) and training and development areas. Before her current position, she worked for several years as an HRM specialist with the NUS, teaching HRM to graduating students. She has extensive experience providing assistance in executive development and organization development to organizations in Singapore and countries around the region.

Chi-Ching Edith Yuen is a Senior Lecturer in the Department of Organizational Behaviour, in the Faculty of Business Administration, National University of Singapore. She obtained her Ph.D. at the University of Sydney, Australia, and has taught in universities in Australia, Hong Kong and Singapore. Her current research interests are in women in management, human resource management practices and comparative management.